Annual Reports in
Computational Chemistry

Annual Reports in Computational Chemistry

Volume 2

Editor
David C. Spellmeyer
Almaden Services Research
IBM Almaden Research Center
San Jose, California
USA

Section Editors
Heather A. Carlson, T. Daniel Crawford, Jeffry D. Madura
Yvonne Martin, Carlos Simmerling and Theresa Julia Zielinski

Sponsored by the Division of Computers in Chemistry of
the American Chemical Society

ELSEVIER

Amsterdam ● Boston ● Heidelberg ● London ● New York ● Oxford ● Paris
● San Diego ● San Francisco ● Singapore ● Sydney ● Tokyo

Elsevier
Radarweg 29, PO Box 211, 1000 AE Amsterdam, The Netherlands
The Boulevard, Langford Lane, Kidlington, Oxford OX5 1GB, UK

First edition 2006

Library of Congress Cataloging-in-Publication Data
A catalog record for this book is available from the British Library of Congress

British Library Cataloguing in Publication Data
A catalogue record for this book is available from the British Library

ISBN-13:   978-0-444-52879-7
ISBN-10:   0-444-52879-2
ISSN: 1574-1400

For information on all Elsevier publications
visit our website at books.elsevier.com

Printed and bound in the USA

06 07 08 09 10 10 9 8 7 6 5 4 3 2 1

Working together to grow
libraries in developing countries

www.elsevier.com | www.bookaid.org | www.sabre.org

ELSEVIER   BOOK AID International   Sabre Foundation

CONTENTS

1. CHEMICAL EDUCATION

Section Editor: Theresa Julia Zielinski, Department of Chemistry,
                  Medical Technology, and Physics, Monmouth
                  University, 400 Cedar Avenue, West Long Branch,
                  NJ 07764-1898, USA

2. QUANTUM MECHANICAL METHODS

Section Editor: T. Daniel Crawford, Department of Chemistry,
                  Virginia Tech, Blacksburg, VA 24061, USA

3. MOLECULAR MODELING METHODS

Section Editor: Carlos Simmerling, Center for Structural Biology,
                  Stony Brook University, Stony Brook, NY 11794,
                  USA

4. ADVANCES IN QSAR/QSPR

Section Editor: Yvonne Martin, Abbott Laboratories, Abbott Park,
                  IL 60064, USA

5. APPLICATIONS OF COMPUTATIONAL METHODS

Section Editors: Heather A. Carlson, University of Michigan,
College of Pharmacy, 428 Church Street, Ann
Arbor, MI 48109-1065, USA and
Jeffry D. Madura, Duquesne University,
Department of Chemistry and Biochemistry,
Center for Computational Sciences, 600 Forbes
Ave., Pittsburgh, PA 15282, USA

CONTRIBUTORS

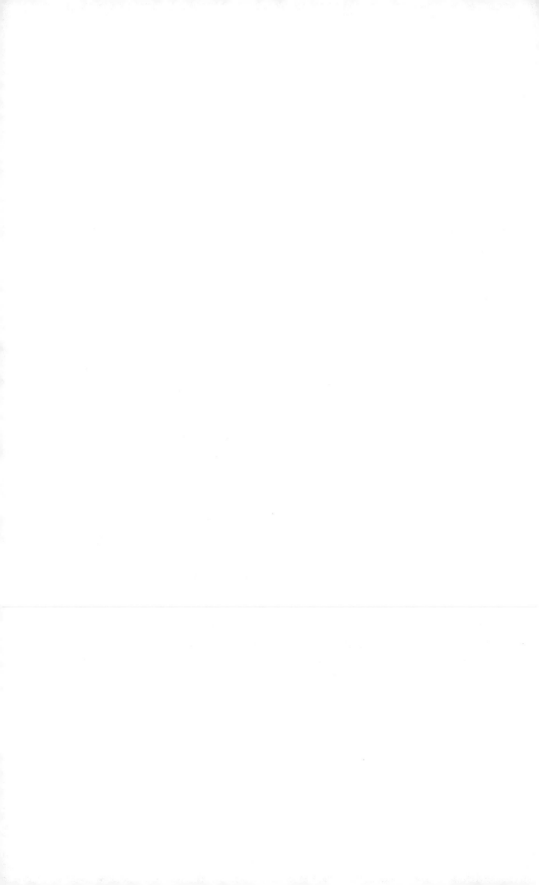

Preface

Annual Reports in Computational Chemistry focuses on providing timely reviews of topics important to researchers in the field of computational chemistry. It is published and distributed by Elsevier and is sponsored by the Division of Computers in Chemistry (COMP) of the American Chemical Society. We are pleased that Volume 1 received a very positive response from our readers. The COMP Executive Committee expects to deliver future volumes of the ARCC which build on the solid contributors of our first two volumes.

In Volume 2, our Section Editors have assembled 16 contributions in five sections. Topics covered include Chemical Education (Theresa Julia Zielinski), Quantum Mechanical Methods (T. Daniel Crawford), Molecular Modeling Methods (Carlos Simmerling), QSAR/QSPR (Yvonne Martin), and Applications of Computational Methods (Heather A. Carlson and Jeffry D. Madura). With Volume 2, we establish a practice of cumulative indexing of both the current and past editions in order to provide easy identification of past reports.

As was the case with our first volume, the Annual Reports in Computational Chemistry has been assembled entirely by volunteers in order to produce a high-quality scientific publication at the lowest cost possible. I would like to thank the many people who have given their time to make this edition of the Annual Reports in Computational Chemistry possible. The authors of each of this year's contributions and the Section Editors have graciously dedicated significant amounts of their time. This year's edition could not have been assembled without the help of Deirdre Clark, of Elsevier. Thank you one and all for your hard work, your time, and your contributions.

I hope that you will find this edition to be interesting and valuable. We are actively planning the third volume and are soliciting input from our readers about future topics. Please contact me with your suggestions and/ or to volunteer to be a contributor.

Sincerely
David C. Spellmeyer

Section 1
Chemical Education

Section Editor: Theresa Julia Zielinski
Department of Chemistry, Medical Technology
and Physics
Monmouth University
400 Cedar Avenue
West Long Branch
NJ 07764-1898, USA

CHAPTER 1

Real-World Kinetics via Simulations

F.A. Houle and W.D. Hinsberg

IBM Almaden Research Center, 650 Harry Road, San Jose, CA 95120, USA

Contents

1. INTRODUCTION

The pressure to include important and interesting new topics of chemistry into the undergraduate curriculum has reduced the time available to teach more traditional fundamental aspects of chemistry. One area in particular that has been reduced to a bare minimum in many chemistry departments (although not so in related engineering departments) is chemical kinetics. This is unfortunate, because although the theoretical physical chemistry of reaction rates and mechanisms has been reasonably well understood for some time and most of the experimental tools required have been developed and published, in practice the field is far from mature. The study of chemical kinetics phenomena remains very much a core activity in chemistry-related fields, whether in catalysis, synthesis scale-up, pharmacology, biochemistry, materials processing or polymerization, to highlight just a few areas. Indeed it is fair to say that a thorough grounding in chemical kinetics and thermodynamics are core competencies for current and future chemical scientists, particularly those who choose positions in industrial chemical research and development. Through our careers we have seen much time and effort wasted when kinetics is overlooked or treated incorrectly due to the lack of knowledge by the chemists involved.

When chemical kinetics is taught, the primary focus is on systems or reaction conditions that can be described with simple mechanisms with

ANNUAL REPORTS IN COMPUTATIONAL CHEMISTRY, VOLUME 2
ISSN: 1574-1400   DOI 10.1016/S1574-1400(06)02001-9

rate laws that are solvable analytically and/or graphically [1].[a] Although well-understood examples of more complex kinetics abound, they call for the application of more advanced numerical methods (such as solution of coupled differential equations) requiring a level of effort and mathematics that is impractical during the few class hours devoted to kinetics overall. Student chemists will likely be faced with the need to analyze and understand such complex systems during their future work, however, and are unlikely to be well-prepared for such tasks if only exposed to the introductory parts of the kinetics curriculum.

To broaden the scope of kinetics taught in the class time available, a number of educators have published excellent computer simulation codes and simulation-based curricula [2–10]. Typically they are dedicated to one particular type of kinetics, with enzyme kinetics being particularly popular, or to simple reaction schemes such as a sequence of reversible first-order reactions. We had developed for our own research use a general purpose kinetics simulator based on the algorithms of Bunker [11] and Gillespie [12] and on a simulator used in kinetics courses at UC Irvine in the early 1970s [2]. In 1996 we began distributing this software package, called "Chemical Kinetics Simulator" (CKS), under a no-cost license over the World Wide Web [13]. Part of our motivation was to provide a new tool that would facilitate teaching of chemical kinetics at a deeper level within the time available in the curriculum by eliminating the need for including numerical methods; to this end we developed and included an extensive set of demonstration simulations. During the ensuing 8 years, the package has been widely downloaded worldwide and is in use in high school to graduate level classrooms. It is also used for research in academic, industrial, government and military research laboratories in fields ranging from chemistry and chemical engineering to physics to environmental engineering to biology – basically anywhere chemistry is studied or applied. CKS also is in daily use in our own laboratories[b], together with a more advanced internal use version that treats coupled reaction-diffusion systems [14,15]. When fully integrated with experiments, simulations have proved invaluable for characterization of the materials reactions we study at a highly rigorous level.

In this article we describe the use of CKS to teach students how to think about kinetic processes. This includes developing and evaluating reaction mechanisms, and building familiarity with typical reaction mechanisms beyond the basic simple cases. We focus on two examples in materials

---

[a] See ref. [1].
[b] Materials kinetics publications using CKS (see ref. 14).

and biomimetic chemistry; however, the same methodology can easily be applied to kinetic problems in other fields [16].[c]

2. SELECTING AND SETTING UP SIMULATION STUDIES

The demonstration simulations included in the CKS package cover a variety of chemically important processes, but primarily are intended to illustrate uses and features of the simulator package and to teach simulation techniques. We view them as a starting point to a deeper set of simulation-based investigations of how kinetic mechanisms are determined from experimental data, and how experiments are designed to reveal the mechanism of a process.

We believe that this focus is uniquely suited for preparing students to apply what they have learned in their courses. By connecting a simulation to experimental data students can begin to appreciate important practical aspects of chemical kinetics studies. These include:

- the ambiguities that come with limited data sets (more than one mechanism can fit the data),
- useful numerical approaches for extracting rate constants from data fits when graphical methods are not possible,
- integrating data from multiple types of time-dependent measurements (e.g. spectroscopies),
- how to use simulations to focus an experimental investigation by identifying the next measurements to make,
- determining the sensitivity of a fit (assumed mechanism and rate constants) to the available data,
- how to make a first guess at a mechanism for an unknown system,
- how to use literature kinetics data to construct a mechanism,
- identifying when a mechanism that seems intuitively right just does not describe the data, and
- distinguishing between thermodynamics and kinetics.

Although ideally simulations would be associated with a laboratory module, it is often not practical to have the students carry out the necessary measurements themselves because of time, chemical cost and equipment constraints. In this case a good second choice is to use data from the literature and assign the task of analysis to the students. This allows the systems to be chosen on the basis of their pedagogical value

---

[c] Extensive references to interesting kinetics systems and methods can be found in the reviews (see ref. 16).

and not their adaptability to an undergraduate lab. Part of the exercise would include interpretation and recommendations for future work, which could then be compared to those found in the original publications and discussed.

3. KINETICS IN MATERIALS CHEMISTRY AND BIOMIMETIC CHEMISTRY

The kinetics processes that dominate in materials systems and intracellular systems have many parallels, and embody phenomena that chemistry students should become familiar with because of their importance for both academic research and industrial research and development. Both involve reactions in condensed phases or at interfaces. In materials systems chemical reactions often go to completion, and the close proximity of reactants and products can lead to secondary reactions that would not be observed in dilute solution or in the gas phase. In both materials and cellular systems the small effective reaction volumes can lead to concentrations that are inherently high, even though absolute amounts are small, and thus high reaction rates even when rate constants are low. Statistical effects can be very important in both classes of reactions. In materials systems significant local inhomogeneities can develop since the reaction can initiate in multiple locations and diffusion is slow or nonexistent. Chemical changes initiated by random events such as atomic displacements are common. Similarly, sporadic events in cells can regulate ion transport and control expression. There are notable differences as well. In materials systems reactions can involve single temperatures or programmed temperature heating, or be driven by irradiation by photons or charged particles. The resulting chemistry can be coupled to concurrent phase changes or morphology changes. In living systems reactions are at or near ambient (physiological) temperature, and consequently involve facile processes with low activation energies.

The demonstration simulations distributed with CKS provide a set of quick exercises introducing particular simulation scenarios, mainly relevant to materials chemistry, but also a sampling of biological chemistry. The collection includes polymerization simulations, thermal deprotection, polyimide curing, surface adsorption, film accretion, thermogravimetric analysis, temperature programmed-desorption, and chemical vapor deposition; enzyme chemistry and chiral synthesis. Many of the kinetics course curricula using CKS that are posted on the World Wide Web are built on these alone. Much more is possible, however, and the demonstrations can be used to introduce specific mechanisms and the capabilities of the simulator, leading the students into more complex projects.

Two examples of CKS-based laboratory course modules are outlined here, one in interfacial materials chemistry [17] and the other involving kinetics in a biomimetic capsule system [18]. Although both reports come from academic laboratories, they are representative of kinetics studies likely to be performed in industry because of their subject matter and experimental methods, and in their focus on reactions that go to completion and must be understood from beginning to end. As the students work through these examples, they will encounter many of the characteristics of real-life kinetics investigations that were noted in the preceding section.

Both modules are structured as open-ended projects, with activities suitable for beginning and advanced students. What is important is that the students become familiar with the methodology used for kinetics studies and develop the best mechanism they can, not that they come to a particular end result. Class presentations and discussions of results at the end of the module would allow students to appreciate the range of well-considered results that might be achieved, and types of follow-up studies that can be used to test them.

3.1. Interfacial reactions on silica nanoparticles

We use a recent study of a titration technique for determination of adsorption kinetics on the surface of 4–10 nm diameter silica nanoparticles [17] as an example of how a materials chemistry simulation lab might be designed. Molecular aggregates such as micelles and colloids play important roles as reaction supports in materials science as well as biology, yet rather few quantitative data are available for their all-important interfacial reaction properties. The authors investigated methyl viologen^{2+} (MV^{2+}) adsorption to silica nanoparticles by measuring the rate of radiolytically generated electron trapping by MV^{2+} in solution in competition with MV^{2+} adsorption and electron trapping on varying concentrations and sizes of nanoparticles. $Ru(bpy)_3^{2+}$ also was studied. Hydrated electron absorbances were measured optically, and a variety of absorption vs. time curves are included in the article. The authors present a mechanism and use it to determine rate constants and adsorption isotherms. The authors selected experimental conditions that allowed pseudo-first-order conditions to be obtained over part of the experimental data range, and used graphical techniques to extract rate constants. Their mechanism as published is not immediately suitable for simulations using CKS because key details such as silica particle surface area are not explicitly included.

For students unfamiliar with surface chemistry, it is valuable to start with an exploration of general interfacial kinetics. The CKS adsorption demonstration simulation provides an introduction to the role of available sites in governing adsorption isotherms, and can be expanded to include competitive adsorption of several adsorbates on sites of varying sizes. The general irreversible adsorption mechanism for a species A on a surface with a fixed number of small and large adsorption sites (indicated by subscripts s and l, respectively) is

$$A + \text{small site} \rightarrow A_s \tag{1}$$

$$A + \text{large site} \rightarrow A_l \tag{2}$$

Rate constant ranges can be chosen to suit the experimental conditions being evaluated; typical surface reaction-controlled adsorption rates are 1 monolayer (approximately 10^{15} surface sites per cm^2) occupied in one second at 10^{-6} torr pressure [20]. Adsorption rates from the liquid phase can be estimated using concentrations to determine incident number densities. When realistic rate constants are used the time base of the simulated kinetics can be compared directly to experimental data. In the case of weakly bound adsorbates where desorption competes with adsorption, the reactions are written as reversible steps. The first-order desorption rate constants should be in the range of 10^{11}–10^{14} sec^{-1} [19].

Moving to the nanoparticle MV^{2+} system, the published mechanism is:

$$H_2O + \text{radiation} \rightarrow e_{aq}^-, \; H, \; OH \tag{3}$$

$$e_{aq}^- + MV^{2+} \rightarrow MV^+ \tag{4}$$

$$(SiO_2)_{coll} + MV^{2+} \rightarrow (MV^{2+})_{ads} \tag{5}$$

$$e_{aq}^- + (MV^{2+})_{ads} \rightarrow (MV^+)_{ads} \tag{6}$$

where e_{aq}^- is a hydrated electron, and the subscripts coll and ads refer to colloidal and adsorbed, respectively.

Step (6), reduction of the adsorbate, has a small rate constant and was neglected in the analysis. Under other experimental conditions, such as large depletion of MV^{2+} from solution by adsorption on nanoparticles, omission of this step might not be justified.

Before they are shown this mechanism, the students should write down a set of steps they think should occur in the titration reaction. They can then be asked to compare their scheme with the published mechanism and examine similarities and differences. This helps build intuition for how reactions proceed, and serves as a starting point for working with the published mechanism.

The first task is to prepare a set of reaction steps suitable for simulation. The level of assistance this requires from the instructor will depend on the level of the students.

Referring to the microscopic kinetic description of adsorption given in steps (1) and (2) above, it can be seen that step (5) is not written in a form amenable to determination of adsorption rate constants or surface site densities on the nanoparticles using simulations because particle adsorption sites are not explicitly included. Assuming the most general case of a reversible process, it can be rewritten as

$$\text{Site} + \text{MV}^{2+} = (\text{MV}^{2+})_{ads} \tag{5$'$}$$

where Site represents the total collection of available sites on all nanoparticles in the solution and " $=$ " denotes a reversible reaction. The initial concentration of Site is given by either the number of sites per particle (unknown initially) times the particle concentration, or by the total particle surface area per gram added to the solution volume times an assumed site density. Another appropriate modification is to omit step (3), which is a process much faster than the subsequent chemistry, and start with an assumed initial hydrated electron concentration calculated from the absorption properties of water and its quantum yield for photolysis.

Turning to Fig. 1 (a schematic representation of data given in Fig. 1 of Reference[17]), the students would be directed to use steps (4) and (5$'$) as a starting point to obtain an estimate of the concentration of initial Site corresponding to each of the nanoparticle loadings, $[\text{SiO}_2]_1$ and $[\text{SiO}_2]_2$, and estimates of rate constants for step (4) and the forward and reverse directions of step (5$'$). As a first step, the students could be instructed to use log plots to graphically assess whether assumptions about reaction order at small extents of reaction are correct in the mechanism. Furthermore, observations of slope changes in the plots as a function of time signal that a multi-step mechanism is operant. It can also be pointed out that there is no step in the mechanism for loss of hydrated electrons in the absence of silica or MV^{2+}, although the data clearly show that this occurs at a significant rate. This is an opportunity for teaching inductive techniques for building mechanisms [20], in which one starts with a minimal mechanism and adds steps to improve the fit, leading to a mechanism with no inactive steps, rather than writing down all possible reactions and having to work with a mechanism too complex to refine or test. Obviously the loss process due to neutralization in water alone is slow, so can be added in later with appropriate adjustments to the rate constants.

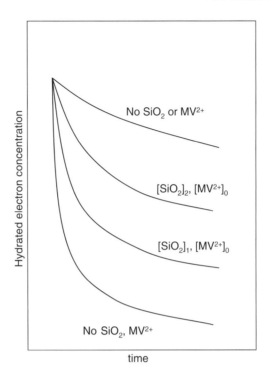

Fig. 1. Experimental decay curves for hydrated electrons in the presence of solution phase and adsorbed MV^{2+}. The bottom trace allows determination of the solution phase reaction kinetics alone, the top trace allows secondary loss kinetics to be measured, and the middle two traces allow the adsorption rate constant and initial Site concentration to be estimated.

Rate constants and Site concentrations would be obtained by trial and error simulations, working inductively to determine first the rate constant for (4) using the bottom trace in Fig. 1, and then the unknown initial number of Site and rate constants for step (5′) using the middle two traces. It should be noted that the equilibrium constant for (5′) is about 1×10^5 M^{-1} [17]. The students should consider how significant the reversibility of this step really is and whether it is necessary to include MV^2 desorption in the initial fits.

Although all elementary reactions are in principle reversible, not all reverse steps are kinetically important. The sensitivity of the fit to assumed variations in the best-fit values for the unknowns and to the inclusion of the reverse step in (5′) will enable students to appreciate how carefully and systematically one must work to obtain reliable kinetics parameters.

The next stage of mechanism development would be to add the slower hydrated electron loss step. The rate constant for this decay process can be estimated by fitting the top curve in Fig. 1 as an apparent single step process, and then all the simulations for the remaining curves repeated with the expanded mechanism to assess sensitivity to the added step. For a more advanced project, students could be asked to look at the radiolysis literature and add in appropriate steps using known kinetics for reactions of e_{aq}^- [21].[d] With the mechanism and rate constants in hand, the students can now compare the results of their kinetics simulations to values reported in the literature, obtained by very different means. They can also use their initial mechanism to identify further experiments, for example over a range of temperatures, that would be useful for determining the uniqueness and completeness of the mechanism for accurately describing what is occurring in the actual physical system. Finally, they can consider what other processes ought to be included in the mechanism, such as diffusion and nanoparticle–nanoparticle interactions. They can consider the relationship between an apparent mechanism that is obviously over-simplified but describes all the experimental data available, and one that includes all microscopic processes, and thus is more realistic physically, but contains too many unknown and unmeasurable steps and thus would be little better than a guess.

3.2. Chemical amplification with encapsulated reagents

Compartmentalization, where a reaction is constrained to take place within a specific volume, is believed to be an important aspect of the chemistry of living systems [18]. The sequestration of reactants into a confined space affects kinetics and reaction paths, introducing an environmental factor into their reactivity. This effect is more than the simple, well-documented solution cage effect, where reactants surrounded by solvent can undergo more efficient reaction by being trapped close together allowing multiple encounters and rapid dissipation of any exothermicity away from the reaction zone [22].

   In this simulation lab, students examine the kinetics of a model system that mimics some aspects of compartmentalization [18]. The authors selected a dimeric capsule system, held together by hydrogen bonds, that resembles a miniature version of the gel capsule used for medications. The capsules and three reactants are introduced into hydrophobic solvent. One of the reactants, dicyclohexylcarbodiimide (DCC) fits selectively into the capsules, and rapidly populates all of them. Encapsulated DCC is unreactive. Since DCC and capsules are present in equal quantities the encapsulation process is not 100% efficient and there will be very small

---

[d] See ref. [21].

amounts of free DCC in solution. Initially, free DCC will react with the other reactants, slowly forming two products that each have greater affinity for the capsule than DCC. The products displace DCC from the capsules, releasing two DCCs into solution per DCC consumed, and increasing the rate of product formation. This is an autoaccelerating reaction and the product concentration as a function of time increases in a characteristic sigmoid functional form. NMR data are given showing the decrease in encapsulated reactant DCC and the increase in one of the encapsulated products as a function of time.

The data presented in the paper are analyzed by a combination of graphical and simulation techniques. The simulations were carried out using order-of-magnitude estimates for rate constants, and therefore are not intended to produce simulated concentration vs. time curves that can be compared directly to experiment. This approach is certainly useful for gaining key insights to overall behaviors, however much more can be learned by attempting to fit the data accurately.

The authors list the mechanism they used for their simulations (rewritten here with different notation for clarity in this context). Reactions involving entering and leaving the capsule are

$$DCC + capsule = ecDCC \tag{7}$$

$$ecDCC + Product1 = DCC + ecProduct1 \tag{8}$$

$$ecDCC + Product2 = DCC + ecProduct2 \tag{9}$$

$$ecProduct1 + Product2 = Product1 + ecProduct2 \tag{10}$$

where ec means "encapsulated," and Product1 is less tightly bound inside the capsule than Product2, so can be displaced by it. The reactions are written as reversible steps. Reactions in solution are

$$DCC + Reactant1 \rightarrow Intermediate1 \tag{11}$$

$$Intermediate1 + Reactant2 \rightarrow Product1 + Product2 \tag{12}$$

$$Intermediate1 + Reactant1 \rightarrow Intermediate2 + Product2 \tag{13}$$

$$Intermediate2 + Reactant2 \rightarrow Product1 \tag{14}$$

As suggested for the nanoparticle system, it is valuable to have the students write a mechanism *before* examining the published one, and then consider how they compare. Then, as an initial exercise, the students can use the rate constants published in the paper and this mechanism to run an initial CKS simulation and evaluate the results. It will be immediately evident that the simulation gives a time base 100 times slower than that observed experimentally, so the rate constants used are too small. Since the only real test of a mechanism is the direct comparison of its predictions to experiment, the students have to decide what is the best approach to modifying the mechanism and rate constants to obtain a better fit. One obvious approach is to simply multiply every rate constant by 100. Since some steps are irreversible and others are equilibria, this can stimulate a discussion of what an equilibrium constant is and whether it is permissible to change its corresponding forward and reverse rate constants at will while keeping their ratio constant. Running a simulation after this scaling exercise shows that while the agreement between NMR data for the encapsulated product and simulation results is improved at this point (Fig. 2 of their article), it still is not quantitative and the disappearance of encapsulated DCC is significantly too slow (Fig. 3(a) of their article). The published model is of clear qualitative value, but must evolve to be quantitative.

This places the students in the situation where they must develop a strategy to extract more quantitative results from these very interesting experiments. It is a situation often encountered in a practical setting: where one has a reliable data set and a concrete idea of what is occurring, but significant differences between initial model predictions and what has been observed.

For beginning students a structured approach to evolving the mechanism is probably most useful in order to provide a framework for thinking about the logic involved. As a first step, they can be instructed to pare down the mechanism in order to understand whether all the steps listed are actually needed to produce the measured curve shapes out to near completion of the reaction. This calls for some reasoning about what to leave out, and can be judged by simply overlaying the data on the various simulation results. The next step would be to assess which steps are needed to reproduce data to between 10% and 20% depletion of encapsulated DCC. The mechanism at early times can be used to extract rate constants from initial decays. These can then be used in the mechanism appropriate for longer times, and attempts made to determine additional rate constants by trial-and-error fits. Finally, the students should evaluate their progress and discuss what should be done to refine their mechanism further. It is important that they understand what their mechanism will and will not predict.

Higher-level students can be allowed to take a more open-ended approach to extending the published work. They should start with a literature search to learn if any of the rate constants have been determined independently. Values confirmed in this way are fixed. Rate constants for which independent determinations do not exist can be considered variables. If the reaction steps described in the literature differ from those in the proposed mechanism the students can construct an alternate version of the mechanism and work to evaluate both side-by-side.

With this knowledge of related studies, the more advanced students can then carry out the same exercise as the beginning students, with the added constraint that not all steps can be varied. Reactions whose rate constants are known should be subject to a sensitivity analysis, that is, a determination of whether the presence of the reaction step makes a difference in the final simulation predictions, but the rate constant cannot be changed.When complete, the students should have two reaction mechanisms that can be merged into one. This is a good opportunity to discuss the apparent kinetics vs. the more detailed mechanism that our knowledge of chemistry says should be operant, and the relative merits of omitting some steps and including others. This is an issue of model development technique: Occam's razor should be used, resulting in a mechanism involving only steps that are kinetically important [20]. Whether the resulting mechanism makes sense chemically and physically should also be evaluated. Mechanisms are never proved, only disproved, so the students should present an experimental plan for testing their mechanism, with predictions of what should be observed. As an example, important experimental variables that can help constrain a proposed mechanism are concentration and temperature. Additional types of measurements can also be proposed – in this workNMR was the only technique used.

4. A FOUNDATION FOR KINETIC MODEL DEVELOPMENT

The two simulation exercises given above are intended as illustrative introductions to the thought processes that can be used to develop and evaluate reaction mechanisms. Other chemical systems can be substituted according to the interests of the instructor and the class. What is key is that students arrive at an understanding that a mechanism is a set of simple steps and accurate rate constants that can be extracted from data and can predict behavior using simulation tools like CKS. When presented in the future with a practical situation where the kinetics of an unknown reaction system must be characterized, the students will be able to draw on such an exercise for guidance on how the problem can be addressed. They will understand that the kinetics of any reaction can be determined, not just the small set of those amenable to analysis using closed form rate laws and graphs.

ACKNOWLEDGMENTS

We are grateful to our physical chemistry instructors and research mentors for having taught us how to think about kinetics and chemical reactivity: the late D. L. Bunker and F. S. Rowland (UC Irvine), M. Stiles (U. Michigan) and J. L. Beauchamp, W. Goddard and P. B. Dervan (California Institute of Technology). We also thank all our collaborators and the CKS user community for valuable insights and comments on kinetics simulations.

REFERENCES

[1] P. Atkins and J. de Paula (eds), *Physical Chemistry*, 7th edition, Oxford University Press, Oxford, 2001; R. Berry, R. Stephen, S. A. Rice and J. Ross, *Physical Chemistry*, 2nd edition, Oxford University Press, Oxford, 2000.

[2] F. A. Houle and D. L. Bunker, Simulation methods in kinetics courses, *J. Chem. Educ.*, 1981, **58**, 405–408.

[3] B. A. Barshop, R. F. Wrenn and C. Frieden, Analysis of numerical methods for computer simulation of kinetic processes: development of KINSIM – a flexible, portable system, *Anal. Biochem.*, 1983, **130**, 134–145.

[4] J. González-Cruz, R. Rodríguez-Sotres and M. Rodríguez-Penagos, On the convenience of using a computer simulation to teach enzyme kinetics to undergraduate students with biological chemistry-related curricula, *Biochem. Mol. Biol. Educ.*, 2003, **31**, 93–101.

[5] J. L. Holmes and N. S. Gettys, KinSimXP, a chemical kinetics simulation, *General Chemistry Collection for Students* (eds R. D. Allendoerfer) 7th edition, *J. Chem. Educ.*, 2003, **80**, 709.

[6] R. S. Macomber and I. Constantinides, Modeling complex kinetics schemes – a computational experiment, *J. Chem. Educ.*, 1991, **68**, 985–988.

[7] O. N. Temkin and D. G. Bonchev, Application of graph theory to chemical kinetics: part 1. Kinetics of complex reactions, *J. Chem. Educ.*, 1992, **69**, 544–550.

[8] R. R. Pavlis, Kinetics without steady-state approximations, *J. Chem. Educ.*, 1997, **74**, 1139–1140.

[9] J. Snoep, P. Mendes and H. Westerhoff, Teaching metabolic control analysis and kinetic modeling. Towards a portable teaching module, *The Biochemist*, 1999, February 25–28.

[10] J. T. Fermann, K. M. Stamm, A. L. Maillet, C. Nelson, S. J. Codden, M. A. Spaziani, M. Ramirez and W. J. Vining, Discovery learning using Chemland simulation software, *Chem. Educator*, 2000, **5**, 31–37.

[11] D. L. Bunker, B. Garrett, T. Kleindienst and G. S. Long III, Discrete simulation methods in combustion kinetics, *Combustion and Flame*, 1974, **23**, 373–379.

[12] D. T. Gillespie, General method for numerically simulating stochastic time evolution of coupled chemical reactions, *J. Comput. Phys.*, 1976, **22**, 403–434.

[13] W. D. Hinsberg and F. A. Houle, Chemical Kinetics Simulator v1.01, IBM, 1996. CKS may be downloaded at no charge at URL http://www.almaden.ibm.com/st/computational_science/ck/msim

[14] G. Wallraff, J. Hutchinson, W. Hinsberg, F. A. Houle, P. Seidel, R. Johnson and W. Oldham, Thermal and acid-catalyzed deprotection kinetics in deep UV resist materials, *J. Vac. Sci. Technol. B,*, 1994, **12**, 3857–3862; F. A. Houle and W. D. Hinsberg, Simulations of thermal decomposition and film growth from the group VI metal hexacarbonyls, *J. Phys. Chem.*, 1995, **99**, 14477–14485; F. A. Houle and W. D. Hinsberg, Stochastic simulations of temperature programmed desorption kinetics, *Surface Science*, 1995, **338**, 329–346; U. Wetterauer, J. Knobloch, P. Hess and F. A. Houle, In situ FTIR spectroscopy and stochastic modelling of surface chemistry of amorphous silicon growth, *J. Appl. Phys.*, 1998, **83**, 6096–6105.

[15] F. A. Houle, W. D. Hinsberg, M. Morrison, G. Wallraff, C. Larson, M. Sanchez and J. Hoffnagle, Determination of coupled acid catalysis-diffusion processes in a positive tone chemically amplified photoresist, *J. Vac. Sci. Technol. B*, 2000, **18**, 1874–1885; F. A. Houle, W. D. Hinsberg, M. I. Sanchez and J. A. Hoffnagle, The influence of resist components on image blur in a patterned positive-tone chemically amplified photoresist, *J. Vac. Sci. Technol. B*, 2002, **20**, 924–931; F. A. Houle, W. D. Hinsberg and M. I. Sanchez, Kinetic model of positive-tone resist dissolution and roughening, *Macromolecules*, 2002, **35**, 3591–3600; G. M. Gallatin, F. A. Houle and J. L. Cobb, Statistical limitations of printing 50 and 80 nm contact holes by EUV lithography, *J. Vac. Sci. Technol. B*, 2003, **21**, 3172–3176; F. A. Houle, W. D. Hinsberg and M. I. Sanchez, Acid-base reactions in a positive tone chemically amplified photoresist and their effect on imaging, *J. Vac. Sci. Technol. B*, 2004, **22**, 747–757.

[16] S. R. Crouch, T. F. Cullen, A. Scheeline and E. S. Kirkor, Kinetic determinations and some kinetic aspects of analytical chemistry, *Anal. Chem.*, 1998, **70**, 53–106; R, and S. R. Crouch, A. Scheeline and E. S. Kirkor, Kinetic determinations and some kinetic aspects of analytical chemistry, *Anal. Chem.*, 2000, **72**, 53–70.

[17] B. H. Milosavljevic and D. Meisel, Kinetic and thermodynamic aspects of adsorption on silica nanoparticles. A pulse radiolysis study, *J. Phys. Chem. B*, 2004, **108**, 1827–1830.

[18] J. Chen, A. Korner, S. L. Craig, S. Lin, D. M. Rudkevich and J. Rebek, Jr., Chemical amplification with encapsulated reagents, *Proc. Nat. Acad. Sci.*, 2002, **99**, 2593–2596.

[19] G. A. Somorjai, *Chemistry in Two Dimensions: Surfaces*, Cornell University Press, Ithaca, 1981.

[20] D. L. Bunker, Simple kinetic models from Arrhenius to the computer, *Acc. Chem. Res.*, 1974, **7**, 195–201.

[21] J. Boyle, J. Ghormley, C. Hochanandel and J. Riley, Production of hydrated electrons by flash photolysis of liquid water with light in the first continuum, *J. Phys. Chem.*, 1969, **73**, 2886–2890; H. Herrmann, Kinetics of aqueous phase reactions relevant for atmospheric chemistry, *Chem. Rev.*, 2003, **103**, 4691–4716; I. Draganic and Z. Draganic, *The Radiation Chemistry of Water*, Academic Press, New York, 1971; G. Buxton, C. Greenstock, W. P. Helman and A. Ross, Critical review of rate constants for reactions of hydrated electrons, *hydrogen atoms and hydroxyl radicals (OH/O⁻) in aqueous solution, J. Phys Chem Ref. Data*, 1988, **17**, 513–886.

[22] J. I. Steinfeld, J. S. Francisco and W. L. Hase, *Chemical Kinetics and Dynamics*, 2nd edition, Prentice-Hall, Upper Saddle River, New Jersey, 1999.

Section 2
Quantum Mechanical Methods

Section Editor: T. Daniel Crawford
Department of Chemistry
Virginia Tech
Blacksburg
VA 24061
USA

CHAPTER 2

Explicitly Correlated Approaches for Electronic Structure Computations

Edward F. Valeev

Center for Computational Molecular Science and Technology, Georgia Institute of Technology, Atlanta, GA 30332, USA and Oak Ridge National Laboratory, Oak Ridge, TN 37831, USA

Contents

1. INTRODUCTION

The basis set problem in standard wave function-based quantum chemistry is a fundamental obstacle, which makes reliable theoretical predictions of many physical and chemical properties exceedingly difficult. Quantitative descriptions of weak nonbonding interactions, thermochemistry, and reaction activation energies are particularly vulnerable to the basis set issues. The origin of the basis set problem is due to inefficient modeling of short-range correlation of electron pairs, which stems from the exclusive use of electronic orbitals to describe many-electron systems. Explicitly correlated electronic structure methods describe such correlations much more efficiently by describing the two-electron correlation directly. Here, I review some fundamental concepts and recent developments, which make chemical applications of such methods feasible.

    The prediction of molecular properties and reaction profiles of interest to chemists places rather stringent demands on theoretical methods. The prediction of chemical equilibria and reaction rates, for example, requires

ANNUAL REPORTS IN COMPUTATIONAL CHEMISTRY, VOLUME 2
ISSN: 1574-1400   DOI 10.1016/S1574-1400(06)02002-0

computation of energies of involved species accurate to kT, or $2.5 \, \text{kJ} \, \text{mol}^{-1}$ at room temperature. This level of accuracy in energy, rounded up to $1 \, \text{kcal} \, \text{mol}^{-1}$, is commonly referred to as *chemical* accuracy. Even computations of zero-temperature electronic enthalpies to this accuracy are, unfortunately, out of the question for systems with five or more atoms because it is prohibitively expensive to solve the electronic structure problem to this accuracy.

Since exact solution to an electronic Schrödinger equation is not feasible, the accuracy of an approximate solution must be estimated from a series of computations of increasing rigor. This is only possible with *ab initio* wave function methods, which can be improved systematically toward the exact solution.[1] Efficient Kohn–Sham Density Functional Theory methods cannot be improved in such a manner, and thus will not be considered here.

The total error of any electronic structure computation is due to (1) analytic approximations to the original molecular Schrödinger equation (relativistic effects are outside the scope of this article), and (2) numerical approximations due to the finite basis set.[2] The analytic approximations reduce one n-electron problem to a set of simpler coupled problems, each involving at least two electrons. The essential difference between conventional electronic structure methods and their explicitly correlated counterparts is in the functional form of the two-particle basis set. The conventional methods use antisymmetrized products of one-particle orbitals (Slater determinants) to construct two-electron and higher-order basis sets. The explicitly correlated methods also add basis functions which include explicit dependence on the distances between electrons. These extra terms are responsible for significantly smaller and faster decreasing basis set errors of the explicitly correlated methods compared to the standard approaches.

2. TWO-ELECTRON SYSTEMS

The helium atom and the isoelectronic ions are the simplest systems with two electrons. The full configuration interaction (FCI) method can be used to obtain solutions to the Schrödinger equation for two electrons without any approximations other than the finite basis set. Unfortunately, FCI energies converge extremely slowly to the basis set limit. For example, if

---

[1] Quantum Monte-Carlo (QMC) methods can, in principle, be used to obtain the exact solution. Recent applications have been very promising, but it is too early to judge how competitive QMC methods will be with the wave function methods.

[2] Other sources of error, such as roundoff error, are typically not important for chemical applications.

the basis set is constructed by saturating each angular momentum level up to L_{max}, where L_{max} is large, then the basis set error in full CI energy is proportional to $(L_{max} + 1)^{-3}$ [1,2]. This convergence rate is extremely slow: the basis set error is reduced by an order of magnitude at the cost of a roughly twofold increase of the maximum angular momentum of the basis! Numerical tests for up to $L_{max} = 11$ [3] fully confirmed these theoretical predictions for He.

The origin of such slow convergence is the inability of conventional wave functions based on Slater determinants to satisfy Kato's electron–electron cusp condition [4,5], e.g. for the ground state helium atom

$$\frac{\partial \Psi(\mathbf{r}_1, \mathbf{r}_2)}{\partial r_{12}}\bigg|_{r_1=r_2=r} = \frac{1}{2}\Psi(\mathbf{r}, \mathbf{r}), \qquad (1)$$

The cusp condition is satisfied by the exact wave function and is a necessary, but not sufficient, condition for fast basis set convergence as $L_{max} \to \infty$.

Equation (1) can be interpreted as a requirement that the kinetic energy of electrons must cancel the singularity of the Coulomb repulsion at the electron–electron coalescence point. Slater followed this logic to argue that the helium ground state wave function is linear in r_{12} near the coalescence point [6]. Subsequently, Hylleraas demonstrated numerically [7], that general expansions which included first and higher powers of r_{12}

$$\Psi = \sum_{klm} c_{klm} e^{-\zeta(r_1+r_2)}(r_1 + r_2)^k (r_1 - r_2)^l r_{12}^m \qquad (2)$$

can be used to easily compute the energy to very high accuracy. Figure 1 demonstrates the superior convergence rate of the Hylleraas method vs. the conventional CI for the ground state of the helium atom.

Hylleraas expansion is a precursor to related, even more compact expansions by Schwartz [9], Pekeris [10], Thakkar [11], and others. The best variational estimate of the He ground state energy is −2.90372 43770341195982930(2)E_h obtained with a 4648-term explicitly correlated expansion [12].

The explicit dependence of the wave function on the interelectronic distance was also recognized early to reduce critically the error in computations on the hydrogen molecule. James and Coolidge used a 13-term explicitly correlated expansion to compute the ground state energy accurate to $1\,mE_h$ [13]. Their approach was later generalized by Kołos and Wolniewicz [14] to yield some of the most accurate expansions known for

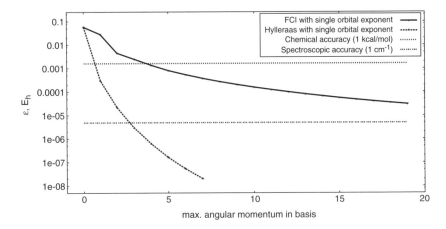

Fig. 1. Convergence of the basis set error in conventional FCI [8] and Hylleraas methods.

the hydrogen molecule, converged to 1 nanohartree [15]. This achievement is a spectacular one, even though not up to the standards of the best helium ground state energies.

3. MANY-ELECTRON SYSTEMS

Basis set convergence rates of correlation energies of many-electron systems computed with conventional, Slater determinant-based methods are just as slow as in two-electron systems. For example, the error in the second-order correlation energy of many-electron atoms due to truncation of the basis set at L_{max} is $\mathcal{O}\left((L_{max} + 1)^{-3}\right)$ [2].

Practical convergence tests in molecules typically use Dunning's correlation-consistent basis sets. The basis set error of the correlation energy computed with a correlation consistent basis is usually expressed as [16]

$$\Delta E(X) = \mathcal{O}(X^{-3}), \tag{3}$$

where X is the principal quantum number of the basis set ($X = 2, 3, \ldots$ for cc-p VDZ, cc-pVTZ, etc.). Equation (3) means that the basis set error is roughly inversely proportional to the number of functions in the basis, or, reduction in basis set error of one-order magnitude increases the cost of the calculation by a factor of 10,000! It is clear that decreasing the typical 20–40% basis set error of the cc-pVDZ set [17] to the 1% desired for chemical accuracy is not possible through brute force.

Extrapolation techniques and other a *posteriori* corrections [18] can be useful to obtain improved estimates of the energy or properties using expressions such as equation (3). These corrections, however, must be derived for each property and cannot be used to reduce basis set error beyond certain limits [19].

The application of explicitly correlated techniques to molecular systems with more than two electrons faces one basic challenge: the need to evaluate numerous and expensive many-electron integrals. For example, the Hylleraas method applied to an n-electron atom requires computation of $3n$-dimensional n-electron integrals. Evaluation of such integrals would clearly be prohibitive for nontrivial systems.

Explicitly correlated methods applicable to many-electron systems overcome the n-electron integral problem via one of the following ways:

- similarity transformation of the Hamiltonian to remove the singularity at $r_{ij} = 0$ (transcorrelated methods)
- restricting each n-electron basis function to depend on one of the interelectronic distances only (Hylleraas-CI, Gaussian geminals, and linear R12 methods).

3.1. Transcorrelated methods

The idea of the transcorrelated method of Boys and Handy [20,21] is to use a similarity transformation

$$\hat{H}_G = e^{-\hat{G}}\hat{H}e^{\hat{G}} \tag{4}$$

to remove the singularity of the electron repulsion term. Boys and Handy chose $\hat{G} = 1/2\sum_{i \neq j} r_{ij}$, although a much more general $\hat{G}$ can be chosen [22]. The transformed Hamiltonian is a three-body, non-Hermitian operator whose spectrum is identical to that of the original Hamiltonian, but whose (right-hand) eigenfunctions are electron-cusp-free.

Original applications of the Boys–Handy method were restricted to a few small systems (LiH, H_2O) [23]. One of the problems with their method was that the potential energy of the transformed Hamiltonian no longer decays with distances between electrons, thus application to larger molecular systems would be prohibitive.

Ten-no has applied the transcorrelated method setting $\hat{G}$ to a linear combination of Gaussian geminals [24]. $\hat{G}$ was optimized to cancel electron repulsion in the vicinity of the coalescence point. Initial applications to small systems (Ne, H_2O) were promising but highlighted the challenge of choosing a *universal* operator $\hat{G}$ (see, however, the somewhat underappreciated Ref. [25]) and the growing importance of three-body terms in the transformed Hamiltonian [24,26]. Future development of the transcorrelated techniques may overcome these difficulties.

3.2. Hylleraas-CI method

The Hylleraas-CI wave function [27] is expanded as a linear combination of *n*-electron basis functions Φ_m

$$\Psi = \sum_m^M \Phi_m, \tag{5}$$

each of which is an *n*-orbital product multiplied by a power of r_{ij} and properly antisymmetrized:

$$\Phi_m = \hat{\mathscr{A}}(r_{i_m j_m})^{k_m} \prod_{i=1}^n \chi_{i_m}(\mathbf{r}_i). \tag{6}$$

Thus, at the most only one r_{ij} appears in each function. In contrast, linked products (r_{ij}, r_{ik}, etc.) appear in the original Hylleraas method (also referred to as Hylleraas-r_{ij} method).

The resulting matrix elements in the Hylleraas-CI method include up to four-electron integrals only, which is a significant improvement over *n*-electron integrals of the Hylleraas-r_{ij} method. More importantly, these integrals can be computed analytically for atoms and numerically for molecules. The number of such integrals is, of course, still dramatically greater than in conventional CI calculations.

The Hylleraas-CI method has been applied successfully to systems with as many as 10 electrons [28]. Most applications, however, have been limited to extremely accurate computations on few-electron atoms (He [12], Li [29], Be [30]), because the expense of numerical integration in molecules with three and more electrons seemingly outweighs possible benefits [31].

Hylleraas-CI studies hinted that a viable explicitly correlated electronic structure method applicable to molecules must avoid painstaking numerical integration. Two approaches have emerged to deal with the many-electron integral problem.

3.3. Gaussian geminal methods

Even before the introduction of the Hylleraas-CI method, Boys [32] and Singer [33] noted that the use of Gaussian correlation factors (Gaussian *geminals*) leads to many-electron integrals, which can be evaluated analytically. A primitive spherical Gaussian geminal

$$g_k(\mathbf{r}_1, \mathbf{r}_2) = \exp(-\alpha_{1k} r_{1A_k}^2 - \alpha_{2k} r_{2B_k}^2 - \gamma_k r_{12}^2) \tag{7}$$

is a product of two *s*-type Gaussians and a Gaussian correlation factor $\exp(-\gamma_k r_{12}^2)$. Although Gaussian geminals do not satisfy the cusp condition (equation (1)), a linear combination of Gaussian geminals can describe the Coulomb hole very efficiently due to the explicit dependence on the interelectronic distance.

Gaussian geminals were initially used in accurate variational computations on two- to four-electron systems using fully correlated *n*-electron basis functions [34]. Modern variational calculations on systems with more than four electrons usually restrict each *n*-electron basis function to include at the most one Gaussian geminal [35], in complete analogy to Hylleraas-CI. The resulting matrix elements include up to four-electron integrals only. Nonfactorizable *n*-electron integrals must be computed in absence of such restrictions, which is a feasible [36], but very expensive proposition.

Second-order Møller-Plesset computations with Gaussian geminals require up to four-electron integrals also. Coupled cluster computations with Gaussian geminals involve up to five-electron integrals, which must be avoided in practical computations [37].

Early applications of Gaussian geminals methods were promising [38]. The full potential of the approach, however, was only realized via thorough optimization of some or all nonlinear parameters [11,39].[3] Modern Gaussian geminals methods can reduce the basis set errors to sub-cm^{-1} level. For example, the most accurate wave function for hydrogen molecule is a 1200-term Gaussian geminal expansion which results in a basis set error of 10^{-4} cm^{-1} [40]. Perturbation theory and coupled cluster methods have generally aimed at very precise calculations on systems with up to four electrons (He, H_2, Be, and LiH) [41]. Calculations on larger systems have been hindered by the high computational cost of nonlinear optimization and evaluating three- and higher-electron integrals [42], although more modest computations have been feasible for a while [43].

---

[3] Each Gaussian geminal in equation (7) has nine such parameters.

3.4. Linear R12 methods

The works of Hylleraas have demonstrated that the electronic energy for two-electron atoms can be calculated to a very high accuracy by including terms dependent on r_{12}^k. The fact that linear r_{12} terms alone are sufficient for high accuracy was not realized until 40 years after Hylleraas. Handy [25] emphasized that variational wave functions for the helium isoelectronic series which included only zeroth and first powers of r_{12} terms recovered more than 98% of correlation energy with only 18 terms! It seemed logical that similar findings could be extended to molecules as well.

Kutzelnigg formulated the idea of linear R12 methods in his groundbreaking 1985 article [44]. He demonstrated that the addition of a single term, namely, the reference determinant multiplied by the r_{12} factor, dramatically improves the basis set convergence of the error in the helium atom FCI energy, from $\mathcal{O}\left((L_{max}+1)^{-3}\right)$ to $\mathcal{O}\left((L_{max}+1)^{-7}\right)$. Such an approach, applied variationally, would require numerical evaluation of up to four-electron integrals. Kutzelnigg also argued how these many-electron integrals can be eliminated or approximated safely using the resolution of the identity (RI). For example, the following typical three-electron integral

$$\langle ijm|r_{12}r_{23}^{-1}|mkl\rangle \approx \sum_p \langle ij|r_{12}|mp\rangle\langle mp|r_{12}^{-1}|kl\rangle, \qquad (8)$$

is approximated via two-electron integrals (i, j, k, l, m are occupied MOs). In the atomic case, the approximation (8) is *exact* if the atom-centered basis $\{p\}$ is saturated to three times the maximum angular momentum of occupied AOs. Proceeding in similar vein, all many-electron integrals reduce to at most four-center two-electron integrals. Such integrals can be evaluated rather efficiently and at comparable cost to the standard electron repulsion integrals [45,46]. Density-fitting techniques, which have been used with great success to speed up conventional computations, can reduce the computational cost of the two-electron integrals even further [47]. It is also possible to diminish the angular momentum requirements on the RI basis set [48].

Early tests of linear R12 methods [49] were extremely positive. Linear R12 analogues of perturbation theory [50], configuration interaction [51], and coupled cluster theory [52] methods were developed shortly thereafter. The number of additional wave function parameters in method X-R12 due to the R12 correction is small relative to the conventional method X. Therefore, fairly large systems can be tackled with linear R12 methods. Initial applications, however, had to use fairly complete, uncontracted Gaussian basis sets (50 and more basis functions per heavy atom) to expand the Hartree–Fock orbitals and to approximate the many-electron integrals. Second-order Møller-Plesset energies could, nevertheless, be computed for rather large molecular systems, such as ferrocene [53] and benzene dimer [54].

The asymptotic convergence rate of the basis error in linear R12 theories is $\mathscr{O}\left((L_{max}+1)^{-7}\right)$, or $\mathscr{O}\left((L_{max}+1)^{-5}\right)$ in the so-called standard approximation A variant, which omits commutators of the exchange operator with r_{12}. These convergence rates are much better than the conventional $\mathscr{O}\left((L_{max}+1)^{-3}\right)$ rate, although slower than the exponential convergence of Gaussian geminals-based methods. Very high accuracy on the order of few cm^{-1} has been attained with linear R12 methods for relative [55,56] and absolute energies [57]. More importantly, basis set errors can be reduced to below the $1\,kcal\,mol^{-1}$ threshold much easier with linear R12 methods than with their conventional counterparts, for properties as difficult as atomization energies and reaction enthalpies [58].

In a major development, Klopper and Samson formulated MP2-R12 theory to use an auxiliary basis set (ABS) for RI [59]. This approach opened a possibility to use linear R12 methods with significantly smaller orbital (Hartree–Fock) basis sets. The error due to RI, however, can be very large if the standard basis sets from early applications of R12 methods are used. Therefore, it is imperative to include Hartree–Fock basis set in ABS and/or use the complementary auxiliary basis set (CABS) approach [60]. Another potentially useful approach is to use numerical quadratures to evaluate three-electron integrals [61].

From the chemists' point of view, linear R12 methods are currently most successful at striking the balance between reduced basis set errors and the associated increase in cost. Practical applications are now becoming possible with the help of several openly available computer programs [62–66].

3.5. Some recent developments

Given the limited scope of this article, it is not possible to even mention all important recent works in the area of explicitly correlated theory. Therefore, I will only concentrate on developments of the past several years which extend applicability of linear R12-type methods in the regime of chemical accuracy.

Linear R12 theories which use a separate basis for the RI [59,60] hold the promise that Hartree–Fock solutions obtained with small orbital basis sets (OBS) can be used to compute accurate correlation energies. Early tests with double- and triple-zeta quality OBSs were somewhat disappointing [59]. MP2-R12/2A' method, for example, recovers 90.1% and 96.6% of the valence second-order correlation energy of Ne atom with the augmented double- and triple-zeta basis sets, respectively. These figures are significantly better than the corresponding MP2 values: 64.6% and 85.1%. One would like, however, to reduce the basis set error to 1% or below.

The relatively poor performance of MP2-R12 method with small OBS is in agreement with a much earlier, seminal study of Persson and Taylor [67]. They discovered that the linear r_{ij} terms are ineffective at correcting *short* CI expansions for the ground state of He atom. Therefore, they argued that the linear r_{ij} correlation factor is not an effective means to reduce basis set error of double- and triple-zeta basis wave functions. Their constructive finding was that Gaussian geminals with fixed exponents were much better correlation factors than r_{ij}: more than 90% of correlation energy was recovered for Ne at the cc-pVDZ MP2 level augmented with six geminals. The attractive feature of their approach compared to other Gaussian geminal-based methods is lack of nonlinear optimization. Unfortunately, the authors did not advance this approach any further.

In a sense, these findings are merely a confirmation of a lesser-known fact that the electron cusp itself is not the reason for poor basis set convergence of conventional methods [68]. For practical basis sets, significant deviations from the exact wave function are observed in the 0.5–1 Bohr vicinity of the cusp for valence pairs, in addition to the higher probability at the coalescence point. Linear r_{ij} terms alone, however, are not sufficient to correct the depth and shape of the Coulomb hole substantially (see Fig. 2). Conclusive quantitative explanation for this observation is still pending.

Several recent studies have recently appeared that use alternative correlation factors, while retaining the practicality of the standard approximations of linear R12 thories [69–71]. A single Slater-type geminal is among the most efficient correlation factors: in excess of 98% of correlation energy can be recovered with a double-zeta basis if standard approximation A' is used [69]. In practice, a linear combination of a few Gaussian geminals can be used effectively to fit the Slater geminal [70,71]. Importantly, May et al. [70] examined standard approximations of linear R12 theory and confirmed their validity even when a very small OBS is used. Although more work remains to be done in this area of research, it is clear now that the goal of 1% basis set error in correlation energy can be achieved with a triple-zeta quality basis.

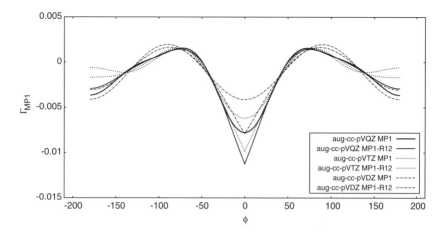

Fig. 2. Angular profile of the Coulomb hole in Ne atom, computed with and without linear r_{ij} terms. Plotted is the diagonal of the first-order two-particle reduced density for the $2s_\alpha 2s_\beta$ electron pair. The nucleus is fixed at the origin, electron 1 is fixed at (1, 0, 0), electron 2 is at (cos ϕ, sin ϕ, 0). Cusps correspond to the r_{ij}-corrected computations.

4. OUTLOOK

This concludes my short introduction to explicitly correlated methods. The main lesson is that the judicious use of the interelectronic distances in the *n*-electron basis greatly reduces the basis set error in wave function computation of electronic structure. Recent progress in the area extends the applicability of explicitly correlated methods to molecules with tens and hundreds of atoms, all with relatively modest (double- and triple-zeta) basis sets. Openly available robust tools have recently become available to general chemical community [62–66]. The future is certain to bring more development in this exciting area of research as well as in complementary subjects – accurate description of strong electron correlation, vibrational contributions to the enthalpy, relativistic effects, among others. Readers interested in an in-depth review of the explicitly correlated theory and its applications in atomic and molecular physics and chemistry should consult a recent book on the subject [72].

ACKNOWLEDGMENTS

Funding for this work was provided in part by the Laboratory Directed Research and Development Program of Oak Ridge National Laboratory, managed by UT-Battelle, LLC, for the U.S. Department of Energy under

Contract No. DE-AC05-00OR22725; and by School of Chemistry and Biochemistry of Georgia Institute of Technology.

REFERENCES

[1] C. Schwartz, Importance of angular correlations between atomic electrons, *Phys. Rev.*, 1962, **126**, 1015.

[2] W. Kutzelnigg and J. D. Morgan, Rates of convergence of the partial-wave expansions of atomic correlation energies, *J. Chem. Phys.*, 1992, **96**, 4484.

[3] D. P. Carroll, H. J. Silverstone and R. M. Metzger, Piecewise polynomial configuration interaction natural orbital study of $1s^2$ helium, *J. Chem. Phys.*, 1979, **71**, 4142.

[4] T. Kato, On the eigenfunctions of many-particle systems in quantum mechanics, *Commun. Pure Appl. Math.*, 1957, **10**, 151.

[5] R. T. Pack and W. B. Brown, Cusp conditions for molecular wavefunctions, *J. Chem. Phys.*, 1966, **45**, 556.

[6] J. C. Slater, Central fields and Rydberg formulas in wave mechanics, *Phys. Rev.*, 1928, **31**, 333.

[7] E. A. Hylleraas, Neue berechnung der energie des heliums im grundzustande, sowie des tiefsten terms von ortho-helium, *Z. Phys.*, 1929, **54**, 347.

[8] E. F. Valeev, W. D. Allen, H. F. Schaefer, A conventional ci study of the ground state of He using basis functions up to $l = 19$. Method is described in Ref. [73].

[9] H. M. Schwartz, Ritz-Hylleraas solutions of the ground state of two-electron atoms involving fractional powers, *Phys. Rev.*, 1960, **120**, 483.

[10] C. L. Pekeris, Ground state of two-electron atoms, *Phys. Rev.*, 1958, **112**, 1649.

[11] A. J. Thakkar and V. H. Smith, Jr., Compact and accurate integral-transform wave functions. i. the 1^1s state of the helium-like ions from H^- through Mg^{10+}., *Phys. Rev. A*, 1977, **15**, 1–15.

[12] J. S. Sims and S. Hagstrom, High-precision Hy-CI variational calculations for the ground state of neutral helium and helium-like ions, *Int. J. Quantum Chem.*, 2002, **90**, 1600–1609.

[13] H. M. James and A. S. Coolidge, The ground state of the hydrogen molecule, *J. Chem. Phys.*, 1933, **1**, 825–835.

[14] W. Kołos and L. Wolniewicz, Potential energy curves for the $x^1\sigma_g{}^+$, $b^3\sigma_u{}^+$ and $c\,^1\pi_u$ states of the hydrogen molecule, *J. Chem. Phys.*, 1965, **43**, 2429–2441.

[15] L. Wolniewicz, Nonadiabatic energies of the ground state of the hydrogen molecule, *J. Chem. Phys.*, 1995, **103**, 1792–1799.

[16] T. Helgaker, W. Klopper, H. Koch and J. Noga, Basis-set convergence of correlated calculation on water, *J. Chem. Phys.*, 1997, **106**, 9639.

[17] A. K. Wilson and T. H. Dunning, Benchmark calculations with correlated molecular wave functions. x. comparison with "exact" mp2 calculations on Ne, HF, H_2O, and N_2, *J. Chem. Phys.*, 1997, **106**, 8718.

[18] W. Klopper, K. L. Bak, P. Jørgensen, J. Olsen and T. Helgaker, Highly accurate calculations of molecular electronic structure, *J. Phys. B: At. Mol. Opt. Phys.*, 1999, **32**, R103–R130.

[19] E. F. Valeev, W. D. Allen, R. Hernandez, C. D. Sherrill and H. F. Schaefer, On the accuracy limits of orbital expansion methods: explicit effects of k-functions on atomic and molecular energies, *J. Chem. Phys.*, 2003, **118**, 8594.

[20] S. F. Boys and N. C. Handy, A condition to remove the indeterminacy in interelectronic correlation functions, *Proc. Roy. Soc. (London) A*, 1969, **309**, 209.

[21] S. F. Boys and N. C. Handy, The determination of energies and wavefunctions with full electronic correlation, *Proc. Roy. Soc. (London) A*, 1969, **310**, 43.

[22] M. Nooijen and R. J. Bartlett, Elimination of coulombic infinities through transformation of the Hamiltonian, *J. Chem. Phys.*, 1998, **109**, 8232.

[23] N. C. Handy, The transcorrelated method for accurate correlation energies using gaussian-type functions: examples on He, H_2, LiH, and H_2O, *Mol. Phys.*, 1972, **23**, 1.

[24] S. Ten-no, A feasible transcorrelated method for treating electronic cusps using a frozen gaussian geminal, *Chem. Phys. Lett.*, 2000, **330**, 169–174.

[25] N. C. Handy, Towards an understanding of the form of correlated wavefunctions for atoms, *J. Chem. Phys.*, 1973, **58**, 279–287.

[26] O. Hino, Y. Tonimura and S. Ten-no, Biorthogonal approach for explicitly correlated calculations using the transcorrelated Hamiltonian, *J. Chem. Phys.*, 2001, **115**, 7865–7871.

[27] J. S. Sims and S. Hagstrom, Combined configuration-interaction-Hylleraas-type wave-function study of the ground state of the beryllium atom, *Phys. Rev. A*, 1971, **4**, 908.

[28] D. C. Clary and N. C. Handy, CI-Hylleraas variational calculations on the ground state of the neon atom, *Phys. Rev. A*, 1976, **14**, 1607.

[29] A. Luchow and H. Kleindienst, Accurate upper and lower bounds to the ^2S states of the lithium atom, *Int. J. Quantum Chem.*, 1994, **51**, 211–224.

[30] G. Busse, H. Kleindienst and A. Luchow, Nonrelativistic energies for the be atom: Double-linked Hylleraas-CI calculation, *Int. J. Quantum Chem.*, 1998, **66**, 241–247.

[31] D. Frye, A. Preiskorn and E. Clementi, The Hylleraas-CI method in molecular calculations. iii. Implementation and numerical verification of a three-electron many-center theory, *J. Comput. Chem.*, 1991, **12**, 560–564.

[32] S. F. Boys, The integral formulae for the variational solution of the molecular many-electron wave equation in terms of gaussian functions with direct electron correlation, *Proc. Roy. Soc. (London) A*, 1960, **258**, 402.

[33] K. Singer, The use of Gaussian (exponential quadratic) wave functions in molecular problems. i. general formulae for the evaluation of integrals, *Proc. Roy. Soc. (London) A*, 1960, **258**, 412.

[34] K. M. Karunakaran and R. E. Christoffersen, Explicitly correlated configuration interaction wavefunctions using spherical gaussians. Formulation and initial application to lih, *J. Chem. Phys.*, 1975, **62**, 1972–1973.

[35] W. Cencek and J. Rychlewski, Many-electron explicitly correlated gaussian functions. i. General theory and test results, *J. Chem. Phys.*, 1993, **98**, 1252.

[36] P. M. Kozlowski and L. Adamowicz, An effective method for generating nonadiabatic many-body wave function using explicitly correlated Gaussian-type functions, *J. Chem. Phys.*, 1991, **95**, 6681–6698.

[37] K. Szalewicz, J. G. Zabolitzki, B. Jeziorski and H. J. Monkhorst, Atomic and molecular correlation energies with explicitly correlated gaussian geminals. iv. a simplified treatment of strong orthogonality in MBPT and coupled cluster calculations, *J. Chem. Phys.*, 1984, **81**, 2723–2731.

[38] N. C. Handy, Correlated Gaussian wavefunctions, *Mol. Phys.*, 1973, **26**, 169.

[39] B. Jeziorski and K. Szalewicz, High-accuracy compton profile of molecular hydrogen from explicitly correlated Gaussian wave function, *Phys. Rev. A*, 1979, **19**, 2360–2365.

[40] W. Cencek and W. Kutzelnigg, Accurate relativistic energies of one- and two-electron systems using Gaussian wave functions, *J. Chem. Phys.*, 1996, **105**, 5878–5885.

[41] R. Bukowski, B. Jeziorski and K. Szalewicz, Gaussian geminals in explicitly correlated coupled cluster theory including single and double excitations, *J. Chem. Phys.*, 1999, **110**, 4165.

[42] R. Bukowski, B. Jeziorski, S. Rybak and K. Szalewicz, Second-order correlation energy for H_2O using explicitly correlated Gaussian geminals, *J. Chem. Phys.*, 1995, **102**, 888.

[43] L. Adamowicz and A. J. Sadlej, Perturbation calculation of molecular correlation energy using gaussian-type geminals. Second-order pair energies of LiH and BH, *J. Chem. Phys.*, 1978, **69**, 3992–4000.

[44] W. Kutzelnigg, r_{12}-dependent terms in the wave function as closed sums of partial wave amplitudes for large l, *Theor. Chim. Acta*, 1985, **68**, 445.

[45] W. Klopper and R. Röhse, Computation of some new two-electron Gaussian integrals, *Theor. Chim. Acta*, 1992, **83**, 441.

[46] E. F. Valeev and H. F. Schaefer, Evaluation of two-electron integrals for explicit r_{12} theories, *J. Chem. Phys.*, 2000, **113**, 3990.

[47] F. R. Manby, Density fitting in second-order linear-r_{12} Møller-Plesset perturbation theory, *J. Chem. Phys.*, 2003, **119**, 4607–4613.

[48] S. Ten-no and F. R. Manby, Density fitting for the decomposition of three-electron integrals in explicitly correlated electronic structure theory, *J. Chem. Phys.*, 2003, **119**, 5358–5363.

[49] W. Klopper and W. Kutzelnigg, Møller-Plesset calculations taking care of the correlation cusp, *Chem. Phys. Lett.*, 1987, **134**, 17.

[50] W. Kutzelnigg and W. Klopper, Wave functions with terms linear in the interelectronic coordinates to take care of the correlation cusp. i. general theory, *J. Chem. Phys.*, 1991, **94**, 1985.

[51] R. J. Gdanitz, A formulation of multiple-reference CI with terms linear in the inter-electronic distances, *Chem. Phys. Lett.*, 1993, **210**, 253.

[52] J. Noga, W. Klopper and W. Kutzelnigg, *Recent Advances in Coupled-Cluster Methods*, World Scientific, Singapore, 1997, p. 1.

[53] W. Klopper and H. P. Lüthi, Towards the accurate computation of properties of transition metal compounds: the binding energy of ferrocene, *Chem. Phys. Lett.*, 1996, **262**, 546.

[54] M. O. Sinnokrot, E. F. Valeev and C. D. Sherrill, Estimates of the *ab initio* limit for pi–pi interactions: the benzene dimer, *J. Am. Chem. Soc.*, 2002, **124**, 10887.

[55] W. Klopper, M. Quack and M. A. Suhm, A new *ab initio* based six-dimensional semi-empirical pair interaction potential for HF, *Chem. Phys. Lett.*, 1996, **261**, 35.

[56] E. F. Valeev, W. D. Allen, H. F. Schaefer and A. G. Császár, The second-order Møller-Plesset limit for the barrier to linearity of water, *J. Chem. Phys.*, 2001, **114**, 2875.

[57] R. Röhse, W. Kutzelnigg, R. Jaquet and W. Klopper, Potential energy surface of the H_3^+ ground state in the neighborhood of the minimum with microhartree accuracy and vibrational frequencies derived from it, *J. Chem. Phys.*, 1994, **101**, 2231–2243.

[58] J. Noga, P. Valiron and W. Klopper, The accuracy of atomization energies from explicitly correlated coupled-cluster calculations, *J. Chem. Phys.*, 2001, **115**, 2022–2032.

[59] W. Klopper and C. C. M. Samson, Explicitly correlated second-order Møller-Plesset methods with auxiliary basis sets, *J. Chem. Phys.*, 2002, **116**, 6397.

[60] E. F. Valeev, Improving on the resolution of the identity in linear r12 *ab initio* theories, *Chem. Phys. Lett.*, 2004, **395** (4–6), 190–195.

[61] S. Ten-no, Explicitly correlated second order perturbation theory: introduction of a rational generator and numerical quadratures, *J. Chem. Phys.*, 2004, **121**, 117–129.

[62] C. L. Janssen, I. B. Nielsen, M. L. Leininger, E. F. Valeev and E. T. Seidl, *The Massively Parallel Quantum Chemistry Program (MPQC): Version 2.2*, Sandia National Laboratories, Livermore, CA USA, http://www.mpqc.org/(2003).

[63] J. Noga, P. Valiron, W. Klopper and T. Helgaker, DIRCCR12-OS is a direct CCSD(T)-R12 program, 2003.

[64] R. J. Gdanitz, G. D. Black, C. S. Lansing, B. J. Palmer and K. L. Schuchardt, Registering the amica electronic structure code in the extensible computational chemistry environment, *J. Comp. Chem.*, 2005, **26**, 214–225.

[65] T. D. Crawford, C. D. Sherrill, E. F. Valeev, J. T. Fermann, R. A. King, M. L. Leininger, S. T. Brown, C. L. Janssen, E. T. Seidl, J. P. Kenny and W. D. Allen, PSI 3.2, http://www.psicode.org/(2003).

[66] H. -J. Werner, P. J. Knowles, R. Lindh, M. Schütz, P. Celani, T. Korona, F. R. Manby, G. Rauhut, R. D. Amos, A. Bernhardsson, A. Berning, D. L. Cooper, M. J. O. Deegan, A. J. Dobbyn, F. Eckert, C. Hampel, G. Hetzer, A. W. Lloyd, S. J. McNicholas, W. Meyer, M. E. Mura, A. Nicklass, P. Palmieri, R. Pitzer, U. Schumann, H. Stoll, A. J. Stone, R. Tarroni and T. Thorsteinsson, Molpro, developmental version 2002.9, a package of *ab initio* programs, see http://www.molpro.net/(2005).

[67] B. J. Persson and P. R. Taylor, Accurate quantum-chemical calculation: the use of Gaussian-type geminal functions in the treatment of electron correlation, *J. Chem. Phys.*, 1996, **105**, 5915.

[68] T. L. Gilbert, Interpretation of the rapid convergence of correlated wave functions, *Rev. Mod. Phys.*, 1963, **35**, 491.

[69] S. Ten-no, Initiation of explicitly correlated Slater-type germinal theory, *Chem. Phys. Lett.*, 2004, **398**, 56–61.

[70] A. J. May, E. Valeev, R. Polly and F. R. Manby, Analysis of the errors in explicitly correlated electronic structure theory, *Phys. Chem. Chem. Phys.*, 2005, **7**, 2710–2713.

[71] D. P. Tew and W. Klopper, New correlation factors for explicitly correlated electronic wavefunctions, *J. Chem. Phys.*, 2005, **123**, 074101.

[72] J. Rychlewski (ed.), Explicitly correlated wave functions in chemistry and physics. Theory and applications. In *Progress in Theoretical Chemistry and Physics*, Springer, New York, 2003, Vol. 13.

[73] R. T. Brown and P. R. Fontana, Configuration interaction in two- and three-electron atoms, *J. Chem. Phys.*, 1966, **45**, 4248.

CHAPTER 3

Hybrid Methods: ONIOM(QM:MM) and QM/MM

Thom Vreven[1] and Keiji Morokuma[2]

[1]Gaussian, Inc., 340 Quinnipiac Street, Building 40, Wallingford, CT 06492, USA
[2]Cherry Emerson Center for Scientific Computation and Department of
Chemistry, Emory University, Atlanta, GA 30322, USA

Contents

1. INTRODUCTION

One of the main themes in computational chemistry is to find a balance
between the accuracy of the results and the computational cost. However,
the computational costs of accurate methods scale very unfavorably with
the size of the system. Molecular Mechanics (MM), semiempirical,
and independent particle models such as Hartree-Fock (HF) or Density
Functional Theory (DFT) methods scale linearly, but MP2, MP3, MP4, and
MP5 scale N^5, N^6, N^7, and N^8, respectively. It is clear that the scaling
problem becomes more severe with increasing N, and it is often not possible to increase the accuracy of the calculation when large systems
are considered. Although linear scaling implementations are available
for semi-empirical and DFT methods, they have pre-factors that are too

ANNUAL REPORTS IN COMPUTATIONAL CHEMISTRY, VOLUME 2
ISSN: 1574-1400   DOI 10.1016/S1574-1400(06)02003-2

high for (dynamics) calculations on very large systems, and often more accurate methods are needed.

The so-called hybrid methods offer a solution to the scaling problem. The basic idea starts with the realization that various regions of the system often play very different roles in the process under investigation. Examples of such cases are most enzymatic reactions, where the bond breaking and forming takes place only in the active site, and the effect of the protein environment is usually only steric or electrostatic. Other examples are processes in solution, where the role of the solute is clearly very different from that of the solvent. With hybrid methods, each region is treated with a different computational method. It often turns out that expensive computational methods are only required for the part of the system 'where the action takes place', while less expensive methods can be used for the supporting regions. The result is that very accurate results can be obtained for a fraction of the computational cost of conventional methods.

Over the years, a variety of hybrid methods have been presented, which are conceptually quite similar but differ in a number of details. Most methods can only combine a Quantum Mechanical (QM) method with a MM method, which is generally referred to as QM/MM. Only several hybrid methods can also combine QM with QM, or more than two different computational methods. Other distinctions involve the description of the interaction between the regions, or how the regions are connected when there is covalent interaction between them.

In this chapter we will briefly discuss the history of hybrid methods, the main differences between the various schemes, and how they are used for the investigation of potential surfaces or properties. We will focus on our own hybrid method, called ONIOM, which can in principle use any computational method, combine QM with QM as well as QM with MM, and do so for any number of layers (although there are some restrictions in the current implementation).

2. DEFINING THE POTENTIAL SURFACE

2.1. QM/MM

Three papers, by Warshel and Levitt [1], Singh and Kollman [2], and Field, Bash, and Karplus [3], are usually credited with having introduced QM/MM methods. In these papers the QM/MM potential was presented as:

$$E^{QM/MM-EE} = E^{v,QM} + E^{MM} + E^{QM-MM} \tag{1}$$

$E^{v,QM}$ is the QM energy of the QM region, in the field v generated by the partial charges of the MM region, and E^{MM} is the MM energy of the MM region (containing all the bonded and non-bonded MM terms that involve exclusively centers from the MM region). E^{QM-MM} describes the interaction between the two regions and has two components. First, if there is covalent bonding between the QM and MM region, it contains the 'border crossing' bonded MM terms that involve both QM and MM centers. Second, E^{QM-MM} contains all the MM van der Waals terms that involve one QM center and one MM center. Because $E^{v,QM}$ already includes it, E^{QM-MM} does not contain the electrostatic interaction between the QM and MM region.

Kollman also suggested a simplified potential [2], with was further explored by Thiel [4]:

$$E^{QM/MM-ME} = E^{MM} + E^{QM} + E^{Q,QM-MM} \qquad (2)$$

The QM energy, E^{QM}, no longer involves the potential from the MM region. Instead, the electrostatic interaction between the regions is calculated in $E^{Q,QM-MM}$, by assigning partial charges to the QM atoms, and using the regular expressions for point charge interactions from the MM force field. Thiel referred to the QM/MM potential using equation (1), $E^{QM/MM-EE}$, as electronic embedding QM/MM, and to the potential using equation (2), $E^{QM/MM-ME}$, as mechanical embedding QM/MM. The advantages of electronic embedding are that the wave function can be polarized by the charge distribution from the MM region, and that it provides a more accurate description of the electrostatic interaction between the two regions. On the other hand, it appears that in many cases the accuracy of the mechanical embedding version is sufficient, and the simplified expression facilitates the implementation of methods to explore the potential surfaces.

When covalent interaction exists between the QM region and the MM region, the dangling bonds need to be capped in the QM calculation. Analogous to conventional model system calculations, the simplest solution is to use hydrogen atoms, which are then referred to as link atoms (LA). A further complication of covalent interaction is that there may be partial charges from the MM region very close to the QM region. Since in molecular mechanics force fields the interactions between partial charges are scaled when they are less then three bonds apart, full inclusion of the partial charges in the boundary region in $E^{v,QM}$ may lead to overestimation of the electrostatic interaction, while also the polarization of the wave function can be unphysical. Kollman zeroed the charges that are less than three bonds away from the QM region. Although this will avoid overpolarization, it is rather arbitrary and also may lead to underestimation of the electrostatic interaction between the regions. Alternatives to zeroing the charges are to use delocalized (gaussian) charges instead of point charges [5,6], or to redistribute the charges close to the boundary (see ref. [7] for recent work).

2.2. ONIOM

Morokuma and co-workers wrote the QM/MM expression as an extrapolation, instead of equations (1) and (2) [8–11]:

$$E^{\text{ONIOM}} = E^{\text{model,QM}} + E^{\text{real,MM}} - E^{\text{model,MM}} \tag{3}$$

real and *model* refer to the full system and the QM region, respectively. ONIOM uses link atoms to saturate the dangling bonds, which together with the QM region form the model system. In Fig. 1 (based on the work in ref. [12]) we illustrate the various components of the ONIOM scheme. Besides some details concerning the bonded MM terms that involve both QM and MM atoms, the ONIOM expression (3) is essentially the same as the QM/MM-ME expression (2). $E^{\text{model,QM}}$ is equivalent to E^{QM}, and $(E^{\text{real,MM}} - E^{\text{model,MM}})$ in equation (3) describes both the MM region and the interaction between the two regions, similar to $(E^{\text{MM}} + E^{\text{Q,QM}-\text{MM}})$ in equation (2).

   An important realization was that, unlike equations (1) and (2), all three terms in equation (3) involve 'chemically realistic systems'. That allows us to substitute the MM method in equation (3) for any other computational method:

$$E^{\text{ONIOM}} = E^{\text{real,low}} + E^{\text{model,high}} - E^{\text{model,low}} \tag{4}$$

Now *high* denotes a high level computational method (the QM method in QM/MM), and *low* a lower level method (the MM method in QM/MM). *high* and *low* are no longer restricted to QM and MM, respectively, so that QM methods can also be combined with other QM methods, to form QM/QM. From equation (3) it is clear that the interaction between the layers is included at the low level method, and that the method defaults to mechanical embedding for QM/MM combinations. The method is referred to as ONIOM, *Our own N-layered Integrated molecular Orbital molecular Mechanics*. As the name indicates, ONIOM can also be used for more

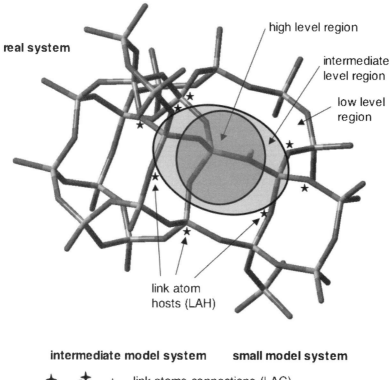

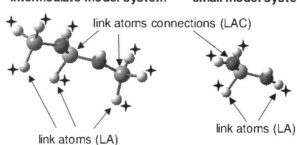

Fig. 1. Example of a three layer ONIOM partitioning of a zeolite model for the study of O1-O4 proton transfer, based on the work presented in ref. [12].

than two layers, for example:

$$E^{ONIOM3} = E^{real,low} - E^{int-model,low} + E^{int-model,intermediate}$$
$$- E^{model,intermediate} + E^{model,high} \tag{5}$$

int-model indicates an intermediate model system (defining the 'middle layer'), which is treated with the *intermediate* computational level.

Recently, Tschumper extended ONIOM to include distinct high level regions [13]. Each of these regions is calculated at the high computational level, but the interaction between them is included at the low computational level.

The QM/MM and QM/QM hybrid methods appear to be very similar, but QM/QM combinations can be even more powerful because also electronic effects can cross the border. This will, of course, only be included at the low level method, and one must ensure that all three sub-calculations describe the correct electronic structure and state. Pushing the limits, we showed that even phenyl groups can be partitioned into two different regions (in the prediction of the dissociation energy of hexaphenylethane) and that the delocalization of an excited state of a conjugated polyene can cross the border region [11].

Although ONIOM in its original formulation follows the mechanical embedding scheme, we extended the formalism of ONIOM(QM:MM) to include electronic embedding [14,15]. Because the model system needs to be identical for both the QM and MM calculation, we include the environment charges in both, and do not change the real system calculation from equation (3):

$$E^{\text{ONIOM(QM:MM)}-EE} = E^{v,\text{model,QM}} + E^{\text{real,MM}} - E^{v,\text{model,MM}} \qquad (6)$$

To avoid overpolarization of the wave function, we may scale charges close to the QM region. Because these charges will then be scaled in both the $E^{v,\text{model,QM}}$ and $E^{v,\text{model,MM}}$ terms, the balance will not change. The charge interactions that are overcounted or undercounted at the QM level in the $E^{v,\text{model,QM}}$ will be balanced at the MM level in the $E^{v,\text{model,MM}}$ term.

ONIOM is implemented in the Gaussian package for electronic structure calculations [16]. Most methods that are available in the package can be used in ONIOM, for either two or three layer calculations. Also most methods for the investigation of the potential surfaces can be used. However, not all the developments presented in this chapter are available in the distributed version of Gaussian.

2.3. Capping the dangling bonds

ONIOM uses link atoms to cap the dangling bonds that result from covalent interaction between the regions. Several other QM/MM implementations use localized orbitals at the boundary instead of link atoms, which are located on the MM atom or along the bond at the boundary [17–19]. The localized orbitals can represent the substituted MM fragment more accurately than a link atom, and because the charge is delocalized, also somewhat alleviate overpolarization. For this accuracy, localized orbitals are often preferred over link atoms, although the number of studies that directly compare link atoms with frozen orbital methods is limited [19,20]. The implementation is, however, more complicated than link atoms, and due to the required parameterization, much less general.

In order for the potential surface to be well defined, the link atom must not introduce additional degrees of freedom. The simplest solution is always to minimize the energy with respect to the link atom coordinates, but this is not feasible in dynamics calculations, and the link atom may end up in an orientation very different from the group it replaces. In ONIOM, we place the link atom on the line between the atom it is connected to (the link atom connection, LAC) and the atom it replaces (the link atom host, LAH), and obtain the LAC-LA distance by scaling the LAC-LAH distance [8,21]. Besides the correct number of degrees of freedom, this scheme has the advantage that compression/elongation effects of the MM part onto the LAC-LAH bond are transferred to the QM calculation, through compression/elongation of the LAC-LA bond.

Although most QM/MM schemes use either localized orbitals and link atoms, some implementations use other techniques such as pseudo-potentials [22,23], or adjusted link atoms in the case of semi-empirical methods [24]. For ab initio QM methods, the 'shift operator' would provide a way to adjust the link atom [25]. Finally, one particular boundary problem occurs in solid state studies, such as zeolites and surfaces, where a single LAH may have bonds to more than one QM atom. Because two (or more) link atoms for the same LAH would be too close together, an interesting solution appears to be the oligovalent link atoms [26], which saturate multiple dangling bonds simultaneously.

3. INVESTIGATING POTENTIAL SURFACES

3.1. Monte Carlo and molecular dynamics

In the study of large systems, such as a solute with explicit solvent molecules, proteins, or other biochemical systems, it is often necessary to include kinetic effects and to sample the configuration space carefully. This is done through the use of molecular dynamics (MD) or Monte Carlo (MC) methods. This poses no problem for QM/MM potentials when the computational time of the QM contribution is of similar order as the MM contributions to the energy and gradient, and indeed the first QM/MM studies involved dynamics calculations with semi-empirical QM methods.

On the other hand, if the QM contribution is much more expensive than the MM contributions, it becomes a bottleneck that makes the QM/MM simulation prohibitively expensive.

QM/MM MD can be made feasible through a Car-Parrinello (CP) approach [27], in the same way CP makes QM dynamics calculations feasible. Several groups presented CP QM/MM methods using plane-wave (PW) expansions [28–30]. A particular concern with a PW based QM/MM scheme with electronic embedding is the electron spill-out from the QM region, due to the non-local character of the basis set [29]. Recently, we presented the ONIOM-ADMP method [31], which is based on the Atom-centered Density Matrix Propagation approach (ADMP). Though similar to CP-MD, ADMP uses localized basis functions, which reduce the problem of electron spill-out in the QM/MM version.

A particular problem with QM/MM dynamics is that the definition of the QM region may need to change over the course of the simulation. For example, when a solute/solvent system is studied with QM/MM methods, the accuracy is often improved by inclusion of a select number of solvent molecules in the QM region. However, when the system is studied dynamically, the "QM solvent" atoms can migrate away from the solute. To avoid this problem, one can employ a switching function that exchanges QM solvent molecules and MM solvent molecules when they cross a predefined border around the solute [32]. A refined version of this mechanism was presented in the ONIOM framework, called ONIOM-XS [33].

3.2. Geometry optimization

Despite the need for MD or MC in many QM/MM studies, it is often required to locate critical points, such as minima and transition states [34], in particular when very accurate and expensive QM methods are used. For large QM/MM systems, one could use geometry optimization methods that are generally used for MM potential surfaces, while for smaller QM/MM systems, one could use methods that are generally used for QM potential surfaces. Alternatively, one can use a geometry optimizer that is a hybrid of the typical QM and MM optimizers. It turns out that in most cases, this hybrid optimizer is much more efficient than either the conventional QM optimizer or the conventional MM optimizer. In this section we will outline the principle of the hybrid geometry optimizer, and discuss some of the recent developments.

Conventional geometry optimization of large systems is usually carried out with a first order algorithm, such as Steepest Descent or Conjugate Gradient, in the Cartesian coordinate space. This requires only energy

and gradient evaluations, and avoids the need for coordinate transformations. The computational time needed to calculate the geometry step is
small compared to the energy and gradient evaluation at the MM level.

QM potential surfaces usually involve a smaller number of variables,
and one can use a second order procedure, such as Newton-Raphson
or Rational Function Optimization, which employ both the gradient and
Hessian. The coupling introduced by the latter improves the convergence
behavior significantly. The Hessian can be obtained either analytically, or
through an update procedure along the optimization path, using only (analytical) gradients. The optimization is usually carried out in the redundant
internal coordinate system, which contains 'chemically relevant' coordinates that improve the quality of the updated Hessian, and reduce the
(neglected) third and higher order coupling. Because the computational
time and memory storage of the geometry step and the coordinate transformations scale each at least quadratically with the number of optimization variables, these procedures can only be used for relatively small
systems.

It is clear that only MM-style geometry optimizers can be used for large
QM/MM systems. However, if the computational time needed for the QM
contributions to the QM/MM energy and gradient is much larger than the
MM contributions, we can use it to our advantage and employ a hybrid
optimizer. We start the optimization with a QM-style (second order, redundant internal) 'macro-iteration', involving only the atoms in the QM
region. This is followed by a full minimization ('micro-iterations') of the
atoms in the MM region using a MM-style optimizer. Because the QM
atoms are kept fixed in this step, only MM energy and gradient evaluations
are needed. The QM step and MM minimization are alternated until the
forces on all atoms are zero. Although the total number of optimization
cycles in this hybrid scheme is larger than it is with a conventional
MM-style optimizer, most of the extra cycles involve only inexpensive MM
calculations. The number of expensive QM energy and gradient calculations, on the other hand, will be reduced, which speeds up overall calculation, provided there is a sufficiently large difference between the
computational time for the QM and MM energy and gradient calculations.

The macro/micro hybrid optimizer was first used by Maseras and
Morokuma [35], and has since then been implemented in many QM/MM
codes. Recently, we presented refinements to deal efficiently with frozen
MM regions [36]. However, there are several problems with the standard
macro/micro scheme that compromise the convergence behavior. First,
there is no explicit second order (Hessian) coupling between the QM
region and the MM region. Second, the updated Hessian can be of poor
quality because the forces on the QM atoms depend on the positions of

the MM atoms, while the latter are not included as variables in the update procedure. In practice, the standard macro/micro procedure works adequately for minimizations, but it turns out to be very hard or impossible to locate transition states or higher order saddle points. Lluch addressed this issue by allowing the part of MM region close to the TS to be treated by redundant internal coordinates [37]. This introduces coupling between the QM atoms and those MM coordinates that are close to the TS region, which is often sufficient for the TS search to succeed. We followed a formally more rigorous approach and included all the second order coupling between the QM and MM variables explicitly and analytically in the macro step [38], which is made feasible through linear scaling and direct methods. We observe that the convergence behavior is improved significantly, but for the time being the algorithm is only available for mechanical embedding QM/MM schemes.

4. PROPERTIES

Since the potential surfaces are well defined for most implementations of hybrid methods, vibrational and IR spectra can be computed provided the second derivative matrices fit in memory. Most local properties can be computed as well, if the 'parent QM program' can do so. Conceptually there are usually no problems, either for QM/MM or QM/QM(/QM) schemes [8]. However, only the calculation of chemical shifts has received much attention in the literature, ranging from large systems studied with QM/MM methods [39], to small organic systems, studied with QM/QM methods [40].

Many chemical processes of interest take place in the presence of a solvent. Although some QM/MM studies are specifically designed to include discrete description of the solvent, the solvent effects can be included through continuum models as well. In most cases, models are used that were initially developed for MM methods. In our ONIOM framework, we adapted the Polarizable Continuum Model (PCM) for QM/QM hybrid methods, called ONIOM-PCM. The continuum in the method interacts with the true QM/QM charge density, and is self-consistent with the wave function [41].

Finally, QM/MM methods have been used in numerous studies on excited state surfaces, including the dynamical investigation of surface crossings. Recently, also the geometry optimization of conical intersections was extended to QM/MM methods [42]. In our groups, we are developing QM/QM schemes to investigate excited state surfaces and locate conical intersections [43].

5. EXAMPLES OF APPLICATIONS

5.1. Structure and reactivity of zeolites

Chemical processes that take place in zeolites are often studied using model systems of fixed size. These small clusters, however, may not sufficiently represent the steric constraints of the zeolite cavity, and even adopt qualitatively wrong conformations in the course of the geometry optimizations. One solution is to use larger clusters that maintain the structural integrity, but this can make the calculation unnecessarily expensive. A second way to deal with this problem is to freeze the Cartesian coordinates of the atoms at the boundary of the cluster. Although these 'hard constraints' avoid optimization to the wrong conformations, it is not always clear where to place the constraints, while they also prohibit the relaxation of the zeolite lattice in response to the chemical processes.

In a recent study, we used ONIOM to impose 'soft constraints' onto cluster models of various sizes [12]. Although many other QM/MM studies on zeolites have been reported, we wish to specifically investigate the effect of the constraints, and use a general method like ONIOM so that the studies can easily be extended to other zeolite reactions. The QM clusters were calculated with B3LYP and embedded in a larger lattice described by the Universal Force Field (UFF). We did not include electrostatic interactions in the MM force field, so that the effect of the UFF layer is purely steric. We investigated the effect of the size of the QM cluster and the UFF layer on the O(1) to O(4) proton jump in the H-Y zeolite (Fig. 1 in Section 2 shows the model), looking at structural data and reaction energies and barriers. We found that the soft constraints through the ONIOM scheme allow us to use smaller QM clusters than required in conventional QM calculations with hard constraints. Having benchmarked an ONIOM combination to study these processes, we are now investigating the possibility to use a three-layer ONIOM scheme to reduce the computational cost even further.

5.2. Enantioselectivity in transition metal-catalyzed hydrogenation

The stereoselectivity in chemical reactions is often controlled by the use of bulky ligands (or substituents) that make one stereoisomer of the stereodetermining transition state more stable than the other. In order to theoretically study the factors that determine stereoselectivity, one has to adopt the bulky real ligands in the calculation. The ONIOM or QM/MM approach is ideally suited for this purpose, treating the large substituents at the MM level that can take care of the van der Waals interaction. Such approaches have been successfully applied to elucidate the origin of stereoselectivity in transition metal-catalyzed reactions [44,45]. In our recent example, we have studied the origin of enantioselectivty in BINAP-rhodium(I)-catalyzed asymmetric hydrogenation of enamides [46]. As shown in Fig. 2, the transition states of two important steps, the oxidative addition of hydrogen molecule (**TSo**) and the insertion of the enamide into the Rh-H bond (**TSi**), were compared between the pathway leading to the major enantiomer (designated by **M**) and that leading to the minor enantiomer (**m**). Both the oxidative addition and the insertion transition states assign the lower energy to the major pathway; either step could be the enantiodetermining step that is consistent with the experimental

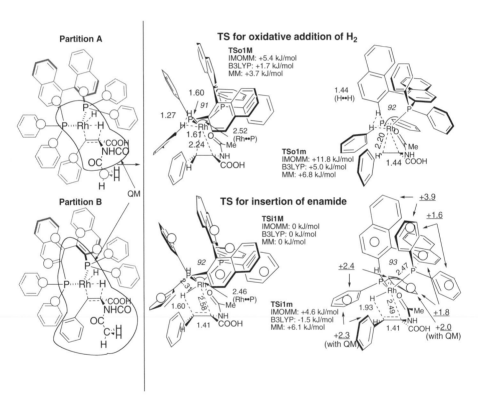

Fig. 2. (A) QM/MM partition A is used for geometry optimization and partition B for the energy evaluation. (B) Structures of transition states of oxidative addition and insertion with bond lengths in Å and bond angles (in italic) in deg. The energy differences between the major and the minor TS are divided into the model QM energy and the peripheral MM energy. The MM energy is further divided into the contributions between particular groups (in parentheses).

enantioselectivity. The difference between the major and minor transition states in the mechanical embedding can be divided into the QM contribution of the "model" part and the MM contribution, which can be further separated into contributions from different pairs of groups. In Fig. 2, one sees that for **TSo** both the QM part and the MM part favor the major pathway. On the other hand, for **TSi** the MM contribution dominates the difference; in particular the steric repulsion between the naphthyl group on a phosphorus and the phenyl group on the other phosphorus makes the largest contribution. Such an analysis of the determining factor may lead to the theoretical design of efficient enantioselective catalysts.

5.3. Enzymatic reaction mechanism of glutathione peroxidase (GPx)

Enzymatic reactions, chemical reactions in protein environment, were in the past often studied computationally using the active site model, which consists of only a limited number of atoms in the active sites, and neglects the remainder of the protein environment. The active-site model has been considered to be reasonable in particular for reactions of metalloenzymes, which take place in the ligand sphere of metal atoms in the protein, and are controlled mainly by the reactivity of the central metal atoms. However, as one tries to improve the approximation, the effects of the remainder of the protein need to be taken into account. Considering the fact that the effect of the protein environment mainly consists of the electrostatic interaction between charged and polar protein residues and the van der Waals interaction (weak attraction and steric repulsion), ONIOM(QM:MM) is a reasonable approach for this purpose.

As our recent example, we used ONIOM(QM:MM) to study the structure and reactivity of Glutathione Peroxidase (GPx), a selenium-containing protein which reduces reactive oxygen species like hydrogen peroxide and organic peroxides by utilizing glutathione as the reducing substrate. The active-site structure of the GPx optimized using an ONIOM system containing 3113 atoms (of which 86 are QM "active-site" atoms) was in much better agreement with experiment than the structure from the "active-site only" model [47]. This indicates the importance of the protein-environment in the structure of the enzyme active site. The ONIOM optimized structure however had residual disagreement, which improved when two water molecules were added in the active site, suggesting that these could have been missed in the X-ray analysis. The potential energy profiles for the three steps of the reduction reaction: $E\text{-}SeH + H_2O_2 \rightarrow E\text{-}SeOH + H_2O$, $E\text{-}SeOH + GSH \rightarrow E\text{-}Se\text{-}SG + HOH$ and $E\text{-}Se\text{-}SG + GSH \rightarrow$

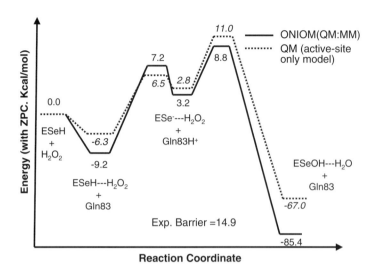

Fig. 3. Potential energy profiles of the first step of the reduction reaction: E-SeH + H$_2$O$_2$ → E-SeOH + H$_2$O, calculated for the "active-site only" model using the B3LYP/ B3LYP/6-311 + G(d,p)//B3LYP/6-31G(d) level and for the 3113-atom model using the ONIOM(B3LYP/6-311 + G(d,p):Amber)//ONIOM(B3LYP/6-31G(d):Amber) level of theory.

E-SeH + GS-SG (GSH: glutathione), were computationally studied with both the "active-site only" QM calculation and the 3113-atom ONIOM calculation [48,49]. The ONIOM optimization of the transition states was facilitated by the "fully coupled" scheme discussed in section 3.2. As shown in Fig. 3, in the first step of the reaction: E-SeH + H$_2$O$_2$ → E-SeOH + H$_2$O of this particular example, the effects of the protein environments did not make a large difference in the potential energy profile, suggesting that the active-site only model was a reasonable model for this reaction. However, we are finding some other cases that protein environment makes a decisive difference in the potential energy profile, and essentially controls the reaction mechanism [50].

6. CONCLUSIONS

The field of hybrid methods has matured immensely during the past decade. Although the foundation for QM/MM potentials was laid much earlier, practical ways for using the surfaces needed to be developed. Indeed, the number of application and 'post-potential methods' studies has increased much relative to the attention for QM-MM interaction terms and capping methods. Judging from the continuous work in our and other groups, QM/MM methods will eventually impact almost every field of chemistry.

REFERENCES

[1] A. Warshel and M. Levitt, Theoretical Studies of Enzymatic Reactions: Dielectric, Electrostatic and Steric Stabilization of the Carbonium Ion in the Reaction of Lysozyme, *J. Mol. Biol.*, 1976, **103**, 227–249.

[2] U. C. Singh and P. A. Kollman, A Combined Abinitio Quantum-Mechanical and Molecular Mechanical Method for Carrying out Simulations on Complex Molecular-Systems - Applications to the $Ch3Cl + Cl-$ Exchange-Reaction and Gas-Phase Protonation of Polyethers, *J. Comput. Chem.*, 1986, **7**, 718–730.

[3] M. J. Field, P. A. Bash and M. Karplus, A Combined Quantum-Mechanical and Molecular Mechanical Potential for Molecular-Dynamics Simulations, *J. Comput. Chem.*, 1990, **11**, 700–733.

[4] D. Bakowies and W. Thiel, Hybrid models for combined quantum mechanical and molecular mechanical approaches, *J. Phys. Chem.*, 1996, **100**, 10580–10594.

[5] P. Amara and M. J. Field, Evaluation of an *ab initio* quantum mechanical / molecular mechanical hybrid-potential link-atom method, *Theor. Chem. Acc.*, 2003, **109**, 43–52.

[6] D. Das, K. P. Eurenius, E. M. Billings, P. Sherwood, D. C. Chatfield, M. Hodoscek and B. R. Brooks, Optimization of quantum mechanical molecular mechanical partitioning schemes: Gaussian delocalization of molecular mechanical charges and the double link atom method, *J. Chem. Phys.*, 2002, **117**, 10534–10547.

[7] H. Lin and D. G. Trulahr, Redistributed Charge and Dipole Schemes for Combined Quantum Mechanical and Molecular Mechanical Calculations, *J. Phys. Chem. A*, 2005, **109**, 3991–4004.

[8] S. Dapprich, I. Komáromi, K. S. Byun, K. Morokuma and M. J. Frisch, A new ONIOM implementation in Gaussian98. Part I. The calculation of energies, gradients, vibrational frequencies and electric field derivatives, *J. Mol. Struct. (Theochem.)*, 1999, **461–462**, 1–21.

[9] M. Svensson, S. Humbel, R. D. J. Froese, T. Matsubara, S. Sieber and K. Morokuma, ONIOM: A multilayered integrated MO + MM method for geometry optimizations and single point energy predictions. A test for Diels-Alder reactions and Pt(P(t-Bu)(3))(2) + H-2 oxidative addition, *J. Phys. Chem.*, 1996, **100**, 19357–19363.

[10] S. Humbel, S. Sieber and K. Morokuma, The IMOMO method: Integration of different levels of molecular orbital approximations for geometry optimization of large systems: Test for n-butane conformation and S(N)2 reaction: RCl + Cl, *J. Chem. Phys.*, 1996, **105**, 1959–1967.

[11] T. Vreven and K. Morokuma, On the Application of the IMOMO (Integrated Molecular Orbital + Molecular Orbital) Method, *J. Comput. Chem.*, 2000, **21**, 1419–1432.

[12] J. T. Fernmann, T. Moniz, O. Kiowski, T. J. McIntire, S. M. Auerbach, T. Vreven and M. J. Frisch, Modeling Proton Transfer in Zeolites: Convergence Behavior of Embedded and Constrained Cluster Calculations, *J. Chem. Theory Comput.*, 2005, **1**, 1232–1239.

[13] B. W. Hopkins and G. S. Tschumper, Multicentered Approach to Integrated QM/QM Calculations. Applications to Multiply Hydrogen Bonded Systems, *J. Comput. Chem.*, 2003, **24**, 1563.

[14] T. Vreven, K. S. Byun, I. Komáromi, S. Dapprich, J. A. Montgomery Jr., K. Morokuma and M. J. Frisch, Combining Quantum Mechanics Methods with Molecular Mechanics Methods in ONIOM, *J. Chem. Theory Comput.* in press.

[15] T. Vreven and K. Morokuma, Investigation of the $S_0 \rightarrow S_1$ Excitation in Bacteriorhodopsin with the ONIOM(MO:MM) Hybrid Method, *Theor. Chem. Acc.*, 2003, **109**, 125–132.

[16] M. J. Frisch et al., Gaussian 03, Revision C.02, Gaussian, Inc.: Wallingford CT, 2004.

[17] V. Thery, D. Rinaldi, J. L. Rivail, B. Maigret and G. G. Ferenczy, Quantum-Mechanical Computations on Very Large Molecular-Systems - the Local Self-Consistent-Field Method, *J. Comput. Chem.*, 1994, **15**, 269–282.

[18] J. Gao, P. Amara, C. Alhambra and M. J. Field, A generalized hybrid orbital (GHO) method for the treatment of boundary atoms in combined QM/MM calculations, *J. Phys. Chem. A*, 1998, **102**, 4714–4721.

[19] N. Reuter, A. Dejaegere, B. Maigret and M. Karplus, Frontier bonds in QM/MM methods: A comparison of different approaches, *J. Phys. Chem. A*, 2000, **104**, 1720–1735.

[20] R. M. Nicoll, S. A. Hindle, G. MacKenzie, I. H. Hillier and N. A. Burton, Quantum mechanical/molecular mechanical methods and the study of kinetic isotope effects: modelling the covalent junction region and application to the enzyme xylose isomerase, *Theor. Chem. Acc.*, 2000, **106**, 105–112.

[21] E. Derat, J. Bouquant and S. Humbel, On the link atom distance in the ONIOM scheme. An harmonic approximation analysis, *J. Mol. Struct. (Theochem.)*, 2003, **632**, 61–69.

[22] Y. K. Zhang, T. S. Lee and W. T. Yang, A pseudobond approach to combining quantum mechanical and molecular mechanical methods, *J. Chem. Phys.*, 1999, **110**, 46–54.

[23] G. A. DiLabio, M. M. Hurley and P. A. Christiansen, Simple one-electron quantum capping potentials for use in hybrid QM/MM studies of biological molecules, *J. Chem. Phys.*, 2002, **116**, 9578–9584.

[24] I. Antes and W. Thiel, Adjusted connection atoms for combined quantum mechanical and molecular mechanical methods, *J. Phys. Chem. A*, 1999, **103**, 9290–9295.

[25] N. Koga and K. Morokuma, A Simple Scheme of Estimating Substitution or Substituent Effects in the abinitio MO Method Based on the Shift Operator, *Chem. Phys. Lett.*, 1990, **172**, 243–248.

[26] T. Kruger and A. F. Sax, Oligovalent Link Atoms in Embedding Calculations, *J. Comput. Chem.*, 2001, **23**, 371–377.

[27] R. Car and M. Parrinello, Unified Approach for Molecular Dynamics and Density-Functional Theory, *Phys. Rev. Lett.*, 1985, **55**, 2471–2474.

[28] M. Eichinger, P. Tavan, J. Hutter and M. Parrinello, A hybrid method for solutes in complex solvents: Density functional theory combined with empirical force fields, *J. Chem. Phys.*, 1999, **110**, 10452–10467.

[29] A. Laio, J. Vandevondele and U. Rothlisberger, A Hamiltonian electrostatic coupling scheme for hybrid Car-Parrinello molecular dynamics simulations, *J. Chem. Phys.*, 2002, **116**, 6941–6947.

[30] T. K. Woo, P. M. Margl, P. E. Bloch and T. Ziegler, A Combined Car-Parrinello QM/MM Implementation for ab Initio Molecular Dynamics Simulations of Extended Systems: Application to Transition Metal Catalysis, *J. Phys. Chem. B*, 1997, **101**, 7877–7880.

[31] N. Rega, S. S. Iyengar, G. A. Voth, H. B. Schlegel, T. Vreven and M. J. Frisch, Hybrid Ab-Initio/Empirical Molecular Dynamics: Combining the ONIOM Scheme with the Atom-centered Density Matrix Propagation (ADMP) Approach, *J. Phys. Chem. B*, 2004, **108**, 4210–4220.

[32] T. Kerdcharoen, K. R. Liedl and B. M. Rode, A QM/MM simulation method applied to the solution of Li+ in liquid ammonia, *Chemical Physics*, 1996, **211**, 313–323.

[33] T. Kerdcharoen and K. Morokuma, ONIOM-XS: an extension of the ONIOM method for molecular simulation in condensed phase, *Chem. Phys. Lett.*, 2002, **355**, 257–262.

[34] H. B. Schlegel, Exploring potential energy surfaces for chemical reactions: An overview of some practical methods, *J. Comput. Chem.*, 2003, **24**, 1514–1527.

[35] F. Maseras and K. Morokuma, IMOMM - a New Integrated Ab-Initio Plus Molecular Mechanics Geometry Optimization Scheme of Equilibrium Structures and Transition-States, *J. Comput. Chem.*, 1995, **16**, 1170–1179.

[36] T. Vreven, K. Morokuma, Ö. Farkas, H. B. Schlegel and M. J. Frisch, Geometry Optimization with QM/MM, ONIOM, and Other Combined Methods. I. Microiterations and Constraints, *J. Comput. Chem.*, 2003, **24**, 760–769.

[37] X. Prat-Resina, J. M. Bofill, A. Gonzalez-Lafont and J. M. Lluch, Geometry Optimization and Transition State Search in Enzymes: Different Options in the Microiterative Method, *Int. J. Quantum Chem. Quantum Chem. Symp.*, 2004, **98**, 367–377.

[38] T. Vreven, M. J. Frisch, K. N. Kudin, H. B. Schlegel and K. Morokuma, Geometry Optimization with QM/MM Methods II: Explicit Quadratic Coupling, *Mol. Phys.*, 2006, **104**, 701–714.

[39] Q. Cui and M. Karplus, Molecular Properties from Combined QM/MM Methods. 2. Chemical Shifts in Large Molecules, *J. Phys. Chem. B*, 2000, **104**, 3721–3743.

[40] P. B. Karadakov and K. Morokuma, ONIOM as an efficient tool for calculating NMR chemical shielding constants in large molecules, *Chem. Phys. Lett.*, 2000, **317**, 589–596.

[41] T. Vreven, B. Mennucci, C. O. da Silva, K. Morokuma and J. Tomasi, The ONIOM-PCM method: Combining the hybrid molecular orbital method and the polarizable continuum model for solvation. Application to the geometry and properties of a merocyanine in solution, *J. Chem. Phys.*, 2001, **115**, 62–72.

[42] A. Toniolo, G. Granucci and T. J. Martinez, Conical Intersections in Solution: A QM/MM Study Using Floating Occupation Semiempirical Configuration Interaction Wave Functions, *J. Phys. Chem. A*, 2003, **107**, 3822–3830.

[43] S. Larkin, M. J. Bearpark and T. Vreven, Excited states and conical intersections using the ONIOM method, Part 1, in preparation.

[44] C. R. Landis, P. Hilfenhaus and S. Feldgus, Structures and Reaction Pathways in Rhodium(I)-Catalyzed Hydrogenation of Enamides: A Model DFT Study, *J. Am. Chem. Soc.*, 1999, **121**, 8741–8754.

[45] G. Drudis-Sole, G. Ujaque, F. Maseras and A. Lledos, A QM/MM study of the Asymmetric Dihydroxylation of Terminal Aliphatic n-Alkenes with OsO4.(DHQD)2PYDZ: Enantioselectivity as a Function of Chain Length, *Chem. Eur. J.*, 2005, **11**, 1017–1029.

[46] S. Mori, T. Vreven and K. Morokuma, Transition states of BINAP-rhodium(I)-catalyzed asymmetric hydrogenation. Theoretical studies on the origin of the enantioselectivity, submitted.

[47] R. Prabhakar, D. G. Musaev, I. V. Khavrutskii and K. Morokuma, Does the Active Site of Mammalian Glutathione Peroxidase (GPx) Contain Water Molecules?, *J. Phys. Chem. B*, 2004, **108**, 12643–12645.

[48] R. Prabhakar, T. Vreven, K. Morokuma and D. G. Musaev, Elucidation of the Mechanism of Selenoprotein Glutathione Peroxidase (GPx) Catalyzed Hydrogen Peroxide Reduction by Two Glutathione Molecules: A Density Functional Study, *Biochemistry*, 2005, **44**, 11864–11871.

[49] R. Prabhakar, T. Vreven, M. J. Frisch, K. Morokuma and D. G. Musaev, Is the Protein Surrounding the Active-Site Critical for Hydrogen Peroxide Reduction by Selenoprotein Glutatione Peroxidase (GPx)? An ONIOM Study, Submitted.

[50] J. Li, J. B. Cross, T. Vreven, S. O. Meroueh, S. Mobashery and H. B. Schlegel, Lysine Carboxylation in Proteins: OXA-10 β-Lactamase, *Proteins*, 2005, **61**, 246–257.

CHAPTER 4

On the Selection of Domains and Orbital Pairs in Local Correlation Treatments

Hans-Joachim Werner[*] and Klaus Pflüger

Institut für Theoretische Chemie, Universität Stuttgart, Pfaffenwaldring 55, D-70569 Stuttgart, Germany

Contents

1. INTRODUCTION

Local correlation treatments, as originally proposed by Pulay [1] and first implemented by Pulay and Saebø [2–6] employ local orbital spaces to restrict the number of excited configurations in the wave function. The occupied orbitals are localized using standard procedures (e.g. Boys [7] or Pipek-Mezey [8] localization), while the virtual space is spanned by non-orthogonal projected atomic orbitals (PAOs). By fully exploiting the

---

[*]Corresponding author.
E-mail: werner@theochem.uni-stuttgart.de

ANNUAL REPORTS IN COMPUTATIONAL CHEMISTRY, VOLUME 2
ISSN: 1574-1400   DOI 10.1016/S1574-1400(06)02004-4

locality, our group has achieved linear scaling of the computational effort with molecular size for all standard single-reference methods [9–16]. This has extended the applicability of high-level methods such as local coupled cluster with single and double excitations and perturbative treatment of triple excitations [LCCSD(T)] to molecules with 50–100 atoms and far over 1000 basis functions. This progress is based on two approximations: First, the excitations are restricted to subspaces of PAOs (domains). The size of these domains and therefore the number of excitations per electron pair is independent of the molecular size, while in conventional methods the number of excitations increases quadratically. Second, the correlation energy decreases quickly with the distance between two correlated localized orbitals, and therefore distant orbital pairs can be neglected or treated at a lower level than the pairs which describe the strong correlation of electrons which are close. More generally, based on distance or energy criteria, a hierarchy of *strong*, *close*, *weak*, and *distant* pairs can be defined. The number of pairs in each class increases linearly with molecular size, except for the remaining *very distant* pairs, which are neglected. This means that the total number of excitations and amplitudes increases linearly with molecular size, and this forms the basis for achieving linear scaling of all computational resources.

Using standard criteria for selecting the domains as proposed by Boughton and Pulay [17] and outlined in the next section, about 98–99% of the correlation energy obtained without local approximations and the same method and basis set are recovered. Most of the error is due to the use of finite domains. It has been demonstrated in previous work that this has very little effect on near equilibrium properties, such as equilibrium geometries [18–20], harmonic vibrational frequencies [21–23], dipole moments and polarizabilities [24,25], or NMR chemical shifts [26]. However, energy differences like reaction energies or reaction barriers might be more affected if the electronic structure and the domains are different in the reactants and products, since then the absolute errors of the correlation energy may be different in reactants and products. Furthermore, the domains and thus the energy along a reaction path may not be contiguous [27]. The latter problems can be avoided by defining extended domains, which are appropriate and fixed along the whole reaction path, as will be demonstrated in a forthcoming publication [28].

In the current work, we discuss and compare different strategies to improve the accuracy by domain extensions at fixed geometries. In principle, this allows to approach the non-local solution to arbitrary precision. However, the computational effort increases rather quickly with the domain sizes, in particular for LCCSD(T), and therefore it is important to find a best compromise between accuracy and cost. In contrast to conventional coupled-cluster calculations for small systems, the bottle-neck of local coupled-cluster calculations is usually the (direct) integral transformation, and the cost for this transformation depends strongly on the domain sizes. It is important to realize that in order to achieve low-order scaling in the integral transformation it is essential to ciroose the domains once in the beginning of a local calculation. Also the computation of the residuals in each coupled-cluster iteration profits enormously if the domains are known in advance. Screening procedures applied during the coupled-cluster iterations have also been proposed [29,30], and it has been shown that this leads to linear scaling of the number of amplitudes to be optimized. However, low-order scaling of the total computational effort has not been demonstrated for this method, and we believe that it cannot be achieved unless the domains are fixed in advance.

The transformation bottleneck has recently been much reduced by local density fitting (DF) approximations [20,31–34]. In this method, the 4-index two-electron integrals are approximated by products of 2-index and 3-index integrals. These are not only easier and faster to compute and transform, but also the scaling of the computational cost with basis set size per atom is reduced from N_{AO}^4 to N_{AO}^3. If large basis sets are used (triple or quadruple zeta) this reduces the transformation times by 1–2 orders of magnitude. The method is particularly fast for local second-order Møller–Plesset perturbation theory (DF-LMP2) [31]. This makes it possi-ble to perform first an DF-LMP2 with large (or even full) domains, and to select the domains to be used in the subsequent DF-LCCSD(T) on the basis of the magnitude of LMP2 amplitudes or energy contributions. The price one has to pay is that an extra integral evaluation for the initial DF-LMP2 is necessary, but the cost for this is usually small as compared to the time for the subsequent DF-LCCSD(T). In the present paper, it will be explored whether this method offers any advantages as compared to simpler methods in which the domains are determined only once.

2. METHOD

In the following sections, we summarize the criteria used to define the local orbital spaces and domains as implemented in the MOLPRO package of *ab initio* programs [35]. The keywords for thresholds are the same as used in this program.

2.1. Orbital spaces

In the following, we will denote occupied molecular orbitals by indices i, j, atomic orbitals (AOs) and PAOs by indices r, s, and basis functions by indices μ, ν. The localized occupied orbitals (LMOs) are represented in a basis $\{\chi_\mu\}$ by a coefficient matrix $\mathbf{L}$. This is related to the occupied canonical orbitals, which are represented by the MO coefficient matrix $\mathbf{C}_o$, by a unitary transformation $\mathbf{W}$

$$| \phi_i^{LMO} > = \sum_\mu | \chi_\mu > L_{\mu i}, \quad \mathbf{L} = \mathbf{C}_o \mathbf{W} \tag{1}$$

In this work, $\mathbf{W}$ is determined by Pipek–Mezey localization [8], which has the advantage that σ and π orbitals stay usually unmixed. Only the correlated orbitals are localized, in order to avoid artificial mixing with core orbitals.

In the case that large and diffuse basis sets are used (e.g. augmented correlation consistent basis sets), poor and non-physical Pipek–Mezey localization may arise due to large MO coefficients arising from near linear dependencies of the basis. We have encountered such problems, for instance in calculations for substituted benzenes (e.g. aniline). This problem can be avoided by excluding the contributions of the diffuse basis functions from the localization. Technically, this can simply be achieved by zeroing the corresponding rows and columns in the AO overlap matrix, which is used in the Pipek–Mezey localization.

The virtual space is spanned by PAOs $\{\phi_r^{PAO}\}$, obtained by projecting a set of AOs against the occupied space:

$$| \phi_r^{AO} > = \sum_\mu | \chi_\mu > C_{\mu r}^{AO}, \tag{2}$$

$$| \phi_r^{PAO} > = \left[1 - \sum_i^{occ} | \phi_i^{LMO} > < \phi_i^{LMO} | \right] | \phi_r^{AO} > = \sum_\mu | \chi_\mu > C_{\mu r}^{PAO} \tag{3}$$

Inserting the expansions yields for the coefficients of the PAOs

$$\mathbf{C}^{PAO} = \left[1 - \mathbf{L} \mathbf{L}^\dagger \mathbf{S} \right] \mathbf{C}^{AO} = \mathbf{P} \mathbf{C}^{AO} \tag{4}$$

If the basis functions are generally contracted and correspond to the atomic Hartree–Fock (HF) orbitals, as is for instance the case for the correlation consistent basis sets of Dunning [36], the matrix $\mathbf{C}^{AO}$ is taken to be the unit matrix. For segmented basis sets $\mathbf{C}^{AO}$ is often assumed to be a unit matrix as well, but it may be advantageous to generate atomic HF orbitals since then inner-shell (core) orbitals can be eliminated. In the current work, we only use the correlation consistent basis sets and

$\mathbf{C}^{AO} = 1$. Core orbitals are eliminated from the set of AOs since the corresponding PAOs would be almost zero and are not well defined. The resulting set of PAOs are orthogonal to all occupied orbitals, but mutually non-orthogonal

$$< \phi_r^{PAO} \mid \phi_i^{LMO} > = 0 \tag{5}$$

$$< \phi_r^{PAO} \mid \phi_s^{PAO} > = \left[\mathbf{S}^{PAO} \right]_{rs} = \left[\mathbf{C}^{PAO\dagger} \mathbf{S} \mathbf{C}^{PAO} \right]_{rs} \tag{6}$$

where $S_{\mu\nu} = < \chi_\mu \mid \chi_\nu >$ is the overlap matrix of the basis functions. Due to the projection, the PAOs are linearly dependent, i.e. $\mathbf{S}^{PAO}$ has m zero eigenvalues, where m is the number of occupied orbitals minus the number of eliminated core orbitals. The number of redundant functions is smaller (or zero) if PAO subspaces are considered. Therefore, redundant functions are eliminated individually for each domain as described in the next section.

3. SELECTION OF DOMAINS USING LOCALIZED ORBITALS

3.1. Standard domains

For each correlated occupied orbital ϕ_i^{LMO} an *orbital domain* [i] is generated according to the procedure proposed by Boughton and Pulay [17]. Some modifications were made in our program, which are outlined in the following. The purpose of the method is to include all PAOs in the domain, which arise from AOs (basis functions), that significantly contribute to the considered LMO. The PAOs arising from AOs at a given atom are considered as a group. Therefore, the first step is to select a set of atoms, and then the PAOs generated from all AOs at these atoms are included in the domain. First, for a given LMO, the atoms are ordered according to decreasing Löwdin charges

$$z_A^{(i)} = 2 \sum_{\mu \in A} \left[\mathbf{S}^{1/2} \mathbf{L} \right]_{\mu i}^2 \tag{7}$$

Here the sum runs over all basis functions at atom A. Mulliken gross charges could also be used, but we found the Löwdin charges to be somewhat less basis set dependent. All atoms with charges greater than a threshold CHGMAX (default 0.4) are immediately added to the domain list for orbital i. Furthermore, atoms with charge CHGMIN (default 0.01) are eliminated from the list and never included. For H-atoms, a separate threshold CHGMINH (default 0.03) is used. The elimination of atoms with small charges is particularly useful for diffuse basis sets, since then neighboring atoms often receive artificially large charges due to or-thogonalization tails. Further atoms are added step by step in the order of decreasing charges until the Boughton and Pulay (BP) criterion

$$T^{(i)} = 1 - \min \left[\int \left(\phi_i - \tilde{\phi}_i \right)^2 d\mathbf{r} \right] \geq \text{THRBP} \qquad (8)$$

is fulfilled, where $\tilde{\phi}_i$ is an approximate orbital represented by just the basis functions at the already selected atoms

$$| \tilde{\phi}_i > = \sum_{A \in [i]} \sum_{\mu \in A} | \chi_\mu > \tilde{L}_{\mu i} \qquad (9)$$

The coefficients $\tilde{L}_{\mu i}$ are determined by a simple least squares fitting pro-cedure [17]. The default value for THRBP is 0.98. If larger basis sets are used, the BP criterion is fulfilled more quickly, and values of 0.985 (aug-cc-pVTZ) or 0.99 (aug-cc-pVQZ) may be needed to obtain sufficiently accurate domains.

In the following, we denote the PAO subspaces selected according to these criteria as *standard* or *primary* orbital domains.

3.2. Extended domains

In order to increase the accuracy, the standard orbital domains as defined in the previous section can be extended by adding the PAOs centered at neighboring atoms. In our program, two possibilities exist to select the additional atoms: either a distance criterion is used, or connectivity infor-mation is used. In the first case, all atoms are added to the atom domain list which are within the given distance REXT from any primary atom se-lected by the standard procedure. In the second case, all atoms are added which are bound to any of the primary atoms. Two atoms A, B are con-sidered to be bound if their distance is smaller than $1.2 \times (r_A + r_B)$, where r_A and r_B are the covalent radii. It is possible to add just the first shell of neighboring atoms (IEXT=1), or the first two shells (IEXT=2), and so on. For simple organic molecules containing just C, N, O, and H atoms, usually REXT=3 Bohr is equivalent to IEXT=1, and REXT=5 Bohr to IEXT=2. The use of connectivity has the advantage that the selection is independent of bond lengths, and works for atoms of different rows of the periodic system without change of the parameter. On the other hand, the use of distance criteria (REXT) may be advantageous in cases where atoms are close for sterical reasons, or if weak bonds are present.

3.3. Pair and triple domains

Domains for double and triple excitations are the union of the orbital domains from which the excitations are made, i.e. for doubles $[ij] = [i] \cup [j]$, and for triples $[ijk] = [i] \cup [j] \cup [k]$. If domains have been extended as described in Section 3.2, the extended orbital domains are used by default. It is possible, however, to use the extended domains just for strong pairs, or for *strong* and *close* pairs. In these cases, the keywords REXT or IEXT are replaced by REXTS, IEXTS or REXTC, IEXTC, respectively.

3.4. Domain merging

For aromatic molecules with high symmetry, for instance benzene, the localization may not be unique, i.e. some orbital rotation parameter is redundant. In benzene, this corresponds to a rotation of the localized π-orbitals in the ring, which does not change the localization criterion. Such redundancies can cause problems in geometry optimizations, since the orbitals and domains may change discontinuously. Mathematically, redundancies lead to zero eigenvalues of the matrix of second derivatives of the localization criterion with respect to orbital rotations, and this can in principle be used to detect redundancies. An easier and recommended way to eliminate redundancies is to merge the three π-orbital domains in benzene into one domain, which is then used for all three orbitals. The correlation energy is then invariant with respect to unitary transformations among the π-orbitals. A simple automatic way to detect critical cases without constructing and diagonalizing the second-derivative matrix is to merge all orbital domains which overlap by more than one center, and to use the merged domains for all the contributing orbitals (option MERGE-DOM=1). Normally, such overlapping domains only occur in conjugated systems. Note that domain merging is done with the standard domains, and any domain extensions apply to the merged domains.

3.5. Redundancy check

As mentioned in Section 2.1, the PAOs in a domain may be linearly dependent. Redundancies are removed for each pair and triples domain individually by constructing and diagonalizing the PAO overlap matrix $[\mathbf{S}^{PAO}]_{rs}$, $rs \in [ij]$ (equation (6), unnormalized PAOs are used). For each eigenvalue which is smaller than a threshold THRLOC (default 10^{-6}) one function is removed. Two different methods are possible: in the first case (IBASO$=1$), individual PAOs are eliminated. The advantage is that minimal domain sizes can be used in the integral transformation and LCCSD calculation, and the domains can be kept fixed across different geometries in order to obtain strictly smooth potentials. However, there are various problems related to this: unless the small eigenvalues of $\mathbf{S}^{PAO}$ are exactly zero (within numerical accuracy of the machine), the correlation energy will slightly depend on the choice of the deleted functions. In our algorithm, the functions are selected in the order of decreasing coefficients in the corresponding eigenvector. This choice may be affected, however, by artificial mixing of degenerate eigenvectors. Furthermore, the energy may not be rotationally invariant if individual p- or d-functions are eliminated. This can be avoided by deleting whole shells of functions, but this may cause an additional loss of correlation energy. Other useful restrictions are not to eliminate 1s functions at H-atoms, but to eliminate only basis functions corresponding to atomic valence orbitals.

A better method (IBASO$=0$), which avoids all these problems, is to eliminate the linear combinations of PAOs which correspond to the eigenvectors with small eigenvalues. This can be done by projection during the update of the LMP2 or LCCSD amplitudes (for details see Ref. [9]). A slight disadvantage of this method is that the LCCSD residual must be computed in the redundant basis, and is transformed to the non-redundant basis only at an intermediate stage. This may lead to some increase of the computational effort and disk space needed to store the amplitudes and transformed integrals.

3.6. Fixing domains

In geometry optimizations, the domains are automatically kept fixed once the geometry step size is smaller than a certain threshold (default 0.01 Bohr). In numerical frequency (Hessian) calculations the domains are always fixed. If eigenvectors of $\mathbf{S}^{PAO}$ are eliminated, the number of deleted eigenvectors is kept fixed. In this way, it is guaranteed that the potential energy surface is microscopically smooth and numerical artifacts in the finite difference calculation of the Hessian are avoided. This procedure is very similar to density functional theory (DFT), in which case the definition of the grid is frozen under the same conditions in order to ensure microscopically smooth potentials.

3.7. Selection of domains using energy thresholds

The procedure outlined in the previous sections to determine the domains was entirely based on the locality of the occupied orbitals. Previous applications, as well as results in the present paper, demonstrate that this works well for a large variety of applications. As an alternative, one could determine the domains for LCCSD calculations on the basis of an initial LMP2 calculation with full domains (i.e. including the full virtual space) using energy thresholds. This would then be independent of the BP procedure and the localization of the occupied orbitals, but would lead to higher scaling and high expense in the LMP2. A compromise is to perform the initial LMP2 with extended domains and use this to select the important parts of the domains using energy thresholds. The LMP2 correlation energy is given by

$$E_{corr} = \sum_{i \geq j \in P} (2 - \delta_{ij}) \sum_{rs} \left[2K_{rs}^{ij} - K_{sr}^{ij} \right] T_{rs}^{ij} \tag{10}$$

where $K_{rs}^{ij} = (ri|sj)$ are the two-electron integrals in the LMO/PAO basis, T_{rs}^{ij} the LMP2 amplitudes, and P the list of orbital pairs (ij) which are included in the calculation. One can now further split this sum into contributions of centers A

$$E_{corr} = \sum_{i \geq j \in P} \sum_{A} E_A^{ij} \tag{11}$$

with

$$E_A^{ij} = \left(1 - \tfrac{1}{2}\delta_{ij}\right) \sum_{r \in [A]} \sum_{s} (1 + \tau_{rs}) \left[2K_{rs}^{ij} - K_{sr}^{ij} \right] T_{rs}^{ij} \tag{12}$$

where τ_{rs} permutes the indices r and s, and $[A]$ denotes all PAOs at center A. Then all centers A are included in the domain $[ij]$ for which E_A^{ij} is above a certain threshold T_s. This results in pair-specific domains $[ij]$, which are not necessarily the union of the orbital domains $[i] = [ii]$ and $[j] = [jj]$. However, $[ij]$ must be (at least) the union of $[i]$ and $[j]$ in order to be able to form in the LCCSD intermediates like $C_{rs}^{ij} = T_{rs}^{ij} + t_r^i t_s^j$, where the singles amplitudes t_r^i and t_s^j are restricted to the domains $[i]$ and $[j]$, respectively. Therefore, we have adopted an alternative orbital-based approach: for each LMO i and center A the energies are accumulated. The energy contribution E_A^{ij} is assigned to orbital i if A is closer to any atom contained in the primary (standard) domain $[i]$ than to any atom in the primary orbital domain [j] (and vice versa). If both distances happen to be the same, the energy contribution is shared between orbitals i and j. Finally, once the contributions of all pairs have been added, the atoms in the orbital domains [i] are selected according to the energy threshold (the primary domains are always kept). Pair or triples domains can then be generated in the usual way by forming the union of the corresponding orbital domains.

In order to keep the linear scaling behavior, extended domains may be used in the initial LMP2. In this case, the summations over r and s in equations (10) and (12) are restricted to the extended domains.

4. PAIR CLASSES

The orbital pairs (ij) are classified according to the closest distance $R^{(ij)}$ between atoms in the primary domains [i] and [j]. This classification is independent of domain extensions. Furthermore, only atoms in the primary domains are considered for the pair classification if the atomic Löwdin charge is larger than CHGMIN_PAIRS (default value 0.2). This criterion was introduced in order to reduce the dependence of the pair selection on localization tails. The *strong pairs* $(0 \leq R^{(ij)} < \text{RCLOSE})$ contribute most to the correlation energy and are treated at highest level, e.g. LCCSD(T). *Close pairs* $(\text{RCLOSE} \leq R^{(ij)} < \text{RWEAK})$, *weak pairs* $(\text{RWEAK} \leq R^{(ij)} < \text{RDIST})$, and *distant pairs* $(\text{RDIST} \leq R^{(ij)} < \text{RVDIST})$ are normally optimized at the LMP2 level. It is also possible to determine the close pair amplitudes at the LMP4 level.

The close pair list as determined by RCLOSE has by default no effect on the LCCSD energy but affects the treatment of triple excitations (cf. Section 5). If option KEEPCL=1 is set, the LMP2 amplitudes of the close pairs are included in the calculation of the LCCSD residuals of the strong pairs. This includes couplings between strong and close pairs, which are otherwise entirely neglected. As will be demonstrated in Section 6, the inclusion of this coupling may significantly improve the results. The additional computational effort is much less than for the full treatment of all strong and close pairs, since for close pairs the residuals need not be computed. In particular, the most expensive contributions, namely those of the integrals over four PAOs, are not needed for the close pairs.

The weak and distant pairs are treated exclusively at the LMP2 level. Optionally, the integrals for distant pairs are approximated by multipole approximations [10,12] (option MULTP). Very distant pairs $(R^{(ij)} \geq \text{RVDIST})$ are neglected. Note that only the number of very distant pairs scales quadratically with molecular size. The pairs in each of the other classes scales linearly, independent of the choice of the distance criteria. The default values for the distance criteria are RCLOSE=1, RWEAK=3, RDIST=8, and RVDIST=15 (all distances in Bohr; note that RDIST has no effect unless the MULTP option is used). This means that in strong pairs the orbital domains [*i*] and [*j*] share at least one atom, while in close pairs the domains [*i*] and [*j*] are separated by at most one bond. Setting a distance criterion to zero means that all pairs up to the corresponding class are treated as strong pairs. For instance, RCLOSE=0 means that strong and close pairs are fully included in the LCCSD (in this case KEEPCL=1 has no effect).

As an alternative to the distance criteria, the classification can also be based on connectivity criteria, i.e. depending on the minimum number of bonds between the two orbital domains. The corresponding parameters are denoted ICLOSE, IWEAK, IDIST, and IVDIST (default values 1,2,5, and 8, respectively). This means that strong pairs are separated by no bonds, close pairs by 1 bond, weak pairs by 2–4 bonds, distant pairs by 5–7 bonds, and very distant pairs by at least 8 bonds. As already discussed in the context of domain extensions, the advantage of using connectivity criteria is the independence of the bond lengths, while the advantage of distance criteria (default in our program) is that they are also effective in non-bonding situations.

5. TRIPLE EXCITATIONS

As for the double excitations, the triple excitations are restricted to domains (cf. Section 3.3) and by a triples list (*ijk*) of LMOs, so that the total number of triple excitations scales linearly with molecular size. As discussed in detail in Ref. [14], the triples list (*ijk*) is defined by the condition that the pairs (*ij*), (*ik*), or (*jk*) must be either strong or close pairs. Additionally, at least one of these pairs must be strong. Second, the close pair amplitudes as determined in the initial LMP2 calculation are included in the triples calculation. This approximation turns out to be important for getting accurate triples corrections, but avoids the inclusion of all close pairs in the LCCSD. This is similar to the option KEEPCL (cf. Section 4), which allows the inclusion of the close pair LMP2 amplitudes in the LCCSD residuals for the strong pairs.

In the local orbital basis the Fock matrix is non-diagonal, and therefore the perturbative treatment of triple excitations requires to solve a set of linear equations [13,14]. This is computationally expensive and also makes it necessary to store all amplitudes of triple excitations. Therefore, two possible approximations have been introduced. In the (T0) approximation [13], the triple excitations arising from different LMO triples (*ijk*) and ($i'j'k'$) are entirely decoupled. This means that couplings via off-diagonal elements f_{ij} of the Fock matrix are neglected [13] (here i, j refer to occupied orbitals only), but all couplings within each triple (ijk) are fully included. The (T0) approximation is non-iterative and does not require to store the triples amplitudes.

A compromise between the full iterative (T) treatment and the simple (T0) approximation is the (T1) method. In this case, the couplings f_{ij} are included to first order. This corresponds to the first iteration of the (T) method, but a paging algorithm can be used to avoid storage of the triples amplitudes [14]. We found in numerous applications that the (T0) approximation works very well and yields results which are very close to the computationally much more demanding (T1) and (T) methods. In cases of doubt, the (T1) method may be used to test the accuracy of the (T0) approximation.

A final note concerns the computational cost: despite linear scaling, the computational effort for the triples can be substantial, in particular, for large basis sets or with extended domains. It should be kept in mind that the CPU times scales with the fourth power of the domain sizes; therefore, calculations with extended domains may take one order of magnitude more time than with standard domains. In calculations for large molecules, it may be helpful to compute the triples correction with a smaller basis set than used in the LCCSD. In recent calculations of barrier heights in enzymes [37] we found that this works well and hardly affects the results.

6. APPLICATIONS AND DISCUSSION

6.1. Dependence of the correlation energy on the domain approximation

In order to demonstrate the effect of the domain approximation on correlation and reaction energies, we have studied 52 chemical reactions involving 59 molecules [38]. Here we present only a representative subset of the results. The geometries of all molecules have been optimized at the MP2/aug-cc-pV(T + d)Z level. Tables 1–3 show the computed correlation energies of 22 molecules for LMP2, LCCSD, and LCCSD(T0). In each case, the results are compared to the full non-local calculations. For the s and p shells the aug-cc-pVTZ basis sets were used, while for d and f the standard cc-pVTZ sets were employed. For second-row atoms, additional hard d functions were included [39]. The resulting basis is denoted as aug[sp]-cc-pV(T + d)Z. The diffuse s and p functions were found to be particularly important for oxygen-containing molecules; without them the

Table 1. LMP2 energies as function of the domain size

Molecule	MP2	LMP2		
		IEXTS = 0	IEXTS = 1	IEXT = 1
C$_2$H$_2$	-0.311213	-0.309642 (99.50)	-0.311136 (99.98)	-0.311136 (99.98)
C$_2$H$_4$	-0.336334	-0.332675 (98.91)	-0.336096 (99.93)	-0.336162 (99.95)
C$_2$H$_6$	-0.370764	-0.366111 (98.74)	-0.370071 (99.81)	-0.370405 (99.90)
H$_2$CO	-0.397511	-0.395534 (99.50)	-0.397459 (99.99)	-0.397464 (99.99)
CH$_3$NH$_2$	-0.406442	-0.401554 (98.80)	-0.405616 (99.80)	-0.406101 (99.92)
CH$_3$OH	-0.430764	-0.426533 (99.02)	-0.430076 (99.84)	-0.430465 (99.93)
H$_2$O$_2$	-0.500681	-0.497630 (99.39)	-0.500313 (99.93)	-0.500538 (99.97)
CH$_3$CN	-0.519120	-0.515115 (99.23)	-0.518504 (99.88)	-0.518656 (99.91)
C$_2$H$_3$Cl	-0.517689	-0.513164 (99.13)	-0.517021 (99.87)	-0.517266 (99.92)
H$_2$CCO	-0.541430	-0.537787 (99.33)	-0.541102 (99.94)	-0.541140 (99.95)
HNCO	-0.581119	-0.578557 (99.56)	-0.580987 (99.98)	-0.581011 (99.98)
CH$_3$CHO	-0.570019	-0.565149 (99.15)	-0.569271 (99.87)	-0.569518 (99.91)
C$_2$H$_4$O	-0.577946	-0.572522 (99.06)	-0.577399 (99.91)	-0.577651 (99.95)
HCONH$_2$	-0.606922	-0.602279 (99.24)	-0.606527 (99.93)	-0.606637 (99.95)
C$_2$H$_5$OH	-0.604622	-0.597066 (98.75)	-0.602717 (99.68)	-0.603745 (99.86)
HCOOH	-0.633158	-0.629535 (99.43)	-0.632855 (99.95)	-0.632966 (99.97)
C$_2$H$_3$CN	-0.661225	-0.655179 (99.09)	-0.660227 (99.85)	-0.660501 (99.89)
COCl$_2$	-0.766275	-0.762349 (99.49)	-0.765222 (99.86)	-0.765833 (99.94)
HCONHCH$_3$	-0.780409	-0.773522 (99.12)	-0.779097 (99.83)	-0.779622 (99.90)
HCOOCH$_3$	-0.803457	-0.796554 (99.14)	-0.801773 (99.79)	-0.802562 (99.89)
NH$_2$CONH$_2$	-0.813438	-0.806032 (99.09)	-0.812265 (99.86)	-0.812730 (99.91)
C$_2$H$_4$(OH)$_2$	-0.839214	-0.828236 (98.69)	-0.835590 (99.57)	-0.837641 (99.81)
CH$_3$NO$_2$	-0.858234	-0.852897 (99.38)	-0.857021 (99.86)	-0.857576 (99.92)
C$_6$H$_{12}$	-1.045942	-1.026304 (98.12)	-1.038709 (99.31)	-1.042408 (99.66)
Average[a]		(99.12 ± 0.33)	(99.84 ± 0.14)	(99.92 ± 0.07)

[a] Average fraction of correlation energy relative to MP2 in percent. The error bounds are standard deviations.

Table 2. LCCSD energies as function of the domain size

Molecule	CCSD	IEXTS = 0	LCCSD|LMP2[a]	
			IEXTS = 1	IEXT = 1
C_2H_2	-0.322948	-0.321504 (99.55)	-0.322874 (99.98)	-0.322876 (99.98)
C_2H_4	-0.360599	-0.357982 (99.27)	-0.361004 (100.11)	-0.361077 (100.13)
C_2H_6	-0.401843	-0.399422 (99.40)	-0.402999 (100.29)	-0.403326 (100.37)
H_2CO	-0.407090	-0.405201 (99.54)	-0.406972 (99.97)	-0.406979 (99.97)
CH_3NH_2	-0.430262	-0.427842 (99.44)	-0.431448 (100.28)	-0.431923 (100.39)
CH_3OH	-0.448749	-0.446227 (99.44)	-0.449411 (100.15)	-0.449793 (100.23)
H_2O_2	-0.507312	-0.505233 (99.59)	-0.507763 (100.09)	-0.507982 (100.13)
CH_3CN	-0.532250	-0.531361 (99.83)	-0.534496 (100.42)	-0.534649 (100.45)
C_2H_3Cl	-0.550382	-0.548913 (99.73)	-0.552350 (100.36)	-0.552597 (100.40)
H_2CCO	-0.549266	-0.546455 (99.49)	-0.549481 (100.04)	-0.549517 (100.05)
$HNCO$	-0.577266	-0.575304 (99.66)	-0.577494 (100.04)	-0.577526 (100.04)
CH_3CHO	-0.589670	-0.587092 (99.56)	-0.590885 (100.21)	-0.591132 (100.25)
C_2H_4O	-0.595732	-0.593008 (99.54)	-0.597507 (100.30)	-0.597749 (100.34)
$HCONH_2$	-0.616527	-0.613322 (99.48)	-0.617170 (100.10)	-0.617299 (100.13)
C_2H_5OH	-0.632951	-0.629493 (99.45)	-0.634604 (100.26)	-0.635620 (100.42)
$HCOOH$	-0.637004	-0.634419 (99.59)	-0.637514 (100.08)	-0.637621 (100.10)
C_2H_3CN	-0.676157	-0.675902 (99.96)	-0.680494 (100.64)	-0.680765 (100.68)
$COCl_2$	-0.789483	-0.791779 (100.29)	-0.794310 (100.61)	-0.794924 (100.69)
$HCONHCH_3$	-0.800478	-0.796843 (99.55)	-0.801969 (100.19)	-0.802481 (100.25)
$HCOOCH_3$	-0.818812	-0.815630 (99.61)	-0.820413 (100.20)	-0.821204 (100.29)
NH_2CONH_2	-0.825674	-0.821861 (99.54)	-0.827515 (100.22)	-0.827967 (100.28)
$C_2H_4(OH)_2$	-0.864727	-0.859758 (99.43)	-0.866409 (100.19)	-0.868437 (100.43)
CH_3NO_2	-0.865569	-0.863578 (99.77)	-0.867420 (100.21)	-0.867976 (100.28)
C_6H_{12}	-1.106198	-1.103528 (99.76)	-1.114741 (100.77)	-1.118381 (101.10)
Average[b]		(99.60 ±0.21)	(100.24±0.20)	(100.31±0.25)

a LCCSD\|LMP2 using IWEAK=2, ICLOSE=1.
b Average fraction of correlation energy relative to CCSD in percent. The error bounds are standard deviations.

Table 3. LCCSD(T0) energies as function of the domain size

Molecule	CCSD(T)	LCCSD(T0)|LMP2[a]		
		IEXTS = 0	IEXTS = 1	IEXT = 1
C$_2$H$_2$	-0.339615	-0.338003 (99.53)	-0.339443 (99.95)	-0.339443 (99.95)
C$_2$H$_4$	-0.375751	-0.372737 (99.20)	-0.376013 (100.07)	-0.376084 (100.09)
C$_2$H$_6$	-0.415408	-0.412527 (99.31)	-0.416392 (100.24)	-0.416752 (100.32)
H$_2$CO	-0.423993	-0.421630 (99.44)	-0.423569 (99.90)	-0.423575 (99.90)
CH$_3$NH$_2$	-0.445378	-0.442216 (99.29)	-0.446252 (100.20)	-0.446784 (100.32)
CH$_3$OH	-0.463960	-0.460634 (99.28)	-0.464238 (100.06)	-0.464668 (100.15)
H$_2$O$_2$	-0.526470	-0.523453 (99.43)	-0.526395 (99.99)	-0.526646 (100.03)
CH$_3$CN	-0.557876	-0.556557 (99.76)	-0.559697 (100.33)	-0.559869 (100.36)
C$_2$H$_3$Cl	-0.575719	-0.573305 (99.58)	-0.577096 (100.24)	-0.577361 (100.29)
H$_2$CCO	-0.575956	-0.572202 (99.35)	-0.575464 (99.91)	-0.575506 (99.92)
HNCO	-0.606660	-0.603389 (99.46)	-0.605784 (99.86)	-0.605810 (99.86)
CH$_3$CHO	-0.614158	-0.610674 (99.43)	-0.614795 (100.10)	-0.615068 (100.15)
C$_2$H$_4$O	-0.620367	-0.616660 (99.40)	-0.621591 (100.20)	-0.621858 (100.24)
HCONH$_2$	-0.642937	-0.638640 (99.33)	-0.642931 (100.00)	-0.643051 (100.02)
C$_2$H$_5$OH	-0.655761	-0.650568 (99.21)	-0.656257 (100.08)	-0.657350 (100.24)
HCOOH	-0.663816	-0.660095 (99.44)	-0.663530 (99.96)	-0.663651 (99.98)
C$_2$H$_3$CN	-0.711718	-0.709890 (99.74)	-0.714840 (100.44)	-0.715133 (100.48)
COCl$_2$	-0.828566	-0.828447 (99.99)	-0.831335 (100.33)	-0.831975 (100.41)
HCONHCH$_3$	-0.834752	-0.828825 (99.29)	-0.834419 (99.96)	-0.834960 (100.02)
HCOOCH$_3$	-0.853381	-0.847756 (99.34)	-0.853069 (99.96)	-0.853901 (100.06)
NH$_2$CONH$_2$	-0.860759	-0.854820 (99.31)	-0.861162 (100.05)	-0.861651 (100.10)
C$_2$H$_4$(OH)$_2$	-0.896933	-0.888724 (99.08)	-0.896253 (99.92)	-0.898407 (100.16)
CH$_3$NO$_2$	-0.907362	-0.902179 (99.43)	-0.906443 (99.90)	-0.907023 (99.96)
C$_6$H$_{12}$	-1.151504	-1.144232 (99.37)	-1.156460 (100.43)	-1.160306 (100.76)
Average[b]		(99.42 ± 0.19)	(100.09 ± 0.17)	(100.16 ± 0.21)

[a] LCCSD(T0)\|LMP2 using IWEAK = 2, ICLOSE = 1.
[b] Average fraction of correlation energy relative to CCSD(T) in percent. The error bounds are standard deviations.

Hartree–Fock errors of energy differences were often larger than the correlation errors. On the other hand, diffuse polarization functions had rather little effect, and therefore we found this basis to provide a suitable compromise between accuracy and cost. Similar calculations were also performed with larger basis sets and will be published elsewhere [38]. The BP criterion for domain selection was chosen to be THRBP= 0.985. The diffuse s and p functions were not included in the Pipek–Mezey localization (cf. Section 2.1, options CPLDEL=1, CPLMAXDL=1).

Table 1 shows that with standard domains on the average 99.12% of the full MP2 energy for the same basis set is recovered. When the domains of the strong pairs are augmented by the PAOs at the next neighbors (IEXTS=1), the fraction increases to 99.84%, and if the domains of all pairs are augmented (IEXT=1) even to 99.92%. At the same time, the scatter becomes smaller, as indicated by the standard deviations of the average percentages. In general, it is found that the fraction is larger for molecules containing double bonds than for saturated molecules. This is somewhat surprising, since the orbitals in saturated molecules can be very well localized, and one would intuitively assume that for such molecules the local approximations have a small effect. However, the opposite is true. We believe that this is due to the fact that unsaturated molecules, in particular those with conjugated bonds, have often planar structures or at least planar subgroups. This leads to smaller basis set superposition errors (BSSE) as compared to saturated molecules with three-dimensional structures. The BSSE is fully present in canonical calculations but small in local calculations [9,40–42]. In addition, in molecules with conjugated double bonds the domains are often larger than for single bonds and may extend over 3–4 atoms. The worst case in the set is cyclohexane C_6H_{12}. For this molecule, only 98.1% of the correlation energy is recovered with standard domains. Furthermore, the convergence towards 100% with increasing domain size is slower than in most other cases. This particular case will be further investigated in Section 6.4.

Tables 2 and 3 show similar results for LCCSD and LCCSD(T0), respectively. In these calculations, only strong pairs were treated at the LCCSD level, and the triples list (ijk) was restricted as described in Section 4. The weak pairs were treated by LMP2, and no coupling between weak and close pairs were included. We denote this approximation LCCSD(T0)|LMP2. Table 2 demonstrates that with LCCSD apparently a larger fraction of correlation energy (99.6% with standard domains) than with LMP2 (99.1%) is recovered. Clearly, this is due to error compensation. It is well known that MP2 overestimates long-range dispersion effects. Thus, the contributions of close and weak pairs, which are treated by LMP2, are overestimated relative to full LCCSD. With extended domains, this even leads to an overestimation of the total correlation energy relative to CCSD. On the other hand, it is also known that CCSD underestimates long-range correlation effects, and this error is largely corrected when perturbative triple excitations are included. Consequently, the overestimation of the correlation energy in LCCSD(T0)|LMP2 relative to full CCSD(T) is smaller than for LCCSD|LMP2; with standard domains, LCCSD(T0)|LMP2 yields an average of 99.4% of the full non-local correlation energy. We may also note that with full LCCSD and LCCSD(T0) (i.e. without weak-pair approximations), 99.2% and 99.1%, respectively, of the correlation energy are obtained, consistent with the LMP2 result.

In contrast to LMP2, the scatter of the fraction of correlation energy obtained with the LCCSD and LCCSD(T0) methods does not decrease with increasing domain size. This indicates that part of this scatter is due to the weak-pair approximation, which will be investigated in the next section.

6.2. Dependence of the correlation energy on the weak-pair approximation

Table 4 demonstrates the effect of relaxing the weak-pair approximations for LCCSD and LCCSD(T0). In all cases, the domains were extended (IEXT=1). In the columns denoted (a) all strong and close pairs were treated by LCCSD and LCCSD(T0); also, the triples list (*ijk*) included all pairs (*ij*), (*ik*), and (*jk*) which are either strong or close. In the columns denoted (b), the pair and triples list were the same as in Tables 1–3, i.e. only strong pairs were fully treated by LCCSD(T0), and the triples list was restricted such that at least one of the three pairs is a strong pair. However, in this case the close pair amplitudes, as optimized at the LMP2 level, were included in the computation of the LCCSD residual of the strong pairs (KEEPCL=1) and also in the (T0) calculation (which is the default). It is found that including the close pairs (case (a)) in the LCCSD eliminates most of the overshooting effect of the LCCSD|LMP2 approximation. Comparison with Tables 2 and 3 shows that the average fraction of correlation energy is reduced from 100.31% (ICLOSE=1) to 99.96% (ICLOSE=2) for LCCSD|LMP2, and from 100.16% to 99.77% for LCCSD(T0)|LMP2. Also, the standard deviations from the average value are now very small. Almost the same improvement is achieved in case (b) (KEEPCL=1). This demonstrates that the coupling of close and strong pairs has an effect that is not entirely negligible. It should be noted that the calculations in the latter case (b) are less expensive than in case (a) since the residuals and contributions of four-external integrals are only needed

Table 4. Effect of weak pair approximations on LCCSD energies

Molecule	LCCSD|LMP2		LCCSD(T0)|LMP2	
	ICLOSE = 0[a]	ICLOSE = 1[b]	ICLOSE = 0[a]	ICLOSE = 1[b]
C_2H_2	−0.322862 (99.97)	−0.322841 (99.97)	−0.339431 (99.95)	−0.339405 (99.94)
C_2H_4	−0.360441 (99.96)	−0.360361 (99.93)	−0.375356 (99.89)	−0.375287 (99.88)
C_2H_6	−0.401508 (99.92)	−0.401746 (99.98)	−0.414718 (99.83)	−0.415006 (99.90)
H_2CO	−0.407040 (99.99)	−0.406998 (99.98)	−0.423625 (99.91)	−0.423584 (99.90)
CH_3NH_2	−0.429943 (99.93)	−0.430137 (99.97)	−0.444575 (99.82)	−0.444809 (99.87)
CH_3OH	−0.448461 (99.94)	−0.448373 (99.92)	−0.463191 (99.83)	−0.463086 (99.81)
H_2O_2	−0.507154 (99.97)	−0.507118 (99.96)	−0.525711 (99.86)	−0.525644 (99.84)
CH_3CN	−0.531795 (99.91)	−0.532502 (100.05)	−0.556546 (99.76)	−0.557374 (99.91)
C_2H_3Cl	−0.550124 (99.95)	−0.550473 (100.02)	−0.574476 (99.78)	−0.574917 (99.86)
H_2CCO	−0.548965 (99.95)	−0.548767 (99.91)	−0.574765 (99.79)	−0.574523 (99.75)
HNCO	−0.577120 (99.97)	−0.576955 (99.95)	−0.605271 (99.77)	−0.605067 (99.74)
CH_3CHO	−0.589216 (99.92)	−0.589481 (99.97)	−0.612831 (99.78)	−0.613129 (99.83)
C_2H_4O	−0.595454 (99.95)	−0.596062 (100.06)	−0.619246 (99.82)	−0.619968 (99.94)
$HCONH_2$	−0.616266 (99.96)	−0.616385 (99.98)	−0.641809 (99.82)	−0.641941 (99.85)
C_2H_5OH	−0.632406 (99.91)	−0.632795 (99.98)	−0.653743 (99.69)	−0.654199 (99.76)
HCOOH	−0.636813 (99.97)	−0.636740 (99.96)	−0.662644 (99.82)	−0.662562 (99.81)
C_2H_3CN	−0.676049 (99.98)	−0.677009 (100.13)	−0.709633 (99.71)	−0.710760 (99.87)
$COCl_2$	−0.789971 (100.06)	−0.790742 (100.16)	−0.826156 (99.71)	−0.827006 (99.81)
$HCONHCH_3$	−0.800101 (99.95)	−0.800713 (100.03)	−0.832190 (99.69)	−0.832899 (99.78)
$HCOOCH_3$	−0.818387 (99.95)	−0.818739 (99.99)	−0.850621 (99.68)	−0.851027 (99.72)
NH_2CONH_2	−0.825267 (99.95)	−0.825889 (100.03)	−0.858491 (99.74)	−0.859191 (99.82)
$C_2H_4(OH)_2$	−0.863853 (99.90)	−0.864383 (99.96)	−0.893263 (99.59)	−0.893875 (99.66)
CH_3NO_2	−0.865443 (99.99)	−0.865899 (100.04)	−0.903933 (99.62)	−0.904484 (99.68)
C_6H_{12}	−1.106354 (100.01)	−1.109230 (100.27)	−1.146770 (99.59)	−1.150110 (99.88)
Average[c]	(99.96 ± 0.03)	(100.01 ± 0.08)	(99.77 ± 0.09)	(99.83 ± 0.08)

[a] LCCSD\|LMP2, IWEAK = 2, ICLOSE = 0, IEXTS = 1
[b] LCCSD\|LMP2, IWEAK = 2, ICLOSE = 1, IEXTS = 1, KEEPCL = 1
[c] Average fraction of correlation energy in percent. The error bounds are standard deviations.

for the strong pairs. In large molecules, this leads to substantial savings not only in CPU time, but also in the disk space requirements.

6.3. Reaction energies

More important than the errors of the individual correlation energies are errors of energy differences, for instance reaction energies. Small differences in the percentage of correlation energy recovered for reactants and products can lead to significant errors in computed energy differences. Here we present results for 33 reactions; a more extensive study will be presented elsewhere [38]. The reactions along with the experimental reaction energies are listed in Table 5. Experimental reaction enthalpies were computed from standard enthalpies of formation taken from [43,44]. Zero point and thermal corrections were computed using DFT/BP86 with the SV(P) [45] basis set. These corrections were subtracted from the experimental reaction enthalpies to obtain reaction energies which can be directly compared to the computed energy differences. The errors introduced by the BP86 zero-point corrections were tested in several cases and found to be negligible when compared to other errors in the calculations. Table 5 also shows the minimum, maximum, and average deviations between the computed and experimental values. The average errors of CCSD(T) with the aug[sp]-cc-pV(T+d)Z basis set used here are 1.34 ± 1.34 kcal/mol. Part of this error is attributed to basis set effects. Using aug-cc-pV(Q+d)Z reduces the error to 1.28 ± 1.05 kcal/mol. While in most cases the CCSD(T) values obtained with large basis sets approach the experimental ones closely, there are some exceptions. In particular, for the reactions involving C_2H_3Cl and HNCO the deviations between the calculated and experimental values amount to more than 4 kcal/mol, even with the full aug-cc-pV(5+d)Z basis set. The enthalpies of formation of these molecules reported in the literature show a large scatter, and it can be concluded that the experimental data are not reliable. If the reactions involving these two molecules (reactions 12, 16, 30, 31) are excluded from the statistics, the average errors for the aug[sp]-cc-pV(T+d)Z and aug-cc-pV(Q+d)Z bases reduce to 0.9 ± 0.7 kcal/mol and 0.6 ± 0.5 kcal/mol, respectively.

In Tables 6 and 7 the minimum, maximum, and average errors along with standard deviations of the LMP2 and LCCSD(T)|LMP2 reaction energies relative to (i) the conventional results and (ii) the experimental data are presented. The corresponding error statistics for the conventional MP2 and CCSD(T) methods, respectively, are shown in the last columns. Using standard domains, the average deviation of LMP2 from MP2

Table 5. Reference values for reaction energies[a] (in kcal/mol)

Reaction	MP2	CCSD	CCSD(T)	Exp.
$C_2H_2 + H_2 \rightarrow C_2H_4$	0.41	−2.64	−1.69	−48.06
$CO + H_2 \rightarrow H_2CO$	−0.60	−0.22	0.06	−4.73
$H_2O_2 + H_2 \rightarrow 2\ H_2O$	−5.38	−2.68	−0.93	−86.27
$C_2H_6 + H_2 \rightarrow 2\ CH_4$	0.08	−0.90	−0.37	−18.16
$C_2H_4 + H_2 \rightarrow C_2H_6$	−1.59	−1.05	−0.06	−39.45
$H_2CO + H_2 \rightarrow CH_3OH$	−0.43	−0.89	0.18	−29.31
$CH_3CHO + H_2 \rightarrow C_2H_5OH$	−2.09	−2.72	−1.66	−23.34
$CO + H_2O \rightarrow CO_2 + H_2$	−1.50	4.99	2.73	−7.40
$C_2H_2 + H_2O \rightarrow CH_3CHO$	2.13	0.31	0.53	−39.10
$C_2H_4 + H_2O \rightarrow C_2H_5OH$	−0.36	0.23	0.56	−14.38
$C_2H_4O + H_2O \rightarrow C_2H_4(OH)_2$	2.54	0.84	1.22	−26.73
$CO_2 + NH_3 \rightarrow HNCO + H_2O$	−4.13	−3.91	−4.20	24.86
$CO + NH_3 \rightarrow HCONH_2$	−0.85	2.23	1.56	−9.57
$HCOOH + NH_3 \rightarrow HCONH_2 + H_2O$	−1.19	−0.41	−0.28	−0.35
$NH_3 + 4\ H_2O_2 \rightarrow HNO_3 + 5\ H_2O$	−16.62	2.17	0.63	−176.83
$HNCO + NH_3 \rightarrow NH_2CONH_2$	6.62	4.05	5.49	−24.74
$CO + H_2O_2 \rightarrow CO_2 + H_2O$	−6.87	2.31	1.81	−93.68
$CH_4 + 4\ H_2O_2 \rightarrow CO_2 + 6\ H_2O$	−20.68	−3.65	−0.65	−288.43
$C_2H_4 + H_2O_2 \rightarrow C_2H_4O + H_2O$	−5.94	−0.86	0.08	−50.90
$C_2H_5OH + H_2O_2 \rightarrow CH_3CHO + 2\ H_2O$	−3.29	0.03	0.73	−62.94
$C_2H_4 + H_2O_2 \rightarrow C_2H_4(OH)_2$	−3.40	−0.02	1.30	−77.62
$H_2CCO + H_2CO \rightarrow C_2H_4O + CO$	0.08	−1.73	−0.72	−3.74
$C_2H_2 + HCN \rightarrow C_2H_3CN$	1.92	1.86	1.54	−45.95
$CO + CH_3OH \rightarrow HCOOCH_3$	−0.70	2.53	1.27	−13.21
$HCOOH + CH_3OH \rightarrow HCOOCH_3 + H_2O$	−1.04	−0.12	−0.57	−3.99
$cis\text{-}CH_3CH = CHCH_3$ $\rightarrow trans\text{-}CH_3CH = CHCH_3$	−0.91	−1.02	−0.92	−0.96
$CS_2 + 2\ H_2O \rightarrow CO_2 + 2\ H_2S$	6.03	−3.80	0.08	−11.85
$SO_2 + CO_2 \rightarrow SO_3 + CO$	2.72	−0.83	0.69	44.88
$SO_2 + H_2O_2 \rightarrow SO_3 + H_2O$	−4.15	1.48	2.49	−48.80
$C_2H_2 + HCl \rightarrow C_2H_3Cl$	−2.67	−2.87	−3.24	−27.56
$C_2H_4 + Cl_2 \rightarrow C_2H_3Cl + HCl$	−7.26	−4.52	−4.67	−24.51
$CO + Cl_2 \rightarrow COCl_2$	−4.49	3.52	1.19	−27.47
$COCl_2 + 2\ NH_3 \rightarrow NH_2CONH_2 + 2\ HCl$	1.29	−2.67	−0.28	−24.81
Minimum error	0.08	0.02	0.06	
Maximum error	20.68	4.99	5.49	
Average error	3.64	1.94	1.34	
σ	4.83	1.41	1.34	

[a] Basis aug[sp]-cc-pV(T + d)Z; the MP2, CCSD, and CCSD(T). Values are the errors relative to the experimental ones.

Table 6. Errors of LMP2 reaction energies[a] (in kcal/mol)

	Relative to MP2			Relative to experiment			
Error	IEXT=0	IEXTS=1	IEXT=1	IEXT=0	IEXTS=1	IEXT=1	MP2
Minimum	0.04	0.01	0.01	0.28	0.03	0.05	0.08
Maximum	2.68	1.93	0.80	22.61	21.55	21.00	20.68
Average	1.02	0.45	0.21	3.85	3.70	3.64	3.64
σ	0.77	0.47	0.19	4.86	4.60	4.47	4.83

[a] Basis aug[sp]-cc-pV(T + d)Z.

Table 7. Errors of LCCSD(T0) reaction energies[a] (in kcal/mol)

	Relative to CCSD(T)				Relative to experiment				
Error	`IEXT=0`	`IEXT=1`	`IEXT=1`	`IEXT=1`[b]	`IEXT=0`	`IEXT=1`	`IEXT=1`	`IEXT=1`[b]	CCSD(T)
Minimum	0.01	0.04	0.02	0.04	0.14	0.01	0.01	0.00	0.06
Maximum	1.73	2.54	2.35	1.51	5.73	4.52	4.53	5.31	5.49
Average	0.60	0.77	0.62	0.33	1.49	1.50	1.45	1.49	1.34
σ	0.51	0.60	0.53	0.30	1.38	1.33	1.36	1.33	1.34

[a] Basis aug[sp]-cc-pV(T+d)Z, `IWEAK=2`, `ICLOSE=1`.
[b] Using `KEEPCL=1`, see text.

amounts to 1.02 ± 0.77 kcal/mol. With `IEXTS=1` or `IEXT=1` these errors are reduced to 0.45 ± 0.47 kcal/mol and 0.21 ± 0.19 kcal/mol, respectively. In all the three cases the errors are small when compared to the errors relative to the experimental values. The errors are only slightly reduced by extending the domains, and these small improvements would normally not justify the increased computational effort.

A rather similar situation is seen in Table 7 for LCCSD(T0). Interestingly, in this case the average error of 0.6 ± 0.5 kcal/mol relative to canonical CCSD(T) obtained with standard domains is even smaller than the corresponding error of LMP2. This points to some error compensation: the reduction of correlation energy by the domain approximation is partly compensated by the overestimation of the LMP2 weak-pair contributions and neglecting the couplings between strong and close pairs. When the domains are extended (`IEXTS=1` or `IEXT=1`) the errors slightly increase since this error compensation becomes less balanced. On the other hand, if the coupling of strong and close pairs is included in the LCCSD residuals (`KEEPCL=1`), the errors are reduced to 0.33 ± 0.30 kcal/mol and are almost as small as the errors of LMP2 (which are independent of weak-pair approximations). As in the case of LMP2, the latter improvement of the computational model does not lead to a significant improvement of the agreement with experimental values. We therefore believe that in most cases the standard local approximations (standard domains and treatment of only strong pairs by LCCSD) are sufficient with basis sets of this size. Only when highly accurate results are required and large basis sets are used should the convergence of the local approximations be tested. It is then recommended to first check the domain approximation by comparing DF-MP2 and DF-LMP2 results (full DF-MP2 calculations should always be possible for cases where LCCSD(T0) is feasible). Second, the convergence of the LCCSD(T0) results with respect to the parameters `ICLOSE` and `IWEAK` can be tested. Such a systematic procedure was recently applied in accurate QM/MM calculations of barrier heights in enzymes [37].

6.4. A case study: the $C_6H_6 + 3H_2 \rightarrow C_6H_{12}$ reaction

In Section 6.1 we discussed the surprisingly large errors in the correlation energy of C_6H_{12} introduced by the domain approximation. Since the loss of correlation energy is much smaller in planar and aromatic molecules like benzene, a particular large error results for the reaction energy of $C_6H_6 + 3H_2 \rightarrow C_6H_{12}$. We have argued above that this effect is probably caused by BSSE effects, which are strongly reduced in local calculations [9,40–42]. In this section, we support this view by further calculations, in which the domain size and the basis set have been systematically varied.

Table 8 shows the convergence of the reaction energies as a function of the domain size for LMP2, LCCSD, and LCCSD(T0), using the cc-pVTZ basis set, THRBP$=0.98$, and MERGEDOM$=1$. We will first discuss the LMP2 results. With standard domains (IEXT$=0$) the LMP2 exothermicity is 5 kcal/mol less than for conventional MP2. There are several effects contributing to the over-stabilization of the reactants relative to the product: (i) as already mentioned above, the domain error is smaller in C_6H_6 than in C_6H_{12}; (ii) the domain merging procedure (cf. Section 3.4) increases the domains of the π-orbitals in benzene, but does not affect C_6H_{12}; and (iii) there is no domain error for H_2 by construction. Furthermore, as will be shown below, the basis set errors of MP2 and LMP2 have opposite sign and are additive. Therefore, this reaction represents a worst-case scenario.

If the domains are extended by the next neighbors (IEXT$=1$) the LMP2 error is reduced to 1 kcal/mol, and for IEXT$=2$ it amounts only to 0.2 kcal/mol. The dependence of the LCCSD|LMP2 and LCCSD(T0)|LMP2 reaction energies on the domain size is very similar as for LMP2. This supports our view that the domain approximation can be faithfully tested at the LMP2 level. For LCCSD|LMP2 and LCCSD(T0)|LMP2 the results with standard

Table 8. Reaction energies for $C_6H_6 + 3\,H_2 \rightarrow C_6H_{12}$ as function of domain size and weak-pair approximations[a] (in kcal/mol without ZPC)

IEXT	LMP2	LCCSD			LCCSD(T0)		
		[210][b]	[200]	[211]	[210]	[200]	[211]
0	−60.2	−75.7	−70.9	−72.2	−70.3	−65.0	−66.5
1	−64.3	−79.4	−74.4	−75.7	−74.5	−69.0	−70.5
2	−65.1	−80.2			−75.4		
3	−65.3						
Full	−65.3		−74.0			−69.5	

[a] All calculation using density fitting and cc-pVTZ basis sets.
[b] The notation [IWEAK ICLOSE KEEPCL] is used.

domains ($\texttt{IEXT}=0$) are apparently in better agreement with the conventional calculations than in the LMP2 case. Clearly, this is due to an error compensation between the domain approximation and the weak-pair approximation, as already discussed in the previous section. If the domains are extended, the LCCSD and LCCSD(T0) reaction energies become too negative. This effect is compensated, however, if close pairs are included in the LCCSD(T0) treatment (case [200] in Table 8; here we use the notation [$\texttt{IWEAK ICLOSE KEEPCL}$]). The [200] reaction energy with $\texttt{IEXT}=1$ is again in close agreement with the canonical result. Almost the same improvement is achieved if only strong pairs are treated by LCCSD, but the close pair LMP2 amplitudes are included in the calculation of the LCCSD residuals ($\texttt{KEEPCL}=1$). This is consistent with the findings in the previous section.

A more complete picture emerges if one considers the dependence of the reaction energy on the basis set, as shown in Fig. 1. The DF-MP2 and DF-LMP2 energies were computed with the cc-pVnZ basis sets up to quintuple zeta. An estimate for the MP2 complete basis set (CBS) limit was obtained by extrapolating the MP2/cc-pVQZ and MP2/cc-pV5Z correlation energies assuming $E_n = E_{CBS} + An^{-3}$. The figure shows that the basis set convergence is qualitatively different for MP2 and LMP2. While MP2 yields for small basis sets much too negative values and converges from below to the CBS limit, the opposite is true for LMP2 with standard

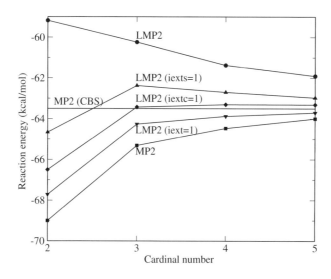

Fig. 1. Dependence of the MP2 and LMP2 reaction energies for C_6H_6 + 3 H_2 → C_6H_{12} on the basis set. The cc-pVnZ basis sets have been used for $n = 2-5$.

domains ($\text{IEXT} = 0$). In fact, for the cc-pVDZ basis ($n = 2$) the error of the LMP2 reaction energy relative to the CBS limit is smaller than that of MP2 and the basis set dependence of LMP2 is weaker than for MP2. It should be noted, however, that both methods seem not to converge to exactly the same limit; there is some intrinsic error in LMP2 due to the domain approximation, but this is much smaller than the apparent error observed for small basis sets. The exceptionally large difference between the LMP2 and MP2 results for small basis sets is due to the addition of the basis set errors of the two methods, which have different sign and origin. In MP2, the large BSSE in the product molecule C_6H_{12} leads to too large an exothermicity. We believe that this is due to the fact that the basis functions at the neighbors of an atom with tetrahedral environment can to a certain extent mimic the effect of missing higher angular momentum functions in the basis. On the other hand, in LMP2 these BSSE effects are small, and the correlation energy of the product converges more slowly with basis set size than the energy of the reactants. If the domains are extended, some of the BSSE effects are introduced back into the LMP2 calculation, and the results approach the MP2 values. This leads to the interesting finding that in case the domains of the strong and close pairs are extended ($\text{IEXTC} = 1$) the CBS limit is already reached with the triple zeta basis set.

Finally, we tested the selection of domains using energy criteria, as described in Section 3.7. Since, as shown above, the dependence of the LMP2 and LCCSD(T0) energies on the domain size is very similar, these tests were performed only at the LMP2 level. The results are shown in Table 9. As expected, the results converge toward the canonical ones with decreasing energy threshold. However, this convergence is less systematic than with the domain extension method. With selection threshold 10^{-3} E_h exactly the same domains and energies as with the standard BP method are obtained. If one considers the energy contributions of individual centers in the domains, one finds that the atoms in the standard domains have by far the largest contributions; those of the next important atoms are about one order of magnitude smaller. They vary somewhat from molecule to molecule, and therefore at certain thresholds more atoms may be added for the reactants or products, leading to unbalanced results. This is most clearly seen in Table 9 for the threshold 3.3×10^{-4} E_h. Of course, for smaller thresholds these effects become less pronounced, but the domains needed to achieve a certain accuracy are not smaller than those determined by the standard procedure with extensions. Therefore, despite the appealing possibility to control the accuracy of a local calculation by an energy threshold, we do not consider this a useful procedure. Controlling the accuracy of the domain approximation is possible by another single parameter, namely the domain extension (IEXT),

Table 9. LMP2 energies[a] as function of the domain selection threshold

THRSEL[b]	$E(C_6H_6)$	$E(C_6H_{12})$	ΔE^c	$N_{av}{}^d(C_6H_6)$	$N_{av}(C_6H_{12})$
1.0×10^{-3}	−231.716592	−235.306494	−60.2	123	87
3.3×10^{-4}	−231.723150	−235.306494	−56.1	167	87
1.0×10^{-4}	−231.723932	−235.320147	−64.2	184	193
3.3×10^{-5}	−231.725079	−235.322537	−65.0	235	255
1.0×10^{-5}	−231.725079	−235.323101	−65.3	235	274
Full	−231.726506	−235.324493	−65.3	263	348

[a] All values (in Hartree) calculated using density fitting and cc-pVTZ basis sets.
[b] Energy threshold for domain selection (in Hartree, see text) using LMP2 (IEXTS=2) as reference.
[c] Reaction energy for C_6H_6 + 3 H_2 → C_6H_{12} in kcal/mol (without ZPC).
[d] Average domain sizes.

and this leads to much more systematic convergence. The weak-pair approximation can also be controlled by an energy threshold, but again we do not find that this leads to a systematic improvement of the method.

7. CONCLUSIONS

We have reviewed the approximations made in the linear scaling local correlation methods developed in our group. The accuracy of local coupled-cluster calculations depends on (i) the domain sizes and (ii) the definition of the strong-pair list included in the LCCSD. These approximations can be controlled using connectivity or distance criteria. The domain sizes can be determined by a single parameter (IEXT or REXT), and we have shown that domain extensions lead to rapid and systematic convergence toward the canonical results. The list of strong pairs depends on parameters IWEAK and ICLOSE (or RWEAK and RCLOSE), and again convergence toward the canonical result with respect to these parameters has been demonstrated. It has been found that in most cases the domain and the weak-pair approximations in LCCSD(T0)|LMP2 calculations compensate each other to a large extent. Therefore, rather accurate results are obtained with the standard approximation, in which the domains are determined by the BP procedure and strong orbital pairs are determined by the condition that the domains of the two orbitals overlap. This may be considered a well-defined new computational model, distinct from conventional CCSD(T). Extensive tests on 33 chemical reactions have shown that the errors introduced by these standard local approximations are usually small when compared to basis set errors and the deviations from experimental values. For the 33 reactions studied here, the average and maximum errors of the reaction energies relative to experimental values are very similar for CCSD(T) and LCCSD(T0). In cases in which high accuracy is required and large basis sets are used, it is recommended first to test the domain approximation at the LMP2/MP2 level, and then to test the convergence of the LCCSD(T) with respect to the weak-pair parameters.

It has also been demonstrated that convergence of the results with basis set size may be qualitatively different for LMP2 and MP2, and faster convergence is found for LMP2. This effect is attributed to a reduction of basis set superposition errors in the local calculations. In a recent study on the influence of local approximations on vibrational frequencies [23] similar effects have been found, and it has been demonstrated that for some modes, which are sensitive to BSSE, the local calculations also yielded better basis set convergence and more accurate results than conventional calculations. Other studies have demonstrated that the effect of local approximations on equilibrium geometries [18–20], dipole moments and polarizabilities [24,25], and NMR chemical shifts [26] are small. The combination of local and DF approximations makes it now possible to perform DF-LCCSD(T0) calculations with large basis sets for molecules of chemical interest (50–100 atoms), as has recently been demonstrated in a QM/MM study of the enzymes chorismate mutase and *para*-hydroxybenzoate hydroxylase [37]. Further work to extend these methods to open-shell cases is in progress.

ACKNOWLEDGEMENTS

This work has been supported by the Deutsche Forschungsgemeinschaft and the Fonds der Chemischen Industrie. The authors thank Dr. A. Schäfer for providing the experimental data as well as zero-point and thermodynamic corrections for the reaction enthalpies.

REFERENCES

[1] P. Pulay, Localizability of dynamic electron correlation, *Chem. Phys. Lett.*, 1983, **100**, 151–154.
[2] S. Saebø and P. Pulay, Local configuration-interaction: an efficient approach for larger molecules, *Chem. Phys. Lett.*, 1985, **113**, 13–18.
[3] P. Pulay and S. Saebø, Orbital-invariant formulation and second-order gradient evaluation in Møller–Plesset perturbation theory, *Theor. Chim. Acta*, 1986, **69**, 357–368.
[4] S. Saebø and P. Pulay, Fourth-order Møller–Plesset perturbation theory in the local correlation treatment. I. Method, *J. Chem. Phys.*, 1987, **86**, 914–922.
[5] S. Saebø and P. Pulay, The local correlation treatment. II. Implementation and tests, *J. Chem. Phys.*, 1988, **88**, 1884–1890.

[6] S. Saebø and P. Pulay, Local treatment of electron correlation, *Annu. Rev. Phys. Chem.*, 1993, **44**, 213–236.

[7] S. F. Boys, Localized orbitals and localized adjustment functions, *In Quantum Theory of Atoms, Molecules, and the Solid State* (ed. P. O. Löwdin), Academic Press, New York, 1966, p. 253–262.

[8] J. Pipek and P. G. Mezey, A fast intrinsic localization procedure applicable for ab initio and semiempirical linear combination of atomic orbital wave functions, *J. Chem. Phys.*, 1989, **90**, 4916–4926.

[9] C. Hampel and H.-J. Werner, Local treatment of electron correlation in coupled cluster theory, *J. Chem. Phys.*, 1996, **104**, 6286–6297.

[10] G. Hetzer, P. Pulay and H.-J. Werner, Multipole approximation of distant pair energies in local MP2 calculations, *Chem. Phys. Lett.*, 1998, **290**, 143–149.

[11] M. Schütz, G. Hetzer and H.-J. Werner, Low-order scaling local electron correlation methods. I. Linear scaling local MP2, *J. Chem. Phys.*, 1999, **111**, 5691–5705.

[12] G. Hetzer, M. Schütz, H. Stoll and H.-J. Werner, Low-order scaling local correlation methods. II: Splitting the Coulomb operator in linear scaling local second-order Møller–Plesset perturbation theory, *J. Chem. Phys.*, 2000, **113**, 9443–9455.

[13] M. Schütz and H.-J. Werner, Local perturbative triples correction (T) with linear cost scaling, *Chem. Phys. Lett.*, 2000, **318**, 370–378.

[14] M. Schütz, Low-order scaling local electron correlation methods. III. Linear scaling local perturbative triples correction (T), *J. Chem. Phys.*, 2000, **113**, 9986–10001.

[15] M. Schütz and H.-J. Werner, Low-order scaling local electron correlation methods. IV. Linear scaling local coupled-cluster (LCCSD), *J. Chem. Phys.*, 2001, **114**, 661–681.

[16] M. Schütz, Linear scaling local connected triples beyond local (T): Local CCSDT-1b with O(N) scaling, *J. Chem. Phys.*, 2002, **116**, 8772–8785.

[17] J. W. Boughton and P. Pulay, Comparison of the Boys and Pipek–Mezey localizations in the local correlation approach and automatic virtual basis selection, *J. Comput. Chem.*, 1993, **14**, 736–740.

[18] A. ElAzhary, G. Rauhut, P. Pulay and H.-J. Werner, Analytical energy gradients for local second-order Møller–Plesset perturbation theory, *J. Chem. Phys.*, 1998, **108**, 5185–5193.

[19] G. Rauhut and H.-J. Werner, Analytical energy gradients for local coupled-cluster methods, *Phys. Chem. Chem. Phys.*, 2001, **3**, 4853–4862.

[20] M. Schütz, H.-J. Werner, R. Lindh and F. R. Manby, Analytical energy gradients for local second-order Møller–Plesset perturbation theory using density fitting approximations, *J. Chem. Phys.*, 2004, **121**, 737–750.

[21] G. Rauhut, A. E. Azhary, F. Eckert, U. Schumann and H.-J. Werner, Impact of local approximations on MP2 vibrational frequencies, *Spectrochim. Acta A*, 1999, **55**, 647–658.

[22] G. Rauhut and H.-J. Werner, The vibrational spectra of furoxan and dichlorofuroxan: a comparative theoretical study using density functional theory and local electron correlation methods, *Phys. Chem. Chem. Phys.*, 2003, **5**, 2001–2008.

[23] T. Henar, G. Rauhut and H.-J. Werner, Impact of local and density fitting approximations on harmonic vibrational frequencies, *J. Phys. Chem. A*, 2006, **110**, 2060–2064.

[24] T. Korona, K. Pflüger and H.-J. Werner, The effect of local approximations in coupled-cluster wavefunctions on dipole moments and static dipole polarisabilities, *Phys. Chem. Chem. Phys.*, 2004, **6**, 2059–2065.

[25] N. J. Russ and T. D. Crawford, Local correlation in coupled cluster calculations of molecular response properties, *Chem. Phys. Lett.*, 2004, **400**, 104–111.

[26] J. Gauss and H.-J. Werner, NMR chemical shift calculations within local correlation methods: the GIAO-LMP2 approach, *Phys. Chem. Chem. Phys.*, 2000, **2**, 2083–2090.

[27] N. J. Russ and T. D. Crawford, Potential energy surface discontinuities in local correlation methods, *J. Chem. Phys.*, 2004, **121** (2), 691–696.

[28] R. Mata and H.-J. Werner, Application of local electron correlation methods to chemical reactions, to be published.

[29] P. Y. Ayala and G. E. Scuseria, Linear scaling second-order Møller–Plesset theory in the atomic orbital basis for large molecular systems, *J. Chem. Phys.*, 1999, **110**, 3660–3671.

[30] G. E. Scuseria and P. Y. Ayala, Linear scaling coupled cluster and perturbation theories in the atomic orbital basis, *J. Chem. Phys.*, 1999, **111**, 8330–8343.

[31] H.-J. Werner, F. R. Manby and P. Knowles, Fast linear scaling second-order Møller–Plesset perturbation theory (MP2) using local and density fitting approximations, *J. Chem. Phys.*, 2003, **118**, 8149–8160.

[32] M. Schütz and F. R. Manby, Linear scaling local coupled cluster theory with density fitting. I : 4-external integrals, *Phys. Chem. Chem. Phys.*, 2003, **5**, 3349–3358.

[33] R. Polly, H.-J. Werner, F. R. Manby and P. J. Knowles, Fast Hartree–Fock theory using local density fitting approximations, *Mol. Phys.*, 2004, **102**, 2311–2321.

[34] H.-J. Werner and M. Schütz, Density fitting approximations in local coupled cluster (LCCSD(T)) calculations, to be published.

[35] H.-J. Werner, P. J. Knowles, R. Lindh, M. Schütz, P. Celani, T. Korona, F. R. Manby, G. Rauhut, R. D. Amos, A. Bernhardsson, A. Berning, D. L. Cooper, M. J. O. Deegan, A. J. Dobbyn, F. Eckert, C. Hampel, G. Hetzer, A. W. Lloyd, S. J. McNicholas, W. Meyer, M. E. Mura, A. Nicklass, P. Palmieri, R. Pitzer, U. Schumann, H. Stoll, A. J. Stone, R. Tarroni and T. Thorsteinsson, Molpro, version 2006.1, a package of *ab initio* programs, 2006, see http://www.molpro.net.

[36] T. H. Dunning, Jr., Gaussian basis sets for use in correlated molecular calculations. I. The atoms boron through neon and hydrogen, *J. Chem. Phys.*, 1989, **90**, 1007–1023.

[37] F. Claeyssens, J. N. Harvey, F. R. Manby, R. A. Mata, A. J. Mulholland, K. E. Ranaghan, M. Schütz, S. Thiel, W. Thiel and H.-J. Werner, Converged quantum chemistry for enzymatic catalysis using local correlation methods, to be published.

[38] K. Pflüger, H.-J. Werner, A. Schäfer and M. Schütz, The effect of local approximations on reaction energies, to be published.

[39] J. T. H. Dunning, K. A. Peterson and A. Wilson, Gaussian basis sets for use in correlated molecular calculations. X. The atoms aluminum through argon revisited, *J. Chem. Phys.*, 2001, **114**, 9244–9253.

[40] W. Meyer and L. Frommhold, Ab initio calculation of the dipole moment of He–Ar and the collision-induced absorption spectra, *Phys. Rev. A*, 1986, **33**, 3807–3814.

[41] S. Saebø, W. Tong and P. Pulay, Efficient elimination of basis set superposition errors by the local correlation method: accurate ab initio studies of the water dimer, *J. Chem. Phys.*, 1993, **98**, 2170–2175.

[42] M. Schütz, G. Rauhut and H.-J. Werner, Local treatment of electron correlation in molecular clusters: structures and stabilities of $(H_2O)_n$, $n = 2$–4, *J. Phys. Chem. A*, 1998, **102**, 5997–6003.

[43] I. Barin, *Thermochemical Data of Pure Substances*, Verlag Chemie, Weinheim, 1989.

[44] D. R. Lide, *Handbook of Chemistry and Physics*, 76th edition, CRC Press, Boca Raton, FL, 1995.

[45] A. Schäfer, H. Horn and R. Ahlrichs, Fully optimized contracted gaussian basis sets for atoms Li to Kr, *J. Chem. Phys.*, 1992, **97**, 2571–2577.

Section 3
Molecular Modeling Methods

Section Editor: Carlos Simmerling
Center for Structural Biology
Stony Brook University
Stony Brook, NY 11794
USA

CHAPTER 5

Simulations of Temperature and Pressure Unfolding of Peptides and Proteins with Replica Exchange Molecular Dynamics

Angel E. Garcia,[1] Henry Herce[1] and Dietmar Paschek[2]

[1]Department of Physics, Applied Physics and Astronomy, and Center for Biotechnology and Interdisciplinary Studies, Rensselaer Polytechnic Institute, Troy, NY 12180, USA
[2]Department of Physical Chemistry, Otto-Hahn-Street 6, University of Dortmund, D-44221 Dortmund, Germany, UK

Contents

1. INTRODUCTION

The use of enhanced sampling methods has enabled the sampling of the conformational space of proteins and peptides in an efficient way, overcoming sampling limitations due to the multiple time scales involved in protein folding [1]. Umbrella sampling [2], replica exchange molecular dynamics (REMD) [3–5] (which can be derived as an umbrella sampling technique [6]), and multicanonical ensemble methods [7,8] are efficient methods for modeling thermodynamic equilibrium at the cost of dynamics information. Replica dynamics and its variations have also been effectively used to explore the folding kinetics of peptides and mini proteins [9–11]. The replica exchange (RE) algorithm has been described independently many times in different contexts [3–5,12–14]. To our knowledge, the first description was by Swendsen and Wang [12,15]. The first use of biomolecules was by Hansmann [4], within the context of Monte Carlo (MC) simulations. The extension of the method to molecular dynamics (MD) simulations was first done by Sugita and Okamoto [3].

ANNUAL REPORTS IN COMPUTATIONAL CHEMISTRY, VOLUME 2
ISSN: 1574-1400   DOI 10.1016/S1574-1400(06)02005-6

Enhanced sampling methods and equilibrium MD simulations have been employed to validate (or invalidate) and modify semiempirical force fields [16–19], and to explore the free-energy landscape of proteins and peptides [11,16,20–23]. The REMD method has been used to describe the energy landscape of peptides [16,18,24–26], proteins [27], mini-proteins [28], protein membrane systems [6,29], amyloid formation [30,31], protein structure prediction [30–34], NMR refinement [35,36], protein design [37], and binding [38]. For more information we refer the reader to recent reviews on the topic [1,6].

Here we will describe the use of REMD methods and describe issues surrounding the use of REMD, its advantages, and limitations. We will discuss system-size limitations, the efficient selection of temperatures, sampling of a canonical ensemble, thermodynamic equilibrium, and convergence of averages. We will also describe extensions of the REMD that allows for the sampling density and T and density states. This chapter is not intended as a review of all the literature in the field, since there are more than 200 articles published since the year 2000.

2. THE REPLICA EXCHANGE ALGORITHM

Let us assume that we are performing MC simulations of a system whose energy is defined by a potential energy function, $U(x)$. In the MC replica exchange method, one simulates multiple copies of the system at different thermodynamic states. For simplicity, we will describe replicas that differ only in temperature, T. We can preserve detailed-balance, which is a sufficient condition for sampling from a Boltzmann distribution, if the exchange moves between any two replicas are accepted with probability min(1, exp($\Delta U \Delta \beta$)), where $\Delta U = U(x_j) - U(x_i)$ is the difference in energy and $\Delta \beta = (1/\kappa_B T_j - 1/\kappa_B T_j)$ the difference in inverse temperature between the two replicas. To extend this method to MD simulations Sugita and Okamoto used the same exchange probability function, which is obtained for MD if we scale the kinetic energy terms during the exchange such that the changes in kinetic energy during the exchange is zero. That is all velocities in replica j are multiplied by $\sqrt{(T_i/T_j)}$, and the velocities in replica i are multiplied by $\sqrt{(T_j/T_i)}$. This is the method most commonly implemented in biomolecular simulation codes. In practice, the exchanges are done by exchanging temperatures rather than by exchanging configurations.

The replica exchange algorithm allows the system to sample configurational space more efficiently. Owing to the coupling between replicas, the REMD is similar to a simulated annealing calculation where the system self-regulate its heating and cooling schedule. The exchange between systems is driven by the system energy, with high-energy configurations pushed toward high T and low-energy configurations are cooled down, except when driven by thermal fluctuations. At high T the system can overcome energy barriers and samples more configurations. In alpha-helical systems, we found that alpha helices were nucleated at high T and once formed, the system adopted low T. In systems where water is treated explicitly, most of the high-energy conformations of the protein can be accommodated within the thermal fluctuations of the much larger water bath. Therefore, it is not uncommon to observe completely unfolded conformations at low T, or folded configurations at very high T. It has been argued that REMD enhances the sampling by a factor of 20–100, when compared to constant T MD [21,23,39]. This would be the case if one is really interested in sampling different T, since we need to simulate multiple copies of the system, while constant we can perform multiple constant T MD simulations and spend equal amounts of computer time sampling at only one T [40]. As we apply REMD to new systems we find that REMD also needs long-time simulations to reach equilibrium.

To implement the REMD we must decide the number of replicas to be simulated, the temperatures of the replicas, and the number of replicas. These parameters are not independent of each other. First, the T range must be decided based on the expected properties of the energy landscape of the system.

The definition of parameters in REMD is guided by statistical mechanics. A quantity central to the application is the energy histograms and their dependence on temperature. The energy probability histograms, $P(E|N, T, V)$ for a system at constant N, V, T is given by

$$P(E|N, V, T) = \frac{1}{Z(T)} \Omega(E)\exp(-E/\kappa_B T) \qquad (1)$$

where $Z(T)$ is the partition function, $\Omega(E)$ the density of states, κ_B the Boltzmann constant, and E the energy. Figure 1a shows a set of energy histograms at various T for 12-nucleotide RNA molecule in water (a system of approximately 12 K atoms). Notice that these histograms shift to higher energy as T increases. If we approximate the probability histograms by Gaussian distributions we can define two main quantities, the average energy, $\bar{E}(T)$ (see Fig. 1b), and the standard deviation, $\sigma(T)$ (see Fig. 1c). The difference in $\bar{E}(T)$ (between two systems at temperatures differing by ΔT is given by $\Delta E = \bar{E}(T+\Delta T) - \bar{E}(T) = C_V m\Delta T$, where C_V is the coordinate space contribution to the specific heat at constant volume and m the mass of the system. The mean-square fluctuations are given by $\Delta E^2 = \langle E^2 - <E>^2 \rangle = C_V m\kappa_B T^2$. To have an overlap between the two probability distributions, $\Delta E/\sqrt{\Delta E^2} \approx 1$, and the difference

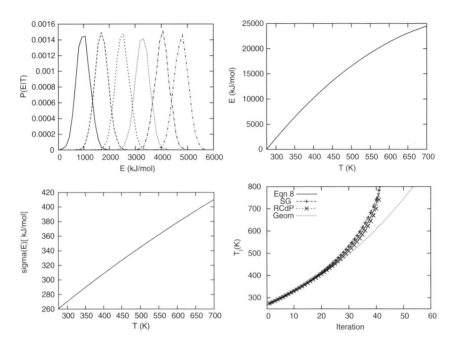

Fig. 1. (a) Potential energy histograms sampled at various T, (b) average, and (c) energy variance as a function of T for a 12 K atoms RNA system in TIP3P water. (d) Calculated optimal replica temperatures using a geometric distribution (equation (3)), the GS (equation (4)), the Rathora, Chopra and de Pablo (RCdP) (equation (7)), and a Gaussian approximation for the exchange rate (equation (8))

$\Delta T \approx \sqrt{\kappa_B T^2 / m C_v}$, that is, the T spacing required for energy distributions to have an overlap decreases proportionally to $1/\sqrt{m} \approx 1/\sqrt{N}$. This implies that for large systems the number of replicas required to cover a broad temperature range get prohibitedly large, thus limiting the use of REMD to relatively small systems (20 K atoms). This limitation can be overcome by using a method called REST (Replica exchange with solute tempering). This approach can be used to enhance the sampling efficiency, but limits the calculation of thermodynamic properties [41].

The energy probability distribution can also be useful to determine if a Boltzmann distribution is being sampled by the MD. Using Bennett's histogram overlap method we can verify that the log of the ratio of the distributions (for energies where there is an overlap) can be fitted to

$$\log\left[\frac{P(E, T_1)}{P(E, T_2)}\right] = (1/\kappa_B T_2 - 1/\kappa_B T_1)E + \text{constant} \qquad (2)$$

That is, the slope must equal $\Delta\beta = (1/\kappa_B T_2 - 1/\kappa_B T_1)$. We have found that Nose–Hoover and the Anderson thermostat satisfy this condition, but Berendsen heat coupling method does not [42].

2.1. Assignment of temperatures to replicas

A simple way of assigning the replica's T is by using a geometric distribution.

$$T_j = T_1 \left(1 + \frac{(T_2 - T_1)}{T_1} \right)^{(j-1)} \tag{3}$$

Other methods have been described by Sanbonmatsu and Garcia (SG) [39], and by Rathore, Chopra, and de Pablo (RCdP) [43]. SG used the averaged values of the energy as a function of T to estimate iteratively the T_{i+1} given T_i using

$$\exp(\Delta\beta(i-1,i)\Delta\bar{E}(i-1,i)) = \exp(\Delta\beta(i,i+1)\Delta\bar{E}(i,i+1)) \tag{4}$$

where $\Delta\bar{E}(i,j) = \bar{E}(T_j) - \bar{E}(T_i)$. Here it is assumed that R_{acc} will be constant and is determined by the choice of two neighboring temperatures.

RCdP used Gaussian approximations of the energy distributions at various T to approximate the overlap integral. Within this approximation

$$P(E \mid \bar{E}, \sigma) = \frac{1}{\sqrt{2\pi}\sigma} \exp\left[\frac{-(E - \bar{E})^2}{2\sigma^2} \right] \tag{5}$$

and

$$
\begin{aligned}
A_{\text{overlap}} &= \int_{\infty}^{E_i} dE P(E \mid \bar{E}_2, \sigma_2) + \int_{E_i}^{\infty} dE P(E \mid \bar{E}_1, \sigma_1) \\
&= \frac{1}{2} erfc\left[\frac{E_i - \bar{E}_1}{\sqrt{2}\sigma_1} \right] + \frac{1}{2} erfc\left[\frac{E_i - \bar{E}_2}{\sqrt{2}\sigma_2} \right] \\
&\approx erfc\left[\frac{\Delta E}{2\sqrt{2}\sigma_m} \right]
\end{aligned}
\tag{6}
$$

where ΔE is the difference between energy means and $\sigma_m = (\sigma_1 + \sigma_2)/2$. However, the relevant quantity is not the A_{overlap}, but the rate of acceptance R_{acc}. RCdP illustrated that for different systems the probability of acceptance as a function of $\Delta E/\sigma_m$ collapse on a single curve. Based on this observation they suggest a protocol where

$$[\Delta E/\sigma_m]_{T_i} = [\Delta E/\sigma_m]_{T_{\mathrm{target}}} \tag{7}$$

Following this iterative method it is simple to assign temperatures while maintaining a constant pre-selected value for R_{acc}. This method proved superior than the geometric distribution in that it provides a uniform R_{acc}.

An extension of the RCdP method is based on the calculation of R_{acc} using Gaussian energy distributions. That is,

$$
\begin{aligned}
R_{\mathrm{acc}} &= \int_{-\infty}^{\infty} dx\, P(x|\bar{E}_1, \sigma_1)\left[\int_{-\infty}^{x} dy\, P(y|\bar{E}_2, \sigma_2) + \int_{x}^{\infty} dy\, P(y|\bar{E}_2, \sigma_2)\exp(\Delta\beta(x-y))\right] \\
&= \frac{1}{2}\left[1 + erf\left[\frac{\bar{E}_2 - \bar{E}_1}{\sqrt{2\sigma_1^2 + 2\sigma_2^2}}\right]\right] \\
&\quad + \frac{1}{2}\left[\exp\left[\Delta\beta(\bar{E}_2 - \bar{E}_1) + \left(\frac{\Delta\beta}{2}\right)^2(2\sigma_1^2 + 2\sigma_2^2)\right]\right. \\
&\quad \left. erfc\left[\frac{\Delta\beta(\sigma_1^2 + \sigma_2^2) + \bar{E}_2 - \bar{E}_1}{\sqrt{2\sigma_1^2 + 2\sigma_2^2}}\right]\right]
\end{aligned} \tag{8}
$$

Using this formula and given $\bar{E}$ and σ as a function of T we can iteratively solve for T_{i+1} given T_i. Figure 1d shows three curves for T assignments using the geometric distribution, SG, RCdP, and equation (8). The plot show curves of T_j as a function of the iteration index j for the geometric (solid line), SG (dot dashed curve), the RCdP (dashed line), and equation (8) (solid circles). All approximations give very similar curves, except the geometric distribution, which underestimates the temperatures at high T and will require a larger number of replicas to span the same temperature range as with the other methods. At low T all methods give the same curves. These curves were obtained by solving equation (8) for $R_{\mathrm{acc}} = 0.15$.

3. CONVERGENCE OF AVERAGES

Although REMD dramatically enhances sampling, it may take quite long simulation times to establish a converged folding/unfolding equilibrium, particularly when starting from a set of completely unfolded protein configurations. To illustrate this, we show very recent results of a simulation of the methyl-capped 20-residue Trp-cage protein using the AMBER94 force field [44] and 2637 TIP3P [45] water molecules as a solvent. Trp-cage (more precisely TC5b) is a 20-residue protein created by Neidigh, Fesinmeyer, and Andersen [46], which currently holds the record as the smallest peptide with a cooperatively folded tertiary structure. The Trp-cage simulation is starting from an artificially prepared compact coil structure. The initial structure is found to be completely unfolded with a (CNO)-backbone RMSD from the first NMR structure of 6.0 Å. Moreover, it lacks any regular secondary structure elements in particular, it has none of the helical structure elements that is present in the native state. Our simulation uses 40 replicas distributed over a temperature range from 280.0 K to 539.7 K. The temperature spacing between each of the replicas was chosen such that the energy distributions overlap sufficiently and state exchange attempts are (on average) accepted with a 20 percent probability. State exchange attempts were undertaken with a probability of 0.05 (every 20th step on average), leading to a time of about 1.6 ps for each replica between two state exchanges. The time step used in the MD steps is 2 fs and a Nosé–Hoover [47,48] thermostat is used with a time coupling of $\tau_T = 0.5$ ps. The total simulation is performed for 50 ns. Using our GROMACS implementation the simulation as discussed above takes about 10.9 h/ns when distributed over 40 processors of our Opteron 2.2 GHz Linux Cluster.

Figure 2a shows a time evolution of the CNO-backbone RMSD with respect to the NMR structure (#1 of PDB-code "1L2Y") [46] for each of the

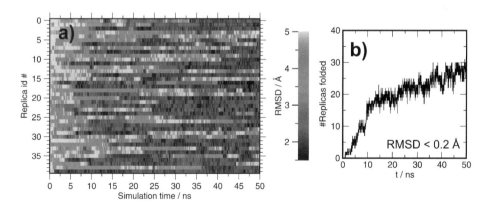

Fig. 2. Convergence of the Trp-cage folding obtained from a 40-replica REMD simulation. (a) Time evolution of the CNO-backbone RMSD value for each of the 40 replicas. (b) Total number of folded replicas (with RMSD ≤ 2.2 Å) as a function of simulation time.

40 replicas. The gray shading coding indicates that the simulation starts with a completely unfolded ensemble with an RMSD > 0.5 nm. Although some of the replicas fold rather quickly, we denote a rapid folding rate particularly in the very first 12 ns of the simulation runs. From a very well-pronounced minimum in the RMSD distribution function at lower temperatures (not shown), the folded configurations can be well separated from the unfolded configurations by a RMSD threshold of RMSD ≤ 2.2 Å. Please note that the total number of folded replicas (Fig. 2b) increases quickly during the 12 ns period. Over the final 38 ns of the simulation run we observe folding and unfolding events. However, the total number of folded configurations indicates that the equilibrium value is still not achieved. As can be roughly concluded from Fig. 2b, the lifetime of a folded configuration is probably of the order of 20 ns. So we conclude that a proper representation of the folding/unfolding equilibrium of the Trp-cage might require simulation times of about 200 ns, or even longer.

4. VOLUME AND TEMPERATURE REPLICA EXCHANGE MOLECULAR DYNAMICS

Pressure effects on proteins are of interest in the physical chemistry of proteins since pressure provides a way of reversibly changing the equilibrium of protein configurations without increasing thermal fluctuations. Changes in hydrostatic pressure provide a way of probing the effect of hydration on protein stability. Paschek and Garcia extended the REMD method to include exchanges between states at different temperatures and volumes and allow the evaluation of a protein $P-T$ diagram for folding/unfolding. They called this method the Volume–Temperature REMD (VTREMD) [49]. The VTREMD simulations are conducted using a grid of different (V, T) states; each state is characterized by its volume V and temperature T. The acceptance rule for state-swapping moves between two states i and j is given by the acceptance probability

$$P_{acc} = \min\{1, \exp[\beta_i(U(\vec{s}_i^N; L_i) - U(\vec{s}_j^N; L_i))$$
$$+ \beta_j(U(\vec{s}_j^N; L_j) - U(\vec{s}_i^N; L_j))]\} \qquad (9)$$

Here, $\vec{s}_i^N$ represents the set of scaled coordinates $\vec{s}_N = L^{-1}\vec{r}_N$ of the entire N-particle system belonging to state i. $U(\vec{s}_i^N; L_i)$ denotes the potential energy of configuration $\vec{s}_i^N$ at volume $V_i = L_i^3$, whereas $U(\vec{s}_i^N; L_j)$ represents the configurational energy belonging to $\vec{s}_i^N$ at volume V_j. The volume change is performed in such a way that only intermolecular distances are changed. Considering that only small volume changes are made, the energies can be approximated as

$$U(\vec{s}_j^N; L_i) \approx U(\vec{s}_j^N; L_j) - \left(P_j - \frac{M}{\beta_j' V_j}\right) \times (V_i - V_j) \tag{10}$$

and

$$U(\vec{s}_i^N; L_j) \approx U(\vec{s}_i^N; L_i) - \left(P_i - \frac{M}{\beta_i' V_i}\right) \times (V_j - V_i) \tag{11}$$

Here M represents the number of molecules in the simulation box and P_i and P_j denote the pressures of states i and j. β' represents the *instantaneous* temperature, whereas β corresponds to the *average* temperature characterizing the states i and j. In order to fulfill the detailed balance condition, the decision whether a state-swapping move or an MD move is executed, is chosen at random. VTREMD have been carried out using the GROMACS 3.2 program [50], modified to allow for V, T-state-swapping moves. The GROMACS 3.2 program has also been modified to use the AMBER force field [44] in addition to the GROMOS [51] force field. It is preferable to simulate constant at volume (or density, ρ) and temperature (V, T) states against the typical (P, T) to avoid gas to liquid transitions in water, which will slow down the convergence of the simulations. In the VTREMD method the number of replicas to be considered increases by one order of magnitude. That is, in addition to the replicas spanning the T range, there are replicas spanning the V space.

The VTREMD has been used to describe the $P-T$ free-energy diagram of the GB-1 beta hairpin (using 253 replicas, 23 temperatures, and 11 volumes) [49] and for the AK peptide – an alpha-helix forming peptide (using 360 replicas, 36 temperatures, and 10 densities) [52]. The $P-T$ phase diagram for the GB-1 peptide is shown in Fig. 3. Notice that the free-energy diagram for the GB-1 peptide exhibits an ellipsoidal shape, characteristic of the $P-T$ diagram of proteins [53]. This diagram shows protein destabilization upon cooling (i.e., cold denaturation), at high P and low T. To get this diagram, we converted the calculated (ρ, T) diagram to a $(<P>, T)$ diagram, which we fit to a second-order expansion of the free energy,

$$\Delta G_U(P, T) = \Delta G_U^0 - \Delta S_U(T - T_0) + \Delta C_p T \log(T/T_0)$$
$$+ \ \Delta V_U(P - P_0) + \frac{1}{2}\Delta \bar{\beta}(P - P_0)^2 + \Delta \alpha(P - P_0)(T - T_0) \tag{12}$$

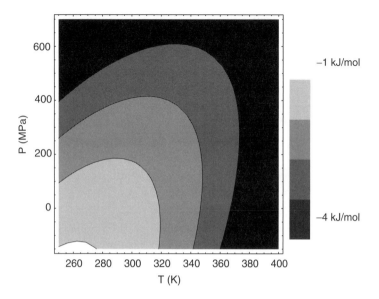

Fig. 3. $\Delta G_U(P, T)$ contours for the GB-1 beta hairpin peptide. Pressure is given in megapascals (MPa), and T in Kelvins. The unfolded hairpin is always the lowest free-energy state for all P–T states sampled with the VTREMD. Notice that the stability of the folded state can be reduced by increasing the pressure at low T, or by increasing the T at low pressures. The folded state can also become less stable by lowering T at high P (400 MPa) – thus describing cold denaturation.

where ΔC_p is the heat capacity, ΔS_U the entropy of unfolding, ΔG_U^0 the Gibbs free energy of unfolding at the reference temperature T_0, $\Delta\bar{\beta}$ the compressibility change (not to be confused with the difference in inverse temperatures), ΔV_U the volume change upon unfolding, and $\Delta\alpha$ the temperature-independent expansivity change upon unfolding [53]. The values for ΔC_p, ΔS_U, $\Delta\bar{\beta}$, ΔV_U, and $\Delta\alpha$ upon unfolding are of the same order of magnitude as those measured for proteins [54]. Interestingly, the phase diagram for the alpha-helical peptide shows no pressure-induced denaturation [52].

5. CONCLUSIONS

The increasing popularity of the REMD method should enable us to better discover the advantages, limitations, and further extensions of the method to study protein-folding thermodynamics. Initial applications showed that the REMD was able to quickly form secondary structural elements such as alpha helices and beta hairpins. Further studies showed that tens of nanoseconds are not sufficient to obtain convergence of detailed free-energy surfaces and that longer simulation times are required. We have shown here that for the Trp-cage mini-protein the mean time for replicas to sample folding and unfolding basins is of the order of 20 ns, which implies that 'equilibrium' calculations should be extended for many times this time. Unfortunately, these calculations, when done in explicit solvent models, require calculations that extend for months in today's computers.

ACKNOWLEDGEMENTS

DP gratefully acknowledges support by DFG FOR436. AEG and HH are supported by the National Science Foundation, grant MCB-0543769.

REFERENCES

[1] S. Gnanakaran, H. Nymeyer, J. Portman, K. Y. Sanbonmatsu and A. E. Garcia, Peptide folding simulations, *Curr. Opt. Struct. Biol.*, 2003, **13**, 168–174.
[2] E. M. Boczko and C. L. Brooks III, First-principles calculation of the folding free energy of a three-helix bundle protein, *Science*, 1995, **269**, 393–396.
[3] Y. Sugita and Y. Okamoto, Replica-exchange molecular dynamics methods for protein folding, *Chem. Phys. Lett.*, 1999, **314**, 141–151.
[4] U. H. E. Hansmann, Parallel tempering algorithm for conformational studies of biological molecules, *Chem. Phys. Lett.*, 1997, **281**, 140–150.
[5] K. Hukushima and K. Nemoto, Exchange Monte Carlo method and application to spin glass simulation, *J. Phys. Soc. Japan*, 1996, **65**, 1604–1608.
[6] H. Nymeyer, S. Gnanakaran and A. E. Garcia, Atomic simulations of protein folding, *using the replica exchange algorithm, Methods Enzymol. Numer. Comput. Methods, Pt D*, 2004, **383**, 119.
[7] B. A. Berg and T. Neuhaus, Multicanonical algorithms for first order phase transitions, *Phys. Lett. B*, 1991, **267**, 249–253.
[8] R. Faller, Q. L. Yan and J. J. de Pablo, Multicanonical parallel tempering, *J. Chem. Phys.*, 2002, **116**, 5419–5423.
[9] A. F. Voter, Parallel replica method for dynamics of infrequent events, *Phys. Rev. B*, 1998, **57**, R13985–R13988.
[10] M. R. Shirts and V. S. Pande, Mathematical analysis of coupled parallel simulation, *Phys. Rev. Lett.*, 2001, **86**, 4983–4987.
[11] C. D. Snow, E. J. Sorin, Y. M. Rhee and V. S. Pande, How well can simulation predict protein folding kinetics and thermodynamics?, *Ann. Rev. Biophys. Biomol. Struct.*, 2005, **34**, 43–69.
[12] R. Swendsen and J. Wang, Replica Monte Carlo of spin-glasses, *Rev. Lett.*, 1986, **57**, 2607–2609.
[13] E. Marinari and G. Parisi, Simulated tempering – a new Monte Carlo scheme, *Europhys. Lett.*, 1992, **19**, 451–458.
[14] C. J. Geyer, Markov-chain Monte-Carlo maximum-likelihood. In *23RD Symposium on the Interface between Computing Science and Statistics – Critical Applications of Scientific Computing: Biology, Engineering, Medicine, Speech; April 21–24, 1991* (ed. E. M. Keramidas), Interface Foundation North America, Seattle, WA, 1991, pp. 156–163.

[15] J. S. Wang and R. H. Swendsen, Replica Monte Carlo simulation (revisited), *Prog. Theor. Phys. Supp.*, 2005, **157**, 317–323.

[16] A. E. Garcia and K. Y. Sanbonmatsu, Alpha-helical stabilization by side chain shielding of backbone hydrogen bonds, *Proc. Natl. Acad. Sci. USA*, 2002, **99**, 2782–2787.

[17] M. Feig, A. D. MacKerell and C. L. Brooks, Force field influence on the observation of pi-helical protein structures in molecular dynamics simulations, *J. Chem. Phys. B*, 2003, **107**, 2831–2836.

[18] S. Gnanakaran, R. M. Hochstrasser and A. E. Garcia, Nature of structural inhomogeneities on folding a helix and their influence on spectral measurements, *Proc. Natl. Acad. Sci. USA*, 2004, **101**, 9229–9234.

[19] S. Gnanakaran and A. E. Garcia, Helix-coil transition of alanine peptides in water: force field dependence on the folded and unfolded structures, *Proteins*, 2005, **59**, 773–782.

[20] C. Simmerling, B. Strockbine and A. E. Roitberg, All-atom structure prediction and folding simulations of a stable protein, *J. Am. Chem. Soc.*, 2002, **124**, 11258–11259.

[21] W. Zhang, C. Wu and Y. Duan, Convergence of replica exchange molecular dynamics, *J. Chem. Phys.*, 2005, **123**, 154105.

[22] P. H. Nguyen, Y. G. Mu and G. Stock, Structure and energy landscape of a photoswitchable peptide: a replica exchange molecular dynamics study, *Proteins*, 2005, **60**, 485–494.

[23] M. M. Seibert, A. Patriksson, B. Hess and D. van der Spoel, Reproducible polypeptide folding and structure prediction using molecular dynamics simulations, *J. Mol. Biol.*, 2005, **354**, 173–183.

[24] A. E. Garcia and K. Y. Sanbonmatsu, Exploring the energy landscape of a beta hairpin in explicit solvent, *Proteins*, 2001, **42**, 345–354.

[25] R. H. Zhou, B. J. Berne and R. Germain, The free energy landscape for beta hairpin folding in explicit water, *Proc. Natl. Acad. Sci. USA*, 2001, **98**, 14931–14936.

[26] H. Nymeyer and A. E. Garcia, Simulation of the folding equilibrium of alpha-helical peptides: a comparison of the generalized Born approximation with explicit solvent, *Proc. Natl. Acad. Sci. USA*, 2003, **100**, 13934–13939.

[27] A. E. Garcia and J. N. Onuchic, Folding a protein in a computer: an atomic description of the folding/unfolding of protein A, *Proc. Natl. Acad. Sci. USA*, 2003, **100**, 13898–13903.

[28] R. H. Zhou, Trp-cage: folding free energy landscape in explicit water, *Proc. Natl. Acad. Sci. USA*, 2003, **100**, 13280–13285.

[29] W. Im and C. L. Brooks, Interfacial folding and membrane insertion of designed peptides studied by molecular dynamics simulations, *Proc. Natl. Acad. Sci. USA*, 2005, **102**, 6771–6776.

[30] M. Cecchini, F. Rao, M. Seeber and A. Caflisch, Replica exchange molecular dynamics simulations of amyloid peptide aggregation, *J. Chem. Phys.*, 2004, **121**, 10748–10756.

[31] H. H. Tsai, M. Reches, C. J. Tsai, K. Gunasekaran, E. Gazit and R. Nussinov, Energy landscape of amyloidogenic peptide oligomerization by parallel-tempering molecular dynamics simulation: significant role of asn ladder, *Proc. Natl. Acad. Sci. USA*, 2005, **102**, 8174–8179.

[32] J. Skolnick, A. Kolinski, D. Kihara, M. Betancourt, P. Rotkiewicz and M. Boniecki, Ab initio protein structure prediction via a combination of threading, lattice folding, clustering, and structure refinement, *Proteins*, 2001, **45** (5), 149–156.

[33] H. Fukunishi, O. Watanabe and S. Takada, On the Hamiltonian replica exchange method for efficient sampling of biomolecular systems: application to protein structure prediction, *J. Chem. Phys.*, 2002, **116**, 9058–9067.

[34] M. Nanias, M. Chinchio, S. Oldziej, C. Czaplewski and H. A. Scheraga, Protein structure prediction with the UNRES force-field using replica-exchange Monte Carlo-with-minimization; comparison with MCM, *CSA, and CFMC, J. Comp. Chem.*, 2005, **26**, 1472–1486.

[35] X. L. Cheng, G. L. Cui, V. Hornak and C. Simmerling, Modified replica exchange simulation methods for local structure refinement, *J. Phys. Chem. B*, 2005, **109**, 8220–8230.

[36] J. H. Chen, W. Im and C. L. Brooks, Refinement of NMR structures using implicit solvent and advanced sampling techniques, *J. Am. Chem. Soc.*, 2004, **126**, 16038–16047.

[37] X. Yang and J. G. Saven, Computational methods for protein design and protein sequence variability: biased Monte Carlo and replica exchange, *Chem. Phys. Lett.*, 2005, **401**, 205–210.

[38] G. M. Verkhivker, P. A. Rejto, D. Bouzida, S. Arthurs, A. B. Colson, S. T. Freer, D. K. Gehlhaar, V. Larson, B. A. Luty, T. Marrone and P. W. Rose, Parallel simulated tempering dynamics of ligand–protein binding with ensembles of protein conformations, *Chem. Phys. Lett.*, 2001, **337**, 181–189.

[39] K. Y. Sanbonmatsu and A. E. Garcia, Structure of met-enkephalin in explicit aqueous solution using replica exchange molecular dynamics, *Proteins*, 2002, **46**, 225–234.

[40] E. Lyman, F. M. Ytreberg and D. M. Zuckerman, Resolution exchange simulation, *Phys. Rev. Lett.*, 2006, **96**, 0281051–0281054.

[41] P. Liu, B. Kim, R. A. Friesner and B. J. Berne, Replica exchange with solute tempering: a method for sampling biological systems in explicit water, *Proc. Natl. Acad. Sci. USA*, 2005, **102**, 13749–13754.

[42] H. Nymeyer and A. E. Garcia, Replica exchange dynamics with the Nose–Hoover thermostat, Unpublished.

[43] N. Rathore, M. Chopra and J. J. de Pablo, Optimal allocation of replicas in parallel tempering simulations. *J. Chem. Phys.* 122, 0241111–0241118.

[44] W. D. Cornell, P. Cieplak, C. I. Bayly, I. R. Gouls, K. M. Merz, Jr., D. M. Fergueson, D. C. Spellmeyer, T. Fox, J. W. Caldwell and P. A. Kollman, A second generation force field for the simulation of proteins nucleic acids and organic molecules, *J. Am. Chem. Soc.*, 1995, **117**, 5179–5197.

[45] W. L. Jorgensen, J. Chandrasekhar, J. D. Madura, R. W. Impey and M. L. Klein, Comparison of simple potential functions for simulating liquid water, *J. Chem. Phys.*, 1983, **79**, 926–935.

[46] J. W. Neidigh, R. M. Fesinmeyer and N. H. Andersen, Designing a 20-residue protein, *Nat. Struct. Biol.*, 1983, **9**, 425–430.

[47] S. Nosé, A unified formulation of the constant temperature molecular dynamics methods, *J. Chem. Phys.*, 1984, **81**, 511–519.

[48] W. G. Hoover, Canonical dynamics: equilibrium phase-space distributions, *Phys. Rev. A*, 1984, **31**, 1695–1697.

[49] D. Paschek and A. E. Garcia, Reversible temperature and pressure denaturation of a protein fragment: a replica exchange molecular dynamics simulation study, *Phys. Rev. Lett.*, 2004, **93**, 2381051–2381054.

[50] D. van der Spoel, E. Lindahl, B. Hess, A. R. van Buuren, E. Apol, P. J. Meulenhoff, D. P. Tieleman, A. L. T. M. Sijbers, K. A. Feenstra, R. van Drunen and H. J. C. Berendsen, Gromacs User Manual version 3.2. http://www.gromacs.org, 2004.

[51] W. F. van Gunsteren, S. R. Billeter, A. A. Eising, P. H. Hünenberger, P. Krüger, A. E. Mark, W. R. P. Scott and I. G. Tironi, *Biomolecular Simulation: The GROMOS96 Manual and User Guide*, Hochschulverlag AG an der ETH Zürich, Zürich, Switzerland, 1996.

[52] D. Paschek, S. Gnanakaran and A. E. Garcia, Simulations of the pressure and temperature unfolding of an alpha-helical peptide, *Proc. Natl. Acad. Sci. USA*, 2005, **102**, 6765–6770.

[53] L. Smeller, Pressure-temperature phase diagrams of biomolecules, Biochim. Biophys. Acta. Prot. 1595 (2002) 11–29.

[54] G. Panick, G. J. A. Vidugiris, R. Malessa, G. Rapp, R. Winter and C. A. Royer, Exploring the temperature–pressure phase diagram of staphylococcal nuclease, *Biochemistry*, 1999, **38**, 4157–4164.

CHAPTER 6

Hybrid Explicit/Implicit Solvation Methods

Asim Okur and Carlos Simmerling

Department of Chemistry, Stony Brook University, Stony Brook, NY 11794, USA

Contents

1. INTRODUCTION

Interactions with solvent play a central role in the thermodynamics and structure of macromolecules. In particular, the stability and functionality of proteins and nucleic acids are dictated by both specific and bulk solvent effects. The effects and importance of solvents for proteins and nucleic acids have been summarized by Makarov *et al.* [1]. Solvent properties in the proximity of protein surfaces can differ significantly from bulk solvent (e.g. see a recent review by Bagchi [2]). Therefore, it is important to include solvent effects as accurately as possible for successful simulation studies.

Another important consideration when choosing a method to treat solvation is the impact it may have on the system size and thus the computational requirement of the simulations. Explicit representation of solvent molecules significantly increases the number of atoms in the simulated system. Periodic Boundary Conditions (PBC) are usually applied together with an Ewald method [3] such as Particle Mesh Ewald (PME) [4] or Particle–Particle Particle Mesh Ewald (P3ME) [5], which take advantage of the system periodicity to efficiently calculate long-range electrostatic interactions. While this may be reasonable for simulations of compact states, it can become prohibitive when the solvent box is made large enough to enclose unfolded conformations of peptides and proteins. The growth in system size results in increased computational cost to calculate forces and integrate equations of motion for the solvent molecules.

ANNUAL REPORTS IN COMPUTATIONAL CHEMISTRY, VOLUME 2
ISSN: 1574-1400   DOI 10.1016/S1574-1400(06)02006-8

As a result, large explicitly solvated systems typically cannot be simulated for biologically relevant timescales.

Continuum solvent models, like those based on Poisson Boltzmann (PB) formalism or the semi-analytical Generalized Born (GB) model [6], estimate the free energy of solvation based solely on coordinates of the solute atoms. The neglect of explicit solvent molecules can significantly reduce the computational cost of evaluating energies and forces for the system. Continuum solvent models are thus an attractive approach to enabling the study of larger systems with molecular dynamics (MD). Among the various models that have been developed, the GB approach is commonly used with MD due to its computational efficiency, permitting use at each time step. However, continuum models can also have significant limitations. Since the atomic detail of the solvent is not considered, modeling specific effects of structured water molecules with any implicit model can be challenging [7,8].

In the case of protein and peptide folding, it appears likely that the current generation of GB models do not have as good a balance between protein–protein and protein–solvent interactions as do the more widely tested explicit solvent models [9,10]. More particularly, it has been reported [10–13] that ion pairs were frequently too stable in the GB implicit water model, causing salt-bridged conformations to be oversampled in MD simulations, thus altering the thermodynamics and kinetics of folding for small peptides. A clear illustration was given by Zhou and Berne [10], who sampled the C-terminal β-hairpin of protein G (GB1) with both a surface-GB (SGB) [14] continuum model and explicit solvent. The lowest free energy state with SGB was significantly different from the lowest free energy state in explicit solvent, with incorrect salt bridges formed at the core of the peptide, in place of hydrophobic contacts. Zhou extended this study on GB1 by examining several force field–GB model combinations, with all GB models tested showing erroneous salt bridges [12]. However, it should be noted that it may be possible to resolve these problems with careful reparameterization of the models, and they continue to evolve. One example of this type of refitting was shown by Geney et al., where potentials of mean force for salt-bridge formation in a GB model were significantly improved following modification of the intrinsic Born radii for certain hydrogen atoms [15].

More rigorous models based on PB equations are generally considered to be more accurate. Historically, the increased cost of evaluating solvation free energy with these methods resulted in their use primarily to post-process a small number of conformations, or snapshots sampled during an MD simulation in explicit solvent [16]. Some researchers have recently reported using PB as a solvent model for MD simulation [17,18].

However, since solvent has non-bulk properties in the first solvation shell [1], implicit approaches (both GB and PB) may have intrinsic limitations that are difficult to overcome.

In order to benefit from the efficiency of implicit solvents for replacing the bulk water that gives rise to much of the computational cost, while also directly modeling structural effects of water in the proximity of the solute, several hybrid explicit/implicit models have been proposed. Hybrid methods have been implemented to improve the computational accuracy and efficiency of MD and Monte Carlo (MC) simulations and are usually employed in one of several ways. The most common approach, which we will refer to as the solvation shell method, typically employs explicit solvent only for the first 1–2 solvation shells of the solute, often surrounded by a continuum representation of various types to model bulk effects beyond the shell. The number of simulated particles is significantly reduced with shell methods and large savings in computational cost may be obtained as compared to simulations in a full box of explicit solvent.

However, these methods have drawbacks in that the explicit water typically must be restrained to remain close to the solute to avoid diffusion into the "bulk" continuum. These restraints, as well as boundary effects at the explicit/implicit solvent interface, can have a dramatic effect on solute behavior. Definition of the simulation volume is another challenge for hybrid models since simple geometric shapes make it possible to incorporate rigorous continuum treatments such as PB. However, large volumes with a significant number of explicit water molecules may be required to fully enclose irregularly shaped solutes with a simple shape. For solutes that are expected to undergo large conformational changes during the simulation, the change in the surface area of the solute may introduce a need to add or delete explicit water molecules in the shell in order to maintain pressure.

In this review, we will focus on the hybrid shell approaches and briefly summarize recent progress in this area. We also describe a recent method that draws on ideas from these hybrid shell methods in order to reduce the computational cost of Replica Exchange Molecular Dynamics (REMD), an enhanced sampling method that has gained popularity for peptide and small protein folding studies. In this case the hybrid treatment is only applied during the calculation of exchange probability in the REMD simulations. This method does not reduce the size of the simulated system like the solvent shell methods during dynamics, but the number of replicas required for the overall REMD simulation is reduced. For further details on REMD, the reader is encouraged to consult another chapter in this volume that deals with REMD in greater detail.

In the next section, we introduce the basic concepts of these hybrid approaches, provide some examples of how they have been applied and briefly summarize their advantages and limitations.

2. HYBRID SOLVATION METHODS

2.1. Solvation shell approach

Solvation shell methods usually include a sufficient number of explicit water molecules to account for the first one or two solvation shells. The main motivation for replacing the remainder with a continuum model is that radial distribution functions of the solvent molecules do not show deviation from bulk solvent past the second shell [1]. Since water molecules close to the protein surfaces display different structural and dynamic properties than the bulk solvent, it is assumed that explicit inclusion of these nearest solvent molecules should be sufficient to capture these effects. These explicit water molecules are enclosed in a fixed simulation volume, often spherical in shape, surrounded by a dielectric continuum [19–22]. Early studies showed that simulations with a small number of explicit water molecules surrounded by a reaction field provided good agreement with data from fully solvated systems for the solvation free energies of water and ions, as well as conformational preferences of short peptides (such as alanine dipeptide) [19,23].

However, certain aspects of shell models require careful consideration. The primary savings using shell methods over conventional periodic boundary approaches is obtained due to reduction in the system size with fewer explicit water molecules [19,22]. For larger systems, however, these savings may be eliminated if all interactions need to be calculated (i.e. no cutoff on nonbonded interactions) as compared to efficient Ewald summation that is typically used for long-range interactions for periodic boundary calculations.

The most significant problem of shell models is the treatment of the explicit/implicit solvent boundary. Unlike periodic boundary conditions, solvent molecules in a hybrid shell approach need to be restrained near the solute surface to avoid diffusion into the bulk. These restraints may give rise to artifacts [24] in properties such as distribution functions, which can be partially corrected by modifying the boundary potential [19,21,22,25]. Another boundary issue arises from the shape of the surface defined by the outer surface of the shell. Spherical boundaries have often been used because the reaction field of a spherical dielectric can be solved analytically [19,26], where the solvent molecules are usually restrained with respect to the center of the sphere. However, for non-spherical solutes such as biomolecules, this treatment may be inefficient since a large number of solvent molecules may be required to fill a sphere that encloses a non-spherical solute. Incorporation of only the layer of water in contact with the solute would make the simulated system smaller, but efficiently using an accurate reaction field treatment on such shapes remains a challenge. To employ solvation shells with irregular shapes, the Poisson equation needs to be solved numerically at every simulation step, which can become more computationally intensive than standard explicit solvent simulations with periodic boundary conditions (depending on the system size).

Beglov and Roux developed an approach called the primary hydration shell (PHS) method, where a half-harmonic potential is used to restrain solvent molecules to the nearest solute atom [27]. This type of restraint potential allows irregular shapes for the simulation volumes and can adjust to conformational changes of the solute. By adjusting the force constant, it is possible to maintain constant pressure in the system. Difficulties arising from the irregular boundary were avoided by not including a reaction field treatment.

The PHS method was tested on short peptides (alanine dipeptide and tripeptide) using umbrella sampling and the results were compared to standard explicit solvent simulations using PBC. The model was shown to be able to accurately capture most of the solvent effects. This method has been extended further to include temperature dependence in the restraining potential, and combined with simulated annealing and locally enhanced sampling (LES) [28]. The resulting PHS/LES/simulated annealing method was tested on Thyrotropin-releasing hormone and the low-temperature structures had dihedral angles in good agreement with NMR experiments and standard PHS simulations [29].

The PHS method has also been combined with Monte Carlo (MC-PHS) and was tested on small biological molecules. This combination was able to reproduce the experimentally observed native structure of a β-hairpin pentapeptide [30]. However, it should be noted that lack of a reaction field treatment outside of the explicit water shell in the PHS approach may cause problems for large solute molecules, as long-range electrostatic interactions will not get proper dielectric screening and water at the interface may show even larger artifacts than in shell models that do employ a reaction field.

The shell approximation for protein hydration (SAPHYR) method developed by Lounnas et al. [31] uses a similar approach as PHS, showing successful implementation of a flexible hydration shell at constant pressure. The simulation volume is defined similar to PHS, but an important difference is that the shell is maintained using repulsive van der Waals interactions between explicit solvent molecules and virtual solvent molecules placed at the simulation boundary along the line connecting the solvent molecule and the closest solute atom. The positions of the virtual solvent molecules are updated at every simulation step. Electrostatic contributions are included through interactions of explicit solvent molecules and the virtual solvent molecules, which are assumed to be freely rotating dipoles.

This model was tested on various systems ranging from a single argon atom to ubiquitin using TIP3P and SPC/E water models. Comparison was made to fully solvated PBC/PME calculations and to experimental data. Radial distribution functions (argon – water oxygen and protein heavy atoms – water oxygen distribution functions) from SAPHYR were similar to those from the fully solvated calculations, suggesting that the virtual solvent molecules performed adequately for incorporating bulk solvent properties. Stable trajectories for ubiquitin with fluctuations in agreement with crystallographic B-factors were obtained. The inclusion of the reaction field treatment (even if only for the solvent molecules) improves the model significantly even for large systems like cytochrome P450cam (more than 400 residues), where a stable trajectory and again fluctuations in agreement with experimental B-factors were obtained using a 5 Å thick hydration shell.

To be able to efficiently include a full reaction field treatment with irregular simulation volumes, Lee *et al.* developed a hybrid solvation scheme using the GB solvation model [32]. The simulation volume was defined with a sum-over-spheres approach similar to the PHS method described above, where solvent molecules are restrained with respect to the closest solute atom position. They also introduced the multigrid of pairwise Interactions approach derived from the multigrid method for Coulomb electrostatics [33] to approximate the long-range component of the electrostatic and GB interactions to further reduce the computational cost.

This methodology was tested on single ion simulations (Na^+ and Cl^-) and on simulations of the B1 domain of protein L. The hybrid results were compared to full explicit solvent simulations using PBC/PME. The ion–oxygen radial distribution functions for the ion hybrid simulations with various shell radii were compared to PME simulations and good agreement was obtained, but some deviations were observed near the shell boundaries. Stable 2 ns trajectories were obtained for protein L with a good correlation between fluctuations and X-ray crystallographic B-factors. In a later study, these shell results were used to evaluate Poisson-based implicit solvation models [34].

Shell methods may also be used to simulate sections of a large system such as binding pockets or ion channels as shown by Im *et al.* in their generalized solvent boundary potential (GSBP) method [35]. This method can be considered as the implementation of the spherical boundary potential approach by Beglov and Roux [19], where this time the simulation volume is defined as a section of a large macromolecule instead of a small solute in uniform solvent. The model was tested on the active site region of aspartyl-tRNA synthetase with a spherical inner region and the interior of the KcsA potassium channel with an orthorhombic inner region. Long-range electrostatic interaction energies from GSBP were compared to numerical finite-difference PB calculations and good agreement was observed.

In summary, shell methods are an efficient way of performing molecular simulations at a reduced cost. Importantly, this increased efficiency comes with some drawbacks that need to be carefully considered before deciding whether current shell models are consistent with the goals of the calculation. For example, current shell models have not been shown to be applicable for solutes which undergo large conformational changes. Using fixed shape shell models would require large simulation volumes to properly solvate the different conformations, and with irregular shape shell models the number of water molecules needed to solvate the first (and second) shell may depend strongly on the conformation of the solute. It may be necessary to frequently add or remove water molecules to maintain pressure or avoid large restraint energies. For the latter case Woo *et al.* introduced the Grand Canonical MC algorithm into the GSBP method described above in order to vary the number of water molecules in the simulation volume [36]. They tested the algorithm on a spherical shell with water, alanine peptide solvated in a spherical shell and the KcsA potassium channel simulations. They were able to show frequent exchanges between the water molecules on simulation boundary and solvent molecules in the "bulk" solvent phase.

It should also be noted that since shell methods have an explicit/implicit interface quite near the solute and also require restraints to keep water molecules close to the solvent, solvent properties such as radial density and dipole distributions typically show significant artifacts as compared to fully solvated simulations. A central assumption of the shell models is that inclusion of the shell will properly account for behavior at the solute/solvent interface, but this may fail if the shell waters are themselves affected by the implicit/explicit interface. A final issue is the treatment of long-range electrostatic interactions; shell models may require the use of a cutoff for nonbonded interactions to be practical for large solutes while PBC simulations can avoid cutoffs and use efficient Ewald summation methods. All of these are the subject of ongoing research.

It should also be noted that the hybrid approaches involve many approximations and complete statistical mechanical treatments have not been reported. For example, solvation shells that change based on the solute conformation (such as PHS and SAPHYR methods) result in significant complication of the partition function integral. These issues have been addressed in detail by some of the authors [19,36].

2.2. Hybrid solvation with replica exchange

An approach that has seen a recent increase in use for biomolecular simulation is the replica exchange method [37–39], described in detail in another chapter in this volume. In REMD [40] (also called parallel tempering [37]), a series of MD simulations (replicas) are performed for the system of interest. In the original form of REMD, each replica is an independent realization of the system, coupled to a heat bath at a different temperature. The temperatures of the replicas span a range from low values of interest (such as 280 K or 300 K) up to high values (such as 600 K) at which the system can rapidly overcome potential energy barriers that would otherwise impede conformational transitions on the timescale simulated. Due to these advantages, REMD has been applied to many studies of peptide and small protein folding [9,11,13,37,40–47].

For large systems, however, REMD becomes intractable since the number of replicas needed to span a given temperature range increases with the square root of the number of degrees of freedom in the system [48–51]. Several promising techniques have been proposed [50,52–54] to deal with this apparent disadvantage to REM.

Recognizing that the main difficulty in applying REMD with explicit solvent lies in the number of simulations required, rather than just the complexity of each simulation, a new approach has been proposed [55], in which each replica is simulated in explicit solvent using standard methods such as PBC and PME. However, the calculation of exchange probabilities (which determines the temperature spacing and thus the number of replicas) is handled differently. Only a subset of closest water molecules is retained (such as those in the first shell), with the remainder *temporarily* replaced by a continuum representation. The exchange probability is calculated using the hybrid model energy. The original solvent coordinates are then restored and the simulation proceeds as a continuous trajectory with fully explicit solvation. Since the solvation shell is determined from the fully solvated structure being sampled at each exchange calculation, no restraints are required and the explicit water at the solute interface is free to exchange with the bulk.

The key advantage of this approximation is that it allows dramatic reduction of the perceived system size for evaluation of exchange probability, and fewer replicas are needed to cover same temperature range as standard explicit solvent REMD. However, since the Hamiltonian used for the exchange calculation differs from that employed during dynamics, these simulations are approximate and are not guaranteed to provide correct canonical ensembles, depending on the degree to which the bulk solvent can be accurately treated with the continuum model.

This approach has been tested on several model systems (alanine polymers of 1, 3 and 10 residues) and the performance of the hybrid approach was compared to fully solvated explicit solvent REMD simulations. For Ala_{10}, a fivefold reduction in number of replicas provided similar exchange probability. Due to the scaling of REMD with system size, even greater efficiency gains would be expected for larger systems. Detailed results for Ala_3 are provided in Table 1.

Good agreement was found for populations of various secondary structure minima on the ϕ/ψ Ramachandran free energy surfaces. Likewise, cluster analysis showed that the populations of conformation families were highly similar in the hybrid and standard approach. The importance of including the explicit shell and the reaction field were both tested. Use of only a continuum model without a shell of explicit water provided poor results for Ala_3 and Ala_{10} with a significant bias favoring α-helix, suggesting that first shell effects are critical for these systems. It has been shown that alternate backbone conformations have differences in first shell solvent structure [56]. Likewise, using only the solvation shells and no

Table 1. Data for the central alanine in alanine tetrapeptide (blocked Ala3). Populations of basins on the ϕ/ψ energy landscape corresponding to alternate secondary structures are shown. Uncertainties were obtained from independent simulations with different initial conformations

Alanine tetrapeptide	α	β	P^{II}	α^L
Explicit Solvent PBC/PME	23.6 ± 0.1	23.4 ± 1.3	40.2 ± 1.4	5.1 ± 0.1
GB only (no explicit water)	50.5 ± 2.4	17.5 ± 0.9	22.9 ± 0.6	1.1 ± 0.4
1st shell noGB	41.4 ± 0.8	13.5 ± 0.9	23.4 ± 1.0	13.1 ± 0.8
1st and 2nd shells noGB	29.5 ± 0.2	14.1 ± 0.2	24.1 ± 0.5	23.4 ± 0.3
Hybrid 1st Shell + GB	21.6 ± 0.9	21.2 ± 0.2	41.1 ± 0.3	7.6 ± 1.0
Hybrid 1st and 2nd Shells + GB	28.3 ± 1.7	22.2 ± 0.9	37.7 ± 0.2	3.8 ± 0.1

reaction field outside the shell resulted in ensembles that also differed significantly from the standard explicit solvent data (too much α^L and not enough P^{II}), highlighting the need for proper solvation of the explicit water molecules themselves. Ensembles obtained from the hybrid model were in very close agreement with the explicit solvent data, predominantly populating polyproline II conformation. Inclusion of a second shell of explicit solvent was found to give similar results, suggesting that explicit modeling of only the first shell is sufficient. As expected no artifacts were seen in solvent properties such as radial distribution functions since the hybrid REMD simulations were performed with PBC and a fully explicit solvent box, and the hybrid potential was only used during the exchange step.

3. CONCLUSIONS

In recent years, there has been a significant increase in the development and use of hybrid solvent models for biomolecular simulations. Shell methods reduce system size by explicitly including solvent molecules only for the first 1–2 solvent shells. Early examples required fixed and simple simulation volumes to employ a reaction field outside the simulation volume. Irregular shapes can be accommodated either by omitting the reaction field term or using semi-analytical methods like the GB approximation. Shell methods can be extremely useful in studies requiring extensive conformational sampling at a reduced cost. However, current implementations may not yet be ready for simulation of large-scale conformational changes since the number of water molecules in the solvent shell depends strongly on solute conformation. Another challenge that remains is overcoming artifacts at the implicit/explicit solvent boundary, which can arise from restraints at the boundary. Since the central motivation of shell models is that continuum models are inadequate to treat water at the solute interface, it is important to consider the extent to which the continuum model can provide accurate solvation for water in the first shell that is itself assumed to be non-bulk in behavior.

Current shell methods seem suitable for conformational search in short peptides. Similar application to larger systems remains challenging. However, modeling local fluctuations of a biomolecule with a stable structure using a hybrid method has been shown to be successful. Many of the methods described were shown to be able to reproduce experimental B-factors with similar accuracy as simulations with fully explicit solvent.

Hybrid solvation can also be used with other methods to improve computational efficiency as seen with REMD simulations using hybrid exchange potential. Even though this method is new and further testing with different peptides and proteins is required, it shows great potential for becoming an efficient enhanced conformational sampling tool.

ACKNOWLEDGMENTS

Financial support from the NIH (GM6167803) and supercomputer time at NCSA (NPACI MCA02N028) are gratefully acknowledged. C.S. is a Cottrell Scholar of Research Corporation.

REFERENCES

[1] V. Makarov, B. M. Pettitt and M. Feig, Solvation and hydration of proteins and nucleic acids: A theoretical view of simulation and experiment, *Acc. Chem. Res.*, 2002, **35** (6), 376–384.

[2] B. Bagchi, Water dynamics in the hydration layer around proteins and micelles, *Chem. Rev.*, 2005, **105** (9), 3197–3219.

[3] P. P. Ewald, The calculation of optical and electrostatic grid potential, *Annalen Der Physik*, 1921, **64** (3), 253–287.

[4] U. Essmann, L. Perera, M. L. Berkowitz, T. Darden, H. Lee and L. G. Pedersen, A smooth particle mesh Ewald method, *J. Chem. Phy.*, 1995, **103** (19), 8577–8593.

[5] R. W. Hockney and J. W. Eastwood, *Computer Simulation Using Particles*, IOP, Bristol, 1988.

[6] W. C. Still, A. Tempczyk, R. C. Hawley and T. Hendrickson, Semianalytical treatment of solvation for molecular mechanics and dynamics, *J. Am. Chem. Soc.*, 1990, **112** (16), 6127–6129.

[7] A. Masunov and T. Lazaridis, Potentials of mean force between ionizable amino acid side chains in water, *J. Am. Chem. Soc.*, 2003, **125** (7), 1722–1730.

[8] Z. Y. Yu, M. P. Jacobson, J. Josovitz, C. S. Rapp and R. A. Friesner, First-shell solvation of ion pairs: Correction of systematic errors in implicit solvent models, *J. Phys. Chem. B.*, 2004, **108** (21), 6643–6654.

[9] H. Nymeyer and A. E. Garcia, Simulation of the folding equilibrium of alpha-helical peptides: A comparison of the generalized Born approximation with explicit solvent, *Proc. Natl. Acad. Sci. USA*, 2003, **100** (24), 13934–13939.

[10] R. H. Zhou and B. J. Berne, Can a continuum solvent model reproduce the free energy landscape of a beta-hairpin folding in water?, *Proc. Natl. Acad. Sci. USA*, 2002, **99** (20), 12777–12782.

[11] J. W. Pitera and W. Swope, Understanding folding and design: Replica-exchange simulations of Trp-cage miniproteins, *Proc. Natl. Acad. Sci. USA*, 2003, **100** (13), 7587–7592.

[12] R. H. Zhou, Free energy landscape of protein folding in water: Explicit vs. implicit solvent, *Proteins-Structure Function and Genetics*, 2003, **53** (2), 148–161.

[13] R. H. Zhou, B. J. Berne and R. Germain, The free energy landscape for beta hairpin folding in explicit water, *Proc. Natl. Acad. Sci. USA*, 2001, **98** (26), 14931–14936.

[14] A. Ghosh, C. S. Rapp and R. A. Friesner, Generalized born model based on a surface integral formulation, *J. Phys. Chem. B.*, 1998, **102** (52), 10983–10990.

[15] R. Geney, M. Layten, R. Gomperts, V. Hornak and C. Simmerling, Investigation of salt bridge stability in a generalized Born solvent model, *J. Chem. Theory Comput.*, 2006, **2** (1), 115–127.

[16] J. Srinivasan, T. E. Cheatham, P. Cieplak, P. A. Kollman and D. A. Case, Continuum solvent studies of the stability of DNA, RNA, and phosphoramidate – DNA helices, *J. Am. Chem. Soc.*, 1998, **120** (37), 9401–9409.

[17] R. Luo, L. David and M. K. Gilson, Accelerated Poisson-Boltzmann calculations for static and dynamic systems, *J. Comput. Chem.*, 2002, **23** (13), 1244–1253.

[18] K. Sharp, Incorporating solvent and ion screening into molecular-dynamics using the finite-difference Poisson-Boltzmann method, *J. Comput. Chem.*, 1991, **12** (4), 454–468.

[19] D. Beglov and B. Roux, Finite Representation of an infinite bulk system – Solvent boundary potential for computer-simulations, *J. Chem. Phys.*, 1994, **100** (12), 9050–9063.

[20] C. L. Brooks, A. Brunger and M. Karplus, Active-site dynamics in protein molecules – a stochastic boundary molecular-dynamics approach, *Biopolymers*, 1985, **24** (5), 843–865.

[21] C. L. Brooks and M. Karplus, Deformable stochastic boundaries in molecular-dynamics, *J. Chem. Phys.*, 1983, **79** (12), 6312–6325.

[22] G. King and A. Warshel, A surface constrained all-atom solvent model for effective simulations of polar solutions, *J. Chem. Phys.*, 1989, **91** (6), 3647–3661.

[23] G. Hummer, L. R. Pratt and A. E. Garcia, Free energy of ionic hydration, *J. Phys. Chem.*, 1996, **100** (4), 1206–1215.

[24] T. Darden, D. Pearlman and L. G. Pedersen, Ionic charging free energies: Spherical versus periodic boundary conditions, *J. Chem. Phys.*, 1998, **109** (24), 10921–10935.

[25] J. W. Essex and W. L. Jorgensen, An empirical boundary potential for water droplet simulations, *J. Comput. Chem.*, 1995, **16** (8), 951–972.

[26] J. G. Kirkwood, Statistical mechanics of liquid solutions, *Chem. Rev.*, 1936, **19** (3), 275–307.

[27] D. Beglov and B. Roux, Dominant solvation effects from the primary shell of hydration – Approximation for molecular-dynamics simulations, *Biopolymers*, 1995, **35** (2), 171–178.

[28] R. Elber and M. Karplus, Enhanced sampling in molecular-dynamics – use of the time-dependent Hartree approximation for a simulation of carbon-monoxide diffusion through myoglobin, *J. Am. Chem. Soc.*, 1990, **112** (25), 9161–9175.

[29] A. Rosenhouse-Dantsker and R. Osman, Application of the primary hydration shell approach to locally enhanced sampling simulated annealing: Computer simulation of thyrotropin-releasing hormone in water, *Biophys. J.*, 2000, **79** (1), 66–79.

[30] A. Kentsis, M. Mezei and R. Osman, MC-PHS: A Monte Carlo implementation of the primary hydration shell for protein folding and design, *Biophys. J.*, 2003, **84** (2), 805–815.

[31] V. Lounnas, S. K. Ludemann and R. C. Wade, Towards molecular dynamics simulation of large proteins with a hydration shell at constant pressure, *Biophys. Chem.*, 1999, **78** (1–2), 157–182.

[32] M. S. Lee, F. R. Salsbury and M. A. Olson, An efficient hybrid explicit/implicit solvent method for biomolecular simulations, *J. Comput. Chem.*, 2004, **25** (16), 1967–1978.

[33] R. D. Skeel, I. Tezcan and D. J. Hardy, Multiple grid methods for classical molecular dynamics, *J. Comput. Chem.*, 2002, **23** (6), 673–684.

[34] M. S. Lee and M. A. Olson, Evaluation of Poisson solvation models using a hybrid explicit/implicit solvent method, *J. Phys. Chem. B*, 2005, **109** (11), 5223–5236.

[35] W. Im, S. Berneche and B. Roux, Generalized solvent boundary potential for computer simulations, *J. Chem. Phys.*, 2001, **114** (7), 2924–2937.

[36] H. J. Woo, A. R. Dinner and B. Roux, Grand canonical Monte Carlo simulations of water in protein environments, *J. Chem. Phys.*, 2004, **121** (13), 6392–6400.

[37] U. H. E. Hansmann, Parallel tempering algorithm for conformational studies of biological molecules, *Chem. Phys. Lett.*, 1997, **281** (1–3), 140–150.

[38] R. H. Swendsen and J. S. Wang, Replica Monte-Carlo simulation of spin-glasses, *Phys. Rev. Lett.*, 1986, **57** (21), 2607–2609.
[39] M. C. Tesi, E. J. J. vanRensburg, E. Orlandini and S. G. Whittington, Monte Carlo study of the interacting self-avoiding walk model in three dimensions, *J. Stat. Phys.*, 1996, **82** (1–2), 155–181.
[40] Y. Sugita and Y. Okamoto, Replica-exchange molecular dynamics method for protein folding, *Chem. Phys. Lett.*, 1999, **314** (1–2), 141–151.
[41] M. Feig, J. Karanicolas and C. L. Brooks, MMTSB tool set: enhanced sampling and multiscale modeling methods for applications in structural biology, *J. Mol. Graphic. Model.*, 2004, **22** (5), 377–395.
[42] A. E. Garcia and K. Y. Sanbonmatsu, Exploring the energy landscape of a beta hairpin in explicit solvent, *Prot.-Struc. Func. Genet.*, 2001, **42** (3), 345–354.
[43] A. E. Garcia and K. Y. Sanbonmatsu, Alpha-helical stabilization by side chain shielding of backbone hydrogen bonds, *Proc. Natl. Acad. Sci. USA*, 2002, **99** (5), 2782–2787.
[44] J. Karanicolas and C. L. Brooks, The structural basis for biphasic kinetics in the folding of the WW domain from a formin-binding protein: Lessons for protein design?, *Proc. Natl. Acad. Sci. USA*, 2003, **100** (7), 3954–3959.
[45] B. S. Kinnear, M. F. Jarrold and U. H. E. Hansmann, All-atom generalized-ensemble simulations of small proteins, *J. Mol. Graphic Model.*, 2004, **22** (5), 397–403.
[46] Y. Sugita, A. Kitao and Y. Okamoto, Multidimensional replica-exchange method for free-energy calculations, *J. Chem. Phys.*, 2000, **113** (15), 6042–6051.
[47] D. R. Roe, V. Hornak and C. Simmerling, Folding cooperativity in a three-stranded beta-sheet model, *J. Mol. Biol.*, 2005, **352** (2), 370–381.
[48] N. Rathore, M. Chopra and J. J. de Pablo, Optimal allocation of replicas in parallel tempering simulations, *J. Chem. Phys.*, 2005, **122** (2), 024111.
[49] H. Fukunishi, O. Watanabe and S. Takada, On the Hamiltonian replica exchange method for efficient sampling of biomolecular systems: Application to protein structure prediction, *J. Chem. Phys.*, 2002, **116** (20), 9058–9067.
[50] X. Cheng, G. Cui, V. Hornak and C. Simmerling, Modified replica exchange simulation methods for local structure refinement, *J. Phys. Chem. B.*, 2005, **109** (16), 8220–8230.
[51] D. A. Kofke, On the acceptance probability of replica-exchange Monte Carlo trials, *J. Chem. Phys.*, 2002, **117** (15), 6911–6914.
[52] Y. Sugita and Y. Okamoto, Replica-exchange multicanonical algorithm and multicanonical replica-exchange method for simulating systems with rough energy landscape, *Chem. Phys. Lett.*, 2000, **329** (3–4), 261–270.
[53] A. Mitsutake, Y. Sugita and Y. Okamoto, Replica-exchange multicanonical and multicanonical replica-exchange Monte Carlo simulations of peptides. I. Formulation and benchmark test, *J. Chem. Phys.*, 2003, **118** (14), 6664–6675.
[54] S. M. Jang, S. Shin and Y. Pak, Replica-exchange method using the generalized effective potential, *Phys. Rev. Lett.*, 2003, **91** (5), 058305.
[55] A. Okur, L. Wickstrom, M. Layten, R. Geney, K. Song, V. Hornak and C. Simmerling, Improved efficiency of replica exchange simulations through use of a hybrid explicit/implicit solvation model, *J. Chem. Theory and Comput.*, 2006, **2**, 420–433.
[56] M. Mezei, P. J. Fleming, R. Srinivasan and G. D. Rose, Polyproline II helix is the preferred conformation for unfolded polyalanine in water, *Proteins*, 2004, **55** (3), 502–507.

Section 4
Advances in QSAR/QSPR

Section Editor: Yvonne Martin
Abbott Laboratories
Abbott Park
IL 60064
USA

CHAPTER 7

Variable Selection QSAR Modeling, Model Validation, and Virtual Screening

Alexander Tropsha

Laboratory for Molecular Modeling, CB # 7360 School of Pharmacy, University of North Carolina at Chapel Hill, Chapel Hill, NC 27599, USA

Contents

1. INTRODUCTION

Modern Quantitative Structure–Activity Relationship (QSAR) approaches are characterized by the use of multiple descriptors of chemical structure combined with the application of both linear and non-linear optimization approaches, and a strong emphasis on rigorous model validation [1] to afford robust and predictive models. Important recent developments in the field are driven by both a substantial increase in the size of experimental datasets available for the analysis, and also by an increased application of QSAR models as virtual screening tools to discover biologically active molecules in chemical databases and/or virtual chemical libraries. This recent focus differs substantially from the traditional emphasis on developing the so-called explanatory QSAR models characterized by high statistical significance as applied only to training sets of molecules with known chemical structure and known biological activity.

Recent trends in QSAR studies have focused on the development of optimal models through variable selection. This procedure selects only a subset of available chemical descriptors – those that are most meaningful and statistically significant in terms of correlation with biological activity. The optimal selection of variables is achieved by combining stochastic search methods such as simulated annealing [2], genetic algorithms [3], or evolutionary algorithms [4] with the correlation methods such as multiple linear regression (MLR), partial least squares (PLS) analysis, or artificial neural networks (ANN) [2–5]. Such methods used in combination with various chemometric tools have been shown to improve QSAR models, as compared to those without variable selection.

Many reviews discussing different QSAR modeling methodologies have been published [6,7]. This chapter focuses on the QSAR model validation as an integral component of model development. We discuss and illustrate that rigorously validated QSAR models with statistically significant external predictive power ultimately afford their application as reliable virtual screening tools for database mining or chemical library design.

2. BUILDING PREDICTIVE QSAR MODELS: THE APPROACHES TO MODEL VALIDATION

The process of QSAR model development is divided into three key steps: (1) data preparation, (2) data analysis, and (3) model validation. The implementation and relative merit of these steps is generally determined by the researcher's interests, experience, and software availability. The resulting models are then frequently employed, at least in theory, to design new molecules based on chemical features or trends found to be statistically significant with respect to underlying biological activity.

The first stage includes the selection of a dataset for QSAR studies and the calculation of molecular descriptors. The second stage deals with the selection of a statistical data analysis technique, either linear or non-linear such as PLS or ANN. A variety of different algorithms and computer software are available for this purpose. In all approaches, descriptors are considered as independent variables, and biological activities as dependent variables.

Typically, the final part of QSAR model development is model validation [1,8] in which estimates of the predictive power of the model are calculated. This predictive power is one of the most important characteristics of QSAR models. Ideally, it should be defined as the ability of the model to predict accurately the target property (e.g., biological activity) of compounds that were not used in model development. The typical problem of QSAR modeling is that at the time of model building a researcher has only the training set molecules, so predictive ability can be characterized only by statistical characteristics of the training set model, and not by true external validation.

Most QSAR modeling methods implement the leave-one-out (LOO), or leave-some-out, cross-validation procedure. The outcome from this procedure is a cross-validated correlation coefficient q^2, which is calculated according to the following formula:

$$q^2 = 1 - \frac{\sum(y_i - \hat{y}_i)^2}{\sum(y_i - \bar{y}_i)^2} \qquad (1)$$

where y_i, $\hat{y}_i$, and $\bar{y}$ are the actual activities, the estimated activities by LOO cross-validation procedure, and the average activities, respectively. The summations in equation (1) are performed over all compounds used to build a model (i.e., the training set). Frequently, q^2 is used as the criterion of both robustness and predictive ability of the model. Many authors consider high q^2 (for instance, $q^2 > 0.5$) as an indicator or even as the ultimate proof of the high predictive power of a QSAR model. They do not test the models for their ability to predict the activity of compounds of an external test set (i.e., compounds which have not been used in the QSAR model development). For instance, in several publications [9–12] models were claimed to have high predictive ability in the absence of validation using an external test set. In other examples, models were validated using only one or two compounds that were not used in the QSAR model development [13,14], and the claim was made that these models were highly predictive.

Thus, it is still not common to test QSAR models characterized by a reasonably high q^2 for their ability to accurately predict biological activities of compounds not included in the training set. However, it has been shown [15,16] that various commonly accepted statistical characteristics of QSAR models derived for a training set are insufficient to establish and estimate the predictive power of QSAR models. Contrary to expectations, evidence would seem to indicate that no correlation exists between the LOO cross-validated q^2 and the correlation coefficient R^2 between the predicted and observed activities even when a test set of compounds with known biological activities is available for prediction (Fig. 1). Furthermore, experience suggests [1,17] that this phenomenon is characteristic of many datasets and is independent of the descriptor types and optimization techniques used to develop training set models. Several recent publications [8,15,16,18–20] suggest that the only way to ensure the high predictive power of a QSAR model is to demonstrate a significant correlation between predicted and observed activities for a validation set of compounds, which were not employed in model development.

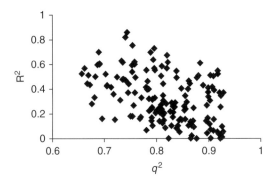

Fig. 1. Beware of q^2! External R^2 (for the test set) shows no correlation with the "predictive" LOO q^2 (for the training set). Adopted from Reference [1].

The Y-randomization of response is another important validation approach that is widely used to establish model robustness [21]. This method consists of repeating the QSAR model derivation calculation procedure, but with randomized activities. The subsequent probability assessment of the resultant statistics is then used to gauge the robustness of the model developed with the actual activities. It is often used along with the cross-validation. In many cases, models based on the randomized data have high q^2 values, which can be explained by a chance correlation or structural redundancy [22]. If all QSAR models obtained in the Y-randomization test have relatively high R^2 and LOO q^2, it implies that an acceptable QSAR model cannot be obtained for the given dataset by the current modeling method. A recent publication [23] provides examples of training set models that had high internal q^2, but were still unacceptable based on the Y-randomization test criteria.

We should emphasize that both Y-randomization and external validation must be made a mandatory part of model development. This goal can be achieved by a division of an experimental SAR dataset into the training and test sets, which are used for model development and validation, respectively. We believe that special approaches should be used to select a training set to ensure the highest significance, robustness, and predictive power of QSAR models [1,17]. Recent reviews and publications describe several algorithms that can be employed for such division [15–17].

As follows from the above discussion, in order to estimate the true predictive power of a QSAR model, one needs to compare the predicted and observed activities of a sufficiently large external test set of compounds that were not used in the model development. One convenient parameter is an external q^2 defined as follows (similar to equation (1) for the training set):

$$q_{ext}^2 = 1 - \frac{\sum_{i=1}^{test}(y_i - \hat{y}_i)^2}{\sum_{i=1}^{test}(y_i - \bar{y}_{tr})^2} \tag{2}$$

where y_i and $\hat{y}_i$ are the measured and predicted activities (over the test set), respectively, values of the dependent variable and $\bar{y}_{tr}$ the averaged value of the dependent variable for the training set; the summations run over all compounds in the test set. Certainly, this formula is only meaningful when $\bar{y}_{tr}$ does not differ significantly from the similar value for the test set [24]. In principle, given the entire collection of compounds with known structure and activity, there is no particular reason to select one particular group of compounds as the training (or test) set; thus, the division of the dataset into multiple training and test sets [17] or interchangeable definition of these sets [25] is recommended.

The use of the following statistical characteristics of the test set was also recommended [17]:

   (i) correlation coefficient R^2 between the predicted and observed activities;
   (ii) coefficients of determination (predicted Versus observed activities, R_0^2, and observed Versus predicted activities, $R_0'^2$); and
   (iii) slopes k and k' of the regression lines through the origin.

In summary, we consider a QSAR model predictive, if the following conditions are satisfied [17]:

$$q^2 > 0.5 \tag{3}$$

$$R^2 > 0.6 \tag{4}$$

$$\frac{(R^2 - R_0^2)}{R^2} < 0.1 \quad \text{or} \quad \frac{(R^2 - R_0'^2)}{R^2} < 0.1 \tag{5}$$

$$0.85 \leq k \leq 1.15 \quad \text{or} \quad 0.85 \leq k' \leq 1.15 \tag{6}$$

It has been demonstrated [15,17] that all of the above criteria are indeed necessary to adequately assess the predictive ability of a QSAR model.

3. DEFINING MODEL APPLICABILITY DOMAIN

It needs to be emphasized that no matter how robust, significant, and validated a QSAR model may be, it cannot be expected to be applicable to the entire universe of chemicals. Therefore, before any QSAR model is used to predict biological activity of any untested compound, its domain of application must be defined and predictions for only those chemicals that fall into this domain may be considered reliable. Described below are some approaches that aid in defining the applicability domain.

3.1. Extent of extrapolation

For a regression-like QSAR, a simple measure of a chemical being too far from the applicability domain of the model is its leverage, h_i [26], which is defined as

$$h_i = x_i^T (\mathbf{X}^T \mathbf{X})^{-1} x_i \qquad (i = 1, \ldots, n) \qquad (7)$$

where x_i is the descriptor row-vector of the query compound, and $\mathbf{X}$ the $n \times k-1$ matrix of k model descriptor values for n training set compounds. The superscript T refers to the transpose of the matrix/vector. The warning leverage h^* is, generally, fixed at $(3k)/n$, where n is the number of training compounds, and k the number of model parameters. A leverage greater than the warning leverage h^* means that the predicted response is the result of substantial extrapolation of the model and, therefore, may not be reliable [27,28].

3.2. Effective prediction domain

Similarly, for regression-like models, especially when the model descriptors are significantly correlated, Mandel [29] proposed the formulation of effective prediction domain, EPD. It has been demonstrated, with examples, that a regression model is justified inside and on the periphery of the EPD. Clearly, if a compound is determined to be too far from the EPD, its prediction from the model should not be considered reliable.

3.3. Residual standard deviation

Another important approach that can be used to evaluate the applicability domain is the degree-of-fit method developed originally by Lindberg et al. [30] and modified subsequently [31]. According to the original method, the predicted y values are considered to be reliable if the following condition is met:

$$s^2 < s_a^2(E_x)F \qquad (8)$$

where s^2 is the residual standard deviation (RSD) of descriptor values generated for a test compound, $s_a^2(E_x)$ the RSD of the **X** matrix after dimensions (components) a, and F the F-statistic at the probability level α and $(p-a)/2$, and $(p-a)(n-a-1)/2$ degrees of freedom. The RSD of descriptor values generated for a test compound is calculated using the following equation:

$$s^2 = ||e||/(p - a) \qquad (9)$$

where p is the number of x variables, a the number of components, and $||e||$ the sum of squared residuals e_i expressed as

$$e_i = x_i - x_i \mathbf{BB'} \qquad (10)$$

where x_i is the ith x variable, and **B** and **B'** represent the weight matrix and transposed weight matrix of x variables, respectively. Since the lowest possible value of F is 1.00 at $\alpha = 0.10$ (when both degrees of freedom are equal to infinity), the authors [31] decided to replace F with the degree-of-fit factor f to simplify the above condition. Thus, the modified degree-of-fit condition [31] is as follows: predicted y values are considered to be reliable if

$$s^2 < s_a^2(E_x)f \qquad (11)$$

3.4. Similarity distance

Domain applicability can also be determined based on chemical similarity. Non-linear methods such as k Nearest Neighbor (kNN) QSAR [32] employ models based on chemical similarity calculations. As such, a large similarity distance could signal that query compounds are too dissimilar to the training set compounds, and thus are not within the domain of applicability. A proposed [32] cutoff value, D_c (equation (12)), defines a similarity distance threshold for external compounds

$$D_c = Z\sigma + y \qquad (12)$$

Here y is the average and σ the standard deviation of the Euclidean distances of the k nearest neighbors of each compound in the training set in the chemical descriptor space, and Z is an empirical parameter to control the significance level, with the default value of 0.5. If the distance from an external compound to its nearest neighbor in the training set is above D_c, we label its prediction as unreliable.

4. VALIDATED QSAR MODELING AS AN EMPIRICAL DATA MODELING APPROACH: COMBINATORIAL QSAR

We believe QSAR modeling is an empirical, exploratory research area where the models with the best validated predictive power should be sought by a combinatorial exploration of various pairings of statistical data modeling techniques and different types of chemical descriptors. The next step is consensus prediction of activities for external compounds by averaging the predicted activity values resulting from all validated models [23]. This strategy is driven by the concept that if an implicit structure–activity relationship exists for a given dataset, it can be formally manifested via a variety of QSAR models that use different descriptors and optimization protocols. We believe that multiple alternative QSAR models should be developed (as opposed to a single model using some favorite QSAR method) for each dataset.

Several popular commercial and non-commercial QSAR software packages provide users with various descriptor types and data modeling capabilities. Practically, every package employs only one (or a few) type of descriptors and, typically, a single or a few molecular modeling techniques. Most commercially available programs provide a relatively easy to use interface and allow users to build single models with internal accuracy typically characterized by q^2. As emphasized in the previous section, training-set-only modeling is insufficient to achieve models with validated predictive power; the QSAR model development process has to be modified to incorporate an independent model validation and applicability domain definition [16,17]. Since the process is relatively fast (and in principle, can be completely automated), these alternative models could be explored simultaneously when making predictions for external datasets. Consensus predictions of biological activity for novel compounds on the basis of several QSAR models, especially when predictions converge, provide more confidence in the activity estimates and better justification for the experimental validation of these compounds.

The need to develop and employ the combinatorial QSAR approach is dictated by experience in QSAR modeling, suggesting that QSAR is still an experimental area of statistical data modeling. As such, it is impossible to decide a priori as to which particular QSAR modeling method will prove most successful. Every particular combination of descriptor sets and optimization techniques is likely to capture certain unique aspects of the structure–activity relationship. Since the ultimate goal is to use the resulting models in database mining to discover diverse biologically active molecules, application of different combination of modeling techniques and descriptor sets shall increase the chances for success as demonstrated in recent publications [23,33].

5. VALIDATED QSAR MODELS AS VIRTUAL SCREENING TOOLS

Although combinatorial chemistry and HTS have offered medicinal chemists a much broader range of possibilities for lead discovery and optimization, the number of chemical compounds that can be synthesized and tested is still far beyond today's capability of medicinal chemistry. Therefore, medicinal chemists continue to face the same problem as before: which compounds should be chosen for the next round of synthesis and testing? For cheminformaticians, the task is to develop and utilize computational approaches to evaluate a very large number of chemical compounds and recommend the most promising ones for bench chemists.

Database mining associated with pharmacophore identification is a common and efficient approach for lead compound discovery. Pharmacophore identification refers to the computational approach to identifying the essential 3D structural features and configurations that are responsible for the biological activity of a series of compounds. Once a pharmacophore model has been developed for a particular set of biologically active molecules, it can be used to search databases of 3D structures with the aim of finding new, structurally different lead molecules with the desired biological activity [34].

An obvious parallel can be established between the search for pharmacophore elements, which are thought to describe the specificity of drug action, and the identification of a subset of descriptors contributing the most to the correlation with biological activity in a variable selection QSAR model. Thus, the selection of specific pharmacophore features responsible for biological activity is directly analogous to the selection of specific chemical descriptors that contribute the most to an explanatory QSAR model. It is convenient to establish a concept of the *descriptor pharmacophore* in the context of variable selection QSAR modeling. Thus, by analogy with the conventional definition of pharmacophores, the *descriptor pharmacophore* can be defined as a set of descriptor variables implicated in highly statistically significant and predictive QSAR models.

It has been demonstrated that QSAR models can be used in database mining, i.e., finding molecular structures that are similar in their activity to the probe molecules or even predicting the activities for the compounds in a database [35–37]. First, a pre-constructed QSAR model can be used as a means of screening compounds from existing databases (or virtual libraries) for high-predicted biological activity. Alternatively, variables selected by QSAR optimization can be used for similarity searches to improve the performance of the database mining methods.

It should be noted that despite formal similarity between the common definition of pharmacophores and descriptor pharmacophores, there is also a significant difference in the procedure as well as expected outcome of virtual screening. As mentioned above, traditional approaches to database mining are based on chemical fragment or sub-fragment based similarity searches. While this is an efficient approach that has enjoyed certain successes, it limits the chemical diversity of selected compounds to those that are similar to existing ligands. Search methodologies are based on chemical similarity estimated by Euclidean distance (or any other similarity measure) in multidimensional descriptor space (where descriptors are selected from the entire initial space in the process of variable selection model development) combined with quantitative predictions from combinatorial QSPR models. Due to the nature of the descriptors (e.g., whole molecule-based descriptors as opposed to fragments), such searches are more likely to result in accurate prediction of target properties for diverse novel compounds than traditional fragment-based search methodologies. This strategy was successfully tested in recent studies of anticonvulsant agents [38,39] and on the Ames Genotoxicity dataset [40]. The approach is outlined in Fig. 2. It is important to stress that the outputs of these studies are not models with their statistical characteristics as is typical for most QSAR studies. Rather, the modeling results are the predictions of the target properties for all database or virtual library compounds, which allows for immediate compound prioritization for subsequent experimental verification. Another advantage of using QSAR models for database mining is that this approach affords not only the identification of compounds of interest but also quantitative prediction of compounds' potency. For illustration, we shall discuss recent successes in developing validated predictive models of anticonvulsants [38] and their application to the discovery of novel potent compounds by means of database mining [39].

Fig. 3 summarizes the approach to using validated QSAR models for virtual screening as applied to the anticonvulsant dataset. Initially, the authors applied variable selection kNN and simulated-annealing PLS (SA-PLS) QSAR approaches to a dataset of 48 chemically diverse functionalized amino acids (FAA) with anticonvulsant activity to develop

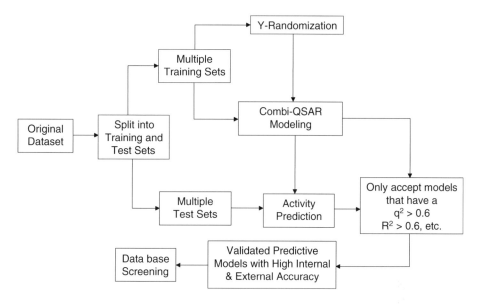

Fig. 2. Flowchart of predictive QSAR workflow based on validated combi-QSAR models.

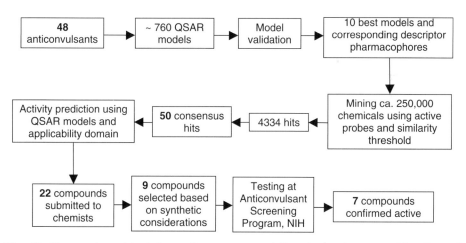

Fig. 3. Computer-aided drug discovery workflow based on combination of QSAR modeling and consensus database mining as applied to the discovery of novel anticonvulsants [39]. The workflow emphasizes the importance of model validation and applicability domain in ensuring high hit rates as a result of database mining with predictive QSAR models.

validated QSAR models [38]. Both methods used multiple descriptors such as molecular connectivity indices or atom-pair descriptors, which are derived from two-dimensional molecular topology. QSAR models with high internal accuracy were generated, with LOO cross-validated R^2 (q^2) values ranging between 0.6 and 0.8. The q^2 values for the actual dataset were significantly higher than those obtained for the same dataset with randomly shuffled activity values, indicating that models were robust. The original dataset was further divided into several training and test sets, and highly predictive models were obtained with q^2 values for the training sets greater than 0.5 and R^2 values for the test sets greater than 0.6.

In the second stage of this process, the validated QSAR models and descriptor pharmacophore concepts were applied [39] to mining of available chemical databases for new lead anticonvulsant agents (Fig. 3). Two databases have been explored: the National Cancer Institute [41] and the Maybridge [42] databases, including 237,771 and 55,273 chemical structures, respectively. Database mining was performed independently using the 10 best-validated QSAR models with the highest values of both q^2 and R^2. First, chemical similarity searches were performed between the training set compounds and database molecules using descriptor pharmacophores only (i.e., Euclidean similarity was calculated using only descriptors implicated in the 10 best-validated kNN QSAR models), and over 4300 compounds found within the same similarity threshold in all 10 independent searches were selected as consensus hits (cf. Fig. 3). Their activities then were predicted using individual QSAR models and the consensus hits with the highest predicted anticonvulsant activity were further explored experimentally. See reference [39] for additional details.

This study [38,39] presents a practical example of the drug discovery workflow that can be generalized for any dataset where sufficient data to develop reliable QSAR models are available. These results certainly appear very promising and reassuring in terms of computational strategies, which emphasize that rigorous validation of QSAR models as well as conservative extrapolation are responsible for a very high hit rate.

6. CONCLUSIONS

In this chapter, we have reviewed modeling approaches for the development of the externally validated and predictive QSAR models that can be ultimately employed in mining chemical databases or virtual compound libraries for novel bioactive compounds. We stress that any approach to QSAR model development should be rigorous and comprehensive. Several criteria of model robustness have been presented, placing particular emphasis on external predictive power of the model. That the traditional LOO q^2 is insufficient statistical characteristic of model predictive power has been demonstrated. Thus, although low values of q^2 almost certainly indicate that the model is not expected to be predictive externally, high values of this parameter alone also provide no guarantee that the underlying models can be used for the reliable external prediction. A particular scheme to validated QSAR model development has been proposed. The application of these principles (Fig. 2) to the development of the predictive QSAR models of anticonvulsant agents [38] followed by the use of these models for database mining was shown to afford the discovery of novel anticonvulsant agents [39] (Fig. 3). We conclude that continuing emphasis on the robustness and *external* predictive power as well as applicability domain as the most important parameters of QSAR models shall increase their practical use as reliable virtual screening tools for pharmaceutical lead identification.

REFERENCES

[1] A. Golbraikh and A. Tropsha, *J. Mol. Graph. Model*, 2002, **20** (4), 269–276.
[2] D. Rogers and A. J. Hopfinger, *J. Chem. Inf. Comput. Sci.*, 1994, **34**, 854–866.
[3] H. Kubinyi, *Quant. Struct-Act. Relat.*, 1994, **13**, 285–294.
[4] S. S. So and M. Karplus, *J. Med. Chem.*, 1996, **39** (7), 1521–1530.
[5] S. S. So and M. Karplus, *J. Med. Chem.*, 1996, **39** (26), 5246–5256.
[6] A. Tropsha, Recent trends in quantitative structure-activity relationships. In *Burger's Medicinal Chemistry and Drug Discovery* (ed. D. Abraham), Wiley, New York, 2003, Vol. 1, pp. 49–77.
[7] T. I. Oprea, 3D-QSAR modeling in drug design. In *Computational Medicinal Chemistry and Drug Discovery* (eds J. Tollenaere, H. De Winter, W. Langenaeker and P. Bultinck), Marcel Dekker, New York, 2004, pp. 571–616.
[8] H. Kubinyi, F. A. Hamprecht and T. Mietzner, *J. Med. Chem.*, 1998, **41** (14), 2553–2564.
[9] X. Girones, A. Gallegos and R. Carbo-Dorca, *J. Chem. Inf. Comput. Sci.*, 2000, **40** (6), 1400–1407.
[10] B. Bordas, T. Komives, Z. Szanto and A. Lopata, *J. Agr. Food Chem.*, 2000, **48** (3), 926–931.
[11] Y. Fan, L. M. Shi, K. W. Kohn, Y. Pommier and J. N. Weinstein, *J. Med. Chem.*, 2001, **44** (20), 3254–3263.
[12] T. Suzuki, K. Ide, M. Ishida and S. Shapiro, *J. Chem. Inf. Comput. Sci.*, 2001, **41** (3), 718–726.
[13] M. Recanatini, A. Cavalli, F. Belluti, L. Piazzi, A. Rampa, A. Bisi, S. Gobbi, P. Valenti, V. Andrisano, M. Bartolini and V. Cavrini, *J. Med. Chem.*, 2000, **43** (10), 2007–2018.
[14] J. A. Moron, M. Campillo, V. Perez, M. Unzeta and L. Pardo, *J. Med. Chem.*, 2000, **43** (9), 1684–1691.
[15] A. Golbraikh and A. Tropsha, *J. Comput. Aided Mol. Des.*, 2002, **16** (5–6), 357–369.
[16] A. Tropsha, P. Gramatica and V. K. Gombar, *Quant. Struct-Act. Relat. Comb. Sci.*, 2003, **22**, 69–77.
[17] A. Golbraikh, M. Shen, Z. Xiao, Y. D. Xiao, K. H. Lee and A. Tropsha, *J. Comput. Aided Mol. Des.*, 2003, **17** (2–4), 241–253.

[18] E. Novellino, C. Fattorusso and G. Greco, *Pharm. Acta Helv.*, 1995, **70**, 149–154.
[19] U. Norinder, *J. Chemomet.*, 1996, **10**, 95–105.
[20] N. S. Zefirov and V. A. Palyulin, *J. Chem. Inf. Comput. Sci.*, 2001, **41** (4), 1022–1027.
[21] S. Wold and L. Eriksson, Statistical validation of QSAR results. In *Chemometrics Methods in Molecular Design* (ed. H. v. d. Waterbeemd), VCH, Weinheim (Germany), 1995, pp. 309–318.
[22] R. D. Clark, D. G. Sprous and J. M. Leonard, Validating models based on large dataset. In *Rational Approaches to Drug Design, Proceedings of the 13th European Symposium on Quantitative Structure-Activity Relationship, Aug 27– Sept 1* (eds H.-D. Höltje and W. Sippl), Prous Science, Düsseldorf, 2001, pp. 475–485.
[23] A. Kovatcheva, A. Golbraikh, S. Oloff, Y. D. Xiao, W. Zheng, P. Wolschann, G. Buchbauer and A. Tropsha, *J. Chem. Inf. Comput. Sci.*, 2004, **44** (2), 582–595.
[24] T. I. Oprea and A. E. Garcia, *J. Comput. Aided Mol. Des.*, 1996, **10** (3), 186–200.
[25] T. I. Oprea, *SAR QSAR Environ. Res.*, 2001, **12** (1–2), 129–141.
[26] A. C. Atkinson, *Plots, Transformations and Regression*, Clarendon Press, Oxford, UK, 1985.
[27] P. Gramatica and E. Papa, *Quant. Struct-Act. Relat.*, 2003, **22** (3), 374–385.
[28] P. Gramatica, P. Pilutti and E. Papa, *Quant. Struct-Act. Relat.*, 2003, **22** (3), 364–373.
[29] J. Mandel, *J. Res. Nat. Bur. Stand.*, 1985, **90**, 465–476.
[30] W. Lindberg, J.-A. Persson and S. Wold, *Anal. Chem.*, 1983, **55**, 643–648.
[31] S. J. Cho, W. Zheng and A. Tropsha, *J. Chem. Inf. Comput. Sci.*, 1998, **38** (2), 259–268.
[32] W. Zheng and A. Tropsha, *J. Chem. Inf. Comput. Sci.*, 2000, **40** (1), 185–194.
[33] P. Lima, A. Golbraikh, S. Oloff, Y. D. Xiao and A. Tropsha, *J. Med. Chem.*, 2006, **46**, 1245–1254.
[34] *Pharmacophore Perception, Development, and Use in Drug Design*, IUL, La Jolla, CA, 2000.
[35] A. Tropsha, S. J. Cho and W. Zheng, New tricks for an old dog: development and application of novel QSAR methods for rational design of combinatorial chemical libraries and database mining. In *Rational Drug Design: Novel Methodology and Practical Applications* (eds A. L. Parrill and M. R. Reddy), ACS Symposium Series, Washington, DC, 1999, Vol. 719, pp. 198–211.
[36] A. Tropsha and W. Zheng, *Curr. Pharm. Des.*, 2001, **7** (7), 599–612.
[37] B. T. Hoffman, T. Kopajtic, J. L. Katz and A. H. Newman, *J. Med. Chem.*, 2000, **43** (22), 4151–4159.
[38] M. Shen, A. LeTiran, Y. Xiao, A. Golbraikh, H. Kohn and A. Tropsha, *J. Med. Chem.*, 2002, **45** (13), 2811–2823.
[39] M. Shen, C. Beguin, A. Golbraikh, J. P. Stables, H. Kohn and A. Tropsha, *J. Med. Chem.*, 2004, **47** (9), 2356–2364.
[40] J. R. Votano, M. Parham, L. H. Hall, L. B. Kier, S. Oloff, A. Tropsha, Q. Xie and W. Tong, *Mutagenesis*, 2004, **19** (5), 365–377.
[41] NCI, see http://dtp.nci.nih.gov/docs/3d_database/structural_information/smiles_strings.html, 2004.
[42] Maybridge, see http://www.daylight.com/products/databases/Maybridge.html, 2004.

CHAPTER 8

Machine Learning in Computational Chemistry

Brian B. Goldman and W. Patrick Walters

Vertex Pharmaceuticals Inc., 130 Waverley St., Cambridge, MA 02139, USA

Contents

1. INTRODUCTION

The objective of machine learning is to infer a function by mapping a collection of input examples to an observed outcome. The natural fit between machine learning and pharmaceutical research leads to the common utilization of learning algorithms to construct quantitative structure activity relationships (QSAR). In a QSAR study, the objective is to relate a set of variables calculated from molecular structure to a known physical property or biological activity. This review provides a survey of machine learning techniques that have recently appeared in the computational chemistry literature.

Three major areas must be addressed prior to the successful application of machine learning methods to QSAR studies: the identification of a relevant molecular descriptor set, the selection of an appropriate learning algorithm and the choice of a technique to validate the inferred model. Selecting an appropriate set of molecular descriptors is nontrivial, as many different types of descriptors exist. For example, a commercial program DRAGON [1] is capable of producing over 1600 different descriptors. It is usually uncertain which descriptors perform best for a particular learning task. Researchers typically use a collection of descriptors sets and evaluate their performance on a given learning problem. Analogous to determining which descriptors to use, selecting an appropriate learning method is also problematic. A large collection of machine learning algorithms with a successful history in QSAR exists. Although each method

ANNUAL REPORTS IN COMPUTATIONAL CHEMISTRY, VOLUME 2
ISSN: 1574-1400   DOI 10.1016/S1574-1400(06)02008-1

has its relative strengths and weaknesses, it is uncertain which particular algorithm will have the best performance on a given problem. Researchers customarily engage a small set of methods and identify the top-performing technique for the particular problem. While a number of machine learning methods have been applied in computational chemistry [2–5], consensus seems to be forming in the community that support vector machines (SVMs), Bayesian methods and ensemble techniques provide consistently high performance. This review will focus on these three methods.

The final step that must be addressed is estimating predictive power of the inferred model. Cross-validation is predominantly used as a means to estimate a test statistic (e.g. q^2, mean-squared error) related to the generalization error of a model. However, Golbraikh and Tropsha [6] question the use of cross-validation as a reliable metric for determining the generalizability of a model. These authors indicate that a reasonable value of a test statistic is a necessary but not sufficient condition for a model to have high predictive power. In a separate review, Hawkins [7] asserts that cross-validation gives a "serviceable and slightly conservative estimate of precision". The contradictory conclusions of these two authors may be understood by appealing to a fundamental assumption of most learning methods. Learning algorithms infer a function mapping patterns to responses by observing examples from a fixed distribution. If the learned function is applied to an example from a different distribution, it will likely generate an inaccurate prediction. A reasonable value of a cross-validated test statistic ensures that a model will provide accurate predictions on new molecules only if they are similar to the original training set. Several research groups have recently reported algorithms for quantifying the applicability of a QSAR model on a per molecule basis. Model applicability is determined based on the similarity of a test molecule to the training set [8–11]. The more similar a molecule is to the training set, the more reliable the prediction will be. To obtain accurate performance from a cross-validated QSAR model, it is essential to apply the model only on molecules within its domain.

2. SUPPORT VECTOR MACHINES

SVMs [12,13] are a relatively recent addition to the computational chemist's tool chest of machine learning algorithms. This method was developed by Vapnik [14] in the 1990s, and can be used for either classification or regression. The fundamental idea of support vector classification is to find a hyperplane that separates examples of two different classes of objects by the widest possible margin. The elegance and power of the technique arises from the fact that during the training process, reference is made to the input patterns exclusively through the use of dot products. This allows for the introduction of nonlinearity through the use of kernel functions. Kernel functions implicitly compute the dot product between two vectors in a high-dimensional feature space without explicitly mapping the vectors to that space. By using these functions, SVMs compute a separating hyperplane in a high-dimensional space, which becomes a nonlinear decision boundary when projected down into the input space of the examples. Popular kernel functions are the radial basis function (RBF) and the polynomial kernel. SVMs contain an adjustable parameter C that governs the trade off between complexity of the decision surface and the number of training errors tolerated. Practical application of the technique requires that the parameters to the kernel function along with the SVM parameter be tuned appropriately. Practitioners typically conduct a grid search over a reasonable range of parameter space, although methods based on gradient descent algorithms have also been utilized [15].

Müller [16] and Byvatov [17] individually reported on using SVMs to classify "drugs" from "nondrugs". These studies are extremely similar to one another, each comparing the performance of the technique to other learning methods. Byvatov compared the performance of SVMs to neural networks, while Müller compared SVMs to linear programming machines, linear discriminant analysis, nearest neighbor classifiers and bagged decision trees. Both studies were based upon a subset of 9208 compounds (4998 "drug" and 4210 "nondrug") selected from a source list of 210,000 molecules originally compiled by Sadowski and Kubinyi [18]. Byvatov used a collection of topological pharmacophores, Ghose-Crippen [19] and MOE [20] descriptors, while Müller used only the Ghose-Crippen descriptors. Byvatov selected autoscaling for descriptor preprocessing, and Müller employed a log transform. Both authors used polynomial kernels, but Müller also used a RBF. Byvatov reported cross-validated error rates of approximately 18% for the SVM, slightly better than the error rate of 20% achieved by a neural network on the same data set. Müller reported cross-validated errors rates of 18.7% for the SVM trained using the polynomial kernel and 18.1% for the SVM trained with the RBF kernel. Müller also trained an SVM using the entire data set of 210,000 molecules (166,000 for training, 10,000 for validation and 10,000 for testing). SVM achieved a cross-validated error rate of 7%. The nearest neighbor and decision tree algorithms yielded error rates of 8.2% on this large data set, while linear discriminant analysis and linear programming machines both produced error rates of approximately 13.6%. In 1998, Sadowski and Kubinyi [18] used a neural network on the same data set and achieved an error rate of 18.1%.

Lind and Maltseva [21] reported using support vector regression to estimate the aqueous solubility of organic compounds. Results were reported on three different data sets: the training data of Huuskonen [22]
compiled from the AQUASOL [23] and PHYSPROP [24] database, the
testing data from the Huuskonen [22] study and a data set provided by
Katritzky [25]. Instead of a standard polynomial or RBF kernel, Lind and
Maltseva used a kernel based upon the Tanimoto similarity of molecules
as calculated by the Accord Software Development kit provided by
Accelrys [26]. Cross-validated results for the different data sets ranged
from a root-mean-squared-error in the log of the solubility of 0.57–0.77
with q^2 in the range of 0.86–0.88. As the authors note, these results are
similar to those reported in previous studies.

Yap and Chen [27] reported on the use of SVMs for the prediction of
inhibitors and substrates of cytochrome P450 isoenzymes CYP3A4,
CYP2D6 and CYP2C9. Data sets were obtained from several literature
sources resulting in a few hundred molecules representing each distinct
class of inhibitor/noninhibitor and substrate/nonsubstrate for each isoen-
zyme. Each molecule was represented by 1607 individual descriptors
calculated using DRAGON [1] and a proprietary program. All descriptors
were normalized into the range $[-1, +1]$. A genetic algorithm was used to
perform feature selection [28]. An initial population of 50 descriptor subsets were selected and evolved for 100 generations. Fitness of the descriptor sets was assessed using the Matthews correlation coefficient [29]
on a held out test set. At the end of the optimization procedure, the highest
ranked descriptor subset was identified and used to train a final SVM. The
above process was repeated 101 times, resulting in a pool of classification
systems, each using a potentially different set of 50 descriptors. A consensus SVM was constructed by randomly selecting 81 individual SVMs
from this pool. The final consensus SVM models were validated using
independent test sets resulting in overall accuracies ranging from 85.7%
to 98.8% for the various systems.

Kriegl and coworkers [30] also reports on a SVM classification system
for the identification of CYP3A4 inhibitors. The data set consisted of 1345
diverse drug-like compounds gathered from internal discovery programs.
This set was divided into three groups consisting of strong ($IC_{50} < 2 \mu M$;
243 molecules), medium ($2 \mu M \leqslant IC_{50} \leqslant 20 \mu M$; 561 molecules) and
weak inhibitors ($IC_{50} > 20 \mu M$; 541 molecules). For the development of
binary SVM classifiers, all inhibitors in the medium category were removed from the data set. Four different sets of descriptors were investigated: 32 2D descriptors generated from an "in-house" program, 114 2D
descriptors generated using MOE, 88 VolSurf [31] descriptors and 68
descriptors representing electrostatic properties calculated using an

in-house quantum mechanics program. All descriptors were scaled to the range of $[-1, +1]$. The SVM and kernel parameters were tuned using a grid search. The best models were identified and subsequently combined into a consensus SVM. Final prediction on a test molecule was determined by majority vote. All models created using the different descriptor sets had cross-validated accuracies exceeding 93%. The best-performing model used all the descriptors combined. A three-class model was also developed which correctly classified more than 70% of the test molecules.

An interesting application of SVMs to classify mutagenic compounds was recently reported by Mahe [32]. In this paper, the author applies a novel kernel function designed specifically for use with chemical structures. Using graph theory, the kernel maps molecules into an infinite-dimensional space, where each dimension corresponds to a unique molecular substructure. In essence, the kernel computes a dot product between two structural fingerprints indexed by all possible molecular fragments. The approach was tested on two mutagenic data sets and compared against linear regression, decision trees, neural networks, three different inductive logic programming (ILP) instances and a version space (VS) algorithm [33]. On one data set, the SVM yielded an accuracy of 91.2%, being outperformed by the VS algorithm (95.7% accurate) and one of the ILP programs (93.3% accurate). On a different but related data set, the method achieved an accuracy of 88.1%, outperforming all other tested methods.

Jorissen and Gilson [34] report using SVMs for the virtual screening of molecular databases. In this setting the learning task is not classification, but the enrichment of active molecules contained in a set of molecules selected from a chemical database. The authors used a RBF kernel and optimized SVM parameter settings using a coarse-grained grid search. Performance was assessed using cross-validation and a novel scoring function related to the model's ability to identify active molecules. Feature selection was used to reduce an initial list of 517 descriptors to 50 features. The method was tested on five different protein–ligand systems. Training and test sets were carefully constructed so that molecules from similar chemical classes were wholly contained within distinct sets. Each training set contained 25 active molecules and 5160 inactive molecules. The validation sets contained 25 active molecules mixed with a background of 25,300 inactive molecules. The method recovered at least half of the known actives in the top-ranked 10% of the test database. The SVM method outperformed other ranking techniques based on the molecular similarity between known active molecules and unknown test compounds. Several other research groups have also used SVMs for compound selection, and reported similar results [35–37].

Saeh and coworkers [38] report on the use of SVMs and 3D pharmacophore fingerprints to perform "scaffold hopping". Scaffold hopping is
defined as morphing one chemical class to a topologically distinct but
pharmacophorically equivalent class without sacrificing activity in the
desired assay. Initially, the group constructed SVMs able to distinguish
between active and inactive compounds of the G-protein coupled receptor
β_1 Adrenoceptor. The initial training data consisted of 200 active molecules and 2000 inactive compounds collected from a proprietary screening
database. A 3D conformation model containing a maximum of 1000 conformers per molecules was generated using the program OMEGA [39].
Binary pharmacophore fingerprints were created from each of these conformational models and used to train a RBF SVM. A modified version of
Güner's [40] goodness of hit score in conjunction with cross-validation
was used to determine optimal parameter settings. The final model was
tested on a database containing a mix of 68 active molecules in a
background pool of 60,000 inactive compounds. The algorithm correctly
identified 45 active compounds out of a total positive prediction of
2836 molecules. To demonstrate the SVM's ability to perform lead hopping, a more challenging experiment was designed. Using MDL Drug Data
Report (MDDR) [41] database, 370 α_2 adrenergic actives were clustered
using a Tanimoto similarity of $T_c = 0.45$, resulting in 35 clusters. One
cluster containing 15 active molecules was removed to a validation set
and mixed with 6800 inactive compounds. The training set contained the
remaining 355 active molecules mixed with 6000 inactive compounds. The
training set was further pruned by removing molecules that had a Tanimoto similarity of greater than $T_c = 0.45$ to any molecule in the validation
set. An SVM model was trained and used to predict on the validation set.
The resulting model identified 68% of the actives and yielded an overall hit
rate of 37.1%. The results indicate that SVMs in combination with
pharmacophore fingerprints can be used to perform scaffold hopping.

3. BAYESIAN METHODS

Bayesian methods [42] operate by utilizing a straightforward "learn by
example" paradigm. A program is presented with a set of examples labeled as "good" or "bad," and a set of features representing each example.
The program then utilizes combinations of features, in conjunction with
Bayes' rule, to learn the difference between good and bad examples. One
of the most widely applied types of Bayesian learning is the naïve Bayes
method. The method is referred to as naïve because it operates on
the assumption that all features are independent, thus allowing prior

probabilities to be calculated from the input data. The method's speed, broad applicability and ability to operate in high-dimensional spaces have made it popular among computational chemists.

One of the primary applications of naïve Bayes method has been as an alternative to similarity searching in chemical databases. Similarity searching has been a mainstay of computational drug discovery for more than 20 years [43]. There are numerous established methods for identifying sets of molecules that are similar to a single query molecule. However, in many cases, an investigator may want to identify compounds similar to set of query molecules. One method of accomplishing this task would be to perform a series of single searches and combine the results. However, a search of this type would not be efficient and would not provide a means of combining the characteristics of several query molecules. In addition, there is no straightforward means of determining the number of database molecules to retain for each query molecule. A number of recent papers describe the application of naïve Bayes to chemical database searching [44–47]. All of these methods operate in a similar fashion. Descriptors are calculated for a set of molecules labeled either "good" (active molecules) or "bad" (inactive molecules), and a model constructed that can differentiate between the two classes. This model is then used to score a new set of molecules, and the resulting rank ordering used to prioritize molecules for purchase or screening.

Glen and coworkers have recently published a series of papers that describe the use of a naïve Bayes classifier for searching 2D and 3D databases. The first such paper describes a method known as MOL-PRINT 2D [44], which employs atom environment descriptors and feature selection combined with a naïve Bayes classifier to perform database searches. The authors compared the MOLPRINT 2D Bayesian method with two other established methods, fusion of ranking scores and binary kernel discrimination. Tests were performed by executing searches in a data set of more than 100,000 molecules from the MDDR [41] database. Queries were performed using 11 compound sets from different therapeutic classes. In each case, 10 active compounds were selected from each class to be used as query molecules. In 10 out of 11 cases, the MOLPRINT 2D method proved to be superior to the other methods studied. Glen's work also demonstrated the importance of feature selection in Bayesian learning. The authors compared the results of MOLPRINT 2D with and without feature selection, and found that in cases where the number of inactive molecules is much greater than the number of active molecules, feature selection provides a significant improvement. In one case, the average retrieval rate was 51% when all features were used, but climbed to 65% when a subset of 250 features was selected.

In a subsequent paper, the same group describes a similar method, MOLPRINT 3D [45], which can be used for virtual screening and pharma-cophore elucidation. MOLPRINT 3D computes descriptors by transform-ing interaction energies at a molecular surface. The descriptors are then used with a naïve Bayes classifier to perform similarity searches using multiple query structures. The authors used a strategy similar to that de-scribed above to evaluate the performance of MOLPRINT 3D. A set of 957 structures from MDDR containing molecules from five different activity classes was used as a test database. This database was augmented with 457 additional MDDR molecules that did not belong to any of the five activity classes. Bayesian learning was performed using a set of five ac-tive molecules and 50% of the inactive molecules as a training set. The learned model was then used to rank order the remaining 50% of the database. Performance of MOLPRINT 3D was compared with a number of established techniques and found to be as good or better than the majority of the methods tested. Only the MOLPRINT 2D methodology (discussed above) produced better results. One commonly cited advan-tage of 3D descriptors, such as those used in MOLPRINT 3D, is the ability to "scaffold hop". The authors provide an example of the ability of MOL-PRINT 3D to identify molecules from other scaffold classes. These mol-ecules would not have been found by a 2D search.

Bayesian learning has also been applied to the design of screening libraries targeted at a single receptor or an entire gene family. A recent paper from Xia and coworkers [47] demonstrates the use of a Bayesian model to classify molecules as kinase inhibitors. The authors used a set of 6236 kinase active compounds from the Amgen corporate collection as the active set, and 193,417 compounds from the same database as the inactive set. A Bayesian learning program was then used to generate a model for kinase activity that rank ordered compounds in the database based on the likelihood that they will be kinase inhibitors. In a validation study involving the results of 22 kinase assays, the authors found that the Bayesian model was typically able to identify 90% of the screening hits in the top 10% of the ranked database.

Similar approaches have also been used to construct models for pre-dicting off-target activity. A recent paper from Sun [48] describes a Bay-esian model for predicting multidrug resistance. In this paper, a set of 609 molecules, of which 371 show multidrug resistance, was used to train the Bayesian model. Under five-fold cross-validation, 78.7% of the mol-ecules were correctly predicted. The authors also evaluated the impact of descriptor selection on model performance, and came to the conclusion that high-dimensional descriptors give better results for large data sets, while low-dimensional descriptors give better results for small data sets.

A paper by O'Brien and coworkers [49] describes the construction of Bayesian models to predict hERG channel blocking and CYP2D6 inhibition. The hERG model, built based on a set of 11,966 compounds was able to achieve an overall accuracy of 82%. The authors also constructed a neural network model for the same data set (accuracy 85%). The rankings from the Bayesian and neural network models were then combined to produce a consensus model with 89% accuracy. A similar procedure was followed to construct a consensus model for CYP2D6 activity (built from 600 compounds) that achieved an overall accuracy of 99%.

Another novel application of Bayesian learning has been in enhancing the results of other virtual screening methods. Klon and coworkers [50–52] recently published a series of papers that describe the use of Bayesian learning to improve hit rates in protein–ligand docking studies. In these studies, a set of molecules is computationally docked into a protein active site. The docked molecules are then rank ordered according to an empirical or force field-based scoring function and divided into two sets. One set, composed of the highest scoring compounds is treated as good, while the remaining set of molecules is considered bad. A set of topological fingerprint descriptors is then calculated for all molecules and used as input to a Bayesian learning program. The learned model is then used to re-rank the docked molecules. Tests were performed using three docking programs (Dock, FlexX and Glide) and two protein targets (PTP-1B and PKB). In the case of PTP-1B, the authors observed a 5–25% improvement in hit rate. However, in the case of PKB, the additional Bayesian step actually brought about a decrease in hit rate. The initial docking run found 48% of the active compounds in the top 10% of the scored database, while the subsequent Bayesian step only uncovered 2% of the hits in the same fraction of the database. The authors attribute this dramatic loss of efficiency to the large number of false positives present in the high-scoring molecules. In a subsequent paper [51], the addition of consensus scoring ameliorated this finding and produced a 20% improvement in hit rate.

A third paper from the same group applied a method similar to that described above to the case of HIV-1 protease [50]. In this case, a database of 175,000 random compounds was seeded with a set of 424 known inhibitors. Once again, the addition of a second Bayesian ranking step led to a significant improvement in docking efficiency. In one case (docking with Glide), the original docking procedure identified 82% of the active molecules in the top 2% of the database. The subsequent Bayesian re-ranking of the hits identified 97% of the hits in the same fraction of the database. The authors also provide a comparison of the coupled docking/Bayesian approach with more traditional topological search strategies including Tanimoto similarity, maximum common subgraph and substructure search. In each case, the Bayesian/docking procedure outperformed the topological searches.

4. ENSEMBLE METHODS

Machine learning researchers have shown that it is possible to achieve significant gains in accuracy by employing sets of classifiers. In these techniques, known as ensemble methods [53], a prediction is generated by combining the output of several individual classifiers. One of the most common methods of constructing multiple classifiers is to use separate sub-samples of the data. One such sampling method is bagging (bootstrap aggregation), where multiple classifiers are constructed by randomly sampling (with replacement) from the original data set. The final classification for each example is then based on voting (for classification) or averaging (for numeric prediction) of the individual classifiers. Boosting [54] is another method that utilizes sampling to improve the accuracy of a learning algorithm. Boosting differs from bagging, in that it is an iterative method where examples are assigned weights based on prediction accuracy. Boosting increases accuracy by adjusting the weights and putting an emphasis on examples that were poorly predicted. The final classification for each example is then based on the weighted votes of the individual classifiers. While ensemble methods can be applied to any machine learning algorithm, they are particularly useful with unstable methods such as decision trees [55,56]. In an unstable method, a small change in the composition of the training set can often bring about a large change in the output of the learned model. Combining several models can largely reduce this sensitivity to data set composition.

One widely used example of an ensemble method is the Random Forest (RF) algorithm developed by Brieman [57]. In RF, a large number (typically several hundred) of decision trees are constructed from the training data. Individual trees are constructed by considering random subsets of available variables. Test examples are then classified by each of the individual trees, and an overall classification is obtained by summing the votes of the individual decision trees. Brieman and others [58,59] have demonstrated that the method is efficient, robust and able to handle thousands of descriptors without having to resort to feature selection [28].

A recent paper by Svetnik and coworkers [60] provided one of the first examples of the use of RF in building QSAR models. The authors built classification and regression models for six literature data sets using RF, Recursive Partitioning (RP) and Partial Least Squares (PLS). The models were then compared on the basis of accuracy (classification models),

Table 1. A sampling of available machine learning programs that implement methods discussed in this review, RF, SVMs and naïve Bayes

Program	Learning algorithms	URL	License
Weka	RF, SVM, NB	http://www.cs.waikato.ac.nz/ml/weka	Open Source
R	RF, SVM, NB	http://www.r-project.org	Open Source
Orange	RF, SVM, NB	http://magix.fri.uni-lj.si/orange	Open Source
LibSVM	SVM	http://www.csie.ntu.edu.tw/~cjlin/libsvm	Open Source
Pipeline Pilot	SVM, NB, Ensemble decision trees Commercial	http://www.scitegic.com	
Chem Tree	Ensemble decision trees	http://www.goldenhelix.com	Commercial

RMS error and correlation coefficient (regression models). Under 50-fold cross-validation, RF consistently outperformed both RP and PLS. The accuracies for the RF Models ranged from 78% to 83%, typically 5–10% better than accuracies obtained with other methods. The regression models built with RF also performed as well or better than models built using RP and PLS. Tong and coworkers [61] have published a similar method called Decision Forest that also employs multiple decision trees.

The application of another ensemble method, Stochastic Gradient Boosting (SGB), is described in a recent paper from Svetnik and coworkers [62]. Like RF, SGB builds ensembles of decision trees. However, where RF constructs trees in parallel and classifies examples based on "votes," SGB iteratively builds a series of trees using a boosting algorithm. Each tree improves upon its predecessors using an error correcting strategy. In this paper the authors evaluated the performance of SGB, for both classification and regression, on 10 QSAR data sets. The performance of SGB was compared with RF, single decision tree, partial least squares, k-nearest neighbors, naïve Bayes and (SVMs). Classification performance was assessed based on the proportion of correctly classified molecules (accuracy), while regression performance was based on RMS error and correlation coefficient. The ensemble methods RF and SGB performed best in terms of both regression and classification.

5. CONCLUSION

Until recently, the application of machine learning methods was primarily the domain of specialists in the Artificial Intelligence or Statistics Fields. Early machine learning software required an intimate knowledge of the algorithms as well as a familiarity with specialized programming languages such as Prolog or Lisp. More recently, a number of easy to use Open Source and commercial machine learning programs and toolkits have appeared. A number of these software tools are listed in Table 1. The availability of easily accessible, high-quality software has led to the widespread adoption of machine learning among computational chemists. Although modern machine learning techniques require minimal parameter adjustment to achieve reasonable results, it is inappropriate to treat these techniques as "black boxes". As with other QSAR techniques, model quality and applicability must be judiciously assessed.

REFERENCES

[1] R. Todeschini and V. Consonnii, *Handbook of Molecular Descriptors*, Wiley-VCH, Weinheim, 2000.
[2] R. D. King, S. H. Muggleton, A. Srinivasan and M. J. Sternberg, Structure-activity relationships derived by machine learning: the use of atoms and their bond connectivities to predict mutagenicity by inductive logic programming, *Proc. Natl. Acad. Sci. USA*, 1996, **93**, 438–442.
[3] R. D. King, S. Muggleton, R. A. Lewis and M. J. Sternberg, Drug design by machine learning: the use of inductive logic programming to model the structure-activity relationships of trimethoprim analogues binding to dihydrofolate reductase, *Proc. Natl. Acad. Sci. USA*, 1992, **89**, 11322–11326.
[4] N. Marchand-Geneste, K. A. Watson, B. K. Alsberg and R. D. King, New approach to pharmacophore mapping and QSAR analysis using inductive logic programming. Application to thermolysin inhibitors and glycogen phosphorylase B inhibitors,, *J. Med. Chem.*, 2002, **45**, 399–409.
[5] J. Zupan and J. Gasteiger, *Neural Networks in Chemistry and Drug Design*, Wiley-VCH, New York, 1999.
[6] A. Golbraikh and A. Tropsha, Beware of q^2!, *J. Mol. Graph Model*, 2002, **20**, 269–276.
[7] D. M. Hawkins, The problem of overfitting, *J. Chem. Inf. Comput. Sci.*, 2004, **44**, 1–12.
[8] S. Dimitrov, G. Dimitrova, T. Pavlov, N. Dimitrova, G. Patlewicz, J. Niemela and O. Mekenyan, A stepwise approach for defining the applicability domain of SAR and QSAR models, *J. Chem. Inf. Model*, 2005, **45**, 839–849.
[9] R. P. Sheridan, B. P. Feuston, V. N. Maiorov and S. K. Kearsley, Similarity to molecules in the training set is a good discriminator for prediction accuracy in QSAR, *J. Chem. Inf. Comput. Sci.*, 2004, **44**, 1912–1928.
[10] R. Guha and P. C. Jurs, Determining the validity of a QSAR model – a classification approach, *J. Chem. Inf. Model*, 2005, **45**, 65–73.
[11] L. He and P. C. Jurs, Assessing the reliability of a QSAR model's predictions, *J. Mol. Graph Model*, 2005, **23**, 503–523.
[12] B. Scholkopf, C. J. C. Burges and A. Smola, *Advances in Kernel Methods Support Vector Learning*, MIT Press, 1999.
[13] N. Cristianini and J. Shawe-Taylor, *An Introduction to Support Vector Machines and Other Kernel-Based Learning Methods*, Cambridge University Press, 2000.
[14] V. Vapnik, *The Nature of Statistical Learning Theory*, Springer, New York, 1995.
[15] O. Chapelle, V. N. Vapnik, O. Bousquet and S. Mukherjee, Choosing multiple parameters for support vector machines, *Mach. Learn.*, 2002, **46**, 131–159.
[16] K. R. Müller, G. Ratsch, S. Sonnenburg, S. Mika, M. Grimm and N. Heinrich, Classifying 'drug-likeness' with Kernel-based learning methods, *J. Chem. Inf. Model*, 2005, **45**, 249–253.

[17] E. Byvatov, U. Fechner, J. Sadowski and G. Schneider, Comparison of support vector machine and artificial neural network systems for drug/nondrug classification, *J. Chem. Inf. Comput. Sci.*, 2003, **43**, 1882–1889.

[18] J. Sadowski and H. Kubinyi, A scoring scheme for discriminating between drugs and nondrugs, *J. Med. Chem.*, 1998, **41**, 3325–3329.

[19] A. K. Ghose and G. M. Crippen, Atomic physicochemical parameters for three-dimensional-structure-directed quantitative-structure-activity relationships. 2. Modeling dispersive and hydrophobic interactions, *J. Chem. Inf. Comput. Sci.*, 1987, **27**, 21–35.

[20] P. Labute, A widely applicable set of descriptors, *J. Mol. Graph Model,*, 2000, **18**, 464–477.

[21] P. Lind and T. Maltseva, Support vector machines for the estimation of aqueous solubility, *J. Chem. Inf. Comput. Sci.*, 2003, **43**, 1855–1859.

[22] J. Huuskonen, Estimation of aqueous solubility for a diverse set of organic compounds based on molecular topology, *J. Chem. Inf. Comput. Sci.*, 2000, **40**, 773–777.

[23] R. Dannenfelser and S. H. Yalkowsky, Database for aqueous solubility of nonelectrolytes, *Comput. Appl. Biosci.*, 1989, **5**, 235–236.

[24] The Physical Properties Database (PHYSPROP), Syracuse Research Corporation, Syracuse, NW, 2005.

[25] A. R. Katritzky, Y. Wang, S. Sild, T. Tamm and M. Karelson, QSPR studies on vapor pressure, aqueous solubility, and the prediciton of water-air partition coefficients, *J. Chem. Inf. Comput. Sci.*, 1998, **38**, 720–725.

[26] Accord SDK., *Accelrys*, San Diego, CA, 2005.

[27] C. W. Yap and Y. Z. Chen, Prediction of cytochrome P450 3A4, 2D6, and 2C9 inhibitors and substrates by using support vector machines, *J. Chem. Inf. Model*, 2005, **45**, 982–992.

[28] W. P. Walters and B. B. Goldman, Feature selection in quantitative structure-activity relationships, *Curr. Opin. Drug Discov. Devel.*, 2005, **8**, 329–333.

[29] B. W. Matthews, Comparison of the predicted and observed secondary structure of T4 phage lysozyme, *Biochim. Biophys. Acta*, 1975, **405**, 442–451.

[30] J. M. Kriegl, T. Arnold, B. Beck and T. Fox, A support vector machine approach to classify human cytochrome P450 3A4 inhibitors, *J. Comput. Aided Mol. Des.*, 2005, **19**, 189–201.

[31] P. Crivori, G. Cruciani, P. A. Carrupt and B. Testa, Predicting blood-brain barrier permeation from three-dimensional molecular structure, *J. Med. Chem.*, 2000, **43**, 2204–2216.

[32] P. Mahe, N. Ueda, T. Akutsu, J. L. Perret and J. P. Vert, Graph kernels for molecular structure-activity relationship analysis with support vector machines, *J. Chem. Inf. Model*, 2005, **45**, 939–951.

[33] T. M. Mitchell, *Machine Learning*, McGraw-Hill, Boston, MA, 1997, pp. 20–51.

[34] R. N. Jorissen and M. K. Gilson, Virtual screening of molecular databases using a support vector machine, *J. Chem. Inf. Model*, 2005, **45**, 549–561.

[35] M. K. Warmuth, J. Liao, G. Ratsch, M. Mathieson, S. Putta and C. Lemmen, Active learning with support vector machines in the drug discovery process, *J. Chem. Inf. Comput. Sci.*, 2003, **43**, 667–673.

[36] J. Weston, F. Perez-Cruz, O. Bousquet, O. Chapelle, A. Elisseeff and B. Schoelkopf, Feature selection and transduction for prediction of molecular bioactivity for drug design, *Bioinformatics*, 2003, **19**, 764–771.

[37] E. Byvatov and G. Schneider, SVM-based feature selection for characterization of focused compound collections, *J. Chem. Inf. Comput. Sci.*, 2004, **44**, 993–999.

[38] J. C. Saeh, P. D. Lyne, B. K. Takasaki and D. A. Cosgrove, Lead hopping using SVM and 3D pharmacophore fingerprints, *J. Chem. Inf. Model*, 2005, **45**, 1122–1133.

[39] Omega, OpenEye Scientific Software.

[40] O. F. Güner, *Pharmacophore Perception, Development, and Use in Drug Design*, International University Line, La Jolla, CA, 2000.

[41] MDL Drug Data Report, MDL Information Systems, San Leandro, CA, 2005.

[42] I. H. Wiitten and E. Frank, *Data Mining*, Morgan Kaufman, San Francisco, CA, 2005, pp. 315–334.

[43] A. Bender and R. C. Glen, Molecular similarity: a key technique in molecular informatics, *Org. Biomol. Chem.*, 2004, **2**, 3204–3218.

[44] A. Bender, H. Y. Mussa, R. C. Glen and S. Reiling, Similarity searching of chemical databases using atom environment descriptors (MOLPRINT 2D): evaluation of performance, *J. Chem. Inf. Comput. Sci.*, 2004, **44**, 1708–1718.

[45] A. Bender, H. Y. Mussa, G. S. Gill and R. C. Glen, Molecular surface point environments for virtual screening and the elucidation of binding patterns (MOLPRINT 3D), *J. Med. Chem.*, 2004, **47**, 6569–6583.

[46] A. Bender, H. Y. Mussa and R. C. Glen, Screening for dihydrofolate reductase inhibitors using MOLPRINT 2D, a fast fragment-based method employing the Naive Bayesian classifier: limitations of the descriptor and the importance of balanced chemistry in training and test sets, *J. Biomol. Screen*, 2005, **7**, 658–666.

[47] X. Xia, E. G. Maliski, P. Gallant and D. Rogers, Classification of kinase inhibitors using a Bayesian model, *J. Med. Chem.*, 2004, **47**, 4463–4470.

[48] H. Sun, A naive Bayes classifier for prediction of multidrug resistance reversal activity on the basis of atom typing, *J. Med. Chem.*, 2005, **48**, 4031–4039.

[49] S. E. O'Brien and M. J. de Groot, Greater than the sum of its parts: combining models for useful ADMET prediction, *J. Med. Chem.*, 2005, **48**, 1287–1291.

[50] A. E. Klon, M. Glick and J. W. Davies, Application of machine learning to improve the results of high-throughput docking against the HIV-1 protease, *J. Chem. Inf. Comput. Sci.*, 2004, **44**, 2216–2224.

[51] A. E. Klon, M. Glick and J. W. Davies, Combination of a naive Bayes classifier with consensus scoring improves enrichment of high-throughput docking results, *J. Med. Chem.*, 2004, **47**, 4356–4359.

[52] A. E. Klon, M. Glick, M. Thoma, P. Acklin and J. W. Davies, Finding more needles in the haystack: a simple and efficient method for improving high-throughput docking results, *J. Med. Chem.*, 2004, **47**, 2743–2749.

[53] T. G. Dietterich, *Ensemble Learning. The Handbook of Brain Theory and Neural Networks,*, MIT Press, Cambridge, MA, 2002.

[54] Y. Freund and R. E. Schapire, *Experiments with a new boosting algorithm*. Proceedings of the Thirteenth Annual Conference on Machine Learning, Morgan Kauffman, Bari, Italy, 1996, pp. 148–156.

[55] L. Breiman, *Classification and Regression Trees*, Chapman & Hall, New York, 1984.

[56] J. R. Quinlan, *C4.5: Programs for Machine Learning,*, Morgan Kaufmann, San Francisco, 1993.

[57] L. Breiman, Random forests, *Mach. Learn.*, 2001, **36**, 5–32.

[58] T. Shi, D. Seligson, A. S. Belldegrun, A. Palotie and S. Horvath, Tumor classification by tissue microarray profiling: random forest clustering applied to renal cell carcinoma, *Mod. Pathol.*, 2005, **18**, 547–557.

[59] G. Izmirlian, Application of the random forest classification algorithm to a SELDI-TOF proteomics study in the setting of a cancer prevention trial, *Ann. NY Acad. Sci.*, 2004, **102**, 154–174.

[60] V. Svetnik, A. Liaw, C. Tong, J. C. Culberson, R. P. Sheridan and B. P. Feuston, Random forest: a classification and regression tool for compound classification and QSAR modeling, *J. Chem. Inf. Comput. Sci.*, 2003, **43**, 1947–1958.

[61] W. Tong, H. Hong, H. Fang, Q. Xie and R. Perkins, Decision forest: combining the predictions of multiple independent decision tree models, *J. Chem. Inf. Comput. Sci.*, 2003, **43**, 525–531.

[62] V. Svetnik, T. Wang, C. Tong, A. Liaw, R. P. Sheridan and Q. Song, Boosting: an ensemble learning tool for compound classification and QSAR modeling, *J. Chem. Inf. Model*, 2005, **45**, 786–799.

CHAPTER 9

Molecular Similarity: Advances in Methods, Applications and Validations in Virtual Screening and QSAR

Andreas Bender,[1,2] Jeremy L. Jenkins,[2] Qingliang Li,[3] Sam E. Adams,[1] Edward O. Cannon[1] and Robert C. Glen[1]

[1]*Unilever Centre for Molecular Science Informatics, Department of Chemistry, University of Cambridge, Lensfield Road, Cambridge CB2 1EW, UK*
[2]*Lead Discovery Center, Novartis Institutes for BioMedical Research Inc., 250 Massachusetts Ave., Cambridge, MA 02139, USA*
[3]*College of Chemistry and Molecular Engineering, Center for Theoretical Biology, Peking University, Beijing 100871, China*

Contents

1. INTRODUCTION

Molecular similarity [1–4] follows, in principle, a simple idea: molecules which are similar to each other exhibit similar properties more often than dissimilar pairs of molecules. This is often written as the relationship

$$Property = f(Structure)$$

ANNUAL REPORTS IN COMPUTATIONAL CHEMISTRY, VOLUME 2
ISSN: 1574-1400   DOI 10.1016/S1574-1400(06)02009-3

Which leaves open two major questions:

1. How to represent molecular structure (the connectivity table or the coordinates of atoms are not *per se* suitable choices)?
2. What is the functional form between structure (or rather structural representation) and the property under consideration so that we can derive an empirical measure of similarity?

In order to explicitly include both challenges mentioned one can reformulate to give

$$m(Property) = f(g(Structure))$$

where m is the measurement outcome of a molecular property concept (such as log P as a surrogate measure of 'lipophilicity'), g represents the transformation of a molecular structure into a 'descriptor' which is amenable to a statistical analysis or machine-learning treatment and f connects experimental measurement and structural representation. Both steps are generally independent of each other, although some combinations of molecular representation and model generation technique are more sensible than others.

The problem in establishing a suitable function g, which translates a molecular structure into a descriptor representation, is that it is usually not known *a priori* which molecular features contribute to a certain property. For example, some functional groups in ligand–receptor binding will establish ligand–receptor interactions, while others simply point into bulk solvent. Often a large number of descriptors need to be calculated in order to (hopefully) capture the relevant factors for a certain molecular property, since often no direct experimental observation is known.

The problem in establishing a function *f*, which correlates descriptor representation and property is that its functional form is also usually not known. Again, no underlying theory exists and its character can vary between two extremes. Linear regression, for example, represents a simple functional form between input and output variables with the advantage of a very small number of free parameters – and following Occam's razor it should be applied in cases where there is a sound physical reason to believe in an underlying linear relationship between input and output variables. At the other end, neural networks are able to model *any* (also nonlinear) relationships between input and output variables. However, they depend on a large number of variables, which may lead to spurious correlations. Often the choice of a functional form, in the absence of physical laws, is governed simply by trial-and-error.

The problems in establishing the optimal choice of f and g are increased by the fact that the relationship between structure and measured property (the only relationship available from experimental data!) is rarely given over a large region of chemical space. Data are sparse – estimations of the size of the chemical space for typical drug molecules [5] (up to 30 heavy atoms) are in the region of 10^{60}, experimental datasets on a property of interest are rarely available for more than 10^6 compounds and are often considerably smaller.

A solution to the problem of identifying the 'best' molecular descriptor will never be fully established – for both practical reasons (the limited size of datasets) and theoretical reasons. A wide variety of different features are important for each property and the functional forms between descriptor representation and property can usually not be established from physical laws (and thus cannot be optimized analytically).

Still, we can establish empirical measures of molecular similarity to predict some particular properties better than others, tested on some of the more or less restricted datasets available. This review deals with both novel molecular representations, function g from above, as well as novel model generation and machine learning methods, function f from above.

As soon as a relationship between molecular representation and a particular property's values is established a crucial question arises: how good are predictions for novel molecules?

Ideally, *all* of chemical space would be covered with *zero error*.

Limits in descriptor generation as well as in experimentally available data clearly prevent us from reaching this goal. Still, in order to establish confidence in models in practical settings, this requirement can be replaced by the question:

Which area of chemical space is covered with *acceptable error?*

Different methods (best known among them are approaches like cross-validation), attempt to provide empirical answers to this question. Intuitively one might guess that for the question *which region* is covered by a given model, the distance of compounds from the training set to the novel compounds whose properties are to be predicted is relevant. This is indeed the case, as has been established in recent articles (see Section 4).

The question of how good predictions for novel compounds are is often established by cross-validation, where portions of the available datasets are, in turn, taken as an external test set, while the remainder of the dataset is used for training purposes. The test set thus attempts to simulate a novel set of molecules, unknown to the training phase of the model and root-mean-square errors (RMSE) or cross-validated correlation coefficients (q^2) on the test set are often reported as a measure of the generalizability of models. Recently, it has emerged that cross-validation actually shows merely that a model is *internally consistent*, but not necessarily predictive for new compounds. The question of how reliability of models can be assured is also discussed in Section 4, and indeed several recent publications propose approaches to determine the 'domain' of models (the area in which they are applicable, see Section 4 for details).

Conventionally, enrichment over random selection is often cited, giving an estimate of how many more active compounds are retrieved from a database than by pure chance. While this measure is correct in the way it is calculated, more recently the performance of 'sophisticated' fingerprints has been compared to trivial features, namely counts of atoms by element, without any structural information [6]. The performance ratio of 'state-of-the-art' methods (i.e., circular fingerprints and Unity fingerprints) to those 'dumb' descriptors can then be interpreted as the 'added value' of more sophisticated methods. Soberingly, on many datasets of actives 'real' fingerprints do not perform significantly better than atom counts (see Fig. 1).

This also relates to the suitability of current databases employed for retrospective virtual screening runs, which are often derived from the MDDR [7,8]. While on the one hand, multiple activity classes are present, those datasets still possess two major disadvantages; first, no information about definite *inactivity* of compounds is contained in the database. Still, if experimental data for retrieved hits are subsequently obtained, many of the 'false-positive' predictions may well be active. Second, following bioisosteric considerations in combination with 'fast follower' approaches to synthesis, it should be noted that this database contains a large number of close analogues. The hit rates obtained on this dataset may thus be overly optimistic compared to real-world libraries employed for virtual screening. Still, the two databases referenced above, which are both subsets of the MDDR, were very important as they enabled comparison of similarity searching approaches on multiple, identical datasets. We would also like to emphasize that more suitable datasets are too often – unfortunately – unavailable from the pharmaceutical and biotechnology companies.

In the following sections, we will also cover other recent developments in some of the areas, which exploit the 'molecular similarity principle'. Section 3 will present novel approaches to capture molecular properties by the use of novel 'descriptors'. Since molecular descriptors and the methods used to analyze the data they represent cannot be separated easily, the second part of this section also covers novel data analysis methods. Section 4 focuses on a crucial aspect of computational models – their validity. In the previous few years, about two dozen publications that focused on 'model validation' have appeared, an area which shall be summarized in this

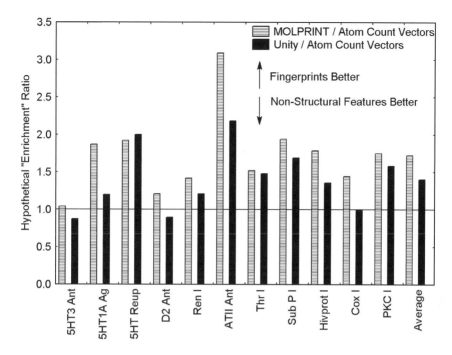

Fig. 1. Comparison of retrieval rates of established descriptors, namely Unity and circular (MOLPRINT 2D) fingerprints, to 'dumb' atom counts. The added value of real descriptors is present in most sets of active compound, although not in all and in many cases only showing low single-digit improvement. Reprinted with permission from J. Chem. Inf. Comput. Sci., 2005, 45, 1372. Copyright 2006 American Chemical Society.

review. Finally, Sections 5 and 6 turn to the application of the methods described earlier. In Section 5, we discuss additional ways to examine data available such as those from high-throughput screening (HTS) campaigns and to gain more knowledge from this data. Section 6 describes some of the recent applications of methods described in the preceding sections, focusing on successes of virtual screening applications, database clustering and comparisons (such as drug- and in-house-likeness) and recent large-scale validations of docking and scoring programs.

2. NOVEL METHODS

We will now describe some of the recent developments in the calculation of molecular descriptors.

2.1. Molecular descriptors

POT-DMC [9] (short for POTency-scaled Dynamic Mapping of Consensus positions) takes not only the (binary) activity of a compound into consideration for virtual screening applications, but also the quantitative activity of a structure. Accordingly, each bit of the descriptor vector (which consists of a combination of one-, two- and three-dimensional (1D, 2D and 3D) features) is multiplied depending on the IC_{50} value of the compound. Scaled bits are summed and normalized at each position. Afterward, the descriptor can be used for virtual screening. When applied to a database of CCR5 chemokine receptor antagonists, serotonin receptor agonists and gonadotropin-releasing hormone agonists, the method overall did not retrieve a larger number of structures – but those which were retrieved were, as intended, of higher activity than in cases where no scaling according to activity was applied.

The FEPOPS[10] (Feature Points of PharmacophoreS) descriptor aims to exploit a (relative) advantage of 3D descriptors, the ability to discover novel scaffolds against a given target, based on active sample structures. After generation of tautomers and conformers, k-means clustering of atomic coordinates is performed. Thus, no knowledge about the active conformation of a structure is necessary. Interaction types are assigned to characteristic 'feature points' in a subsequent step, and are again subject to k-medoids clustering to reduce redundant conformer coverage. Cluster representatives can now be used for similarity searching. Validations are presented using both MDDR (Cox-2, HIV-RT and 5HT3A inhibitors and ligands, respectively) and in-house datasets. In addition, it was shown that inhibitors can be identified from a database, based simply on endogenous ligands (for dopamine and retinoic acid).

A completely different path is followed by the LINGO [11] approach, which is based on a textual representation of molecules. Based on the SMILES string of a structure, and without time-consuming conversion and descriptor generation, a molecule is represented by a set of overlapping 'LINGOs', each of which represents a substring of the complete SMILES structure. While being a straightforward concept (in the best possible sense), favorable performance is presented on log P and solubility datasets, where cross-validated RMS errors are 0.61 and 0.89 log units, respectively. The descriptor also shows applicability to bioactivity, where significant discrimination between bioisosteres and random functional groups can be observed.

Reduced graph descriptors have been the subject of interest for a considerable time, and recently further work was performed in this area with success. Earlier comparison algorithms of reduced graphs represent the graph as a binary fingerprint, sometimes leading to molecules perceived as similar by the algorithm, which are not similar to the eyes of most chemists. This problem was recently addressed [12] by applying 'edit distance' measures to the similarity of compounds – the number of operations needed to transform one reduced graph structure of a molecule into another. Through this emphasis of not only the fragments present in reduced graphs, but also the way in which they are connected, better agreement with the human perception of 'molecular similarity' could be achieved.

Molecular binding can be thought of as being mediated by complementary shapes and matching properties – where, due to solvation and other effects, 'matching' does not only mean complementarity. Accordingly, a 'Shape Fingerprint' method has recently been presented [13] which implements shape similarity measures akin to volume overlap methods, but which, due to the employment of database-derived reference shapes, is several orders of magnitude faster. (Note of course that shape also plays an important role in other areas of science [14].) Employing Gaussian descriptions of molecular shape, about 500 shape comparisons can be performed per second and the resulting shape similarity was shown to be useful in virtual screening applications.

Only some parts of a ligand bound to its target will actually interact with the target, other parts will just be pointing into the bulk solvent. By analyzing the variability of ligands' regions, features which correspond to each of the regions can be inferred – molecular features which are involved in ligand–target interactions will be more highly conserved than those which point into the solvent, due to the stricter requirements imposed on them. The 'Weighted Probe Interaction Energy (WeP) Method' [15] exploits exactly this principle, and can be used to derive ligand-based receptor models. This was applied to the steroid dataset (which is well known from CoMFA studies) a set of dihydrofolate reductase (DHFR) inhibitors as well as hydrophobic chlorinated dibenzofurans. In particular, the DHFR model was able to elucidate interactions relevant to binding which very closely resemble the target-derived model complex.

Previously applied to the calculation of inter-substituent similarities, which might be exploited for the identification of bioisosteric groups [16], the R-group descriptor (RGD) was more recently also the subject of QSAR investigations [17]. The RGD describes the distribution of atomic properties at a distance of n bonds ($n = 1, 2, 3 \ldots$) away from a core that is common to a series of compounds. In combination with partial least squares the descriptor was applied to several datasets for QSAR studies, comprising of benzodiazepin-2-ones active at $GABA_A$, triazines exhibiting anticoccidal activity and a set of tropanes active at serine, dopamine and norepinephrine transporters. RGDss in combination with PLS showed comparable performance overall to HQSAR and EVA models in a cross-validation study, in some cases outperforming the other QSAR approaches.

Another alignment-free method for the time-efficient generation of QSAR models is Fingal [18] (a short and straightforward acronym for 'Fingerprint Algorithm'). Unlike RGDs, a hashed fingerprint is generated which encodes structural features of the molecule, where distances may be measured either topologically or by employing spatial information between atoms. Applied to D2 ligands, the 2D version of Fingal, in particular, was able to outperform CoMFA- and CoMSIA-based approaches. For estrogen ligands, performance was highly dependent on the structural class of compounds, not only for Fingal but also for models based on CoMFA, HQSAR, FRED/SKEYS (Fast Random Elimination of Descriptors/Substructure Keys) and Dragon descriptors. In subsets such as a pesticide subset, no model was obtained via CoMFA (correlation coefficient of zero), whereas Fingal gave correlation coefficients as high as 0.85 in a cross-validation study.

The GRID force field [19] has been the basis of a number of descriptors developed recently, among the best-known ones being the GRIND descriptor [20]. Some extensions of the descriptor have been presented recently, which include the incorporation of shape [21] into the descriptor. It was recognized that molecular shape is a major factor determining ligand–receptor binding, a property that was previously not emphasized enough by the original GRIND descriptors. This was due to the fact that only maximum products of interactions are incorporated into the descriptor, omitting large lipophilic features which do not contribute significantly to calculated interaction energies with probes, but might still have profound influence on binding through steric effects. Introducing the new 'TIP' probe (which is not a probe in the traditional sense but a measure of curvature of the molecular surface) led to significant improvements in QSAR studies of adenosine receptor antagonists (of the xanthine structural class) and *Plasmodium falciparum* plasmepsin inhibitors being observed. Interestingly, TIP–TIP correlations were also found to be the most significant descriptors in case of A_1 antagonists, showing the importance of the shape descriptor on this class. The second development was the 'anchor-GRIND' approach [22], which focuses on user-defined features to calculate a distribution of interaction points relative to it, thereby incorporating pre-existing biological knowledge about a target. Models are found to be both of better quality and easier to interpret on congeneric series of hepatitis C virus NS3 protease and of acetylcholinesterase inhibitors, as well as more discriminatory between factor Xa inhibitors of both high and low affinity. A virtual screening methodology also based on the GRID force field was developed recently [23]. This method was validated on a large dataset containing thrombin inhibitors and also showed potential to select suitable replacements for scaffolds typically encountered in the lead optimization stage.

A molecular 'descriptor' which actually does not employ an explicit transformation of the molecular structure into descriptor space was recently presented [24]. It employs a graph kernel description of the structure in combination with support vector machines (SVMs) for regression analysis. The computational burden is alleviated through employing a Morgan index process as well as the definition of a second-order Markov model for random walks on 2D structures. The method was then validated on two mutagenicity datasets. While already exhibiting the ability to capture molecular features responsible for bioactivity (here mutagenicity) in its current form, future developments might include more abstract representations of the molecular scaffold such as some form of reduced graph representation.

While the bioinformatics area has a multitude of methods which can be applied to the analysis on 1D representations of protein sequences and DNA, due to branching and cyclization the case is far more difficult for small molecules. One of the few 1D representations of molecules [25], based on multidimensional scaling of the structure from 3D into 1D space, has more recently been extended to allow for the alignment of multiple structures [26]. Applied to SKC kinase ligands as well as hERG channel blockers, significant improvement in retrieval rates could be observed in a retrospective study if multiple (in this case 10) ligands were used for screening. The concept of Feature Trees was also recently extended to allow for the incorporation of knowledge derived from multiple ligands into a single query [27], and retrospective screening results on ACE inhibitors as well as adrenergic α_{1a} receptor ligands showed considerable improvements over searches using single queries, both in terms of enrichments as well as the diversity of structures identified.

When structures are encoded in a discrete fashion, 'binning' is often employed in order to convert real-valued distance ranges into binary presence/absence features. This approach is followed in, for example, the CATS autocorrelation descriptor in its 3D version (CATS3D) [28]. However, binning borders may introduce artifacts such that feature distances close to each other but on opposites sides of bin borders being perceived to be as different from each other (simply since features do not match) as much more distant features. Accordingly, a related descriptor termed 'SQUID' was recently introduced which incorporates a variable degree of fuzziness [29]. Applied to Cox-2 ligands considerable retrieval improvement was observed, with best performance at intermediate degrees of fuzziness. Using Cox-2 ligands as well as thrombin inhibitors in combination with graph-based potential pharmacophore point triangles, typed according to interaction types, features responsible for ligand-target binding could be identified [30]. In addition, prospective screening was performed and a benzimidazole identified as a potent Cox-2 inhibitor was experimentally found to be active in a cellular assay with high affinity ($IC_{50} = 200$ nm).

The ultimate descriptor, in the realm of virtual screening, is the response of the biological system. While structure-derived descriptors are quick and (usually) easy to calculate, they are not the final goal – it is the effect that the compound has in a 'real world' setting. Using those biological effects as descriptors, namely percent inhibition values across a range of 92 targets for a number of 1567 molecules, the 'biospectra similarity' (the similarity of effects on the respective targets) was established via hierarchical clustering [31]. It was found that biospectra similarity provides a solid descriptor for forecasting activities of novel compounds and this was validated by removal of some important target classes after which clustering of compounds was overall still very stable. While the response of single targets is already a step toward biology, protein readouts of cell cultures [32] also incorporate cell signaling networks, thus stepping even closer to whole organism systems (of course at the price of increased complexity and cost involved). Also based on biological response data (phenotypic screening) a 'class scoring' technique was recently developed [33], which does not assign binary (hit/non-hit) activities to individual compounds but to classes of compounds instead. This way, more robust assignments are achieved as well as a lower number of false-positive predictions.

2.2. Data analysis and model generation

SVMs have been previously used for distinguishing, for example, between drug- and non-drug-like structures [34] and recently have been applied in virtual screening [35,36]. Using DRAGON descriptors and a modification of the traditional SVM to rank molecules (instead of just classifying them), performance was in this study [35] validated on inhibitors (or ligands) of cyclin-dependent kinase 2, cyclooxygenase 2, factor Xa, phosphodiesterase-5 and of the α_{1a} adrenoceptor. Compared to methods such as Binary Kernel Discrimination in combination with JChem fingerprints the new approach was found to be superior. The ability of lead hopping was also demonstrated recently through the combination of SVMs with 3D pharmacophore fingerprints (defined as SMARTs queries) [36].

There is a trend in the recent cheminformatics literature toward ensemble methods, i.e., methods where multiple models (instead of a single model) are generated and used together (as an ensemble) to make either qualitative or quantitative predictions about new instances. Random Forests [37] are an ensemble of unpruned classification or regression trees created by bootstrapping of the training data and random feature selection during tree induction. Prediction is then made by majority vote or averaging the predictions of the ensemble. On a set of diverse datasets (blood–brain-barrier penetration, estrogen-binding, P-glycoprotein-activity, multidrug-resistance reversal-activity and activity against COX-2 and dopamine receptors) superior results to methods such as decision trees and PLS were reported. More recently, 'Boosting' was applied to the same (and additional) datasets [38], and as a general rule this new method seems to be slightly superior in large regression tasks, whereas Random Forests are claimed to excel in classification problems. Additionally, employing k-nearest neighbor classifiers, SVMs and ridge regression in an ensemble approach [39] gave significant improvement over single classifiers on a 'frequent hitter' dataset.

Most models derived in QSAR studies, for example, ordinary and partial least-squares regression or principal components regression, employ a linear parametric part and a random error part, the latter of which is assumed to show independent random distributions for each descriptor. However, since molecular descriptors never capture 'complete' information about a molecule, this independence assumption is often not valid. Kriging [40] has replaced the independent errors by, for example, Gaussian processes. Applied to a boiling point dataset and compared to other regression methods (ordinary and partial least-squares and principal component regression) improved performance could be observed.

Alongside model generation, feature selection is also an important step in many studies. Since no perfect descriptors of the molecular system are known, often a multitude of descriptors (often several thousands) are calculated and it is hoped that they capture information, which is relevant to the respective classification or regression task.

A comparative study of feature selection methods in drug design appeared recently [41], which compares information gain, mutual information, χ^2-test, odds ratio and the GSS coefficient (named after the authors, Galavotti, Sebastiani and Simi; a simplified version of the χ^2-test) in combination with the Naïve Bayes Classifier as well as SVMs. While SVMs were found overall to perform favorably in higher-dimensional feature spaces (and do not benefit much from feature selection), feature selection is found to be a crucial step for the Bayes Classifier. (Note that this has at the same time been shown empirically in virtual screening experiments

[42,43].) Some of the methods, namely mutual information and genetic programing, have also been evaluated separately for their use in QSAR studies [44] with respect to a dataset which showed some (typical) problems present in the area, such as a very different sizes of 'active' vs. 'inactive' data subsets.

The problem that structure-activity relationships are rarely linear has been addressed previously through the application of nonlinear methods [45,46] such as k-nearest neighbor approaches [47,48]. More recently, k-nn has also been combined with a CoMFA-like approach, termed k-NN MFA, to predict bioactivity of a compound based on its k-nearest neighbors in 'field space' [49]. As discussed by the authors, some of the disadvantages of CoMFA such as alignment problems are retained; nonetheless, multiple models are produced in each run, giving more room for appropriate model selection. Removing limitations of the statistical model is possible using non-parametric models which have recently been used in QSAR studies [50] and were shown to improve results over more conventional regression-type models. Also Bayesian Regularized Networks have been found to be of interest in recent QSAR studies [51–53]. Those networks possess inherent advantages including that they run less risk of being overtrained than non-Bayesian networks (since more complex models are punished by default).

2.3. New properties of old methods

The effect of binary representations of fingerprints has been known for some time, such as combinatorial preferences [54] and size effects [55] (depending on the similarity coefficient used). More recently, another aspect of the binary representation of features in a fingerprint has been analyzed [56]. Integer or real-valued representations of feature vectors were calculated for 12 activity classes and employed CATS2D and CATS3D autocorrelation descriptors as well as Ghose and Crippen fragment descriptors. Afterward, retrospective virtual screening calculations were performed for both the original (quantitative) representations and the binary (presence/absence) fingerprints. Surprisingly, in only 2 out of the 12 cases did significantly different numbers of actives get retrieved (defined as more than 20% difference). In addition, the retrieved actives showed, depending on the activity class, very different overlap, between 0% and 90%, indicating some orthogonality of the same descriptor, differing by its representation (integer/real-values vs. binary format).

Exploiting the 'molecular similarity principle' by not only looking for neighbors of an active compound and assuming they are active (as is usually done in virtual screening) but also using this knowledge further to improve the model, has recently been exploited in a method called 'Turbo Similarity Searching' [57]. By feeding back information about the nearest neighbors of an active compound into the model generation step, an increased number of active compounds can be retrieved in a subsequent step. This is analogous to the re-use of hot air in turbo chargers in cars, where the output (hot gas, nearest neighbor in this case) is fed back into the loop to improve performance.

3. METHOD VALIDATION

A number of publications have appeared recently focusing on the validation of QSAR models. A wealth of parameters exist here, such as training/test/validation set splits, the dimensionality of descriptors used in relation to the number of degrees of freedom of a model, or the way selection of features is performed.

While it has been recognized for some time that a larger number of descriptors increases the likelihood of chance correlations [58], more recently a discussion of the validity of statistical significance tests, such as the F test, has appeared [59] which puts the number of features considered into relation to the significance of a model. This study cautions in agreement with earlier work that one needs to be very careful when judging the statistical significance of correlation models if feature selection is applied – and that statistically 'significant' models can hardly be 'avoided' if too large a variable pool is chosen to select features in the first place.

Since datasets are generally limited in size, a suitable split into training and test set(s) is crucial in order to achieve sufficient training examples on the one hand, and as high as possible a predictivity of the model on the other. Often, leave-one-out cross-validation has been used to judge model performance – where the compound 'left out' was supposed to be a novel compound found for which property predictions had to be made. Unfortunately this is, according to recent studies, not a suitable validation method [60,61]. In the case of leave-one-out cross-validation, where features are selected from a wider range, the tendency exists in every case to select those features which perform best on a particular compound – thus decreasing generalizability of the model. Results were summarized in a simple statement: 'Beware of q^2!', where specifically the cross-validated correlation coefficient of a leave-one-out cross-validation is alluded to. In addition, general guidelines for developing robust QSAR models were developed, namely a high cross-validated correlation coefficient and a regression, which shows slope close to 1 and no significant bias.

Using theoretical considerations as well as empirical evaluations the question of leave-one-out vs. separate test sets was recently considered in detail [62]. Performing repeated cross-validations of both types on a large QSAR dataset, the conclusion was drawn that in the case of smaller datasets, separate test sets are wasteful, but in case of larger datasets (at least large three-digit numbers of data points) it is recommended. This partly contradicts the above conclusion, that separate test sets should always be used. The discrepancy was explained by the fact that in the earlier work only small separate test sets were used (containing 10 compounds), which was not able to provide a sufficiently reliable performance measure.

The finding that cross-validation often overestimates model performance was corroborated in a recent related study [63], in particular, in cases where strong model selection such as variable selection is applied. The main influence on quality overestimation was found to be a (small) dataset size; other factors are the size of the variable pool considered, the object-to-variable-ratio, the variable selection method, and the correlation structure of the underlying data matrix. While in case of conventional stepwise variable selection overconfidence is commonly encountered, as a remedy LASSO (least absolute shrinking and selection operator) selection is proposed, as well as the utilization of ensemble averaging. Both techniques give more reliable estimates of the quality of the developed model. Given that the latter was shown to improve performance in many cases on its own the generation of reliable performance measures is an additional advantage of ensemble techniques.

Overfitting is a problem which describes good model performance on a training set but much worse performance on subsequent data, and thus, mediocre generalizability of the model (the model is not robust). A recent discussion of this problem, with many accessible examples, gives similar guidelines to those above, such as that leave-one-out cross-validation is not sufficient [64]. It also emphasizes the recommendation of multiple training/test set splits even in the case of very large dataset sizes and of performing cross-validation across classes of compounds in the case of close analogues (instead of molecule-by-molecule splits). In order to have some measure of overfitting, the use of 'benchmark models' such as partial least squares is recommended (depending on the particular problem) in order to determine whether there might be simpler models appropriate to the task (indicating that the more complex model overfits the data).

Using a toxicity dataset of phenols against *Tetrahymena pyriformis* [65] the conclusion that q^2 is not a sufficient predictor for the applicability of a QSAR model to unseen compounds is corroborated, and suggests using the RMS error of prediction (RMSEP) instead. This guideline is presented along with additional important points: that outliers should not necessarily be deleted since this step reduces the chemical space covered by the model, that the number of descriptors in a multivariate model needs to be chosen carefully and finally that an 'appropriate' number of dimensions is required for PLS modeling. In addition, the influence of the number of variables on predictive performance for training and test sets is investigated.

Several recent publications have attempted to investigate what the actual scope of a QSAR model is – and attempted to develop guidelines to assess the applicability of a model to a novel compound whose properties are to be predicted [66,67]. Two measures for applicability are proposed: the similarity of the novel molecule to the nearest molecule in the training set and the number of neighbors of the novel compound within the training set with a similarity greater than a certain cutoff. As expected, molecules with the highest similarity are best predicted, and this was found to be true across datasets as well as across methods. The applicability measures described above can also be used numerically to derive error bars for estimations of how likely the prediction of a specific model is within a certain error threshold. The issue of model validity was also briefly reviewed from a regulatory viewpoint [68]. In a similar vein, a 'classification approach' has been presented for determining the validity of a QSAR model for predicting properties of a novel compound [69]. Focusing on linear models (though the underlying concept is more generally applicable), the predictions made for compounds within the initial training set are differentiated between 'good residuals' and 'bad residuals'. Using three different datasets (an artemisinin dataset as well as two boiling point datasets) machine-learning methods were employed to predict whether a novel compound belongs to the 'good' or 'bad' class of residuals, thereby making predictions as to whether its properties can be predicted – with a success rate of between 73% and 94%. A stepwise approach for determining model applicability [70] considers physicochemical properties, structural properties, a mechanistic understanding of the phenomenon and, if applicable, the reliability of simulated metabolism in a step-by-step manner. With several QSAR datasets, it could be shown that for substances that are well covered by the training set improved predictions can be made for novel compounds, in agreement with the conclusions stated above.

The performance of similarity searching methods varies widely, comprising both target- and ligand-based approaches. While large enrichment factors (often in the hundreds) are reported, the question arises of how much 'added value' more sophisticated methods actually provide, compared to very simple approaches, and where the gain-to-cost ratio actually shows an optimum. A recent study illustrated that simple 'atom count descriptors' (which do not capture any structural knowledge but represent a molecule by a set of integers which represent the number of atoms of each element) are able to have comparable performance to state-of-the-art fingerprints [6]. Thus, when averaged over multiple target classes, the added value of virtual screening approaches is probably closer to two (compared to trivial descriptors) than in the region of often published double-digit numbers (compared to random selection). It should be added that performance of 'dumb' and more sophisticated descriptors varied widely, between virtually no difference in performance up to high single-digit performance improvements of state-of-the-art fingerprints (which are, with respect to retrieval rate and on a MDDR-dataset, circular fingerprint descriptors).

4. 'GETTING MORE FROM YOUR DATA'

4.1. Analysis of high-throughput screening data

HTS results are notorious for the amount of noise they contain and methods such as multiple screening runs are routinely applied to alleviate the problem. Still, additional experiments are required. An alternative method was recently presented [71] which, applying purely computational methods, is able to predict truly active compounds with improved reliability in screenings where multiple compounds are screened per well. Using Scitegic circular fingerprints [72], similarities between molecules in wells containing compounds predicted as being active (which may be true positives or, often, just noise) are calculated. The compounds most similar to active compounds are more likely to be active themselves; by predicting (across wells) those compounds which are similar to each other and at the same time are located in wells showing activity, the active compounds out of the mixtures can be estimated. This way, between 29% and 41% of the active compounds could be retrieved in the top 10% of the sorted compounds.

Another approach which attempts to improve knowledge derived from HTS campaigns was recently proposed [73]; the conventional selection of a fixed number of compounds showing activity in a primary screen is replaced for secondary screens ('Top X approach'). Alternatively, methods based on partitioning are frequently employed. In the approach presented here, an ontology-based pattern identification method is employed, which originated from bioinformatics methods (the prediction of gene function based on microarray data). Taking scaffold diversity into account and also applying the 'molecular similarity principle', the overall probability of selecting active compounds from different clusters is maximized. Based on earlier HTS data, significant improvement of hit confirmation rates was demonstrated, compared to a conventional 'Top X' approach. Related work was recently also performed with a focus on scaffold clustering [74].

As discussed below, scoring functions are not yet able to predict binding affinities sufficiently well across the board of target proteins. Still, the identification of active ligands was shown to be improved by a second data post-processing step. First, ligands are docked to the target. Subsequently, predicted active and inactive compounds are subject to model generation via a Naïve Bayesian model [75] based on circular fingerprints. Applied to protein kinase B and protein-tyrosine phosphatase 1B, significant performance improvements could be observed in combination with Dock, FlexX as well as Glide scores on protein-tyrosine phosphatase 1B. On the other hand, results on protein kinase B results were not improved, which was attributed to the fact that the predicted actives used to train the model were 100% false positives. Understandably, performance cannot be improved if the initial enrichments are not able to identify true positive binders. More recently, another step was introduced between scoring and selecting active and inactive compounds for training the Bayes Classifier [76], which is one of the available consensus scoring methods. Since consensus scoring is often able to rescue docking results in cases where a specific scoring function fails, rank-by-median consensus scoring was shown to improve results for protein kinase B considerably. Other consensus approaches (rank-by-mean, and rank-by-vote) did not perform as well. This was attributed to their sensitivity to cases where one of the scoring functions performs badly. (The median of a set of numbers is less sensitive to outliers than its mean.)

An alternative method for post-processing docking scores is the Post-DOCK approach whose final goal is the elimination of false-positive predictions and their discrimination from artifacts [77]. Based on a ligand-target database, derived descriptors (DOCK score, empirical scoring and buried solvent accessible surface area) and models from machine-learning methods were derived to identify false-positive predictions. Validating the method on 44 structurally diverse targets (plus the same number of decoy complexes), 39 of 44 binding and only 2 of 44 complexes were predicted to be of true-positive nature. Compared to purely docking-based methods, DOCK and ChemScore achieve enrichments on the order of five to seven, depending upon the database used, while the method presented here claims to obtain about 19-fold enrichment.

4.2. Consensus predictions

Consensus prediction of docking scores is often able to improve results over single functions and multiple ways have been proposed to combine scores from different functions such as rank-by-rank, rank-by-vote or rank-by-number [78]. Performance improvement could not be observed in every case and a theoretical study [79] to elucidate the way in which consensus scoring improves results, concluded that this was due to the simple reason that multiple samplings of a distribution are closer to its true mean than single samplings. Assumptions made by the study, such as the performance of each individual scoring function is comparable, have led to the work later being criticized [80], and it has been concluded that consensus scoring *can* improve results but that it is not true in every case (as observed in practice). More recently, it was demonstrated [81] that two criteria are important if consensus scoring is to be successful: first, each individual scoring function has to be of high quality, and second, the scoring functions need to be distinctive. Even if no training data are available to judge those points, rank-vs.-score plots were proposed to gauge the success of target-based virtual screening against a particular target.

While consensus predictions for ligand-based virtual screening have been known for some time, a more recent study extended the descriptors employed to include structural, 2D pharmacophore and property-based fingerprints as well as BCUT descriptors and 3D pharmacophores [82]. Logistic regression and rank-by-sum consensus approaches were found to be most advantageous due to repeated samplings, better clustering of actives (since multiple sampling will recover more actives than inactives) and agreement of methods to predict actives but less so inactives. In addition, more stable performance across a range of targets was observed.

If multiple active compounds are known in a virtual screening setting, the question arises of how to combine the retrieved lists of individual compounds. Applied to different activity classes from the MDL Drug Data Report as well as the Natural Products Database [83] it was recently found that the rank-by-max method generally outperforms the rank-by-sum method, while concluding that the Tanimoto coefficient is superior to 10 other similarity coefficients considered. As to the applicability of consensus approaches, it is found that more dissimilar activity classes profit more than more homogeneous classes, where best retrieval performance is already obtained using lower numbers of query structures (which are then already able to cover the 'activity island' inhabited by the particular class of compounds).

5. APPLICATIONS

5.1. Virtual screening

While many applications of virtual screening tools have appeared in the literature, only some examples can be given here.

A phosphodiesterase-4 (PDE4) inhibitor recently has been optimized through the application of small combinatorial libraries [84]. Affinity was increased by three orders of magnitude by screening only 320 compounds after prioritization by FlexX docking. Following the recent SARS scare, a virtual screening procedure via docking (DOCK program) was able to find inhibitors of SARS coronavirus 3C-like proteinase with binding affinities of $K_i = 61 \, \mu M$ out of 40 compounds tested [85]. Virtual screening based on a homology model of the neurokinin-1 (NK1) receptor led to the discovery of submicromolar ligands [86], while even nanomolar binding compounds against Checkpoint kinase 1 (CHK1) could be discovered [87] by applying successive filtering for physicochemical properties, pharmacophore filters and docking stages. Ligand-based pharmacophore models generated by Catalyst [88] were used to discover nanomolar ligands of ERG2, emopamil-binding protein (EBP), and the sigma-1 receptor (σ_1) [89]. Out of 11 compounds tested, 3 exhibited affinities of less than 60 nM. High levels of biliary elimination of a CCK2 antagonist led to the quest for novel compounds, which retained activity and selectivity while improving half-life. Using field points derived from XED charges [90], novel heterocycles were proposed [91] (switching from an indole to pyrrole and imidazole series), which decreased molecular weight and polarity and achieved the desired scaffold hop.

Apart from this list of applications against particular targets, only two further applications shall be described here (since the field is simply too large to capture it in its entirety). First, ligand- and target-based approaches were recently compared in their abilities to identify ligands for G-protein coupled receptors [92]. Evaluating docking into homology models, ligand-based pharmacophore models and Feature Trees, 3D similarity searches as well as models built on 2D descriptors, all ligand-based techniques were shown to outperform the docking-based approaches. However, docking also provided significant enrichment.

Second, the 'HTS Data Mining and Docking Competition' presented its results recently [93–95]. Duplicate residual activities of 50,000 compounds against *Escherichia coli* DHFR in primary screening were released in late 2003 [96], upon which 42 groups submitted activity predictions for a test set of the same size (but with unknown activity). Approaches employed ranged from docking [97,98] to purely ligand-based methods [99,100]. Overall, none of them was able to predict actives from the test set reliably. While this was partly due to difference in chemical composition of the training and test sets, an additional problem was posed by the test set which did not contain real 'actives' (showing proper dose-response curves in secondary assays), thus making predictions difficult.

5.2. Clustering

Several novel clustering algorithms have been presented recently, each of which extends previous approaches in its own way. A combination of fingerprint and maximum common substructure (MCS) descriptors [101] speed up clustering (compared to purely MCS methods) enabling its application to large datasets, and the method was shown to be able to identify the most frequent scaffolds in databases, to select analogues of screening hits and to prioritize chemical vendor libraries. A modification of k-means clustering also showed a considerable speed increase to be possible when processing large libraries [102], as demonstrated on a dataset containing about 60,000 compounds derived from the MDDR. The desired speed-up was observed along with favorable enrichment of activity classes within the clusters. By introducing fuzziness into the clustering process [103], superior results can be obtained compared to the original (non-fuzzy or 'crisp') approaches to k-means and Ward clustering, depending on the particular dataset and the property one attempts to predict. Fuzzy clustering assigns partial memberships to multiple classes (instead of binary values); with a log P dataset the best fuzzy parameterization was shown to clearly outperform the best crisp clustering. In addition, partial class memberships were shown to capture the 'chemical character' of a compound more satisfyingly than conventional (crisp) class assignments.

5.3. Drug-likeness and comparison of databases

While the concept of 'drug-likeness' has to be applied with care (and one needs to be aware of its limitations) it has nonetheless received considerable attention in recent years, based on datasets derived from the Available Chemicals Directory (ACD) and the World Drug Index (WDI). First applications employed Ghose/Crippen descriptors in combination with neural networks for classification, and correct classification was achieved for 83% of the ACD and 77% of the WDI, respectively [104]. Later, the application of SVMs was not able to improve overall performance significantly, but the new method was able to correctly classify compounds that were misclassified by the ANN-based technique [34]. Very recently a further analysis of the drug/non-drug dataset appeared, which analyzed SVM performance (as well as that of other machine-learning methods) in more detail [105]. It was found that, in spite of problems with the dataset (some descriptor representations of compounds were, for example, identical in the drug and non-drug dataset) performance could be improved considerably to about 7% misclassified compounds by optimizing the kernel dimensions employed. An application using 'human-understandable' descriptors of drug- vs. non-drug-like properties has also been presented [106] recently, and was able to distinguish between both datasets with the most important descriptors being proper saturation level and the heteroatom-to-carbon ratio of the molecule. The concept of database comparison is also more generally applicable, as was shown recently when the question of how 'in-house like' external databases are was addressed in order to help to decide whether they should be acquired or not [107].

5.4. Docking validations

A number of validations of docking programs have appeared recently, and it is interesting to observe that they grow in size in every respect – including the number of docking and scoring functions considered as well as the number and diversity of ligand-target complexes employed for their evaluation.

Using DOCK, GOLD and GLIDE in order to evaluate the performance of docking programs in target-based virtual screening on five targets (HIV protease, protein tyrosine phosphatase 1B, thrombin, urokinase plasminogen activator and the human homologue of the mouse double minute 2 oncoprotein), it was concluded that performance is both target- and method-dependent [108]. Performance varied widely, between near-perfect behavior (for example, GOLD in combination with protein tyrosine phosphatase 1b) to negative enrichment (for example, GOLD with HIV protease). Employing FRED, DOCK and Surflex, and adopting the algorithm to the particular binding pocket, it was found that target-based virtual screening is successful in some cases [109], with Surflex probably performing the best overall.

Investigating phosphodiesterase 4B [110] and a set of 19 known inhibitors with 1980 decoys, the scoring functions PMF, JAIN, PLP2, LigScore2 and DockScore were compared with respect to their ability to enrich known ligands. It was found that PMF and JAIN showed high-enrichment factors (greater than four-fold) alone, while a rank-based consensus-scoring scheme employing PMF and JAIN in combination with either DockScore or PLP2 showed more robust results.

In what is probably one of the most extensive studies yet, 14 scoring functions in combination with 800 protein–ligand complexes from the PDBbind database have been compared for evaluation [111]. The scoring functions compared were X-Score and DrugScore, five scoring functions implemented in Sybyl (ChemScore, D-, F- and G-Score and PMF-Score), four implemented in Cerius2 (LigScore, LUDI, PLP and PMF) as well as two scoring functions implemented in GOLD (GoldScore and ChemScore) as well as the HINT function. Performance was assessed by their ability predicting affinity (K_i/K_d values). Overall, X-Score, DrugScore, Sybyl with ChemScore and Cerius2 with PLP performed better than the other combinations, giving standard deviations in the range of 1.8–2.0 log units.

Another very comprehensive evaluation [112] employed 10 docking programs in combination with 37 scoring functions against eight proteins of seven types. Three criteria were used for assessment, namely the ability to predict binding modes, to predict ligands with high affinity and to correctly rank-order ligands by affinity. While nearly all programs were able to generate crystallographic ligand-target complexes, the identification of the correct structure by the scoring function was found to be considerably more error-prone. Averaged over all targets, none of the programs was able to predict more than 35% of the ligands within an RMSD of equal to or less than 2 Å. While active compounds were correctly identified, activity prediction was more difficult – to the extent that 'for the eight proteins of seven evolutionarily diverse target types studied in this evaluation, no statistically significant relationship existed between docking scores and ligand affinity' [112]. Similar results were obtained on five datasets (serine, aspartic and metalloproteinases, sugar-binding proteins and a 'miscellaneous' set) using the scoring functions Bleep, PMF, GOLD and ChemScore [113], where across all complexes on average no function returned a better correlation than $r^2 = 0.32$.

Interestingly, another recent study drew quite different conclusions from similar observations [114]. Docking endogenous ligands into a panel of proteins it was concluded that proteins are often very promiscuous and do not interact with only a single clearly defined small molecule. While this is surely possible, given the limitations of today's scoring functions it might well be the case that predictions are just not yet good enough.

6. CONCLUSIONS AND OUTLOOK

While a great number of descriptors and modeling methods has been proposed until today, the recent trend toward proper model validation is very much appreciated. Applications of the 'Molecular Similarity Principle' do not yet show the power one would like them to have – and although some of their limitations are surely due to underlying principles and limitations of fundamental concepts, others will certainly be eliminated in the future.

REFERENCES

[1] M. A. Johnson and G. M. Maggiora, *Concepts and Applications of Molecular Similarity*, Wiley, New York, 1990.

[2] P. Willett, J. M. Barnard and G. M. Downs, Chemical similarity searching, *J. Chem. Inf. Comput. Sci.*, 1998, **38**, 983–996.

[3] N. Nikolova and J. Jaworska, Approaches to measure chemical similarity – a review, *QSAR Comb. Sci.*, 2004, **22**, 1006–1026.

[4] A. Bender and R. C. Glen, Molecular similarity: a key technique in molecular informatics, *Org. Biomol. Chem.*, 2004, **2**, 3204–3218.

[5] R. S. Bohacek, C. McMartin and W. C. Guida, The art and practice of structure-based drug design: a molecular modeling perspective, *Med. Res. Rev.*, 1996, **16**, 3–50.

[6] A. Bender and R. C. Glen, A discussion of measures of enrichment in virtual screening: comparing the information content of descriptors with increasing levels of sophistication, *J. Chem. Inf. Model.*, 2005, **45**, 1369–1375.

[7] H. Briem and U. Lessel, *In vitro* and *in silico* affinity fingerprints: finding similarities beyond structural classes, *Perspect. Drug Discov. Des.*, 2000, **20**, 231–244.

[8] J. Hert, P. Willett and D. J. Wilton, Comparison of fingerprint-based methods for virtual screening using multiple bioactive reference structures, *J. Chem. Inf. Comput. Sci.*, 2004, **44**, 1177–1185.

[9] J. W. Godden, F. L. Stahura and J. Bajorath, POT-DMC: a virtual screening method for the identification of potent hits, *J. Med. Chem.*, 2004, **47**, 5608–5611.

[10] J. L. Jenkins, M. Glick and J. W. Davies, A 3D similarity method for scaffold hopping from the known drugs or natural ligands to new chemotypes, *J. Med. Chem.*, 2004, **47**, 6144–6159.

[11] D. Vidal, M. Thormann and M. Pons, LINGO, an efficient holographic text based method to calculate biophysical properties and intermolecular similarities, *J. Chem. Inf. Model.*, 2005, **45**, 386–393.

[12] G. Harper, G. S. Bravi, S. D. Pickett, J. Hussain and D. V. S. Green, The reduced graph descriptor in virtual screening and data-driven clustering of high-throughput screening data, *J. Chem. Inf. Comput. Sci.*, 2004, **44**, 2145–2156.

[13] J. A. Haigh, B. T. Pickup, J. A. Grant and A. Nicholls, Small molecule shape-fingerprints, *J. Chem. Inf. Model.*, 2005, **45**, 673–684.

[14] J. Wu, R. Tillett, N. McFarlane, X. Ju, J. P. Siebert and P. Schofield, Extracting the three-dimensional shape of live pigs using stereo photogrammetry, *Comput. Electron. Agricult.*, 2004, **44**, 203–222.

[15] C. H. Chae, S. E. Yoo and W. Shin, Novel receptor surface approach for 3D-QSAR: the weighted probe interaction energy method, *J. Chem. Inf. Comput. Sci.*, 2004, **44**, 1774–1787.

[16] J. D. Holliday, S. P. Jelfs, P. Willett and P. Gedeck, Calculation of intersubstituent similarity using R-group descriptors, *J. Chem. Inf. Comput. Sci.*, 2003, **43**, 406–411.

[17] L. Hirons, J. D. Holliday, S. P. Jelfs, P. Willett and P. Gedeck, Use of the R-group descriptor for alignment-free QSAR, *QSAR Comb. Sci.*, 2005, **24**, 611–619.

[18] N. Brown, B. McKay and J. Gasteiger, Fingal: a novel approach to geometric fingerprinting and a comparative study of its application to 3D-QSAR modelling, *QSAR Comb. Sci.*, 2005, **24**, 480–484.

[19] P. J. Goodford, A computational procedure for determining energetically favorable binding sites on biologically important macromolecules, *J. Med. Chem.*, 1985, **28**, 849–857.

[20] M. Pastor, G. Cruciani, I. McLay, S. Pickett and S. Clementi, GRid-INdependent descriptors (GRIND): a novel class of alignment-independent three-dimensional molecular descriptors, *J. Med. Chem.*, 2000, **43**, 3233–3243.

[21] F. Fontaine, M. Pastor and F. Sanz, Incorporating molecular shape into the alignment-free Grid-Independent Descriptors, *J. Med. Chem.*, 2004, **47**, 2805–2815.

[22] F. Fontaine, M. Pastor, I. Zamora and F. Sanz, Anchor-GRIND: Filling the gap between standard 3D QSAR and the GRid-INdependent Descriptors, *J. Med. Chem.*, 2005, **48**, 2687–2694.

[23] M. M. Ahlstrom, M. Ridderstrom, K. Luthman and I. Zamora, Virtual screening and scaffold hopping based on GRID molecular interaction fields, *J. Chem. Inf. Model.*, 2005, **45**, 1313–1323.

[24] P. Mahe, N. Ueda, T. Akutsu, J. L. Perret and J. P. Vert, Graph kernels for molecular structure-activity relationship analysis with support vector machines, *J. Chem. Inf. Model.*, 2005, **45**, 939–951.

[25] S. L. Dixon and K. M. Merz, Jr., One-dimensional molecular representations and similarity calculations: methodology and validation, *J. Med. Chem.*, 2001, **44**, 3795–3809.

[26] N. Wang, R. K. Delisle and D. J. Diller, Fast small molecule similarity searching with multiple alignment profiles of molecules represented in one-dimension, *J. Med. Chem.*, 2005, **48**, 6980–6990.

[27] G. Hessler, M. Zimmermann, H. Matter, A. Evers, T. Naumann, T. Lengauer and M. Rarey, Multiple-ligand-based virtual screening: methods and applications of the MTree approach, *J. Med. Chem.*, 2005, **48**, 6575–6584.

[28] U. Fechner, L. Franke, S. Renner, P. Schneider and G. Schneider, Comparison of correlation vector methods for ligand-based similarity searching, *J. Comput.-Aided Mol. Des.*, 2003, **17**, 687–698.

[29] S. Renner and G. Schneider, Fuzzy pharmacophore models from molecular alignments for correlation-vector-based virtual screening, *J. Med. Chem.*, 2004, **47**, 4653–4664.

[30] L. Franke, E. Byvatov, O. Werz, D. Steinhilber, P. Schneider and G. Schneider, Extraction and visualization of potential pharmacophore points using support vector machines: application to ligand-based virtual screening for COX-2 inhibitors, *J. Med. Chem.*, 2005, **48**, 6997–7004.

[31] A. F. Fliri, W. T. Loging, P. F. Thadeio and R. A. Volkmann, Biospectra analysis: model proteome characterizations for linking molecular structure and biological response, *J. Med. Chem.*, 2005, **48**, 6918–6925.

[32] E. C. Butcher, Can cell systems biology rescue drug discovery?, *Nat. Rev. Drug Discov.*, 2005, **4**, 461–467.

[33] J. Klekota, E. Brauner and S. L. Schreiber, Identifying biologically active compound classes using phenotypic screening data and sampling statistics, *J. Chem. Inf. Model.*, 2005, **45**, 1824–1836.

[34] E. Byvatov, U. Fechner, J. Sadowski and G. Schneider, Comparison of support vector machine and artificial neural network systems for drug/nondrug classification, *J. Chem. Inf. Comput. Sci.*, 2003, **43**, 1882–1889.

[35] R. N. Jorissen and M. K. Gilson, Virtual screening of molecular databases using a support vector machine, *J. Chem. Inf. Model.*, 2005, **45**, 549–561.

[36] J. C. Saeh, P. D. Lyne, B. K. Takasaki and D. A. Cosgrove, Lead hopping using SVM and 3D pharmacophore fingerprints, *J. Chem. Inf. Model.*, 2005, **45**, 1122–1133.

[37] V. Svetnik, A. Liaw, C. Tong, J. C. Culberson, R. P. Sheridan and B. P. Feuston, Random forest: a classification and regression tool for compound classification and QSAR modeling, *J. Chem. Inf. Comput. Sci.*, 2003, **43**, 1947–1958.

[38] V. Svetnik, T. Wang, C. Tong, A. Liaw, R. P. Sheridan and Q. Song, Boosting: an ensemble learning tool for compound classification and QSAR modeling, *J. Chem. Inf. Model.*, 2005, **45**, 786–799.

[39] C. Merkwirth, H. A. Mauser, T. Schulz-Gasch, O. Roche, M. Stahl and T. Lengauer, Ensemble methods for classification in cheminformatics, *J. Chem. Inf. Comput. Sci.*, 2004, **44**, 1971–1978.

[40] K. T. Fang, H. Yin and Y. Z. Liang, New approach by Kriging models to problems in QSAR, *J. Chem. Inf. Comput. Sci.*, 2004, **44**, 2106–2113.

[41] Y. Liu, A comparative study on feature selection methods for drug discovery, *J. Chem. Inf. Comput. Sci.*, 2004, **44**, 1823–1828.

[42] A. Bender, H. Y. Mussa, R. C. Glen and S. Reiling, Molecular similarity searching using atom environments, information-based feature selection, and a naive Bayesian classifier, *J. Chem. Inf. Comput. Sci.*, 2004, **44**, 170–178.

[43] A. Bender, H. Y. Mussa, R. C. Glen and S. Reiling, Similarity searching of chemical databases using atom environment descriptors (MOLPRINT 2D): evaluation of performance, *J. Chem. Inf. Comput. Sci.*, 2004, **44**, 1708–1718.

[44] V. Venkatraman, A. R. Dalby and Z. R. Yang, Evaluation of mutual information and genetic programming for feature selection in QSAR, *J. Chem. Inf. Comput. Sci.*, 2004, **44**, 1686–1692.

[45] P. Tino, I. T. Nabney, B. S. Williams, J. Losel and Y. Sun, Nonlinear prediction of quantitative structure-activity relationships, *J. Chem. Inf. Comput. Sci.*, 2004, **44**, 1647–1653.

[46] J. D. Hirst, Nonlinear quantitative structure-activity relationship for the inhibition of dihydrofolate reductase by pyrimidines, *J. Med. Chem.*, 1996, **39**, 3526–3532.

[47] W. F. Zheng and A. Tropsha, Novel variable selection quantitative structure-property relationship approach based on the k-nearest-neighbor principle, *J. Chem. Inf. Comput. Sci.*, 2000, **40**, 185–194.

[48] M. Shen, Y. D. Xiao, A. Golbraikh, V. K. Gombar and A. Tropsha, Development and validation of k-nearest-neighbor QSPR models of metabolic stability of drug candidates, *J. Med. Chem.*, 2003, **46**, 3013–3020.

[49] S. Ajmani, K. Jadhav and S. A. Kulkarni, Three-dimensional QSAR using the k-nearest neighbor method and its interpretation, *J. Chem. Inf. Model.*, 2006, **46**, 24–31.

[50] J. D. Hirst, T. J. McNeany, T. Howe and L. Whitehead, Application of non-parametric regression to quantitative structure-activity relationships, *Bioorg. Med. Chem.*, 2002, **10**, 1037–1041.

[51] F. R. Burden and D. A. Winkler, Robust QSAR models using Bayesian regularized neural networks, *J. Med. Chem.*, 1999, **42**, 3183–3187.

[52] F. R. Burden and D. A. Winkler, Predictive Bayesian neural network models of MHC class II peptide binding, *J. Mol. Graph. Model.*, 2005, **23**, 481–489.

[53] T. H. Wang, Y. Li, S. L. Yang and L. Yang, An *in silico* approach for screening flavonoids as P-glycoprotein inhibitors based on a Bayesian-regularized neural network, *J. Comput.-Aided Mol. Des.*, 2005, **19**, 137–147.

[54] J. W. Godden, L. Xue and J. Bajorath, Combinatorial preferences affect molecular similarity/diversity calculations using binary fingerprints and Tanimoto coefficients, *J. Chem. Inf. Comput. Sci.*, 2000, **40**, 163–166.

[55] J. D. Holliday, N. Salim, M. Whittle and P. Willett, Analysis and display of the size dependence of chemical similarity coefficients, *J. Chem. Inf. Comput. Sci.*, 2003, **43**, 819–828.

[56] U. Fechner, J. Paetz and G. Schneider, Comparison of three holographic fingerprint descriptors and their binary counterparts, *QSAR Comb. Sci.*, 2005, **24**, 961–967.

[57] J. Hert, P. Willett, D. J. Wilton, P. Acklin, K. Azzaoui, E. Jacoby and A. Schuffenhauer, Enhancing the effectiveness of similarity-based virtual screening using nearest-neighbor information, *J. Med. Chem.*, 2005, **48**, 7049–7054.

[58] J. G. Topliss and R. P. Edwards, Chance factors in studies of quantitative structure-activity relationships, *J. Med. Chem.*, 1979, **22**, 1238–1244.

[59] D. J. Livingstone and D. W. Salt, Judging the significance of multiple linear regression models, *J. Med. Chem.*, 2005, **48**, 661–663.

[60] A. Golbraikh, M. Shen, Z. Y. Xiao, Y. D. Xiao, K. H. Lee and A. Tropsha, Rational selection of training and test sets for the development of validated QSAR models, *J. Comput.-Aided Mol. Des.*, 2003, **17**, 241–253.

[61] A. Golbraikh and A. Tropsha, *Beware of q2! J. Mol. Graph. Model.*, 2002, **20**, 269–276.

[62] D. M. Hawkins, S. C. Basak and D. Mills, Assessing model fit by cross-validation, *J. Chem. Inf. Comput. Sci.*, 2003, **43**, 579–586.

[63] K. Baumann, Chance correlation in variable subset regression: influence of the objective function, the selection mechanism, and ensemble averaging, *QSAR Comb. Sci.*, 2005, **24**, 1033–1046.

[64] D. M. Hawkins, The problem of overfitting, *J. Chem. Inf. Comput. Sci.*, 2004, **44**, 1–12.

[65] A. O. Aptula, N. G. Jeliazkova, T. W. Schultz and M. T. D. Cronin, The better predictive model: high q(2) for the training set or low root mean square error of prediction for the test set?, *QSAR Comb. Sci.*, 2005, **24**, 385–396.

[66] L. He and P. C. Jurs, Assessing the reliability of a QSAR model's predictions, *J. Mol. Graph.*, 2005, **23**, 503–523.

[67] R. P. Sheridan, B. P. Feuston, V. N. Maiorov and S. K. Kearsley, Similarity to molecules in the training set is a good discriminator for prediction accuracy in QSAR, *J. Chem. Inf. Comput. Sci.*, 2004, **44**, 1912–1928.

[68] J. D. Walker, L. Carlsen and J. Jaworska, Improving opportunities for regulatory acceptance of QSARs: the importance of model domain, uncertainty, validity and predictability, *QSAR Comb. Sci.*, 2003, **22**, 346–350.

[69] R. Guha and P. C. Jurs, Determining the validity of a QSAR model – a classification approach, *J. Chem. Inf. Model.*, 2005, **45**, 65–73.

[70] S. Dimitrov, G. Dimitrova, T. Pavlov, N. Dimitrova, G. Patlewicz, J. Niemela and O. Mekenyan, A stepwise approach for defining the applicability domain of SAR and QSAR models, *J. Chem. Inf. Model.*, 2005, **45**, 839–849.

[71] M. Glick, A. E. Klon, P. Acklin and J. W. Davies, Prioritization of high throughput screening data of compound mixtures using molecular similarity, *Mol. Phys.*, 2003, **101**, 1325–1328.

[72] SciTegic, Inc., San Diego, CA. http://www.scitegic.com.

[73] S. F. Yan, H. Asatryan, J. Li and Y. Zhou, Novel statistical approach for primary high-throughput screening hit selection, *J. Chem. Inf. Model.*, 2005.

[74] S. J. Wilkens, J. Janes and A. I. Su, HierS: hierarchical scaffold clustering using topological chemical graphs, *J. Med. Chem.*, 2005, **48**, 3182–3193.

[75] A. E. Klon, M. Glick, M. Thoma, P. Acklin and J. W. Davies, Finding more needles in the haystack: a simple and efficient method for improving high-throughput docking results, *J. Med. Chem.*, 2004, **47**, 2743–2749.

[76] A. E. Klon, M. Glick and J. W. Davies, Combination of a naive Bayes classifier with consensus scoring improves enrichment of high-throughput docking results, *J. Med. Chem.*, 2004, **47**, 4356–4359.

[77] C. Springer, H. Adalsteinsson, M. M. Young, P. W. Kegelmeyer and D. C. Roe, PostDOCK: a structural, empirical approach to scoring protein ligand complexes, *J. Med. Chem.*, 2005, **48**, 6821–6831.

[78] P. S. Charifson, J. J. Corkery, M. A. Murcko and W. P. Walters, Consensus scoring: a method for obtaining improved hit rates from docking databases of three-dimensional structures into proteins, *J. Med. Chem.*, 1999, **42**, 5100–5109.

[79] R. Wang and S. Wang, How does consensus scoring work for virtual library screening? An idealized computer experiment, *J. Chem. Inf. Comput. Sci.*, 2001, **41**, 1422–1426.

[80] M. L. Verdonk, V. Berdini, M. J. Hartshorn, W. T. M. Mooij, C. W. Murray, R. D. Taylor and P. Watson, Virtual screening using protein-ligand docking: avoiding artificial enrichment, *J. Chem. Inf. Comput. Sci.*, 2004, **44**, 793–806.

[81] J. M. Yang, Y. F. Chen, T. W. Shen, B. S. Kristal and D. F. Hsu, Consensus scoring criteria for improving enrichment in virtual screening, *J. Chem. Inf. Model.*, 2005, **45**, 1134–1146.

[82] J. C. Baber, W. A. Shirley, Y. Gao and M. Feher, The use of consensus scoring in ligand-based virtual screening, *J. Chem. Inf. Model.*, 2006, **46**, 277–288.

[83] M. Whittle, V. J. Gillet, P. Willett, A. Alex and J. Loesel, Enhancing the effectiveness of virtual screening by fusing nearest neighbor lists: a comparison of similarity coefficients, *J. Chem. Inf. Comput. Sci.*, 2004, **44**, 1840–1848.

[84] M. Krier, J. X. de Araujo-Junior, M. Schmitt, J. Duranton, H. Justiano-Basaran, C. Lugnier, J. J. Bourguignon and D. Rognan, Design of small-sized libraries by combinatorial assembly of linkers and functional groups to a given scaffold: application to the structure-based optimization of a phosphodiesterase 4 inhibitor, *J. Med. Chem.*, 2005, **48**, 3816–3822.

[85] Z. Liu, C. Huang, K. Fan, P. Wei, H. Chen, S. Liu, J. Pei, L. Shi, B. Li, K. Yang, Y. Liu and L. Lai, Virtual screening of novel noncovalent inhibitors for SARS-CoV 3C-like proteinase, *J. Chem. Inf. Model.*, 2005, **45**, 10–17.

[86] A. Evers and G. Klebe, Successful virtual screening for a submicromolar antagonist of the neurokinin-1 receptor based on a ligand-supported homology model, *J. Med. Chem.*, 2004, **47**, 5381–5392.

[87] P. D. Lyne, P. W. Kenny, D. A. Cosgrove, C. Deng, S. Zabludoff, J. J. Wendoloski and S. Ashwell, Identification of compounds with nanomolar binding affinity for checkpoint kinase-1 using knowledge-based virtual screening, *J. Med. Chem.*, 2004, **47**, 1962–1968.

[88] Y. Kurogi and O. F. Guner, Pharmacophore modeling and three-dimensional database searching for drug design using catalyst, *Curr. Med. Chem.*, 2001, **8**, 1035–1055.

[89] C. Laggner, C. Schieferer, B. Fiechtner, G. Poles, R. D. Hoffmann, H. Glossmann, T. Langer and F. F. Moebius, Discovery of high-affinity ligands of sigma1 receptor, ERG2, and emopamil binding protein by pharmacophore modeling and virtual screening, *J. Med. Chem.*, 2005, **48**, 4754–4764.

[90] Cresset BioMolecular Discovery Ltd., Letchworth, UK.

[91] C. M. Low, I. M. Buck, T. Cooke, J. R. Cushnir, S. B. Kalindjian, A. Kotecha, M. J. Pether, N. P. Shankley, J. G. Vinter and L. Wright, Scaffold hopping with molecular field points: identification of a cholecystokinin-2 (CCK(2)) receptor pharmacophore and its use in the design of a prototypical series of pyrrole- and imidazole-Based CCK(2) antagonists, *J. Med. Chem.*, 2005, **48**, 6790–6802.

[92] A. Evers, G. Hessler, H. Matter and T. Klabunde, Virtual screening of biogenic amine-binding G-protein coupled receptors: comparative evaluation of protein- and ligand-based virtual screening protocols, *J. Med. Chem.*, 2005, **48**, 5448–5465.

[93] C. N. Parker, McMaster university data-mining and docking competition – computational models on the catwalk, *J. Biomol. Screen*, 2005, **10**, 647–648.

[94] N. H. Elowe, J. E. Blanchard, J. D. Cechetto and E. D. Brown, Experimental screening of dihydrofolate reductase yields a "test set" of 50,000 small molecules for a computational data-mining and docking competition, *J. Biomol. Screen*, 2005, **10**, 653–657.

[95] P. T. Lang, I. D. Kuntz, G. M. Maggiora and J. Bajorath, Evaluating the high-throughput screening computations, *J. Biomol. Screen*, 2005, **10**, 649–652.

[96] M. Zolli-Juran, J. D. Cechetto, R. Hartlen, D. M. Daigle and E. D. Brown, High throughput screening identifies novel inhibitors of *E. coli* dihydrofolate reductase that are competitive with dihydrofolate, *Bioorg. Med. Chem. Lett.*, 2003, **13**, 2493–2496.

[97] R. Brenk, J. J. Irwin and B. K. Shoichet, Here be dragons: docking and screening in an uncharted region of chemical space, *J. Biomol. Screen*, 2005, **10**, 667–674.

[98] K. Bernacki, C. Kalyanaraman and M. P. Jacobson, Virtual ligand screening against *E. coli* dihydrofolate reductase: improving docking enrichment using physics-based methods, *J. Biomol. Screen*, 2005, **10**, 675–681.

[99] D. Rogers, R. D. Brown and M. Hahn, Using extended-connectivity fingerprints with Laplacian-modified Bayesian analysis in high-throughput screening follow-up, *J. Biomol. Screen*, 2005, **10**, 682–686.

[100] A. Bender, H. Y. Mussa and R. C. Glen, Screening for dihydrofolate reductase inhibitors using MOLPRINT2D, a fast fragment-based method employing the naive Bayesian classifier: limitations of the descriptor and the importance of balanced chemistry in training and test sets, *J. Biomol. Screen*, 2005, **10**, 658–666.

[101] M. Stahl and H. Mauser, Database clustering with a combination of fingerprint and maximum common substructure methods, *J. Chem. Inf. Model.*, 2005, **45**, 542–548.

[102] A. Bocker, S. Derksen, E. Schmidt, A. Teckentrup and G. Schneider, A hierarchical clustering approach for large compound libraries, *J. Chem. Inf. Model.*, 2005, **45**, 807–815.

[103] J. D. Holliday, S. L. Rodgers, P. Willett, M. Y. Chen, M. Mahfouf, K. Lawson and G. Mullier, Clustering files of chemical structures using the fuzzy k-means clustering method, *J. Chem. Inf. Comput. Sci.*, 2004, **44**, 894–902.

[104] J. Sadowski and H. Kubinyi, A scoring scheme for discriminating between drugs and nondrugs, *J. Med. Chem.*, 1998, **41**, 3325–3329.

[105] K. R. Muller, G. Ratsch, S. Sonnenburg, S. Mika, M. Grimm and N. Heinrich, Classifying 'drug-likeness' with Kernel-based learning methods, *J. Chem. Inf. Model.*, 2005, **45**, 249–253.

[106] S. Zheng, X. Luo, G. Chen, W. Zhu, J. Shen, K. Chen and H. Jiang, A new rapid and effective chemistry space filter in recognizing a druglike database, *J. Chem. Inf. Model.*, 2005, **45**, 856–862.

[107] S. Muresan and J. Sadowski, "In-house likeness": comparison of large compound collections using artificial neural networks, *J. Chem. Inf. Model.*, 2005, **45**, 888–893.

[108] M. D. Cummings, R. L. DesJarlais, A. C. Gibbs, V. Mohan and E. P. Jaeger, Comparison of automated docking programs as virtual screening tools, *J. Med. Chem.*, 2005, **48**, 962–976.

[109] M. A. Miteva, W. H. Lee, M. O. Montes and B. O. Villoutreix, Fast structure-based virtual ligand screening combining FRED, DOCK, and Surflex, *J. Med. Chem.*, 2005, **48**, 6012–6022.

[110] C. P. Mpamhanga, B. N. Chen, I. M. McLay, D. L. Ormsby and M. K. Lindvall, Retrospective docking study of PDE4B ligands and an analysis of the behavior of selected scoring functions, *J. Chem. Inf. Model.*, 2005, **45**, 1061–1074.

[111] R. X. Wang, Y. P. Lu, X. L. Fang and S. M. Wang, An extensive test of 14 scoring functions using the PDB bind refined set of 800 protein-ligand complexes, *J. Chem. Inf. Comput. Sci.*, 2004, **44**, 2114–2125.

[112] G. L. Warren, C. W. Andrews, A.-M. Capelli, B. Clarke, J. LaLonde, M. H. Lambert, M. K. Lindvall, N. Nevins, S. F. Semus, S. Senger, G. Tedesco, I. D. Wall, J. M. Woolven, C. E. Peishoff and M. S. Head, A critical assessment of docking programs and scoring functions, *J. Med. Chem.*, 2005, ASAP Article; DOI: 10.1021/jm050362n.

[113] P. M. Marsden, D. Puvanendrampillai, J. B. O. Mitchell and R. C. Glen, Predicting protein–ligand binding affinities: a low scoring game?, *Org. Biomol. Chem.*, 2004, **2**, 3267–3273.

[114] A. Macchiarulo, I. Nobeli and J. M. Thornton, Ligand selectivity and competition between enzymes *in silico*, *Nat. Biotechnol.*, 2004, **22**, 1039–1045.

Section 5
Applications of Computational Methods

Section Editors: Heather A. Carlson
University of Michigan
College of Pharmacy
428 Church Street
Ann Arbor
MI 48109-1065
USA

Jeffry D. Madura
Duquesne University
Department of Chemistry and Biochemistry
Center for Computational Sciences
600 Forbes Ave., Pittsburgh
PA 15282
USA

CHAPTER 10

Cytochrome P450 Enzymes: Computational Approaches to Substrate Prediction

Andreas Verras, Irwin D. Kuntz and Paul R. Ortiz de Montellano

Department of Pharmaceutical Chemistry, University of California, 600 16th Street, San Francisco, California 94143-2280

Contents

1. INTRODUCTION

No enzyme family plays a more critical role in xenobiotic metabolism than that of the cytochrome P450 enzymes. Since their discovery in 1963 by Estabrook and coworkers [1], P450 enzymes have inspired the envy of chemists for their ability to perform synthetically difficult hydroxylations at unactivated carbons and have become a focal point for studies of xenobiotic metabolism.

Cytochrome P450 enzymes are best known for their role in phase I metabolism. They hydroxylate lipophilic compounds resulting in increased drug clearance and have been implicated in toxic activation of compounds [2] and drug activation [3]. Furthermore, they play a critical role in several biosynthetic pathways such as steroid biosynthesis [4].

Because of their central role in metabolism, P450 enzymes are a frequent target of absorption, distribution, metabolism, and excretion (ADME) studies [5]. The cost of drug development typically reaches

ANNUAL REPORTS IN COMPUTATIONAL CHEMISTRY, VOLUME 2
ISSN: 1574-1400   DOI 10.1016/S1574-1400(06)02010-X

hundreds of millions of dollars for a single drug [6] and eliminating candidates with poor pharmacokinetics or adverse drug–drug interactions has become a critical goal in pre-clinical studies. Understanding P450 specificity and function also has implications in bioremediation, and the members of this enzyme superfamily are attractive candidates for bioengineering solutions to environmental detoxification [7].

Computational models have been applied to many aspects of these enzymes including inhibitor prediction [8], substrate prediction [9], profiling metabolism [10], determining mechanistic intermediates [11], and generating homology models [12]. This review will focus on structure-based metabolism prediction. We are in an exciting time for this research. Computers continue to grow more powerful and less expensive. More importantly, we have witnessed an unprecedented growth of physiologically relevant P450 structural information in the last few years.

Atomic resolution structures of cytochrome P450 enzymes began with cytochrome P450cam, solved by Poulos in 1985 [13]. The protein has since been crystallized with dozens of ligands and with many mutations. Cytochrome P450cam has been highly characterized, expresses well, and has become an archetypal model for understanding P450 enzymes.

The next structures solved (e.g. P450 BM-3, CYP119, P450nor, and P450 EryF) were all from bacterial systems. The mammalian P450 enzymes, all membrane-associated proteins compared to their soluble bacterial counterparts, remained elusive until 2000 when the structure of cytochrome P450 2C5, was solved [14]. Not only was the structure critical for understanding a new class of P450 enzymes, but the methods used to allow its crystallization were now readily applicable to other mammalian isoforms: deletion of the N-terminus in conjunction with several surface point mutations to generate soluble P450 homologues.

In the last year, two human structures, P450 2C9 and P450 3A4, were resolved to 2 Å [15,16]. While cytochrome P450 enzymes metabolize thousands of xenobiotic compounds, P450 3A4 alone is responsible for approximately 60% of all phase I human drug metabolism [17]. With the wealth of structural information available, new directions and tools must be explored in an effort to increase our predictive power in metabolism.

There are several inherent difficulties in metabolite prediction for P450 enzymes. First, the reactive cycle of P450 enzymes highlights an immediate complexity. The mechanism of P450 enzymes, shown in Fig. 1, illustrates the activated intermediates involved in catalysis. The initial step is substrate binding to the ferric complex, displacing water and changing the redox potential of the protein by approximately 100 mV [18], though in some P450 enzymes the reduction potential is independent of substrate binding [19,20]. This is followed by a single electron transfer yielding the

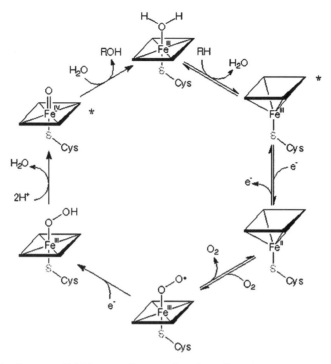

Fig. 1. Cytochrome P450 reaction cycle. Species that are marked with an (*) are most frequently modeled in computational substrate or inhibitor prediction. The heme is represented by the square.

pentacoordinated ferrous complex. Molecular oxygen then binds and a second electron transfer occurs, resulting in oxygen bond cleavage and formation of the reactive ferryl oxygen species. For some of these redox states there is little structural information. In predicting substrate specificity and the regioselectivity of metabolism, should one model the resting ferric state, which initially binds substrate, or the ferryl-oxygen species responsible for hydrogen abstraction? Because of the complicated electrochemistry, the species along the reaction cycle are distinct. There are significant electrostatic and steric differences in their attributes, and conformational changes have been shown to occur in traversing the reaction cycle for at least some P450 enzymes [21]. Model choice can significantly affect prediction of substrates and metabolism.

A second difficulty is the inherent flexibility of P450 enzymes. As was noted, a handful of P450 enzymes are responsible for metabolizing thousands of compounds and have thus evolved to be extremely promiscuous. Much of this promiscuity comes from the malleability of the active site side chains and breathing motions of the backbone. This phenomenon will be discussed later in the review when we describe P450 structures.

Flexibility and substrate orientation also bring us to the third concern in modeling P450–substrate interactions. At several steps in the catalytic cycle uncoupling can occur [22], preventing the oxidation of substrate and instead resulting in the production of water or hydrogen peroxide. Several factors have been implicated in peroxide formation, including substrate–active site complementarity [23], poorly oriented substrates, and water occupancy of the active site [24]. The practice of metabolism prediction requires not only that the substrate be able to bind, but also that the orientation of the substrate be appropriate to allow for hydroxylation by the enzyme. The presence of water molecules in the active site further complicates substrate prediction efforts.

Finally, differentiating ligands and substrates is not trivial. Heteroatom chelation and mechanistic suicide inhibitors may be found to bind in the same manner as substrates, but result in inhibition instead of activity. Methods, which predict inhibitors, shall also be briefly reviewed.

We will begin by summarizing P450 structural information gleaned over the last 20 years from crystallography and homology modeling. In the next section, structure-based approaches predating structural information or including it explicitly will be considered. The final section will discuss new approaches to P450 metabolite prediction. We also hope to highlight some of the ways in which ligand-based models, molecular modeling, and structure-based approaches, working in parallel, can surmount the difficulties of predicting P450 protein–ligand interactions.

2. P450 STRUCTURES

2.1. First crystal structures, bacterial P450 enzymes

P450cam is the archetypal P450 enzyme. The first high-resolution P450 crystal structure was that of P450cam [13,25] and, combined with the wealth of biochemical data on this enzyme, it has shaped the approaches taken to understanding the structure, function, and mechanism of this superfamily. P450cam structures have been solved with alternate substrates [26,27], inhibitors [28], mutations [29], and in the substrate-free form [30].

Other prokaryotic P450 enzyme structures were solved by similar crystallographic methods, including those of P450 BM-3 [31], P450terp [32], and P450EryF [33] (Table 1). While the overall sequence identity of P450 enzymes between various families is generally about 20%, the quaternary structures of these proteins align well (Fig. 2) and exhibit several conserved motifs that are also conserved in the mammalian,

Table 1. Currently available P450 crystal structures

Protein	PDB ID	Ligand	Resolution	References
P450cam				
	1AKD	1-S camphor	1.8	[89]
	1CP4	Phenyl radical	1.9	[90]
Ferric protein	1DZ4	Camphor	1.6	[91]
Ferrous protein	1DZ6	Camphor	1.9	[91]
Oxygen complex	1DZ8	O_2, camphor	1.9	[91]
Ferryl oxygen (putative)	1DZ9	Oxygen, camphor	1.9	[91]
Ferric protein	1GEK	*n*-Butyl-isocyanide	1.5	[92]
Ferrous protein	1GEM	*n*-Butyl-isocyanide	2.0	[92]
Covalently modified protein	1GJM	*n*-2-(Ferrocenylethyl)maleimide)	2.2	[93]
	1K2O	Ruthenium-linker	1.65	[36]
	1QMQ	Ruthenium-linker	1.55	[94]
	1LWL	Fluorescent probe	2.2	[95]
	1O76	Cyanide	1.8	[96]
	1PHA	UK-67254-13(+)	1.63	[28]
	1PHB	UK-67254-13(-)	1.6	[28]
	1PHC	None	1.6	[30]
	1PHD	2-Phenylimidazole	1.6	[37]
	1PHE	2-Phenylimidazole	1.6	[37]
	1PHF	4-Phenylimidazole	1.6	[37]
	1PHG	Metyrapone	1.6	[37]
L358P, C334A	1T85	Camphor, CO	1.8	Poulos, to be published
L358P, C334A	1T86	Camphor	1.9	Poulos, to be published
C334A	1T87	Camphor, CO	1.8	Poulos, to be published
C334A	1T88	Camphor	1.9	Poulos, to be published
T252A	2CP4	Camphor	2.1	[97]
T252A	3CP4	Adamantane	2.3	[97]
	4CP4	Camphor	2.1	[97]
	5CP4	Camphor	1.7	[98]
	2CPP	Camphor	1.63	[25]
	3CPP	Camphor, CO	1.9	[99]
	4CPP	Adamantane	2.11	[27]
	5CPP	Benzofuran adenine	2.08	[100]
D251N	6CP4	Camphor	1.9	[98]
	6CPP	Camphene	1.9	[27]
	7CPP	Norcamphor	2.0	[100]
	8CPP	Thiocamphor	2.1	[27]
P450 BM-3				
Heme domain	1BU7	None	1.65	[31]
Heme-FMN domains	1BVY	None	2.03	[31]
Heme domain	1FAG	Palmitoleic acid	2.7	[21]
Heme domain, T268A	1FAH	None	2.3	[101]
Heme domain, F393H	1JME	None	2.0	[102]
Heme domain	1JPZ	*n*-Palmitoylglycine	1.65	[103]
Heme domain, F393A	1P0V	None	2.05	[104]
Heme domain, F393W	1P0W	None	2.0	[104]
Heme domain, F393Y	1P0X	None	2.0	[104]
Heme domain, A264E	1SMI	None	2.0	[105]
Heme domain, A264E	1SMJ	Palmitoleic acid	2.75	[105]

Table 1. Continued

Protein	PDB ID	Ligand	Resolution	References
P450terp				
1CPT	None	2.3		[32]
P450 2C5				
1DT6	None	3.0		[14]
	1N6B	Sulfaphenazole	1.8	[106]
	1NR6	Diclofenac	2.1	[107]
P450 2C8				
	1PQ2	None (palmitic acid on surface)	2.7	[47]
P450 2C9				
	1OG2	None	2.6	[45]
	1OG5	Warfarin	2.55	[45]
	1R9O	Flurbibrofen	2.0	[15]
P450 3A4				
	1TQN	None	2.05	[16]
	1W0E	None	2.8	[48]
	1W0F	Progesterone	2.65	[48]
	1W0G	Metyrapone	2.74	[48]
P450 2B4				
	1SU0	4-(4-Chlorphenyl)imidazole	1.9	[108]
P450 2B5				
	1PO5	None	1.6	[46]
CYP 51				
1E9X	4-Phenyl	imidazole	2.1	
[40]				
	1EA1	Fluconazole	2.21	[40]
Ferric protein	1H5Z	None	2.05	[41]
C37L, C151T,	1U13	None	2.01	Waterman, to
C442A				be
				published
	1X8V	Estriol	1.55	[41]
P450EryF				
	1EGY	9-Aminophenanthrene (2	2.35	[109]
		molecules)		
	1EUP	Androstenedione (2 molecules)	2.1	[109]
	1JIN	Ketocanazole	2.3	[110]
	1JIO	6-Deoxyerythronolide b	2.1	[110]
P450Epok				
	1Q5D	Epothilone b	1.93	[111]
	1Q5E	None	2.65	[111]
P450Nor				
	1EHE	None	1.7	[112]
S286T	1EHF	None	1.7	[112]
S286V	1EHG	None	1.7	[112]
T243A	1F24	Nitrogen oxide	1.4	Shimizu, to be
				published
T243N	1F25	Nitrogen oxide	1.4	Shimizu, to be
				published
T243V	1F26	Nitrogen oxide	1.4	Shimizu, to be
				published
	1GED	None	2.0	[113]
Ferric protein	1GEI	n-Butyl-isocyanide	1.6	[92]
Ferrous protein	1GEJ	n-Butyl-isocyanide	1.5	[92]
S73G, S75G	1ULW	None	2.0	[114]
	1XQD	3-Pyridinealdehyde adenine	1.8	[114]
CYP 119				
	1F4T	4-Phenyl imidazole	1.93	[43]
	1F4U	Imidazole	2.69	[43]
	1IO7	None	1.5	[115]
F24L	1IO8	None	2.0	[115]
	1IO9	None	2.05	[115]
CYP175A1				
	1N97	None	1.8	[116]
P450 Bsβ				
	1IZO	Palmitoleic acid	2.1	[117]

Table 1. Continued

Protein	PDB ID	Ligand	Resolution	References
P450 Oxyb				
	1LFK	None	1.7	[118]
	1LG9	None	2.0	[118]
	1LGF	None	2.2	[118]
P450 Oxyc				
	1UED	None	1.9	[119]
CYP 121				
	1N4G	Iodopyrazole	1.8	[120]
CYP154A1				
	1ODO	4-Phenyl-imidazole	1.85	[121]

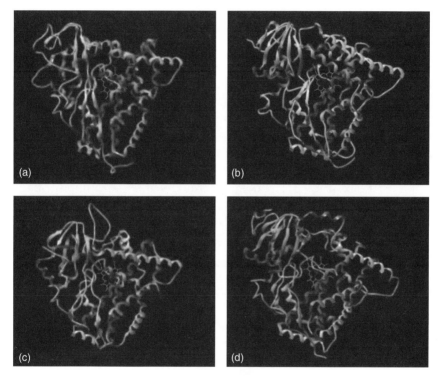

Fig. 2. P450 enzyme alignments. (a) P450cam, (b) P450 BM-3, (c) P450 EryF, and (d) P450 3A4 aligned by superimposition of the heme groups. The overall structure is similar between the four enzymes despite less than 20% sequence identity.

membrane-bound P450 enzymes. The proteins are primarily helical, with 8–9 helices and a small beta sheet region. The active site is formed primarily by the helices with some variation in their position and length depending on the highly variable substrate specificities.

2.2. The active site channel and substrate access

The active site for the protein is buried in the center of the enzyme. A space-filling model of P450cam shows no clear access channel to the heme. Several studies have elucidated the path substrates must navigate to enter the active site and the protein movements that must occur concurrently to allow such access. The question has been approached computationally [34,35] and crystallographically [36]. Using molecular dynamics and random forces on a bound camphor, Ludemann *et al.* computed a most likely path of entrance/exit for the ligand based upon relative energy barriers of expulsion [35,36]. Structural approaches to channel elucidation have included co-crystallization of the protein with a ruthenium linker substrate that is bound to the heme iron atom and extends to the surface of the protein via a 9-carbon alkyl chain [37]. This large ligand stabilized an open form of P450cam that resembles the P450 enzymes with open access channels.

Both studies emphasized the importance of long-chain residues engaged in flexible salt bridges, forming an access channel of 22 Å length. Residues Arg186, Asp251, Lys178, and Asp182 were found to move while maintaining hydrogen bond and salt contacts, stabilizing the channel. At the protein surface, the channel was found to open between the F/G loop and the B' helix (Fig. 3). The studies show the permutable nature of P450cam, flexible enough to bind 7-, 9-, and 13-mer alkyl chains. While the access channel must play a role in filtering potential substrates, the

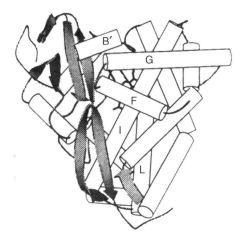

Fig. 3. P450cam. Cartoon representation of P450cam with helices labeled according to P450 tertiary structure nomenclature.

mechanism by which it does so remains elusive. Hydrophobicity seems to be a primary criterion, but to understand substrate specificity we must look at the active site.

2.3. Active site flexibility and promiscuity

With the wealth of P450cam structures bound to a variety of substrates we are able to see structural permutations in a single enzyme and begin to understand the method by which this family adapts to a passel of substrates. Poulos *et al.* co-crystallized P450cam with UK-39671, a large compound found to be an inhibitor [28]. Large deformations of the active site relative to the native, substrate-bound conformation were necessary to bind this ligand. Tyr96, which in the substrate-bound structure forms a hydrogen bond to the camphor ketone group, is inverted in this structure, pointing up into the putative access channel.

In addition to side-chain rearrangements, larger backbone motions have also been observed in co-crystals of P450cam with 1-, 2-, and 4-phenyl-imidazole [37]. With the exception of 2-phenylimidazole, the compounds coordinate to the heme iron through the nitrogen on the imidazole and the phenyl group makes van der Waals contacts in the active site cavity usually occupied by camphor. Compared to the camphor structure the long, axial I-helix is shifted in the presence of 1- and 4-phenylimidazole away from the heme. In the presence of 2-phenylimidazole the I-helix is again shifted but in the opposite direction. The translations are up to 2 Å in magnitude. The motions of the I-helix are mirrored by large increases in the temperature factors in the region. Substrate-induced changes have been observed in other P450 enzymes, including P450BM-3 [38,39] and CYP51 [40].

Of particular interest to this review are substrate-induced changes in the active site [41,42]. One of the most striking examples is CYP119, a thermophilic P450 enzyme. The structure of this enzyme was solved in the presence of imidazole and 4-phenylimidazole [43] and, as the authors note, reveals an unprecedented rearrangement of the active site to adapt to each ligand by side-chain conformer rearrangements, unraveling of the FG helix, and backbone movements of up to 6 Å. For computational chemists pursuing structure-based design methods, these two structures perfectly illustrate the difficulties in substrate or inhibitor prediction. The CYP119 structure in the presence of imidazole, if assumed to be rigid, would suggest an inability to dock the larger 4-phenyl imidazole complex or lauric acid, which has been found to be oxidized by CYP119 [44].

2.4. Mammalian P450 structures

The first mammalian structure solved was rabbit P450 2C5, which was crystallized by removing the N-terminal membrane anchor [14]. The soluble isozyme was resolved to 3.0 Å and represented a monumental breakthrough in P450 structure elucidation. It was followed by co-crystallization of the same construct with a derivatized dimethyl sulfaphenazole ligand resulting in an improved resolution of 2.3 Å. Overall, the tertiary structure of the first mammalian P450 resembled the soluble bacterial enzymes, even though the sequence identity was less than 20%.

In 2003 the first human P450 structure, P4502C9, was published [45]. This protein was also solved as a truncated construct that improved solubility and facilitated crystallization. P4502C9 is one of the prime actors in human metabolism and represented an immense resource for structural biologists predicting metabolism and drug–drug interactions. The structure was solved with bound warfarin, an anti-coagulant drug that the enzyme is known to metabolize; however, the site of metabolism on the drug was positioned 10 Å away from the heme iron suggesting an inactive binding mode. The authors postulated a two-step binding mode, in which a subsequent rearrangement is necessary to bring the substrate adjacent to the heme or a second molecule must bind in a cooperative manner to allow for oxidation.

The coordinates of another mammalian P450, P4502B5, were released in 2003 [46]. The enzyme was isolated as a homodimer and possessed a large open cleft running all the way to the heme. The channel was formed primarily from the B', C, F, and G helices and appeared to represent an open form of the active site channel stabilized by helices contributed by the complementing homodimer. While in the same P450 superfamily as P4502C5, the structures are significantly different, illustrating the dynamic range of these enzymes necessary to promote metabolic flexibility.

Another member of the P4502 superfamily, P4502C8, was solved in 2004 [47]. This enzyme has been implicated in the metabolism of taxol and cerivastatin, as well as retinoic and arachidonic acids. As is suggested by the enzyme's large substrates, the active site volume is twice that of P4502C5, occupying 1438 Å^3.

Finally in June of 2004, structures of P4503A4 were deposited into the Protein Data Bank [48]. In humans, P4503A4 metabolizes more drugs than all other P450 enzymes combined. The protein was crystallized in the substrate-free form, with a bound substrate, and a bound inhibitor. Previous kinetic and binding studies suggested [49] the enzyme could bind multiple substrates, and the crystal structure revealed a large active site in the enzyme consistent with this hypothesis.

Because of the vast numbers of substrates and the inability to crystallize all xenobiotics with all their respective metabolizing P450 enzymes, molecular modeling, docking, and molecular dynamics will always be necessary to elucidate protein–ligand interactions. Also, as we saw with P450cam, the structure of one protein–ligand complex does not immediately suggest a binding mode for alternate ligands; in fact, the static structures from crystallography may seem to preclude the binding of known substrates. As with P4502C9 and warfarin, the structure may yield suggestions for predicting metabolism, but not clearly indicate the mechanism of oxidation. For these reasons reconstructing molecular models remains an important pursuit.

3. COMPUTATIONAL METABOLISM PREDICTION

3.1. Ligand-based techniques

In the absence of protein structural information, several ligand-based approaches have been used to predict metabolism profiles including application of Kohonen maps [50] and neural networks [51]. While a summary of these methods is outside the scope of the review, their success has significantly impacted the field of metabolism prediction and these methods have been combined with structure-based approaches.

3.1.1. Electronic regioselectivity

In the absence of protein structural data at the time, it was possible to predict metabolism profiles based upon the characteristics of the ligand particularly electronic characteristics. Experimentally observed metabolism profiles, isotopic data, and atomic calculations display a tendency for oxidation that follows the potential for radical formation: N-dealkylation > O-dealkylation > secondary carbon oxidation > primary carbon oxidation. Using the AM1* semiempirical basis set, hydrogen abstraction transition sets were modeled using the p-nitrosophenoxy radical to model abstraction [52]. The heat of reaction and activation energy of radical formation correlated well with the experimental bond dissociation energies.

This model was first applied to metabolism prediction of nitrile-bearing compounds [53]. Hydroxylation at the carbon alpha to the nitrile group resulted in rapid loss of a cyanohydrin group as hydrogen cyanide. Experimental LD50 rates had been obtained for a set of nitrile compounds in mice [54]. The data correlated well with log P, but for dinitriles or nitriles containing alkyl groups of four or more carbons, there was a poor correlation with hydrophobicity. A subset of 26 compounds was explored by the electronic model of hydrogen abstraction. The regioselectivity of hydroxylation was evaluated by comparing the potential for oxidation at all potential positions and followed by ranking in comparison to the energy associated with radical formation at the position alpha to the nitrile, hydroxylation, and subsequent release of cyanide. The results correlated poorly to log P alone ($r = 0.59$), but with the addition of electronic parameters of radical formation the correlation improved to an r value of 0.85. A comprehensive review of this method has been published [10].

3.1.2. Pharmacophores and 3d qsar

Pharmacophore and three-dimensional quantitative structure–activity relationships (3D QSAR) have been extensively applied to substrate specificity and regioselectivity prediction. A 3D QSAR technique, often used with cytochrome P450 enzymes, is comparative molecular field analysis (CoMFA) [55] which overlays conformations of known active compounds and builds a molecular field grid about the molecules. The grid is then used in scoring new molecules. With this approach, one is able to approximate the enzyme active-site topology in the absence of a crystal structure.

The promiscuous nature of P450 enzymes makes application of these techniques difficult. Both methods begin with the assumption that compounds will be oriented similarly in the active site, an assumption that is not valid for many P450 enzymes. In fact, multiple hydroxylation of a single molecule by one P450 enzyme has frequently been observed [56] and mandates that even one molecule may bind in multiple orientations. However, both techniques have had reasonable success with P450 enzymes having a stricter substrate specificity and with sets of closely related compounds [57].

A combined pharmacophore-homology modeling technique was applied to CYP2D6 by de Groot et al. [58]. Initially they modeled 57 metabolic pathways based upon 40 substrates. The structures were built and energy minimized by the AM1 method. Debrisoquine and dextromethorphan, compounds with relatively low flexibility compared to the test set, were used as the template over which the other compounds were overlayed. A homology model of CYP2D6 was constructed using the structures of CYPs 101, 102, and 108 as templates. Molecular orbital (MO) calculations using the AM1 method were carried out for all radical intermediates and hydroxylated products.

The substrates were then docked into the CYP2D6 active site and a high complementarity was found between the pharmacophore model and the protein active site. The substrates were energy minimized with some restraints in the presence of protein. Because the final results are ultimately dependent on the conformations and alignment of the test set, and because protein binding can permute the conformation of compounds relative to their free state, energy minimization with a protein model is an important step toward a correct final conformation.

While the MO calculations are important in deriving pharmacophores and in orienting the pharmacophore model in the active site, electronic calculations alone could not reproduce metabolic profiles. MO calculations generally favored O-dealkylation as was seen with several of the compounds, but structural information was critical in elucidating the hydroxylation at alternate sites. The authors conclude that neither pharmacophore, homology model, nor electronic criteria alone are sufficient to predict metabolism and reinforce the inference that these techniques must be merged to produce an accurate depiction of metabolism.

3.2. Homology modeling

Because of the inherent difficulties in crystallizing membrane-bound proteins, such as the mammalian P450 enzymes, homology modeling is commonly employed. The process of homology modeling begins with a sequence alignment generated by methods such as ALIGN [59] or PSI-BLAST [60]. One or more template proteins whose structures are known are chosen against which to align the target. Homology modeling is an iterative process that relies heavily on experimentally derived information to guide the process [61]. In addition to requiring a template of at least 20% identity, mutational analysis and substrate and inhibitor information is important. Several independent assessments of quality exist such as PROCHECK [62], PROSA [63], and WHAT IF [64]. These programs work by checking model characteristics including Ramachandran angles, atom–atom interactions, energy scores of interactions, and protein–solvent interactions. While these provide a method to assess the quality of a predicted structure, the true validity of any model must be judged by its ability to correctly suggest biochemical function, substrate specificity, or novel inhibitors.

An example of integrating experimental data with homology modeling can be found in Gilda Loew's molecular modeling of CYP4A11. The templates used were from P450cam, P450terp, P450 BM-3, and P450 EryF, with a significant portion of backbone and side-chain information derived primarily from P450 BM-3. Two models were generated with identical backbone coordinates, but different side-chain conformers. Previous biochemical data identified lauric acid as a substrate for CYP4A11 and showed that the enzyme promoted the thermodynamically less favorable ω rather than $\omega-1$ hydroxylation. Lauric acid was docked into the active sites of both models and they were submitted to 600 ps of molecular dynamics at 300° K. By PROSA, PROCHECK, and WHAT IF criteria, the models were indistinguishable in quality; however, as restraints in the molecular dynamics simulation were relaxed, one of the models was unable to anchor the lauric acid molecule and the substrate was expelled from the active site within the first 100 ps of the molecular dynamics trajectory. The other model, which was dynamically stable with respect to the ligand, was then used to implicate residues in the active site contributing to the unique regioselectivity of the 4A enzymes.

A later study by Afzelius et al. evaluated homology modeling techniques employed in the construction of several of these models, including single vs. multiple template alignments [65]. The authors used the crystal structures of P450's 2C9 and 2C5 as the metric by which to evaluate the homology models. A total of 15 homology models for each protein were generated using both single templates, 2C9 for 2C5 and vice versa, and multiple template alignments using P450cam, P450terp, P450 BM-3, P450 EryF, P4502C5, and P4502C9. The models were compared to their crystal structures by RMSD and consensus principal component analysis derived from molecular interaction field descriptors of the protein active sites. This analysis gives both the overall fit of the molecules to their target structures as well as a detailed side-chain conformer description of the active site. Both quantifiers of fit illustrated that in all cases the models were more similar to their templates than to their target proteins. Using several proteins in the alignment resulted in higher similarity to the target, reinforcing the trend in the field toward multiple templates.

3.3. Structure-based design, protein-ligand docking

Under the umbrella of structure-based design we will discuss virtual screening methods such as DOCK [66], FlexX [67], GOLD [68], and AutoDock [69]. We will also include molecular dynamics and associated quantum mechanical calculations.

Virtual screening is an attractive approach to substrate prediction or inhibitor design for several reasons. While structural information is required, no ligand test set is necessary though they can be employed for parameterization of scoring functions. Furthermore, depending on the scoring and sampling functions, thousands of compounds can be screened quickly. Because of the scale upon which this method can operate, it can supplement high-throughput assays and when the techniques are used in tandem, either in library design or assay organization, can significantly enrich successful compound discovery [70].

Virtual screening has not been applied extensively to P450 enzymes because of several inherent difficulties. The promiscuity of P450 enzymes makes the assumption of a rigid active site potentially flawed. Also, because the active site is generally modeled in its entirety, selection of its representation is critical. Docking to the ferryl-oxygen vs. ferrous forms can have dramatically different results. The electrostatics in the active site play a large role in virtual screening and have been calculated by several methods including semi-empirical INDO-ROHF calculations by Gilda Loew [71].

Early docking studies were performed with the first crystallized and best-characterized P450 enzyme, P450cam. In 1997, De Voss *et al.* used the DOCK program to predict substrates for P450cam and a P450cam L244A mutant [72]. A total of 16 compounds were evaluated. Seven of the compounds predicted to bind to the wild type were found to be substrates and compounds predicted not to fit were not metabolized. An L244A mutant was able to oxidize some of the larger compounds that were not substrates for the wild type. Retroactive reparameterization of the DOCK scoring function resulted in accurate predictions for 15 of 16 compounds against the wild-type P450cam. To estimate the inherent malleability of the P450 active site, it was found that changing the minimum contact distance for polar and nonpolar interactions from 2.3 to 2.4 Å and 2.8–2.9 Å, respectively, resulted in better fits. With the new parameters the predictions for the L244A mutant also improved.

A survey of docking algorithms for heme-containing proteins was recently conducted [73]. Using a test set of 45 protein–ligand complexes including several P450 enzymes, nitric oxide synthases, peroxidases, and hemoglobin, the authors assessed the GOLD and Chemscore [74] scoring function's ability to return the appropriate ligands within 2 Å of their crystallized structures. The authors found generally poorer results when docking to heme proteins compared to another set of 139 diverse proteins [75]. For the heme-containing test set, they found 57% of the complexes returned successfully by GOLD and 64% by Chemscore compared to 79% by both methods for the diverse protein test set. The authors attributed the discrepancy in predictive power to specific metal chelation factors, such as imidazole binding, not accounted for by the scoring functions, and the high lipophilicity of the P450 active sites. By reparameterizing the scoring function with empirically derived parameters for iron-acceptor contact atoms and modifying the lipophilic term of Chemscore, they were able to successfully return 73% of the corrected complexes.

An alternate method of modeling the iron chelation by which imidazole-based compounds inhibit P450 enzymes was carried out by our laboratory [76]. By introducing a harmonic restraint into the DOCK scoring function we were able to successfully reproduce the experimentally derived binding modes of imidazole-based inhibitors against P450cam. Using the altered form of the DOCK algorithm allowed generation of high-affinity ligands selective between P450cam and a P45cam L244A mutant.

Another example of scoring function validation has been done specifically for P450cam, exploiting the large amount of ligand–protein complex information for the enzyme [77]. The author used FlexX to dock a library of known P450cam substrates against the enzyme and then compared GOLD, DOCK, FlexX, and PMF scoring functions. While PMF scores most often returned correct binding modes, the GOLD-derived ligand scores were found to correlate more closely with experimentally determined affinities. Using the combined methodologies of FlexX to position the ligands, PMF to nominate the top orientation, and GOLD to score it, the methods were applied to the prediction of ligands for P450 3A4. Preliminary results showed good success, though the scoring function could not discriminate between ligands or inhibitors.

One of the strengths of structure-based virtual screening, in comparison with electronic characterization of metabolism and other methods which rely solely upon the ligand [50,51] to predict regioselective oxidation, is its ability to exclude compounds from consideration based upon steric constraints. Ideally, one hopes that ligand docking would be able to correlate regioselectivity with specific P450 enzymes. Knowledge of metabolism at this level would allow for design considerations that avoid drug–drug interactions or toxic activation of compounds by anomalously upregulated P450 enzymes (e.g. acetaminophen). For enzymes such as P450 2D6 which is absent in 5–9% of the Caucasian population [78], knowledge of compounds specifically metabolized by this isoform could have important implications in population sub-group therapy and pharmacogenomics.

While structure-based virtual screening has great potential, traditional methods do not capture the dynamic nature of protein–ligand binding. Induced fit effects, such as side-chain reorganization or breathing motions in the secondary structure, are difficult to model when high-throughput screening is necessary. A study by Knegtel et al. quantitatively illustrates the effects of docking to a single structure [79]. Five HIV protease structures with co-crystallized ligands were used as a test set. DOCK was then employed to score each ligand against all the structures. While all the ligands scored well against their co-crystal structures, they frequently scored poorly against structures crystallized with alternate inhibitors. In some cases, the inhibitors had a large positive score predicting that they could not bind at all to HIV protease. The authors were able to reproduce correct binding modes and computed energies based on energy- or geometry-weighted averages of the composite structure and illustrated the importance of the target structure in virtual screening.

4. CONCLUSIONS

4.1. Summary

The majority of the studies that have been conducted of *in silico* screening of compounds against P450 enzymes have employed pharmacophore and 3D-QSAR methods. Structural approaches are less well represented in the literature. There are several reasons. First, the paucity of crystallographic information on physiologically relevant P450 enzymes has only recently been alleviated. Second, the relative ease with which ligand oxidation can be screened either with rat microsomes or single P450 enzymes in vitro has yielded a wealth of ligand-based data. Last, the conformational liberty enjoyed by the P450 enzymes mandates the need for non-rigid or ensemble approaches to ligand docking. The majority of docking algorithms in use today target single enzyme active sites instead of an ensemble. These enzymes are also considered as rigid to allow for quick screening of thousands of compounds.

One further consideration worth mentioning is the potential of P450 3A4, the prime actor in human metabolism, to bind multiple substrates [80,81]. No docking, or pharmacophore method, has explicit methods for predicting multiple substrates simultaneously in a single active site. Such an approach must be developed for accurate predictions.

After pharmacophore modeling, molecular dynamics methods are most often employed in predicting P450 metabolism. While this method has the advantages of using an ensemble of structures, the ability to reproduce protein flexibility, and quantify reactive geometries necessary for oxidation compared to geometries resulting in uncoupled or inactive orientations, it is extremely time consuming.

4.2. Future prospectives

The last few years have been a watershed in terms of crystallographic data for physiologically relevant P450 enzymes and should lead to an increase in structure-based design approaches. The challenges in substrate prediction outlined in the review are only partially met by the arrival of new structures. While each structure sheds light on problems of flexibility and promiscuity of these enzymes, imagining every P450 enzyme crystallized with every ligand is unrealistic. For this reason predictive methods and computational models will be indispensable in bridging the gap between static structures and protein–ligand complexes.

Incorporation of protein flexibility in ligand design is not a new issue. Modeled protein flexibility has been described by methods including soft-docking [79,82], discrete side-chain sampling [83], continuous side-chain sampling [84], and incorporation of rotomer libraries [85,86]. As noted earlier in this review, several P450 enzymes including P450 BM-3, P450cam, and CYP119 show dramatic backbone rearrangements upon ligand binding. Modeling side-chain motions alone is not enough to capture the binding modes of all ligands.

Work by Gerhard Klebe's lab on Modeling Binding sites Including Ligand information Explicitly (MOBILE) [87] has more rigorously defined a methodology for ligand-guided homology modeling. Using an ensemble of homology models, known ligands are included in the refinement exploiting known spatial restraints and optimizing the protein–ligand interactions. The protein–ligand complexes are used to evaluate the models and derive a final structure.

The techniques of ligand-derived homology modeling are readily applicable to P450 enzymes of known structure. Remodeling the active site using known ligands of disparate shape and electrostatics from those co-crystallized with protein can be used to return unique, various tertiary structures which can then be used for ligand docking, pharmacophore alignments, or molecular dynamics. While structural "resolution" will be compromised by remodeling the protein, several studies, including the previously mentioned pharmacophore-based approaches for P450, have successfully employed homology-derived structures in ligand prediction. Jacobson and Sali present a good review on structure-based docking techniques applied to homology models [88].

We expect to see methodologies that combine the previously described techniques. Molecular orbital calculations of hydrogen abstraction energies used to predict ligand metabolism based on electronic characteristics have already been combined with pharmacophore models and we expect to see such composite techniques to continue and advance in complexity. Furthermore, techniques which predict P450 enzyme inhibitors [76] may be used in tandem to differentiate between substrates and inhibitors.

Novel methods must also be developed, particularly for predicting cooperative binding of ligands to P450 enzymes with large active sites such as P450 EryF and, most importantly, P450 3A4. The nature of cooperative binding in P450 3A4 may present one of the largest hurdles in the future of structure-based ligand prediction.

ACKNOWLEDGMENTS

The preparation of this review and the work of the authors were supported by NIH grants GM56531 and GM25515.

REFERENCES

[1] R. W. Estabrook, D. Y. Cooper and O. Rosenthal, The light reversible carbon monoxide inhibition of the steroid C21-hydroxylase system of the adrenal cortex, *Biochem. Z*, 1963, **338**, 741–755.

[2] H. Jaeschke, G. J. Gores, A. I. Cederbaum, J. A. Hinson, D. Pessayre and J. J. Lemasters, Mechanisms of hepatotoxicity, *Toxicol. Sci.*, 2002, **65** (2), 166–176.

[3] C. S. Chen, J. T. Lin, K. A. Goss, Y. A. He, J. R. Halpert and D. J. Waxman, Activation of the anticancer prodrugs cyclophosphamide and ifosfamide: identification of cytochrome P450 2B enzymes and site-specific mutants with improved enzyme kinetics, *Mol. Pharmacol.*, 2004, **65** (5), 1278–1285.

[4] D. J. Waxman, Interactions of hepatic cytochromes P-450 with steroid hormones. Regioselectivity and stereospecificity of steroid metabolism and hormonal regulation of rat P-450 enzyme expression, *Biochem. Pharmacol.*, 1988, **37** (1), 71–84.

[5] M. A. Wynalda and L. C. Wienkers, Assessment of potential interactions between dopamine receptor agonists and various human cytochrome P450 enzymes using a simple in vitro inhibition screen, *Drug Metab. Dispos.*, 1997, **25** (10), 1211–1214.

[6] K. Kaitlin, Post-Approval R&D Raises Total Drug Development Costs to $897 Million, Tufts Center for the Study of Drug Development, *Impact Report*, 2003, **5** (3) (Boston, MA).

[7] M. Morant, S. Bak, B. L. Moller and D. Werck-Reichhart, Plant cytochromes P450: tools for pharmacology, plant protection and phytoremediation, *Curr. Opin. Biotechnol.*, 2003, **14** (2), 151–162.

[8] S. Rao, R. Aoyama, M. Schrag, W. F. Trager, A. Rettie and J. P. Jones, A refined 3-dimensional QSAR of cytochrome P450 2C9: computational predictions of drug interactions, *J. Med. Chem.*, 2000, **43** (15), 2789–2796.

[9] S. Ekins, G. Bravi, J. H. Wikel and S. A. Wrighton, Three-dimensional-quantitative structure activity relationship analysis of cytochrome P-450 3A4 substrates, *J. Pharmacol. Exp. Ther.*, 1999, **291** (1), 424–433.

[10] J. P. Jones and K. R. Korzekwa, Predicting the rates and regioselectivity of reactions mediated by the P450 superfamily, *Methods Enzymol*, 1996, **272**, 326–335.

[11] S. Shaik, S. P. de Visser, F. Ogliaro, H. Schwarz and D. Schroder, Two-state reactivity mechanisms of hydroxylation and epoxidation by cytochrome P-450 revealed by theory, *Curr. Opin. Chem. Biol.*, 2002, **6** (5), 556–567.

[12] G. D. Szklarz and J. R. Halpert, Molecular modeling of cytochrome P450 3A4, *J. Comput. Aided Mol. Des.*, 1997, **11** (3), 265–272.

[13] T. L. Poulos, B. C. Finzel, B. I. C. Gunsalus, G. C. Wagner and J. Kraut, The 2.6-A crystal structure of *Pseudomonas putida* cytochrome P-450, *J. Biol. Chem.*, 1985, **260** (30), 16122–16130.

[14] P. A. Williams, J. Cosme, V. Sridhar, E. F. Johnson and D. E. McRee, Mammalian microsomal cytochrome P450 monooxygenase: structural adaptations for membrane binding and functional diversity, *Mol. Cell*, 2000, **5** (1), 121–131.

[15] M. R. Wester, J. K. Yano, G. A. Schoch, C. Yang, K. J. Griffin, C. D. Stout and E. F. Johnson, The structure of human cytochrome P450 2C9 complexed with flurbiprofen at 2.0-A resolution, *J. Biol. Chem.*, 2004, **279** (34), 35630–35637.

[16] J. K. Yano, M. R. Wester, G. A. Schoch, K. J. Griffin, C. D. Stout and E. F. Johnson, The structure of human microsomal cytochrome P450 3A4 determined by X-ray crystallography to 2.05-A resolution, *J. Biol. Chem.*, 2004, **279** (37), 38091–38094.

[17] S. A. Wrighton, E. G. Schuetz, K. E. Thummel, D. D. Shen, K. R. Korzekwa and P. B. Watkins, The human CYP3A subfamily: practical considerations, *Drug Metab. Rev.*, 2000, **32** (3–4), 339–361.

[18] K. H. Ruckpaul, H. Rein and J. Blanck, Regulation mechanisms of the endoplasmic cytochrome P-450 systems of the liver, *Biomed. Biochim. Acta*, 1985, **44** (3), 351–379.

[19] D. Kim and F. P. Guengerich, Selection of human cytochrome P450 1A2 mutants with enhanced catalytic activity for heterocyclic amine N-hydroxylation, *Biochemistry*, 2004, **43** (4), 981–988.

[20] K.-F. Aguey-Zinsou, P. V. Bernhardt, J. J. De Voss and K. E. Slessor, Electrochemistry of P450cin: new insights into P450 electron transfer, *Chem. Commun. (Camb)*, 2003 (3), 418–419.

[21] H. Li and T. L. Poulos, The structure of the cytochrome p450BM-3 haem domain complexed with the fatty acid substrate, palmitoleic acid, *Nat. Struct. Biol.*, 1997, **4** (2), 140–146.

[22] W. N. Atkins and S. G. Sligar, Metabolic switching in cyctochrome P-450cam: deuterium isotope effects on regiospecificity and the monooxygenase/oxidase ratio, *J. Am. Chem. Soc.*, 1987, **107** (12), 3754–3760.

[23] M. H. Gelb, P. Malkonen and S. G. Sligar, Cytochrome P450cam catalyzed epoxidation of dehydrocamphor, *Biochem. Biophys. Res. Commun.*, 1982, **104** (3), 853–858.

[24] P. J. Loida and S. G. Sligar, Molecular recognition in cytochrome P-450: mechanism for the control of uncoupling reactions, *Biochemistry*, 1993, **32** (43), 11530–11538.

[25] T. L. Poulos, B. C. Finzel and A. J. Howard, High-resolution crystal structure of cytochrome P450cam, *J. Mol. Biol.*, 1987, **195** (3), 687–700.

[26] M. Strickler, B. M. Goldstein, K. Maxfield, L. Shireman, G. Kim, D. S. Matteson and J. P. Jones, Crystallographic studies on the complex behavior of nicotine binding to P450cam (CYP101), *Biochemistry*, 2003, **42** (41), 11943–11950.

[27] R. Raag. and T. L. Poulos, Crystal structures of cytochrome P-450CAM complexed with camphane, thiocamphor, and adamantane: factors controlling P-450 substrate hydroxylation, *Biochemistry*, 1991, **30** (10), 2674–2684.

[28] R. Raag, H. Li, B. C. Jones and T. L. Poulos, Inhibitor-induced conformational change in cytochrome P-450CAM, *Biochemistry*, 1993, **32** (17), 4571–4578.

[29] X. Chen, A. Christopher, J. A. Jones, S. G. Bell, Q. Guo, F. Xu, Z. Rao and L. L. Wong, Crystal structure of the F87W/Y96F/V247L mutant of cytochrome P-450cam with 1,3,5-trichlorobenzene bound and further protein engineering for the oxidation of pentachlorobenzene and hexachlorobenzene, *J. Biol. Chem.*, 2002, **277** (40), 37519–37526.

[30] T. L. Poulos, B. C. Finzel and A. J. Howard, Crystal structure of substrate-free *Pseudomonas putida* cytochrome P-450, *Biochemistry*, 1986, **25** (18), 5314–5322.

[31] I. F. Sevrioukova, J. T. Hazzard, G. Tollin and T. L. Poulos, Structure of a cytochrome P450-redox partner electron-transfer complex, *Proc. Natl. Acad. Sci. USA*, 1999, **96** (5), 1863–1868.

[32] C. A. Hasemann, K. G. Ravichandran, J. A. Peterson and J. Deisenhofer, Crystal structure and refinement of cytochrome P450terp at 2.3 Å resolution, *J. Mol. Biol.*, 1994, **236** (4), 1169–1185.

[33] J. R. Cupp-Vickery and T. L. Poulos, Structure of cytochrome P450eryF involved in erythromycin biosynthesis, *Nat. Struct. Biol.*, 1995, **2** (2), 144–153.

[34] S. K. Ludemann, V. Lounnas and R. C. Wade, How do substrates enter and products exit the buried active site of cytochrome P450cam? 1. Random expulsion molecular dynamics investigation of ligand access channels and mechanisms, *J. Mol. Biol.*, 2000, **303** (5), 797–811.

[35] S. K. Ludemann, V. Lounnas and R. C. Wade, How do substrates enter and products exit the buried active site of cytochrome P450cam? 2. Steered molecular dynamics and adiabatic mapping of substrate pathways, *J. Mol. Biol.*, 2000, **303** (5), 813–830.

[36] A. R. Dunn, I. J. Dmochowski, A. M. Bilwes, H. B. Gray and B. R. Crane, Probing the open state of cytochrome P450cam with ruthenium-linker substrates, *Proc. Natl. Acad. Sci. USA*, 2001, **98** (22), 12420–12425.

[37] T. L. Poulos and A. J. Howard, Crystal structures of metyrapone- and phenyl-imidazole-inhibited complexes of cytochrome P-450cam, *Biochemistry*, 1987, **26** (25), 8165–8174.

[38] H. Li and T. L. Poulos, Fatty acid metabolism, conformational change, and electron transfer in cytochrome P-450(BM-3), *Biochim. Biophys. Acta*, 1999, **1441** (2–3), 141–149.

[39] K. G. Ravichandran, S. S. Boddupalli, C. A. Hasermann, J. A. Peterson and J. Deisenhofer, Crystal structure of hemoprotein domain of P450BM-3, a prototype for microsomal P450 s, *Science*, 1993, **261** (5122), 731–736.

[40] L. M. Podust, T. L. Poulos and M. R. Waterman, Crystal structure of cytochrome P450 14alpha -sterol demethylase (CYP51) from *Mycobacterium tuberculosis* in complex with azole inhibitors, *Proc. Natl. Acad. Sci. USA*, 2001, **98** (6), 3068–3073.

[41] L. M. Podust, L. V. Yermalitskaya, G. I. Lepesheva, V. N. Podust, E. A. Dalmasso and M. R. Waterman, Estriol bound and ligand-free structures of sterol 14alpha-demethylase, *Structure (Camb)*, 2004, **12** (11), 1937–1945.

[42] C. D. Stout, Cytochrome p450 conformational diversity, *Structure (Camb)*, 2004, **12** (11), 1921–1922.

[43] J. K. Yano, L. S. Koo, D. J. Schuller, H. Li, P. R. Ortiz de Montellano and T. L. Poulos, Crystal structure of a thermophilic cytochrome P450 from the archaeon *Sulfolobus solfataricus*, *J. Biol. Chem.*, 2000, **275** (40), 31086–31092.

[44] L. S. Koo, C. E. Immoos, M. S. Cohen, P. J. Farmer and P. R. Ortiz de Montellano, Enhanced electron transfer and lauric acid hydroxylation by site-directed mutagenesis of CYP119, *J. Am. Chem. Soc.*, 2002, **124** (20), 5684–5691.

[45] P. A. Williams, J. Cosme, A. Ward, H. C. Angove, D. M. Vinkovic and H. Jhoti, Crystal structure of human cytochrome P450 2C9 with bound warfarin, *Nature*, 2003, **424** (6947), 464–468.

[46] E. E. Scott, Y. A. He, M. R. Wester, M. A. White, C. C. Chin, J. R. Halpert, E. F. Johnson and C. D. Stout, An open conformation of mammalian cytochrome P450 2B4 at 1.6-A resolution, *Proc. Natl. Acad. Sci. USA*, 2003, **100** (23), 13196–13201.

[47] G. A. Schoch, J. K. Yano, M. R. Wester, K. J. Griffin, C. D. Stout and E. F. Johnson, Structure of human microsomal cytochrome P450 2C8. Evidence for a peripheral fatty acid binding site, *J. Biol. Chem.*, 2004, **279** (10), 9497–9503.

[48] P. A. Williams, J. Cosme, D. M. Vinkovic, A. Ward, H. C. Angove, P. J. Day, C. Vonrhein, I. J. Tickle and H. Jhoti, Crystal structures of human cytochrome P450 3A4 bound to metyrapone and progesterone, *Science*, 2004, **305** (5684), 683–686.

[49] M. Shou, R. Dai, D. Cui, K. R. Korzekwa, T. A. Baillie and T. H. Rushmore, A kinetic model for the metabolic interaction of two substrates at the active site of cytochrome P450 3A, *J. Biol. Chem.*, 2001, **276** (3), 2256–2262.

[50] K. V. Balakin, S. Ekins, A. Bugrim, Y. A. Ivanenkov, D. Korolev, Y. V. Nikolsky, A. V. Skorenko, A. A. Ivashchenko, N. P. Savchuk and T. Nikolskaya, Kohonen maps for prediction of binding to human cytochrome P450 3A4, *Drug Metab. Dispos.*, 2004, **32** (10), 1183–1189.

[51] L. Molnar and G. M. Keseru, A neural network based virtual screening of cytochrome P450 3A4 inhibitors, *Bioorg. Med. Chem. Lett.*, 2002, **12** (3), 419–421.

[52] K. R. Korzekwa, J. P. Jones and J. R. Gillette, Theoretical studies on cytochrome P-450-mediated hydroxylation: a predictive model for hydrogen atom abstractions, *J. Am. Chem. Soc.*, **112** (1990) 7042–7046.

[53] J. Grogan, S. C. DeVito, R. S. Pearlman and K. R. Korzekwa, Modeling cyanide release from nitriles: prediction of cytochrome P450 mediated acute nitrile toxicity, *Chem. Res. Toxicol.*, 1992, **5** (4), 548–552.

[54] H. Tanii and K. Hashimoto, Studies on the mechanism of acute toxicity of nitriles in mice, *Arch. Toxicol.*, 1984, **55** (1), 47–54.

[55] R. D. Cramer 3rd, D. E. Patterson and J. D. Bunce, Recent advances in comparative molecular field analysis (CoMFA), *Prog. Clin. Biol. Res.*, **291** (1989) 161–165.

[56] K. K. Khan, Y. Q. He, T. L. Domanski and H. R. Halpert, Midazolam oxidation by cytochrome P450 3A4 and active-site mutants: an evaluation of multiple binding sites and of the metabolic pathway that leads to enzyme inactivation, *Mol. Pharmacol.*, 2002, **61** (3), 495–506.

[57] S. Ekins, M. J. de Groot and J. P. Jones, Pharmacophore and three-dimensional quantitative structure activity relationship methods for modeling cytochrome p450 active sites, *Drug Metab. Dispos.*, 2001, **29** (7), 936–944.

[58] M. J. de Groot, M. J. Ackland, V. A. Horne, A. A. Alex and B. C. Jones, Novel approach to predicting P450-mediated drug metabolism: development of a combined protein and pharmacophore model for CYP2D6, *J. Med. Chem.*, 1999, **42** (9), 1515–1524.

[59] B. C. Orcutt, M. O. Dayhoff and W.C. Barker, *ALIGN*, National Biomedical Foundation, Georgetown University Medical Center, Washington, DC, 1982.

[60] S. F. Altschul, T. L. Madden, A. A. Schaffer, J. Zhang, Z. Zhang, W. Miller and D. J. Lipman, Gapped BLAST and PSI-BLAST: a new generation of protein database search programs, *Nucleic Acids Res.*, 1997, **25** (17), 3389–3402.

[61] M. A. F. Marti-Renom, A. M. S. Madhusen, B. John, A. Stuart, N. Eswar, P. Pieper, M. Y. Shen and A. Sali, Modeling Protein Structure from its Sequence, *Curr. Protocol. Bioinform.*, **5**(2003) 5.1.1–5.1.32.

[62] R. A. Laskowski, M. W. MacArthur, D. S. Moss and J. M. Thornton, PROCHECK: a program to check the stereochemical quality of protein structures. *J. Appl. Crystallogr.*, **26** (1993) 283–291.

[63] M. J. Sippl, Recognition of errors in three-dimensional structures of proteins, *Proteins*, 1993, **17** (4), 355–362.

[64] G. Vriend, WHAT IF: a molecular modeling and drug design program, *J. Mol. Graph.*, **8**(1) (1990) 29 52–56.

[65] L. Afzelius, F. Raubacher, A. Karlen, F. S. Jorgensen, T. B. Andersson, C. M. Masimirembwa and I. Zamora, Structural analysis of CYP2C9 and CYP2C5 and an evaluation of commonly used molecular modeling techniques, *Drug Metab. Dispos.*, 2004, **32** (11), 1218–1229.

[66] I. D. Kuntz, J. M. Blaney, S. J. Oatley, R. Langridge and T. E. Ferrin, A geometric approach to macromolecule-ligand interaction, *J. Mol. Biol.*, 1982, **161** (2), 269–288.

[67] M. Rarey, B. Kramer, T. Lengauer and G. Klebe, A fast flexible docking method using an incremental construction algorithm, *J. Mol. Biol.*, 1996, **261** (3), 470–489.

[68] G. Jones, P. Willett, R. C. Glen, A. R. Leach and R. Taylor, Development and validation of a genetic algorithm for flexible docking, *J. Mol. Biol.*, 1997, **267** (3), 727–748.

[69] G. M. Morris, D. S. Goodsell, R. S. Halliday, R. Huey, W. E. Hart, R. K. Belew and A. J. Olson, Automated docking using a Lamarckian genetic algorithm and an empirical binding free energy function, *J. Comput. Chem.*, 1998, **19**, 1639–1662.

[70] E. K. Kick, D. C. Roe, A. G. Skillman, G. Liu, T. J. Ewing, Y. Sun, I. D. Kuntz and J. A. Ellman, Structure-based design and combinatorial chemistry yield low nanomolar inhibitors of cathepsin D, *Chem. Biol.*, 1997, **4** (4), 297–307.

[71] D. L. Harris and G. H. Loew, Investigation of the proton-assisted pathway to formation of the catalytically active, ferryl species of P450 s by molecular dynamics studies of P450eryF, *J. Am. Chem. Soc.*, 1996, **118** (27), 6377–6387.

[72] J. J. De Voss and P. R. Ortiz de Montellano, Substrate docking algorithms and the prediction of substrate specificity, *Methods Enzymol.*, 1996, **272**, 336–347.

[73] S. B. Kirton, C. W. Murray, M. L. Verdonk and R. D. Taylor, Prediction of binding modes for ligands in the cytochromes P450 and other heme-containing proteins, *Proteins*, 2005, **58** (4), 836–844.

[74] M. D. Eldridge, C. W. Murray, T. R. Auton, G. V. Paolini and R. P. Mee, Empirical scoring functions: I. The development of a fast empirical scoring function to estimate

the binding affinity of ligands in receptor complexes, *J. Comput. Aided Mol. Des.*, 1997, **11** (5), 425–445.

[75] J. W. Nissink, C. Murray, M. Hartshorn, M. L. Verdonk, J. C. Cole and R. Taylor, A new test set for validating predictions of protein–ligand interaction, *Proteins*, 2002, **49** (4), 457–471.

[76] A. Verras, I. D. Kuntz and P. R. Ortiz de Montellano, Computer-assisted design of selective imidazole inhibitors for cytochrome p450 enzymes, *J. Med. Chem.*, 2004, **47** (14), 3572–3579.

[77] G. M. Keseru, A virtual high throughput screen for high affinity cytochrome P450cam substrates. Implications for in silico prediction of drug metabolism, *J. Comput. Aided Mol. Des.*, 2001, **15** (7), 649–657.

[78] A. K. Daly, J. Brockmoller, F. Broly, M. Eichelbaum, W. E. Evans, F. J. Gonzalez, J. D. Huang, J. R. Idle, M. Ingelman-Sundberg, T. Ishizaki, E. Jacqz-Aigrain, U. A. Meyer, D. W. Nebert, V. M. Steen, C. R. Wolf and U. M. Zanger, Nomenclature for human CYP2D6 alleles, *Pharmacogenetics*, 1996, **6** (3), 193–201.

[79] R. M. Knegtel, I. D. Kuntz and C. M. Oshiro, Molecular docking to ensembles of protein structures, *J. Mol. Biol.*, 1997, **266** (2), 424–440.

[80] M. Shou, J. Grogan, J. A. Mancewicz, K. W. Krausz, F. J. Gonzalez, H. V. Gelboin and K. R. Korzekwa, Activation of CYP3A4: evidence for the simultaneous binding of two substrates in a cytochrome P450 active site, *Biochemistry*, 1994, **33** (21), 6450–6455.

[81] K. R. Korzekwa, N. Krishnamachary, M. Shou, A. Ogai, R. A. Parise, A. E. Rettie, F. J. Gonzalez and T. S. Tracy, Evaluation of atypical cytochrome P450 kinetics with two-substrate models: evidence that multiple substrates can simultaneously bind to cytochrome P450 active sites, *Biochemistry*, 1998, **37** (12), 4137–4147.

[82] F. Jiang and S. H. Kim, "Soft docking": matching of molecular surface cubes, *J. Mol. Biol.*, 1991, **219** (1), 79–102.

[83] A. R. Leach, Ligand docking to proteins with discrete side-chain flexibility, *J. Mol. Biol.*, 1994, **235** (1), 345–356.

[84] R. Abagyan, M. Totrov and D. Kuznetsov, ICM- a new method for protein modeling and design- applications to docking and structure prediction from the distorted native conformation, *J. Comput. Chem.*, 1994, **15**, 488–506.

[85] J. Desmet, I. A. Wilson, M. Joniau, M. De Maeyer and I. Lasters, Computation of the binding of fully flexible peptides to proteins with flexible side chains, *Faseb J.*, 1997, **11** (2), 164–172.

[86] L. Schaffer and G. M. Verkhivker, Predicting structural effects in HIV-1 protease mutant complexes with flexible ligand docking and protein side-chain optimization, *Proteins*, 1998, **33** (2), 295–310.

[87] A. Evers, H. Gohlke and G. Klebe, Ligand-supported homology modelling of protein binding-sites using knowledge-based potential, *J. Mol. Biol.*, 2003, **334** (2), 327–345.

[88] M. P. Jacobson. and A. Sali, Comparative protein structure modeling and its application to drug discovery, *Annu. Rep. Med. Chem.*, 2004, **39**, 259–276.

[89] I. Schlichting, C. Jung and H. Schulze, Crystal structure of cytochrome P-450cam complexed with the (1S)-camphor enantiomer, *FEBS Lett.*, 1997, **415** (3), 253–257.

[90] R. Raag, B. A. Swanson, T. L. Poulos and P. R. Ortiz de Montellano, Formation, crystal structure, and rearrangement of a cytochrome P-450cam iron–phenyl complex, *Biochemistry*, 1990, **29** (35), 8119–8126.

[91] I. Schlichting, J. Berendzen, K. Chu, A. M. Stock, S. A. Maves, D. E. Benson, R. M. Sweet, D. Ringe, G. A. Petsko and S. G. Sligar, The catalytic pathway of cytochrome p450cam at atomic resolution, *Science*, 2000, **287** (5458), 1615–1622.

[92] D. S. Lee, S. Y. Park, K. Yamane, E. Obayashi, H. Hori and Y. Shiro, Structural characterization of n-butyl-isocyanide complexes of cytochromes P450nor and P450cam, *Biochemistry*, 2001, **40** (9), 2669–2677.

[93] K. Di Gleria, D. P. Nickerson, H. A. O. Hill, L.-L. Wong and V. Fulop, Covalent attachment of an electroactive sulfydryl reagent in the active site of cytochrome P450cam as revealed by the crystal structure of the modified protein, *J. Am. Chem. Soc.*, 1998, **120** (1), 46–52.

[94] I. J. Dmochowski, B. R. Crane, J. J. Wilker, J. R. Winkler and H. B. Gray, Optical detection of cytochrome P450 by sensitizer-linked substrates, *Proc. Natl. Acad. Sci. USA*, 1999, **96** (23), 12987–12990.

[95] A. R. Dunn, A. M. Hays, D. B. Goodin, C. D. Stout, R. Chiu, J. R. Winkler and H. B. Gray, Fluorescent probes for cytochrome p450 structural characterization and inhibitor screening, *J. Am. Chem. Soc.*, 2002, **124** (35), 10254–10255.

[96] R. Fedorov, D. K. Ghosh and I. Schlichting, Crystal structures of cyanide complexes of P450cam and the oxygenase domain of inducible nitric oxide synthase-structural models of the short-lived oxygen complexes, *Arch. Biochem. Biophys.*, 2003, **409** (1), 25–31.

[97] R. Raag, S. A. Martinis, S. G. Sligar and T. L. Poulos, Crystal structure of the cytochrome P-450CAM active site mutant Thr252Ala, *Biochemistry*, 1991, **30** (48), 11420–11429.

[98] M. Vidakovic, S. G. Sligar, H. Li and T. L. Poulos, Understanding the role of the essential Asp251 in cytochrome p450cam using site-directed mutagenesis, *crystallography, and kinetic solvent isotope effect, Biochemistry*, 1998, **37** (26), 9211–9219.

[99] R. Raag and T. L. Poulos, Crystal structure of the carbon monoxide-substrate-cytochrome P-450CAM ternary complex, *Biochemistry*, 1989, **28** (19), 7586–7592.

[100] R. Raag and T. L. Poulos, The structural basis for substrate-induced changes in redox potential and spin equilibrium in cytochrome P-450CAM, *Biochemistry*, 1989, **28** (2), 917–922.

[101] H. Yeom, S. G. Sligar, H. Li, T. L. Poulos and A. J. Fulco, The role of Thr268 in oxygen activation of cytochrome P450BM-3, *Biochemistry*, 1995, **34** (45), 14733–14740.

[102] T. W. Ost, A. W. Munro, C. G. Mowat, P. R. Taylor, A. Pesseguiero, A. J. Fulco, A. K. Cho, M. A. Chessman, M. D. Walkinshaw and S. K. Chapman, Structural and spectroscopic analysis of the F393 H mutant of flavocytochrome P450 BM3, *Biochemistry*, 2001, **40** (45), 13430–13438.

[103] D. C. Haines, D. R. Tomchick, M. Machius and J. A. Peterson, Pivotal role of water in the mechanism of P450BM-3, *Biochemistry*, 2001, **40** (45), 13456–13465.

[104] T. W. Ost, J. Clark, C. G. Mowat, C. S. Miles, M. D. Walkinshaw, G. A. Reid, S. K. Chapman and S. Daff, Oxygen activation and electron transfer in flavocytochrome P450 BM3, *J. Am. Chem. Soc.*, 2003, **125** (49), 15010–15020.

[105] M. G. Joyce, H. M. Girvan, A. W. Munro and D. Leys, A single mutation in cytochrome P450 BM3 induces the conformational rearrangement seen upon substrate binding in the wild-type enzyme, *J. Biol. Chem.*, 2004, **279** (22), 23287–23293.

[106] M. R. Wester, E. F. Johnson, C. Marques-Soares, P. M. Dansette, D. Mansuy and C. D. Stout, Structure of a substrate complex of mammalian cytochrome P450 2C5 at 2.3 A resolution: evidence for multiple substrate binding modes, *Biochemistry*, 2003, **42** (21), 6370–6379.

[107] M. R. Wester, E. F. Johnson, C. Marques-Soares, S. Dijols, P. M. Dansette, D. Mansuy and C. D. Stout, Structure of mammalian cytochrome P450 2C5 complexed with diclofenac at 2.1 A resolution: evidence for an induced fit model of substrate binding, *Biochemistry*, 2003, **42** (31), 9335–9345.

[108] E. E. Scott, M. A. White, Y. A. He, E. F. Johnson, C. D. Stout and J. R. Halpert, Structure of mammalian cytochrome P450 2B4 complexed with 4-(4-chlorophenyl)imidazole at 1.9-A resolution: insight into the range of P450 conformations and the coordination of redox partner binding, *J. Biol. Chem.*, 2004, **279** (26), 27294–27301.

[109] J. R. Cupp-Vickery, R. Anderson and Z. Hatziris, Crystal structures of ligand complexes of P450eryF exhibiting homotropic cooperativity, *Proc. Natl. Acad. Sci. USA*, 2000, **97** (7), 3050–3055.

[110] J. R. Cupp-Vickery, C. Garcia, A. Hofacre and K. McGee-Estrada, Ketoconazole-induced conformational changes in the active site of cytochrome P450eryF, *J. Mol. Biol.*, 2001, **311** (1), 101–110.

[111] S. Nagano, H. Li, H. Shimizu, H. Nishida, H. Ogura, P. R. Ortiz de Montellano and T. L. Poulos, Crystal structures of epothilone D-bound, epothilone B-bound, and substrate-free forms of cytochrome P450epoK, *J. Biol. Chem.*, 2003, **278** (45), 44886–44893.

[112] H. Shimizu, S. Park, D. Lee, H. Shoun and Y. Shiro, Crystal structures of cytochrome P450nor and its mutants (Ser286->Val, Thr) in the ferric resting state at cryogenic temperature: a comparative analysis with monooxygenase cytochrome P450 s, *J. Inorg. Biochem.*, 2000, **81** (3), 191–205.

[113] T. Kudo, N. Takaya, S. Park, Y. Shiro and H. Shoun, A positively charged cluster formed in the heme-distal pocket of cytochrome P450nor is essential for interaction with NADH, *J. Biol. Chem.*, 2001, **276** (7), 5020–5026.

[114] R. Oshima, S. Fushinobu, F. Su, L. Zhang, N. Takaya and H. Shoun, Structural evidence for direct hydride transfer from NADH to cytochrome P450nor, *J. Mol. Biol.*, 2004, **342** (1), 207–217.

[115] S. Y. Park, K. Yamane, S. Adachi, Y. Shiro, K. E. Weiss and S. G. Sligar, Crystallization and preliminary X-ray diffraction analysis of a cytochrome P450 (CYP119) from *Sulfolobus solfataricus*Acta. Crystallogr, *D Biol. Crystallogr*, 2000, **56** (Pt 9), 1173–1175.

[116] J. K. Yano, F. Blasco, H. Li, R. D. Schmid, A. Henne and T. L. Poulos, Preliminary characterization and crystal structure of a thermostable cytochrome P450 from *Thermus thermophilus*, *J. Biol. Chem.*, 2003, **278** (1), 608–616.

[117] D. S. Lee, A. Yamada, H. Sugimoto, I. Matsunaga, H. Ogura, K. Ichihara, S. Adachi, S. Y. Park and Y. Shiro, Substrate recognition and molecular mechanism of fatty acid hydroxylation by cytochrome P450 from *Bacillus subtilis*. Crystallographic, spectroscopic, and mutational studies, *J. Biol. Chem.*, 2003, **278** (11), 9761–9767.

[118] K. Zerbe, O. Pylypenko, F. Vitali, W. Zhang, S. Rouset, M. Heck, J. W. Vrijbloed, D. Bischoff, B. Bister, R. D. Sussmuth, S. Pelzer, W. Wohlleben, J. A. Robinson and I. Schlichting, Crystal structure of OxyB, a cytochrome P450 implicated in an oxidative phenol coupling reaction during vancomycin biosynthesis, *J. Biol. Chem.*, 2002, **277** (49), 47476–47485.

[119] O. Pylypenko, F. Vitali, K. Zerbe, J. A. Robinson and I. Schlichting, Crystal structure of OxyC, a cytochrome P450 implicated in an oxidative C–C coupling reaction during vancomycin biosynthesis, *J. Biol. Chem.*, 2003, **278** (47), 46727–46733.

[120] D. Leys, C. G. Mowat, K. J. McLean, A. Richmond, S. K. Chapman, M. D. Walkinshaw and A. W. Munro, Atomic structure of *Mycobacterium tuberculosis* CYP121 to 1.06 A reveals novel features of cytochrome P450, *J. Biol. Chem.*, 2003, **278** (7), 5141–5147.

[121] L. M. Podust, H. Bach, Y. Kim, D. Lamb, M. Arase, D. H. Sherman, S. L. Kelly and M. R. Waterman, Comparison of the 1.85 A structure of CYP154A1 from *Streptomyces coelicolor* A3(2) with the closely related CYP154C1 and CYPs from antibiotic biosynthetic pathways, *Protein Sci.*, 2004, **13** (1), 255–268.

CHAPTER 11

Recent Advances in Design of Small-Molecule Ligands To Target Protein–Protein Interactions

Chao-Yie Yang and Shaomeng Wang

University of Michigan Comprehensive Cancer Center, Departments of Internal Medicine, Pharmacology and Medicinal Chemistry, University of Michigan, Ann Arbor, MI 48109, USA

Contents

1. INTRODUCTION

Direct interactions between proteins are important for their stability and/or functions. For example, tumor suppressor p53 functions as a tetrameric unit, formation of which is critical for both its stability and function in cells [1]. Interaction of p53 with the MDM2 oncoprotein, for instance, effectively inhibits the cellular functions of p53 [2]. The dimerization of anti-apoptotic Bcl-2 members such as Bcl-2, Bcl-xL and Mcl-1, with pro-apoptotic Bcl-2 members such as Bak, Bax, Bim, Bid and Bad, neutralize their opposing

ANNUAL REPORTS IN COMPUTATIONAL CHEMISTRY, VOLUME 2
ISSN: 1574-1400   DOI 10.1016/S1574-1400(06)02011-1

cellular functions in apoptosis regulation [3]. In addition to such hetero-dimerization between Bcl-2 family members, some Bcl-2 members such as Bax and Bak proteins form homodimers [4], and the delicate balance of hetero- and homodimerization of Bcl-2 family members controls the execution of apoptosis. Protein–protein interactions are therefore not only critical for maintaining normal cellular functions, but also are involved in the pathological processes of many human diseases. Hence, targeting protein–protein interactions with small-molecule ligands has in recent years emerged as an exciting area in chemistry, biology and medicine [5–7].

Because most protein–protein interactions typically involve a large and shallow interface [5,6,8], design and discovery of potent, drug-like, small-molecule ligands to block protein–protein interactions has been a challenging task. However, in recent years, significant progress has been made in this area. We attempt to provide an overview on the design of small-molecule ligands to target protein–protein interactions using both computational and experimental approaches. This review is divided into four sections. First, we review recent computational analysis on the protein–protein interface. Second, we provide an overview on different approaches that have been employed for the design of small-molecule ligands to target protein–protein interactions. Third, we discuss several recent successful examples on the design of small-molecule ligands to interrupt protein–protein interactions. Finally, we summarize what have been accomplished and what challenges remain in this area.

2. COMPUTATIONAL ANALYSIS OF THE PROTEIN–PROTEIN INTERACTION INTERFACE

A recent analysis of 75 homo- and heterodimeric protein complexes [12] showed that 52 of them have a total buried surface area of $1600 \pm 400 \, \text{Å}^2$ in the interface of the protein complexes. The smallest buried surface area is $1150 \, \text{Å}^2$ in the yeast cytochrome peroxydase–cytochrome c complex and the largest is $4660 \, \text{Å}^2$ between phosducin and the $G_{\beta\gamma}$ subunit of transducin. It has also been found that the interfaces of oligomeric proteins are more hydrophobic than other areas on the protein surfaces and in fact are similar in hydrophobicity to the protein cores, an observation consistent with a previous analysis by Jones and Thornton [8]. Interestingly, no large conformational changes are found in most protein–protein complexes, and the packing density of the buried atoms at the interface appears to be similar to that in the protein core.

To investigate the importance of each residue at the protein–protein interface, Clackson and Wells [9] conducted experimental mutational analyses of the hormone–receptor complex and showed that just a few residues in the interface dominate the binding interaction between proteins; in which, 8 of the 31 residues on the hormone protein contribute 85% loss of overall binding affinity when individually mutated to alanine. This study led to a model called "hot spots" of the interface, which refers specifically to those residues, when mutated to alanine [9,10], contributing more than 1.5 kcal/mol to the loss of overall binding free energy. These hot spots are surrounded by energetically less important residues that are often polar and partially hydrated. In an extensive analysis of 2325 alanine mutant data by Bogan and Thorn [11], the existence of "hot spots" was confirmed and the model was extended. In their analysis, Trp, Tyr and Arg are frequently found to be present in hot spots in the interface. In their characterization, the interface is analogous to an "O-ring" where hot-spot residues are surrounded by energetically less important residues, which serve to occlude solvents. Using this O-ring hypothesis, a recent experimental study on the association between anti-hen egg white lysozyme (HEL) antibody H63 and HEL showed that hydrophobicity at the central site is about twice that at the peripheral site (46 *versus* 21 cal/mol/$Å^2$), confirming the dominant contribution of residues at the center of the interface (i.e. the hot spots) to the protein–protein association [13].

To identify structurally conserved residues in the interface, Ma and colleagues [14] analyzed 86 protein complexes in 10 protein families selected from a total of 1629 two-chain interface entries in the Protein Data Bank [15]. For protein complexes in each family, they used MUSTA [16,17] to simultaneously align the protein structures and identify motifs in order to find the largest common substructure in each family. If backbones of residues are aligned within 1.0 Å in more than 80% of family members, they are considered to be conserved in the family. They found that the conservation propensity of each residue on binding sites correlates well with its enrichment in the hot spots reported by Bogan and Thorn [11]. Furthermore, a conserved Trp on the protein surface indicates a highly likely binding site. To a lesser extent are Phe and Met when they are conserved on the protein surfaces. The same approach was used by Keskin and colleagues [18] to characterize the organization and contribution of these structurally conserved hot-spot residues. It was shown that rather than being homogenously distributed in the protein interface, the hot spots are clustered in local tightly packed and separate regions. This suggests that protein–protein associations are contributed cooperatively by several locally optimized, networked and tightly packed structurally conserved residues at the interface.

Although the identification of the hot spots at the protein–protein interface is commonly accomplished by alanine screening, the loss of interactions from the side-chain atoms of the residues may not be well
accounted for and in some cases, a single site mutation to alanine may
result in conformational changes of the protein or unfolding of the native
protein structure [19]. Computational methods combining molecular mechanics and continuum solvation models such as molecular mechanics
and the Poisson–Boltzman surface area (MM-PBSA) method [20] have
been developed to complement experimental alanine screening and assess directly the energetic contribution to the binding affinity of individual
residues at the interface while assuming no dramatic conformational
changes occur after the mutation to alanine. Applications of these methods include the interaction between the peptide from p53 and the MDM2
protein [21] and hormone–hormone receptors [22]. A protocol for MM-
PBSA computation was reported recently by Baker and colleagues [23].

The general applicability of the hot-spot model to protein–protein association remains to be widely tested and validated [19]. Nevertheless, the
"hot-spot" model can be used to guide the development of small-molecule
inhibitors designed to disrupt protein–protein interaction by focusing on
specific locations at the interface. The model also suggests that non-
peptide small-molecule ligands designed to target these hot spots may be
able to effectively interrupt the protein–protein interaction.

3. APPROACHES IN DISCOVERY AND DESIGN OF SMALL-MOLECULE INHIBITORS TARGETING PROTEIN–PROTEIN INTERACTIONS

Several computational and experimental approaches have been employed
to discover and design small-molecule inhibitors to target protein–protein
interactions. Below we briefly review each of these approaches.

3.1. Computational structure-based database screening

Experimental high-throughput screening has become a widely used technique to identify new lead compounds in the pharmaceutical industry, but
structure-based computational virtual screening is a less expensive alternative for lead identification [24,25]. A key advantage of virtual screening
is that it can search very rapidly and with a minimal cost through large
numbers of compounds with diverse chemical structures. It is frequently
used as a powerful tool to reduce the number of compounds to be tested
experimentally and to identify lead compounds.

Key requirements for the success of structure-based virtual screening lie in accurate, three-dimensional (3D) structural information for the protein target and detailed knowledge of the protein–protein interaction site. In a number of reported successful examples, the experimental 3D structure of the protein complex was determined, and provided a solid structural basis for ensuing drug discovery and design efforts. However, computational homology modeling has been used to model the 3D structure of the targeted proteins, as in the cases of the Bcl-2 protein [26,27] and the thyroid hormone receptor [28] where experimental structure information of the proteins or binding sites of the target proteins are lacking.

In virtual database screening, the 3D structural coordinates of small-molecule compounds in chemical databases are always generated using computational modeling tools, whereas the protein structures are either kept fixed or with minimal changes in side-chain conformations. The size and the quality of the database are important for the outcome of virtual database screening. In recent years, attention has been paid to ensure the chemical structural diversity of the compounds in the database, a characteristic which may be analyzed computationally [29]. Docking programs also play a critical role in the success of virtual screening. The widely used programs for virtual screening include DOCK [30], GOLD [31], GLIDE [32,33] and FLEXX [34]. Recently, Kellenberger and colleagues [35] reported a comparative evaluation of eight popular docking programs (DOCK [30], FLEXX [34], FRED (Open Eye Scientific Software, Santa Fe, NM), GLIDE [32,33], GOLD [31], SLIDE [36], SURFLEX [37] and QXP [38]) against 100 known protein–ligand complexes and a virtual screening test on thymidine kinase.

To improve the chances of success for future drug development, a number of strategies have been used in virtual screening. These include elimination from the database of "non-drug-like" [39] compounds, such as highly hydrophobic compounds, and the use of two-stage screening in which the first stage emphasizes speed, while the second stage focuses more on docking accuracy for top-ranked compounds obtained from the first stage. Manual inspection of top-ranked compounds is still used to select "drug-like" candidates for experimental validation. In some cases, similarity analysis of the selected compounds is used to eliminate compounds with similar structures in order to identify structurally diverse compounds from the database.

3.2. Experimental high-throughput screening

Experimental high-throughput screening has been a widely used technique to identify new lead compounds in the last decade. Development and validation of highly efficient and automatic assays make it easier to screen a large number of compounds very rapidly without involving great human efforts. A combination of high-throughput screening with combinatorial and parallel synthesis has succeeded in generating a large number of compounds with much less cost than traditional synthetic approaches.

The main advantage of the experimental approach is to quickly identify a large number of "hits". Potential drawbacks are that identified initial "hits" need to be carefully validated from complementary assays to rule out false positives. To date, very few examples are reported to use experimental high throughput to identify potent small-molecule ligands to target protein–protein interactions. One reason could be that most of the chemical libraries used in high-throughput screening contain compounds that were initially synthesized as enzymatic inhibitors and may not have appropriate chemical scaffolds that are capable of disrupting protein–protein interactions.

3.3. Structure-based design of peptidomimetics to disrupt protein–protein interactions

A direct approach to the design of small-molecule ligands to disrupt protein–protein interactions is to examine the peptide segments involved in their interactions. When a protein–protein complex is known, systematic truncation of one of the proteins into short peptide segments can be readily performed to identify important fragments. After a peptide segment dominating the protein–protein interaction is determined, transformation of the peptide segment into peptidomimetics can proceed in two ways [40]. One approach involves the introduction of unnatural amino acids to explore chemical spaces not accessible to natural amino acids. This may also lead to additional interaction achieving higher affinity and stability to escape proteolysis. The second method is to impose conformational constraints on the peptide, which not only reduces the entropic penalty paid upon complex formation, but also can convert peptides into peptidomimetics, thus increasing their proteolytic stability. In both methods, the template of the ligand is known; thus, 3D structural information of the protein–protein complex is not absolutely necessary. However, structure of the protein–protein complex can be very helpful to avoid unnecessary trial and error designs of such peptidomimetics. In both of these approaches, computational methods can guide designs by assessing strength of additional interaction and providing ideal scaffolds of conformational constrain.

3.4. Lead discovery using fragment library

The low hit rate from the high-throughput screening of chemical libraries for a protein target has prompted development of different strategies to identify new lead compounds [41]. One of them is to screen a library of relatively small fragment compounds against the protein target and to validate the binding via X-ray co-crystallization [41,42] or NMR spectroscopy [43]. In contrast to traditional screening, the major focus of fragment-based screening is not on compound leads with high potency. Instead, the intent is to find high-quality fragments that bind to different subsites in a protein-binding site. These fragments with low affinity are then tethered together to produce larger compounds with high affinity [41,42,44]. The strategy is particularly suitable for the design of small molecules to disrupt protein–protein interactions in which the interface may spread over a large area and the hot spots may not be clustered together.

Four strategies using fragment-based libraries in the design of small-molecule ligands have been used for lead identification and optimization, and have been reviewed recently by Rees and colleagues [41]. They include fragment evolution, fragment linking, fragment self-assembly and fragment optimization. In fragment-based approaches, the preparation of the fragment library is important. Ideally, they should consist of diverse functional groups because they form the basic fragments of tethered compounds. The compounds in the library should also be readily accessible and easy to combine with each other. One direct approach of library preparation is to filter out the redundant commercially available fragments via computational methods (such as similarity analysis) before the screening is performed. Recently, Congreve and colleagues analyzed the properties of 40 fragment fits against a range of targets using high-throughput X-ray crystallography and they suggested a number of rules for selecting fragments to be included in the library [45].

4. EXAMPLES IN DESIGN OF SMALL MOLECULES TO TARGET PROTEIN–PROTEIN INTERACTIONS

4.1. Small-molecule inhibitors targeting Bcl-2 and Bcl-xL proteins

The Bcl-2 family proteins, the master regulators of apoptosis, are classified into pro-apoptotic and anti-apoptotic members based upon their functions in apoptosis [46]. The former include Bax, Bak, Bid, Bad and Bim, while the latter include Bcl-2, Bcl-xL and Mcl-1. The Bcl-2 and Bcl-xL proteins antagonize the functions of pro-apoptotic Bcl-2 protein members through direct dimerization [47]. Overexpression of Bcl-2 and/or Bcl-xL proteins, observed in many human tumors, confers resistance on cancer cells to current therapeutic agents [48,49]. The interaction of Bcl-2/Bcl-xL with pro-apoptotic members of the Bcl-2 family is between a well-defined hydrophobic groove in Bcl-2/Bcl-xL and an α-helical peptide segment (Bcl-2 homology 3, or the BH3 domain) of 16–25 amino acids from its pro-apoptotic members [50,51]. This structural information raises the possibility that drug-like, non-peptide, small molecules may be designed to bind to the surface hydrophobic groove in Bcl-2/Bcl-xL proteins, thus blocking the interactions of Bcl-2/Bcl-xL with pro-apoptotic members of the Bcl-2 family. Such small-molecule inhibitors are thought to have great therapeutic potential for the treatment of many forms of human cancer [51].

Wang and colleagues [26] were the first to employ a computational database screening strategy to discover small-molecule inhibitors to target Bcl-2. They modeled the 3D structure of Bcl-2 protein based on the NMR structure of the homologous Bcl-xL protein complexed with a Bak BH3 peptide and then, using the DOCK program [30], performed computational screening of 193,833 compounds from MDL/ACD 3D database (Molecular Design Limited, San Leandro, CA) followed by experimental bioassay of selected candidates. This work led to the identification of HA14-1 (**1**), which has a binding affinity $IC_{50} = 9\,\mu M$ to Bcl-2 in a fluorescence-polarization-based (FP-based) binding assay, and was shown to induce apoptosis of human acute myeloid leukemia (HL-60) cells. Using a similar strategy, Enyedy and colleagues [27] performed computational screening of 206,876 compounds from the National Cancer Institute 3D database. Seven chemical classes of compounds were identified with IC_{50} values ranging from 1.6 to 14 μM for binding to the Bcl-2 protein as determined in an FP-based binding assay. The binding of one of the most potent inhibitors (**2**) was further confirmed by NMR methods. This particular compound was shown to effectively inhibit cell growth and induce apoptosis in human breast cancer cells.

Experimental high-throughput screening has also been used to identify small-molecule inhibitors of the Bcl-2/Bcl-xL interaction. Degterev and colleagues [52] screened 16,320 compounds from the ChemBridge database (ChemBridge Corporation, San Diego, CA) against Bcl-xL protein using an FP-based assay. They identified two series of compounds (BH3I-1 and BH3I-2) with K_i values ranging from 2.4 to 12.5 μM. Cell-based assays were used to confirm that the BH3I compounds (**3**) interrupt the association of Bcl-xL with other members of Bcl-2 family proteins, such as Bax.

The interaction of Bcl-2/Bcl-xL with pro-apoptotic Bcl-2 members involves a surface-binding groove in the Bcl-2 and Bcl-xL proteins and, from the pro-apoptotic Bcl-2 members, an α-helix segment which is a commonly found motif involved in protein–protein interactions. Since an isolated peptide segment typically has a much-reduced helical propensity, it is essential to stabilize the α-helix conformation for efficient binding if one uses the peptide as the lead for ligand design. One method to achieve this goal is to build a bridge in the peptide between two residues whose side chains do not interact with the binding partner [32,53]. Using this strategy, Walensky and colleagues [54] recently designed a series of peptidomimetics (**4**) based upon the BH3 domain in Bid. These conformationally constrained peptidomimetics (called SAHBs) were found to have much higher helical propensity than the linear Bid BH3 peptide and higher binding affinities to Bcl-2 than the Bid BH3 peptide. Furthermore, it was shown that SAHBs also have much longer half-life in *ex vivo* mouse serum than the Bid peptide. One of the SAHBs showed significant anti-tumor activity in an animal model of human cancer.

Instead of using a BH3 peptide consisting of α-amino acid as a lead, Sadowsky and colleagues designed foldamers by combining α- and β-amino acid residues to mimic the BH3 Bak peptide (16 amino acids) [55]. They found that the 14/15 helix formed by combining segments of α-$/\beta$- and α-amino acids (**5**) achieved much higher affinity to Bcl-xL protein than the Bak 16mer peptide, the measured K_i value of which is 0.7 nM in an FP-based assay. These foldamers are proteolytically stable [56] and may be used as a different strategy to design ligands to interrupt protein–protein interaction.

Recently, efforts have been made to design novel, non-peptide-based scaffolds to mimic the α-helix motif. Hamilton and colleagues [57] used the terphenyl scaffold (**6**) to mimic the backbone of an α-helix in which three consecutive benzenes were linked to each other via their para positions. Substituents are added on the phenyl rings to mimic the side chains of residues on the α-helix. The terphenyl scaffold has poor solubility, and to overcome this, a series of terephthalamide derivatives was prepared (**7**) [58]. In the latter study, terephthalamide derivatives were designed to mimic the BH3 domain of the pro-apototic protein Bak. One of the highly potent compounds was shown in an FP-based binding assay to have a K_i value of 130 nM to Bcl-xL protein.

An SAR by NMR technique [43] combined with structure-based design was used by Oltersdorf and colleagues [59] to develop potent small-molecule inhibitors targeting Bcl-2/Bcl-xL. Initially, two small molecules, 4'-fluoro-biphenyl-4-carboxylic acid and 5,6,7,8-tetrahydronaphthalen-1-ol were identified by high-throughput SAR by NMR to bind to Bcl-xL with dissociation constants of 0.30 and 4.3 mM, respectively. An acyl-sulfonamide was used to replace the biphenyl carboxyl group and act as a linkage between the biphenyl and the naphthalene. Site-directed parallel synthesis was carried out to develop a potent inhibitor (**8**) (see Fig. 1), which binds to Bcl-X_L with a high affinity ($K_i = 36$ nM). It also binds with a high affinity, however, to albumin protein present in human serum, and yields poor cellular activity. Subsequently, 3D structures of **8** in a complex with both Bcl-xL and human serum albumin were determined by NMR. The structural information was used to design ABT-737, which binds more specifically to Bcl-2/Bcl-xL than to albumin. ABT-737 (**9**) binds to Bcl-xL, Bcl-2 and Bcl-w with high affinities ($\leqslant 1$ nM), but has much weaker affinities to Bcl-B, Mcl-1 and A-1, three other anti-apoptotic proteins in the Bcl-2 family [59]. It was shown to potently inhibit cell growth in many cancer cell lines to synergize with a number of chemotherapeutic agents, and shows a robust activity in inhibition of tumor growth in xenograft models of human cancer [59].

4.2. Small molecules targeting the inhibitors of apoptosis proteins

Inhibitor of apoptosis proteins (IAPs) are another family of critical regulators of apoptosis [60]. The X-linked IAP (XIAP) is the best characterized IAP member because of its potent anti-apoptotic activity [60]. XIAP blocks apoptosis at least in part by binding to caspase-3 and caspase-9, inhibiting their caspase activity which is crucial for the execution of apoptosis [61]. The anti-apoptotic function of XIAP and other IAPs can be blocked by Smac (the second mitochondria-derived activator of caspase), which binds directly to the IAP [62]. XIAP consists of three baculovirus inhibitor protein (BIR) domains and a RING domain [60]. Biological [63] and structural studies have determined that the BIR3 domain of XIAP interacts with Smac [64,65] and caspase-9 [66] via a well-defined surface binding groove in XIAP and four residues in Smac and caspase-9 [64–66]. The four-residue AVPI Smac peptide has the same binding affinity to XIAP BIR3 as the full-length Smac protein [67], and the Smac/caspase-9 binding site in XIAP BIR3 domain has been exploited as the targeting site for the design of small-molecule inhibitors of XIAP.

Computational database screening has been used to discover small-molecule inhibitors of XIAP. Nikolovska-Coleska and colleagues [68] performed computational structure-based screening of an in-house 3D structure database of 8221 individual traditional herbal medicine natural products, followed by biochemical testing of selected candidate compounds. Embelin (**10**) from the Japanese Ardisia herb was discovered as a low-molecular-weight inhibitor that binds to the XIAP BIR3 domain

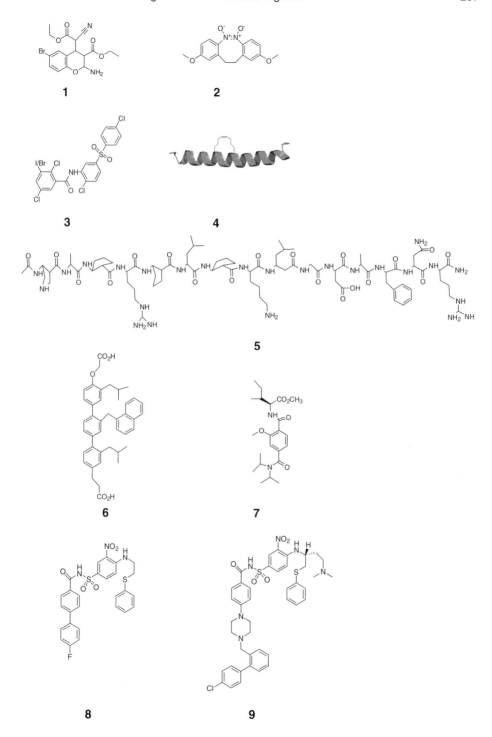

Fig. 1. Small-molecule inhibitors targeting Bcl-2 and Bcl-xL proteins.

(Fig. 2). It was shown to bind to the XIAP BIR3 protein with an affinity similar to that of the natural Smac peptide using an FP-based binding assay, and NMR analysis confirmed that it interacts with several crucial XIAP BIR3 domain residues as Smac and caspsase-9 do. Embelin inhibits cell growth, induces apoptosis and activates caspase-9 in prostate cancer cells with high levels of XIAP, but has a minimal effect on normal prostate epithelial and fibroblast cells with low levels of XIAP. It was probably the first non-peptide small-molecule inhibitor shown to target the XIAP BIR3 domain.

Because only four residues in Smac and caspase-9 are primarily invo-lved in their binding to XIAP BIR3 domain, peptidomimetics based upon these four binding residues have been designed [69–71]. Oost *et al.* [69] have systematically replaced each of the four residues individually using a library of unnatural amino acids or non-amino acids in order to find the optimal side-chain component in each position. Using this approach, they derived a series of highly potent peptidomimetics, the best of which (**11**) has a binding affinity of 5 nM to BIR3 domain of XIAP. It is thus 100 times more potent than the AVPI Smac peptide. One of the very active Smac peptidomimetics was also shown to effectively inhibit cell growth in some cancer cell lines and retard tumor growth in a xenograft model of human

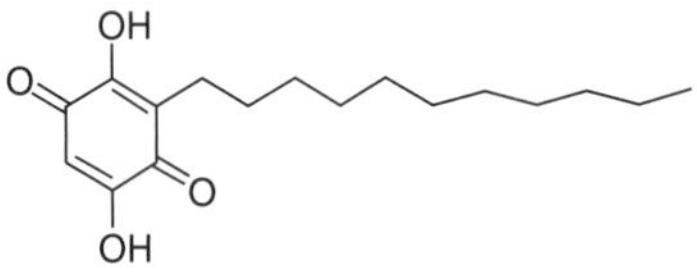

10 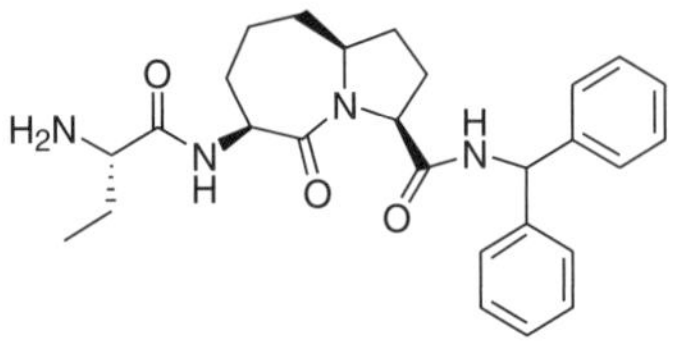   **11**

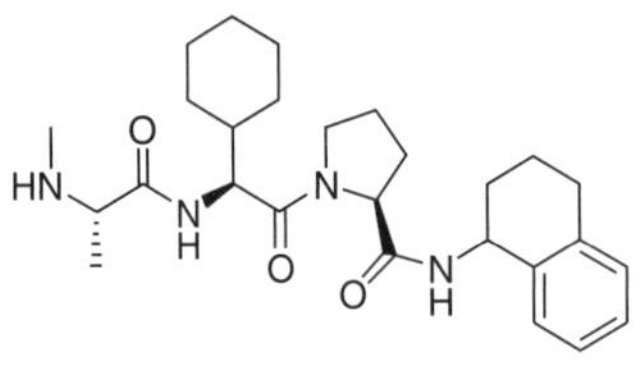

12 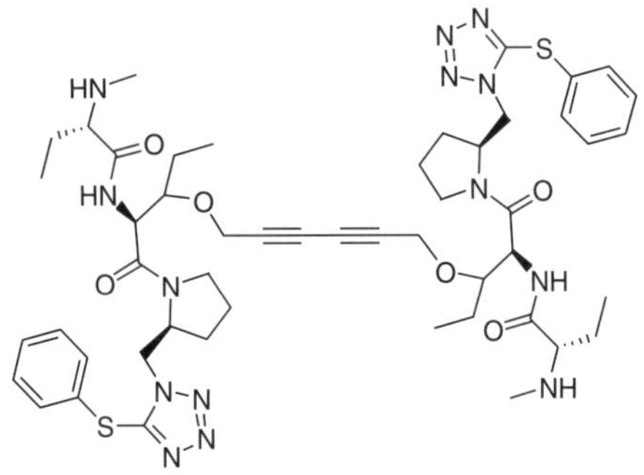   **13**

Fig. 2. Small molecules targeting the inhibitors of apoptosis proteins.

breast cancer. In different studies, Sun *et al.* have successfully designed and synthesized a series of conformationally constrained Smac mimetics employing a computational structure-based design strategy [70,71]. The most potent of these (**12**) has a K_i value of 25 nM to the XIAP BIR3 protein and enhances the activity of cisplatin in cancer cells. Li and colleagues derived a dimeric Smac peptidomimetic containing two AVPI mimetics tethered by a linker (**13**) [72]. They showed that although this dimeric Smac peptidomimetic binds to the XIAP BIR3 protein with only submicromolar affinity, it binds to the full-length XIAP protein with a potency equivalent to that of the Smac protein, which has a K_d value of 300 pM. It was hypothesized that this dimeric Smac peptidomimetic ligand may have a bivalent interaction with both the BIR2 and BIR3 domains of XIAP. Although the precise binding model has not yet been determined, this study provides evidence that design of polyvalent small-molecule ligands [73] that can concurrently target multiple domains in a protein is a very powerful strategy for designing inhibitors to achieve extremely high affinities.

4.3. Small-molecule inhibitors targeting the p53-MDM2 interaction

The p53 tumor suppressor plays a central role in controlling cell cycle progression and apoptosis [74,75], and is an attractive cancer therapeutic target because its tumor suppressing activity can be stimulated to eradicate tumor cells [2,74,75]. A new approach to stimulate the activity of p53 is through inhibition of its interaction with the MDM2 (the Mouse Double Minute-2 or the human MDM2, HDM2) oncoprotein using non-peptide small-molecule MDM2 inhibitors [2]. MDM2 is transcriptionally activated by p53, and in turn inhibits p53 activity by at least one of the three mechanisms and functions as a potent endogenous inhibitor of p53. The design of non-peptide small-molecule MDM2 inhibitors to target the p53-MMD2 interaction is being pursued as a new and attractive strategy for anticancer drug design [76].

A computational strategy has been used to identify non-peptide small-molecule inhibitors. Galatin and Abraham [77] derived a pharmacophore model based upon the three key binding residues (Phe19, Trp23 and Leu26) of p53 in the crystal structure between p53 peptide and MDM2. A pharmacophore search performed on the NCI 3D database identified compounds that met the chemical and geometrical requirements specified in the pharmacophore model. These compounds were further subjected to a structure-based searching and the most promising candidate compounds were tested in an *in vitro* binding assay against the MDM2 protein. One compound (**14**) was discovered to bind to MDM2 and block the interaction between MDM2 and p53 peptide. This compound was also shown to activate p53 in a cellular reporter assay (Fig. 3).

Using a high-throughput screening approach, Vassilev and colleagues have identified synthetic *cis*-imidazolines as inhibitors targeting the MDM2-p53 interaction [78]. Extensive chemical modifications were made on the initial leads, and ultimately yielded potent small-molecule inhibitors (termed Nutlins) with binding affinities (IC_{50} values) of 100–300 nM blocking the MDM2 and p53 interaction. The crystal structure of the complex between MDM2 and one of these (**15**) shows that Nutlins mimic the interactions of Phe19, Trp23 and Leu26 residues in p53 with MDM2. Nutlins were shown to effectively and selectively inhibit cell growth in cancer cells with wild-type p53 over cancer cells with mutated or deleted p53. One of the Nutlins was shown to effectively inhibit tumor growth in a xenograft model of human cancer with wild-type p53 and overexpressed MDM2 protein. The success of the Nutlins demonstrated that potent, cell-permeable small-molecule inhibitors targeting the MDM2-p53 interaction can indeed be designed.

Using a computational *de novo* structure-based strategy, Ding and colleagues have designed a class of potent, non-peptide small-molecule MDM2 inhibitors based upon a core spiro-oxindole structure [79]. First, using substructure searching, they established that oxindole mimics perfectly the side chain of Trp23 of p53 for both hydrogen bonding and

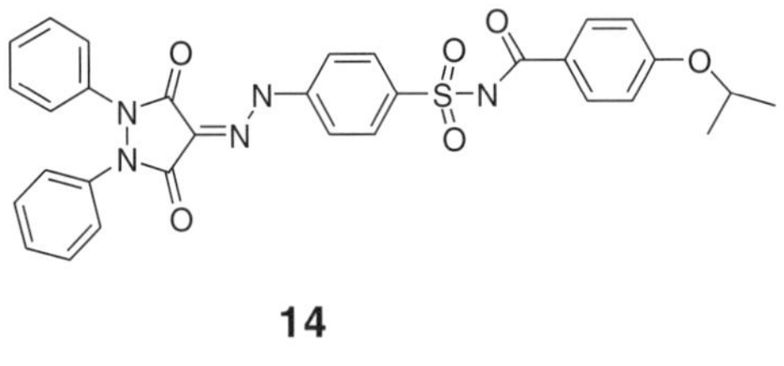

14

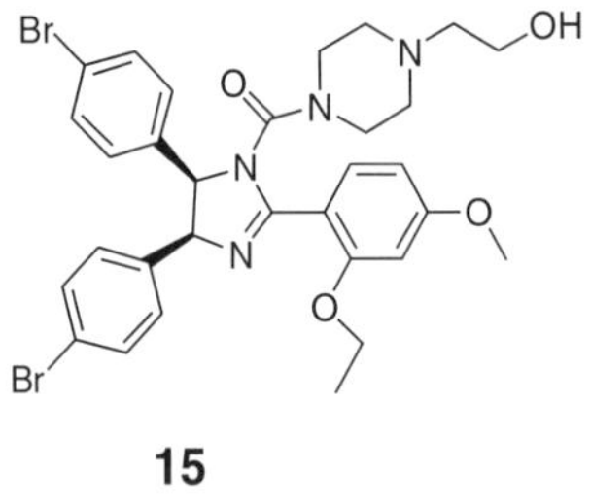

15 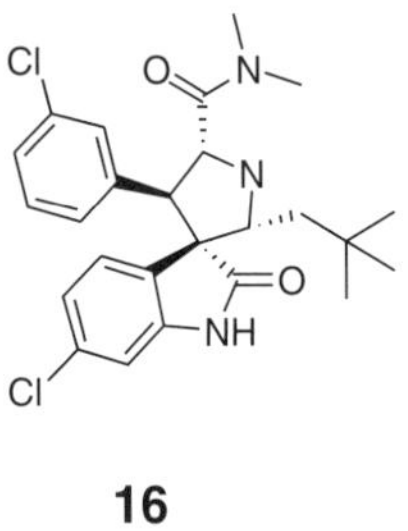   **16**

Fig. 3. Small-molecule inhibitors targeting the p53 – MDM2 interaction.

hydrophobic interaction with MDM2. Second, substructure searching found spiro-oxidole as the core structure in a number of natural products such as spirotrypostatin. Through extensive computational modeling, an initial lead compound was designed to mimic the Phe19, Trp23 and Leu26 residues in p53. This initial lead compound, which contains four chiral centers, was synthesized stereospecifically and was shown to have a K_i value to MDM2 of 7.5 µM. Effective structure-based optimization led to rapid improvement in binding affinity yielding finally an inhibitor (**16**) with a K_i value of 86 nM. Consistent with its mechanism of action, this potent MDM2 inhibitor was shown to selectively inhibit cell growth in cancer cells with wild-type p53 over cancer cells with mutated or deleted p53. It was shown that the experimentally determined binding affinities for this series of compounds correlate well with the scores calculated using the GOLD program [31] based upon predicted binding models. This study provides convincing evidence that a computational structure-based strategy can be used successfully to design potent, non-peptide, drug-like, small-molecule inhibitors targeting protein–protein interactions.

4.4. Antagonists of the thyroid hormone receptor

Overproduction of the thyroid hormone caused by a pathological condition of the thyroid gland is responsible for several diseases, especially of a cardiovascular nature [80]. The activity of the thyroid hormone is regulated by the interaction between L-thyroxin (T4) and L-triiodothyronine (T3) with thyroid hormone nuclear receptors (TRs), which are members of the nuclear hormone receptor (NR) superfamily [81]. Analysis of several NRs reveals that their ligand-binding domains (LBD) are generally unaffected by ligand binding or activation [28]. However, conformational changes of the C-terminal helix (H12) are observed indicating that ligand-bound structures are required to be as templates for homology modeling. Based upon this information and using the crystal structure of raloxifene-bound estrogen receptor α (ERα) as a template, Schapira and colleagues built a model structure of an agonist-bound TRβ-LBD [28]. This structure was used for virtual screening using ICM from Molsoft [82]. Among 250,000 commercially available compounds in ACD database (MDL Information systems, San Leandro, CA), those passed Lipinski rules were selected for virtual screening. Compounds that passed a defined ICM VLS threshold were checked if they were compatible with the active state of the receptor (i.e. satisfying distance criteria with two residues in H12). One thousand compounds were retained. Further refined docking of the 1000 compounds with the receptor allowed both ligand and receptor side-chain flexibility using ICM to eliminate compounds posing unacceptable van der Waals repulsions with the receptor. The remaining 300 top-scoring complexes were inspected visually by considering shape complementarity, hydrogen bond networks and ligand flexibility in the docked conformations. Finally, 100 of them were chosen for *in vitro* testing. Fourteen active TR antagonists were confirmed. This study provided another good example that carefully modeled protein structures are useful to identify novel lead compounds through virtual screening.

4.5. Small-molecule inhibitors targeting the interface of homodimeric proteins

Many proteins in cells function in an oligomeric form. Disrupting the formation of functional homodimers can lead to inhibition of their functions. Recently, Song and colleagues reported the use of a structure-based virtual screening method to identify small-molecule inhibitors, which disrupt the dimerization of the signal transducers and activators of transcription 3 (STAT3) protein [83]. A total of 429,000 small molecules from several database libraries were screened by targeting the dimer interface of STAT3 using the DOCK program [31]. The top 10% scored compounds were rescored using X-Score [84], and the top 200 ranked compounds obtained in this way were selected as candidates. Samples of 100 of these compounds were obtained and tested with a series of cell-based assays. Compound STA-21 (**17**) was found to inhibit STAT3 DNA-binding activity, STAT3 dimerization and STAT3-dependent luciferase activity (Fig. 4).

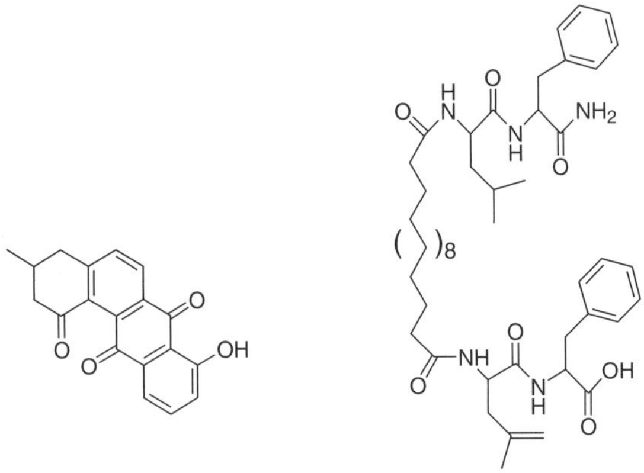

17   **18**

Fig. 4. Small-molecule inhibitors targeting the interface of homodimeric proteins.

In their earlier studies, Chmielewski and her colleagues have designed inhibitors by cross-linking two peptide segments mimicking the resides at the dimer interface in HIV-1 protease [85]. Recently, Hwang and Chmielewski have identified the minimal number of residues for such a class of peptide-based inhibitors to disrupt the dimer formation in HIV-1

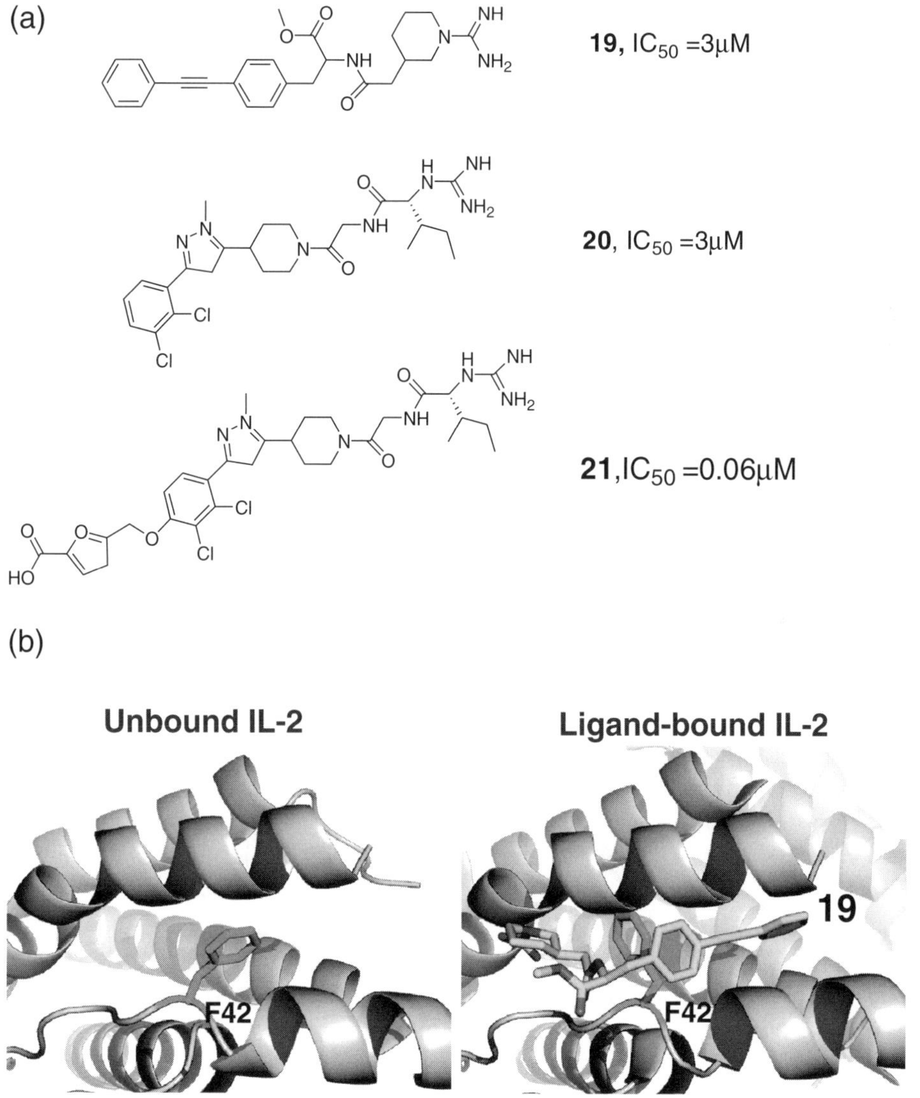

(a)

19, IC$_{50}$ =3µM

20, IC$_{50}$ =3µM

21,IC$_{50}$ =0.06µM

(b)

Unbound IL-2   **Ligand-bound IL-2**

Fig. 5. (a) Small-molecule inhibitors of the interaction between Interleukin-2 and its receptor protein. (b) Structural change of residues Phe42 (F42) in Interleukin-2 upon ligand binding.

protease [86]. The minimal number is four residues consisting of an aliphatic linkage between two two-residue peptides. By focusing on the modification of these four residues, they develop a potent inhibitor (**18**) with a K_i value of 102 nM binding to HIV-1 protease.

4.6. Small-molecule inhibitors of the interaction between Interleukin-2 and its receptor protein

Wells and colleagues recently reported the successful design of small-molecule inhibitors targeting Interleukin-2 (IL-2) [87,88]. Starting with a well-characterized micromolar inhibitor of IL-2, they used a structure-based approach and parallel synthesis to derive novel leads (**19**, **20**) with low micromolar affinity. Further optimization was unsuccessful until a disulfide tethering method was applied to bring another potent fragment into play [88]. The resulting new compound (**21**) has a binding affinity of 60 nM to IL-2 (Fig. 5a). An additional finding from this study is that IL-2 exhibits conformational adaptivity when a ligand binds (Fig. 5b). Specifically, Phe42 was found to be in an up position in the unbound IL-2, and in the complex between IL-2 and the initial novel lead compound. In the complex between IL-2 and the final, more potent compounds, Phe42 was found to be in a down position accompanied with shifting out of a nearby Leu72 [88]. The conformational changes of these two residues created a hydrophobic pocket to accommodate the new fragment.

5. CONCLUSION

In the last several years, there has been an intense effort in the design of small-molecule inhibitors to target protein–protein interactions [5]. Several laboratories have now shown that it is indeed feasible to design potent, non-peptide, drug-like, small molecules which inhibit protein–protein interactions. A number of these designed small-molecule inhibitors are now in advanced pre-clinical development and may move into clinical trials in the near future [89]. Computational virtual screening has played a critical role in the initial lead discovery associated with many of these compounds, and the computational structure-based approach has been found to be particularly effective in lead optimization.

Despite such apparent success, significant challenges remain. Most of the successful cases target protein–protein interactions with well-defined, binding sites on one of the proteins. For most of the protein–protein interactions in which the interface is large and shallow, there is still considerable difficulty to design small molecules (MW <1000) with sufficiently high affinities. Computational methods that have been applied to the design of small-molecule inhibitors to disrupt protein–protein interactions are those that have developed and found successful in the design of enzyme inhibitors. As our understanding of the nature of protein–protein interactions accumulates, new computational methods will undoubtedly be developed to assist the design of small-molecule inhibitors which target the large, shallow interface found in protein–protein complexes. To this end, it is worthwhile to note that the concept of the fragment-based design approach may be particularly effective in the design of small-molecule inhibitors to target protein–protein interfaces with multiple hot spots, both experimentally and computationally.

REFERENCES

[1] A. N. Bullock and A. R. Fersht, Rescuing the function of mutant p53, *Nat. Rev. Cancer.*, 2001, **1**, 68–76.

[2] P. Chène, Inhibiting the p53-MDM2 interaction: an important target for cancer therapy, *Nat. Rev. Cancer.*, 2003, **3**, 102–109.

[3] S. Cory and J. M. Adams, The Bcl2 family: regulators of the cellular life-or-death switch, *Nat. Rev. Cancer.*, 2002, **2**, 647–656.

[4] J.-L. Diaz, T. Oltersdorf, W. Horne, M. McConnel, G. Wilson, S. Weeks, T. Garcia and L. C. Fritz, A common binding site mediates heterodimerization and homodimerization of Bcl-2 family members, *J. Biol. Chem.*, 1997, **272**, 11350–11355.

[5] M. R. Arkin and J. A. Wells, Small-molecule inhibitors of protein–protein interactions: progressing towards the dream, *Nat. Rev. Drug Discov.*, 2004, **3**, 301–317.

[6] L. Pagliaro, J. Felding, K. Audouze, S. Jensby, J. Nielsen, R. B. Terry, C. Krog-jensen and S. Butcher, Emerging classes of protein–protein interaction inhibitors and new tools for their development, *Curr. Opin. Chem. Biol.*, 2004, **8**, 442–449.

[7] S. Buckingham, *Picking the pockets of protein–protein interactions*, Horizon Symposia, Charting Chemical Space, 2004, 1–4.

[8] S. Jones and J. M. Thornton, Principles of protein–protein interactions, *Proc. Natl. Acad. Sci. USA.*, 1996, **93**, 13–20.

[9] T. Clackson and J. A. Wells, A hot spot of binding energy in a hormone–receptor interface, *Science*, 1995, **267**, 383–386.

[10] J. A. Wells, Binding in the growth hormone receptor complex, *Proc. Natl. Acad. Sci. USA.*, 1996, **93**, 1–6.

[11] A. A. Bogan and K. S. Thorn, Anatomy of hot spots in protein interfaces, *J. Mol. Biol.*, 1998, **280**, 1–9.

[12] L. Lo Conte, C. Chothia and J. Janin, The atomic structure of protein–protein recognition sites, *J. Mol. Biol.*, 1999, **285**, 2177–2198.

[13] Y. Li, Y. Huang, C. P. Swaminathan, S. J. Smith-Gill and R. A. Mariuzza, Magnitude of the hydrophobic effect at central versus peripheral sites in protein–protein interfaces, *Structure*, 2005, **13**, 197–307.

[14] B. Ma, T. Elkayam, H. Wolfson and R. Nussinov, Protein–protein interactions: structurally conserved residues distinguish between binding sites and exposed protein surfaces, *Proc. Natl. Acad. Sci. USA.*, 2003, **100**, 5772–5777.

[15] H. M. Berman, J. Westbrook, Z. Feng, G. Gilliland, T. N. Bhat, H. Weissig, I. N. Shindyalov and P. E. Bourne, The Protein Data Bank, *Nucleic Acids Res*, 2002, **28**, 235–242.

[16] N. Leibowitz, Z. Fligelman, R. Nussinov and H. Wolfson, Automated multiple structure alignment and detection of a common substructural motif, *Proteins*, 2001, **43**, 235–245.

[17] N. Leibowitz, R. Nussinov and H. Wolfson, MUSTA – a general, efficient, automated method for multiple structure alignment and detection of common motifs: application to proteins, *J. Comp. Biol.*, 2001, **8**, 93–121.

[18] O. Keskin, B. Ma and R. Nussinov, Hot regions in protein–protein interactions: the organization and contribution of structurally conserved hot spot residues, *J. Mol. Biol.*, 2005, **345**, 1281–1294.

[19] W. L. Delano, Unraveling hot spots in binding interfaces: progress and challenges, *Curr. Opin. Struct. Biol.*, 2002, **12**, 14–20.

[20] P. A. Kollman, I. Massova, C. Reyes, B. Kuhn, S. Huo, L. Chong, M. Lee, T. Lee, Y. Duan, W. Wang, O. Donini, P. Cieplak, J. Srinivasan, D. A. Case and T. E. Cheatham III, Calculating structures and free energies of complex molecules: combining molecular mechanics and continuum models, *Acc. Chem. Res.*, 2000, **33**, 889–897.

[21] I. Massova and P. A. Kollman, Computational alanine scanning to probe protein–protein interactions: a novel approach to evaluating binding free energies, *J. Am. Chem. Soc.*, 1999, **121**, 8133–8143.

[22] S. Huo, I. Massova and P. A. Kollman, Computational alanine scanning of the 1:1 human growth formine-receptor complex, *J. Comp. Chem.*, 2002, **23**, 15–27.

[23] T. Kortemme, D. E. Kim and D. Baker, Computational alanine scanning of protein–protein interfaces, *Sci. STKE.*, 2004, **219**, pl2.

[24] J. Bajorath, Integration of virtual and high-throughput screening, *Nat. Rev. Drug Discov.*, 2002, **1**, 882–894.

[25] B. K. Shoichet, Virtual screening of chemical libraries, *Nature*, 2004, **432**, 862–865.

[26] J.-L. Wang, D. Liu, Z.-J. Zhang, S. Shan, X. Han, S. Srinivasula, C. M. Croce, E. S. Alnemri and Z. Huang, Structure-based discovery of an organic compound that binds Bcl-2 protein and induces apoptosis of tumor cells, *Proc. Natl. Acad. Sci. USA.*, 2000, **97**, 7124–7129.

[27] I. J. Enyedy, Y. Ling, K. Nacro, Y. Tomita, X. Wu, Y. Cao, R. Guo, B. Li, X. Zhu, Y. Huang, Y.-Q. Long, P. P. Roller, D. Yang and S. Wang, Discovery of small-molecule inhibitors of Bcl-2 through structure-based computer screening, *J. Med. Chem.*, 2001, **44**, 4313–4324.

[28] M. Schapira, B. M. Raaka, S. Das, L. Fan, M. Totrov, Z. Zhou, S. R. Wilson, R. Abagyan and H. H. Samuels, Discovery of diverse thyroid hormone receptor antagonists by high-throughput docking, *Proc. Natl. Acad. Sci. USA.*, 2003, **100**, 7354–7359.

[29] D. J. Cummins, C. W. Andrews, J. A. Bentley and M. Cory, Molecular diversity in chemical databases: comparison of medicinal chemistry knowledge bases and databases of commercially available compounds, *J. Chem. Inf. Comput. Sci.*, 1996, **36**, 750–763.

[30] T. J. Ewing, S. Makino, A. G. Skillman and I. D. Kuntz, DOCK 4.0: search strategies for automated molecular docking of flexible molecule database, *J. Comput. Aided Mol. Des.*, 2001, **15**, 411–428.

[31] M. L. Verdonk, J. C. Cole, M. J. Hartshorn, C. W. Murray and R. D. Taylor, Improved protein–ligand docking using GOLD, *Proteins*, 2003, **52**, 609–623.

[32] R. A. Friesner, J. L. Banks, R. B. Murphy, T. A. Halgren, J. J. Klicic, D. T. Mainz, M. P. Repasky, E. H. Knoll, M. Shelley, J. K. Perry, D. E. Shaw, P. Francis and P. S. Shenkin, Glide: a new approach for rapid, accurate docking and scoring. 1. Method and assessment of docking accuracy, *J. Med. Chem.*, 2004, **47**, 1739–1749.

[33] T. A. Halgren, R. B. Murphy, R. A. Friesner, H. S. Beard, L. L. Frye, W. T. Pollard and J. L. Banks, Glide: a new approach for rapid, accurate docking and scoring. 2. Enrichment factors in database screening, *J. Med. Chem.*, 2004, **47**, 1750–1759.

[34] M. Rarey, B. Kramer, T. Lengauer and G. Klebe, A fast flexible docking method using an incremental construction algorithm, *J. Mol. Biol.*, 1996, **261**, 470–489.

[35] E. Kellenberger, J. Rodrigo, P. Muller and D. Rognan, Comparative evaluation of eight docking tools for docking and virtual screening accuracy, *Proteins*, 2004, **57**, 225–242.

[36] M. I. Zavodszky, P. C. Sanschagrin, R. S. Korde and L. A. Kuhn, Distilling the essential features of a protein surface for improving protein–ligand docking scoring, and virtual screening,, *J. Comput. Aided Mol. Des.*, 2002, **16**, 883–902.

[37] A. N. Jain, Surflex: fully automatic flexible molecular docking using a molecular similarity-based search engine, *J. Med. Chem.*, 2003, **46**, 499–511.

[38] C. McMartin and R. S. Bohacek, QXP: powerful rapid computer algorithms for structure-based drug design, *J. Comput. Aided Mol. Des.*, 1997, **11**, 333–344.

[39] C. A. Lipinski, F. Lombardo, B. W. Dominy and P. J. Feeney, Experimental and computational approaches to estimate solubility and permeability in drug discovery and development settings, *Adv. Drug Delivery Rev.*, 1997, **23**, 3–25.

[40] V. J. Hruby, Designing peptide receptor agonists and antagonists, *Nat. Rev. Drug Discov.*, 2002, **1**, 847–858.

[41] D. C. Rees, M. Congreve, C. W. Murray and R. Carr, Fragment-based lead discovery, *Nat. Rev. Drug Discov.*, 2004, **3**, 660–672.

[42] R. Carr and H. Jhoti, Structure-based screening of low-affinity compounds, *DDT*, 2002, **7**, 522–527.

[43] P. J. Hajduk, E. T. Olejniczak and S. W. Fesik, Discovering high-affinity ligands for proteins, *Science*, 1997, **278**, 497–499.

[44] D. A. Erlanson, J. A. Wells and A. C. Braisted, Tethering: fragment-based drug discovery, *Annu. Rev. Biophys. Biomol. Struct.*, 2004, **33**, 199–223.

[45] M. Congreve, R. Carr, C. Murray and H. Jhoti, A 'rule of three' for fragment-based lead discovery?, *Drug Discov. Today.*, 2003, **8**, 876–877.

[46] B. Antonsson and J.-C. Martinou, The Bcl-2 protein family, *Exp. Cell Res.*, 2000, **256**, 50–57.

[47] Y. Tsujimoto and S. Shimizu, Bcl-2 family: life-or-death switch, *FEBS Lett*, 2000, **466**, 6–10.

[48] L. Dong, W. Wang, F. Wang, M. Stoner, J. C. Reed, M. Harigai, I. Samudio, M. P. Kladde, C. Vyhlidal and S. Safe, Mechanisms of transcriptional activation of bcl-2 gene expression by 17 β-estradiol in breast cancer cells, *J. Biol. Chem.*, 1999, **274**, 32099–32107.

[49] R. Kim, M. Emi, K. Tanabe and T. Toge, Therapeutic potential of antisense Bcl-2 as a chemosensitizer for cancer therapy, *Cancer*, 2004, **101**, 2491–2502.

[50] D. Liu and Z. Huang, Synthetic peptides and non-peptidic molecules as probes of structure and function of Bcl-2 family proteins and modulators of apoptosis, *Apoptosis*, 2001, **6**, 453–463.

[51] S. Wang, D. Yang and M. E. Lippman, Targeting Bcl-2 and Bcl-X_L with nonpeptidic small-molecule antagonists, *Semin. Oncology.*, 2003, **30**, 133–142.

[52] A. Degterev, A. Lugovskoy, M. Cardone, B. Mulley, G. Wagner, T. Mitchison and J. Yuan, Identification of small-molecule inhibitors of interaction between the BH3 domain and Bcl-xL, *Nat. Cell Biol.*, 2001, **3**, 173–182.

[53] C. E. Schafmeister, J. Po and G. L. Verdine, An all-hydrocarbon cross-linking system for enhancing the helicity and metabolic stability of peptides, *J. Am. Chem. Soc.*, 2000, **122**, 5891–5892.

[54] L. D. Walensky, A. L. Kung, I. Escher, T. J. Malia, S. Barbuto, R. D. Wright, G. Wagner, G. L. Verdine and S. J. Korsmeyer, Activation of apoptosis in vivo by a hydrocarbon-stapled BH3 helix, *Science*, 2004, **305**, 1466–1470.

[55] J. D. Sadowsky, M. A. Schmitt, H.-S. Lee, N. Umezawa, S. Wang, Y. Tomita and S. H. Gellman, Chimeric ($\alpha/\beta+\alpha$)-peptide ligands for the BH3-recognition cleft of

Bcl-xL: critical role of the molecular scaffold in protein surface recognition, *J. Am. Chem. Soc.*, 2005, **127**, 11966–11968.

[56] J. Frackenpohl, P. I. Arvidsson, J. V. Schreiber and D. Seebach, The outstanding biological stability of β- and γ- peptides toward proteolytic enzymes: an in vitro investigation with fifteen peptidases, *Chembiochem*, 2001, **2**, 445–455.

[57] H. Yin, G.-I. Lee, K. A. Sedey, O. Kutzki, H. S. Park, B. P. Orner, J. T. Ernst, H.-G. Wang, S. M. Sebti and A. D. Hamilton, Terphenyl-based Bak BH3 a-helical proteomimetics as low-molecular-weight antagonists of Bcl-x$_L$, *J. Am. Chem. Soc.*, 2005, **127**, 10191–10196.

[58] H. Yin, G.-I. Lee, K. A. Sedey, J. M. Rodriguez, H.-G. Wang, S. M. Sebti and A. D. Hamilton, Terephthalamide derivatives as mimetics of helical peptides: disruption of the Bcl-xL/Bak interaction, *J. Am. Chem. Soc.*, 2005, **127**, 5463–5468.

[59] T. Oltersdorf, S. W. Elmore, A. R. Shoemaker, R. C. Armstrong, D. J. Augeri, B. A. Belli, M. Bruncko, T. L. Deckwerth, J. Dinges, P. J. Hajduk, M. K. Joseph, S. Kitada, S. J. Korsmeyer, A. R. Kunzer, A. Letai, C. Li, M. J. Mitten, D. G. Nettesheim, S. Ng, P. M. Nimmer, J. M. O'Connor, A. Oleksijew, A. M. Petros, J. C. Reed, W. Shen, S. K. Tahir, C. B. Thompson, K. J. Tomaselli, B. Wang, M. D. Wendt, H. Zhang, S. W. Fesik and S. H. Rosenberg, An inhibitor of Bcl-2 family proteins induces regression of solid tumours, *Nature*, 2005, **435**, 677–681.

[60] G. S. Salvesen and C. S. Duckett, IAP proteins: blocking the road to death's door, *Nat. Rev. Mol. Cell Biol.*, 2002, **3**, 404–410.

[61] N. A. Thornberry and Y. Lazebnik, Caspases: enemies within, *Science*, 1998, **281**, 1312–1316.

[62] E. N. Shiozaki and Y. Shi, Caspases IAPs and Smac/DIABLO: mechanisms from structural biology, *Trends Biochem. Sci.*, 2004, **39**, 486–494.

[63] S. M. Srinivasula, P. Datta, X. J. Fan, T. Fernandes-Alnemri, Z. Huang and E. S. Alnemri, Molecular determinants of the caspase-promoting activity of Smac/DIABLO and its role in the death receptor pathway, *J. Biol. Chem.*, 2000, **275**, 36152–36157.

[64] G. Wu, J. Chai, T. L. Suber, J. W. Wu, C. Du, X. Wang and Y. Shi, Structural basis of IAP recognition by Smac/DIABLO, *Nature*, 2000, **408**, 1008–1012.

[65] Z. Liu, C. Sun, E. T. Olejniczak, R. P. Meadows, S. F. Betz, T. Oost, J. Herrmann, J. C. Wu and S. W. Fesik, Structural basis for binding of Smac/DIABLO to the XIAP BIR3 domain, *Nature*, 2000, **408**, 1004–1008.

[66] E. N. Shiozaki, J. Chai, D. J. Rigotti, S. J. Riedl, P. Li, S. M. Srinivasula, E. S. Alnemri, R. Fairman and Y. Shi, Mechanism of Xiap-mediated inhibition of caspase-9, *Mol. Cell.*, 2003, **11**, 519–527.

[67] R. A. Kipp, M. A. Case, A. D. Wist, C. M. Cresson, M. Carrell, E. Griner, A. Wiita, P. A. ALbiniak, J. Chai, Y. Shi, M. F. Semmelhack and G. L. McLendon, Molecular targeting of inhibitor of apoptosis proteins based on small molecule mimics of natural binding partners, *Biochemistry*, 2002, **41**, 7344–7349.

[68] Z. Nikolovska-Coleska, L. Xu, Z. Hu, Y. Tomita, P. Li, P. P. Roller, R. Wang, X. Fang, R. Guo, M. Zhang, M. E. Lippman, D. Yang and S. Wang, Discovery of Embelin as a cell-permeable, *small-molecular weight inhibitor of XIAP through structure-based computational screening of a traditional herbal medicine three-dimensional structure database*, *J. Med. Chem.*, 2004, **47**, 2430–2440.

[69] T. K. Oost, C. Sun, R. C. Armstrong, A.-S. Al-Assaad, S. F. Betz, T. L. Deckwerth, H. Ding, S. W. Elmore, R. P. Meadows, E. T. Olejniczak, A. Oleksijew, T. Oltersdorf, S. H. Rosenberg, A. R. Shoemaker, K. J. Tomaselli, H. Zhou and S. W. Fesik, Discovery of potent antagonists of the anti-apoptotic protein XIAP for the treatment of cancer, *J. Med. Chem.*, 2004, **47**, 4417–4426.

[70] H. Sun, Z. Nikolovska-Coleska, C.-Y. Yang, L. Xu, Y. Tomita, K. Krajewski, R. R. Roller and S. Wang, Structure-based design, synthesis, and evaluation of conformationally constrained mimetics of the second mitochondria-derived activator of

caspase that target the X-linked inhibitor of apoptosis protein/caspase-9 interaction site, *J. Med. Chem.*, 2004, **47**, 4147–4150.

[71] H. Sun, Z. Nikolovska-Coleska, C.-Y. Yang, L. Xu, M. Liu, Y. Tomita, H. Pan, Y. Yoshioka, K. Krajewski, R. R. Roller and S. Wang, Structure-based design of potent, conformationally constrained Smac mimetics, *J. Am. Chem. Soc.*, 2004, **126**, 16686–16687.

[72] L. Li, R. M. Thomas, H. Suzuki, J. K. De Brabander, X. Wang and P. G. Harran, A small molecule Smac mimic potentiates TRAIL- and TNFα-mediated cell death, *Science*, 2004, **305**, 1471–1474.

[73] M. Mammen, S.-K. Choi and G. M. Whitesides, Polyvalent interactions in biological systems: implications for design and use of multivalent ligands and inhibitors, *Angew. Chem. Int. Ed.*, 1998, **37**, 2754–2794.

[74] B. Vogelstein, D. Lane and A. J. Levine, Surfing the p53 network, *Nature*, 2000, **408**, 307–310.

[75] X. Wu, J. H. Bayle, D. Olson and A. J. Levine, The p53-mdm-2 autoregulatory feedback loop, *Genes Dev*, 1993, **7**, 1126–1132.

[76] L. T. Vassilev, p53 activation by small molecules: application in oncology, *J. Med. Chem.*, 2005, **48**, 1–8.

[77] P. S. Galatin and D. J. Abraham, A nonpeptidic sulfonamide inhibits the p53-mdm2 interaction and activates p53-dependent transcription in mdm2-overexpressing cells, *J. Med. Chem.*, 2004, **47**, 4163–4165.

[78] L. T. Vassilev, B. T. Vu, B. Graves, D. Carvajal, F. Podlaski, Z. Filipovic, N. Kong, U. Kammlott, C. Lukacs, C. Klein, N. Fotouchi and E. A. Liu, In vivo activation of the p53 pathway by small-molecule antagonists of MDM2, *Science*, 2004, **303**, 844–848.

[79] K. Ding, Y. Liu, Z. Nikolovska, S. Qiu, Y. Ding, W. Gao, J. Stuckey, K. Krajewski, P. P. Roller, Y. Tomita, D. A. Parrish, J. R. Deschamps and S. Wang, Structure-based design of potent non-peptide MDM2 inhibitors, *J. Am. Chem. Soc.*, 2005, **127**, 10130–10131.

[80] S. S. Nussey and S. A. Whitehead, *Endocrinology: An Integrated Approach*, BIOS Scientific Publishers Ltd, Oxford, UK, 2001.

[81] P. M. Yen, Physiological and molecular basis of thyroid hormone action, *Physiol. Rev.*, 2001, **81**, 1097–1142.

[82] *Molsoft ICM 2.8 Program Manual,*, Molsoft, San Diego, 2002.

[83] H. Song, R. Wang, S. Wang and J. Lin, A low-molecular-weight compound discovered through virtual database screening inhibits Stat3 function in breast cancer cells, *Proc. Natl. Acad. Sci. USA.*, 2005, **102**, 4700–4705.

[84] R. Wang, L. Lai and S. Wang, Further development and validation of empirical scoring functions for structure-based binding affinity prediction, *J. Comput. Aided Mol. Des.*, 2002, **16**, 11–26.

[85] R. Zutshi, J. Franciskovich, M. Shultz, B. Schweitzer, P. Bishop, M. Wilson and J. Chmielewski, Targeting the dimerization interface of HIV-1 protease: inhibition with cross-linked interfacial peptides, *J. Am. Chem. Soc.*, 1997, **119**, 4841–4845.

[86] Y. S. Hwang and J. Chmielewski, Development of low molecular weight HIV-1 protease dimerization inhibitors, *J. Med. Chem.*, 2005, **48**, 2239–2242.

[87] C. D. Thanos, M. Randal and J. A. Wells, Potent small-molecule binding to a dynamic hot spot on IL2, *J. Am. Chem. Soc.*, 2003, **125**, 15280–15281.

[88] A. C. Braisted, J. D. Oslob, W. L. Delano, J. Hyde, R. S. McDowell, N. Waal, C. Yu, M. R. Arkin and B. C. Raimundo, Discovery of a potent small molecule IL-2 inhibitor through fragment assembly, *J. Am. Chem. Soc.*, 2003, **125**, 3714–3715.

[89] U. Fischer and K. Schulze-Osthoff, New approaches and therapeutics targeting apoptosis in disease, *Pharmcol. Rev.*, 2005, **57**, 187–215.

CHAPTER 12

Accelerating Conformational Transitions in Biomolecular Simulations

Donald Hamelberg and J. Andrew McCammon

Howard Hughes Medical Institute, Center for Theoretical Biological Physics, Department of Chemistry and Biochemistry, and Department of Pharmacology, University of California at San Diego, La Jolla, California 92093–0365, USA

Contents

1. INTRODUCTION

Molecular dynamics simulation is one of the most extensively used bio-physical tools available to computational biologists and chemists due to its ability to accurately sample the conformational space of molecular systems [1]. By integrating Newton's equations of motion, this technique evaluates the time-dependent behavior and evolution of a molecular system as it samples its conformational space. Therefore, with an accurate representation of the system's potential energy landscape, the thermo-dynamic and kinetic properties can be calculated while studying a host of other structural and dynamic phenomena.

Although this method is routinely applied to larger biological systems, the timescale that can be realistically accessed is still limited to tens of nanoseconds, even after the tremendous amount of work that has gone into optimizing several components of the molecular dynamics algorithm. Following the initial applications of molecular dynamics to the study of protein dynamics [2,3] and continuing development of faster computers, much effort has been put into increasing the timescale that can be accessed using this technique. Several approaches have been incorporated into molecular dynamics simulations that have enhanced the sampling of

ANNUAL REPORTS IN COMPUTATIONAL CHEMISTRY, VOLUME 2
ISSN: 1574-1400   DOI 10.1016/S1574-1400(06)02012-3

molecular systems. These include the use of the SHAKE algorithm [4–6] or similar approaches [7,8] that emphasize slow degrees of freedom over high frequency degrees of freedom and thus allow for the use of large integration time steps. Also, reducing the number of degrees of freedom of a system by using a coarse-grained description can increase the time-scale by emphasizing large-scale motions [9–11]. An example of this that is widely used is the reduction of each amino acid of a protein molecule to a single-bead model [11]. Similarly, elimination of the numerous solvent molecules associated with explicit solvation simulations by introducing implicit solvation models like Generalized Born [12–17] have also increased the timescale.

However, despite all of these improvements in the methodology, in an all-atom system we are still limited by the intrinsic roughness [18,19] and multiple minima associated with the potential energy landscape of bio-molecules. In many cases, the minima are separated by high energy barriers. Therefore, during several nanoseconds of molecular dynamics simulation, a biomolecule can easily get trapped in a small number of energy minima for a large number of computational steps, limiting the amount of phase space that can be explored in reasonable amount of computer time. Consequently, many of the interesting large-scale motions of biomolecules that occur in the microsecond to millisecond timescale cannot be observed by doing direct molecular dynamics. With present traditional all-atom simulation, only fast side-chain dynamics and elastic collective motions can be thoroughly sampled. In order to observe long timescale conformational transitions of biological systems, one has to be able to simulate series of rare transition events between potential energy wells. One obvious way of achieving this is to raise the temperature of the system, thus increasing the probability of transition over high-energy barriers [20,21]. Manipulation of the temperature of a system has also been implemented in methods like replica-exchange molecular dynamics [22–24]. However, transitions that are observed at high temperature due to the overestimation of the entropic contribution to the free energy might not be observed at low temperature. In their temperature-accelerated dynamics method, Sorensen and Voter [25] attempted to fix this problem by applying a filtering mechanism to get rid of all the transitions that would not have occurred at the desired low temperature.

A number of other techniques aimed at addressing the problem of crossing high energy barriers have been introduced [26–33], including a promising class of methods that involves modification of the energy land-scape with the sole purpose of limiting the amount of computational time spent in energy wells. This report will focus on the accelerated molecular dynamics approach, which belongs to this class of methods. We begin by examining the basis of this method as it relates to umbrella sampling and subsequent methodologies that have similar roots.

2. UMBRELLA SAMPLING

Umbrella sampling involves increasing the probability of crossing high energy barriers by modifying the potential energy landscape of the system [3,34,35]. This normally involves addition of a compensating energy function to the real potential energy function such that the minimum of a particular conformation is raised. This allows the system to move to another conformation of interest in a nearby potential energy well in a predefined transition path. Therefore, the construction of the umbrella potential usually requires prior knowledge of the conformations of interest and their location on the potential energy landscape, along with the knowledge of the location of the barrier separating them. This would undoubtedly make the construction of a general umbrella potential for biomolecules very challenging, since the potential energy landscape is very rugged. The large number of degrees of freedom required to gain any meaningful insight into complex conformational changes precludes construction of a practical compensating potential function. Therefore, the use of umbrella sampling has been limited to systems wherein the conformational states of interest are well known and the conformational transition coordinate is precisely defined. It is worth noting, however, that the use of an exactly defined umbrella potential allows one to recover unbiased probability distributions and thermodynamic functions from the biased sampling [3,34,35].

3. ACCELERATED MOLECULAR DYNAMICS

3.1. Conformational flooding

Grubmuller [28] extended the ideas of umbrella sampling by raising the free-energy landscape around the basin of a system's initial conformation using prior knowledge of its configuration density. Performing molecular dynamics simulation on the system in the modified basin, the system would therefore then evolve until it escapes to an adjacent basin at an accelerated rate. The free-energy landscape of the new basin is modified by adding to it an artificial or 'flooding' potential that raises the energy without affecting that of the saddle points. This is done so as to study the escape process of the system from its initial well without making any prior assumptions about the transition states and paths connecting the initial basin with other ones. The artificial potential is constructed from a coarse-grained description of the system in its initial configuration obtained from regular molecular dynamics simulations. A configuration density of the system is determined from the molecular dynamics simulations, and the coarse-grained conformation space density is obtained in the form of a multivariate Gaussian from the lowest eigenvectors of the covariance matrix. This method was shown to accelerate sampling of a small argon microcluster at low temperature and complex transitions in some proteins. Nonetheless, when constructing the flooding potential for proteins, one has to keep in mind that the conformation density of each substrate is not always of a Gaussian nature.

3.2. Hyperdynamics

Voter [32,33] later proposed a hyperdynamics scheme to speed up molecular dynamics simulations by decreasing the amount of computational time a system spends in potential energy minima. This allows the system to move over potential barriers at an accelerated rate. Similar to previous approaches, this method modifies the potential energy surface, $V(r)$, by adding a bias potential, $\Delta V(r)$, to the true potential such that the potential surfaces near the minima are raised and those near the barrier or saddle point are left unaffected. This ensures that the relative escape rate to adjacent wells would be unaffected. Unlike umbrella sampling, this method makes no assumptions of the location of the minima and transition state regions. And, unlike conformational flooding, this method modifies the entire potential energy landscape of the system, not just the basins of the initial and subsequent configurations. The bias potential is constructed in order to take advantage of the fact that the lowest eigenvalue of the Hessian matrix is less than zero at the saddle points, and the projection of the gradient onto the lowest eigenvector is equal to zero at the saddle points. The bias potential increases the escape rate of the system from potential basins, and, according to transition state theory, the subsequent state-to-state evolution of the system on the modified potential occurs at an accelerated rate with a nonlinear timescale of Δt^*, where

$$\Delta t_i^* = \Delta t e^{\beta \Delta V[r(t_i)]} \tag{1}$$

This advances the clock at each step depending on the strength of $\Delta V(r)$, where Δt is the actual time step of the simulation on the unmodified potential. Based on the transition state theory, equation (1) is valid only if the bias potential $\Delta V(r)$ is zero near the saddle points as shown in Fig. 1. An acceleration of up to about 8310 times was obtained using this method

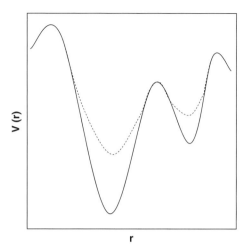

Fig. 1. Schematic representation of the hyperdynamics scheme. The solid line is the original potential energy surface and the dashed line is the modified surface obtained by adding a bias potential to the unmodified potential at points other than the saddle points.

at 300 K for about 70 moving atoms. However, construction of the Hessian-based bias potential for large all-atom biomolecular systems is challenging and very expensive due to their inherently rough and complicated energy landscapes.

3.3. Extension of the hyperdynamics scheme to biomolecules

One of the main objectives of Voter's hyperdynamics technique that sets it apart from other previous methods is the construction of the bias potential across the entire landscape without prior knowledge of the potential energy minima and saddle points. However, construction of the bias potential limits its use to small systems of about 100 atoms because of its computational cost. Alternatively, a prescription for a simpler bias potential was proposed by Steiner *et al.* [36] in which a boost energy E is chosen such that the simulation is performed on a flat modified potential $V^*(r) = V(r) + \Delta V(r) = E$ when $V(r)$ falls below E and is performed on the true potential when $V(\mathbf{r})$ is above E as shown in Fig. 2. Various other similar approaches to define the bias potential based on Voter's scheme have also been studied [37–41]. This implementation is very simple and computationally inexpensive, because the force on the flat "puddle" is zero. However, there are some problems associated with this choice: the derivatives of the potential (forces) are discontinuous at points where the

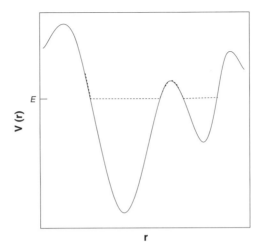

Fig. 2. Schematic illustration of the true potential (solid line), the boost energy E, and the modified potential (dashed line). The molecular dynamics simulation is performed on the flat potential (dashed line) when the energy drops below E, and it is performed on the true potential (solid) when the potential energy is above E.

unmodified potential, $V(\mathbf{r})$, merges with the flat modified potential $V(\mathbf{r}) = E$. Rahman and Tully [37] devised a special integration technique to traverse points where $V(\mathbf{r}) = E$, which however reduces the gain in computational efficiency. It allowed them to extend this flat puddle potential method to a somewhat more complicated molecular system.

In contrast to the flat potential employed to fill energy minima, a modification of the potential energy surface that maintains the underlying shape of the unmodified potential energy surface and merges smoothly with the original potential at the threshold boost energy value E was proposed by Hamelberg $et\ al.$ [42]. A bias potential $\Delta V(\mathbf{r})$ is chosen such that the derivative of $V^*(\mathbf{r})$ has no discontinuity, and the modified potential reflects the shape of the minima even at high values of E. Equation (2) summarizes this scheme:

$$V^*(\mathbf{r}) = \begin{cases} V(\mathbf{r}), & V(\mathbf{r}) \geq E \\ V(\mathbf{r}) + \Delta V(\mathbf{r}), & V(\mathbf{r}) < E \end{cases} \tag{2}$$

where the choice of $\Delta V(\mathbf{r})$ is given by equation (3):

$$\Delta V(\mathbf{r}) = \frac{(E - V(\mathbf{r}))^2}{\alpha + (E - V(\mathbf{r}))} \tag{3}$$

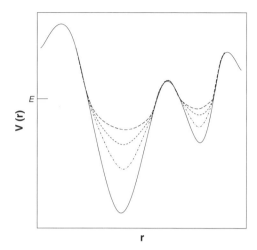

Fig. 3. Schematic depiction of the normal potential (solid line) and several modified potentials (dashed lines) at fixed threshold boost energy E with varying values of α. The larger the value of α, the closer the modified potential is to the original surface.

Here α is a tuning parameter that determines how deep the modified potential energy basin will be. When α is zero, the modified potential is flat, $V^*(\mathbf{r}) = E$. While varying the value of α at a constant value of E, the modified potential becomes smoother as α is decreased as shown in Fig. 3. Conversely, the modified potential surface becomes rougher as α is increased and matches that of the original surface at a very large value of α. The biased potential therefore smoothes the local roughness and lowers the barriers of the potential energy landscape, thus increasing the escape rate of the system from potential energy basins. The state-to-state evolution of the system on the modified potential occurs at an accelerated rate. Therefore, the higher the boost energy E and the smaller the value of α, the greater is the acceleration.

3.3.1. Canonical distribution and conformational sampling

This accelerated molecular dynamics approach provides a general approach for enhancing the conformational transitions of molecular systems without having prior knowledge of the location of the minima and barriers on the potential energy landscape. After performing molecular dynamics simulation on the modified energy surface, at times it is necessary to accurately obtain the correct canonical distribution of the system on the unmodified surface. To recover the correct canonical average of any observable $A(\mathbf{r})$, so that thermodynamics and other equilibrium properties can be accurately determined from the accelerated MD simulations, it is noted that the equilibrium ensemble average on the normal potential $V(\mathbf{r})$ is given by equation (4):

$$\langle A \rangle = \frac{\int d\mathbf{r}\, A(\mathbf{r}) e^{-\beta V(\mathbf{r})}}{\int d\mathbf{r}\, e^{-\beta V(\mathbf{r})}} \tag{4}$$

Similarly, the ensemble average value of any observable $A(\mathbf{r})$ taken on the modified potential can be written as:

$$\langle A^* \rangle = \frac{\int d\mathbf{r}\, A(\mathbf{r}) e^{-\beta V^*(\mathbf{r})}}{\int d\mathbf{r}\, e^{-\beta V^*(\mathbf{r})}} \tag{5}$$

substituting for $V^*(\mathbf{r})$, we get:

$$\langle A^* \rangle = \frac{\int d\mathbf{r}\, A(\mathbf{r}) e^{-\beta V(\mathbf{r}) - \beta \Delta V(\mathbf{r})}}{\int d\mathbf{r}\, e^{-\beta V(\mathbf{r}) - \beta \Delta V(\mathbf{r})}} \tag{6}$$

Therefore, re-weighting the phase space of the modified potential by multiplying each configuration by the strength of the Boltzmann factor of the bias at each position, $e^{\beta \Delta V[r(t_i)]}$, the corrected ensemble average is obtained. When the system is on the normal potential, the bias is zero and the weight factor is one. The relationship between the biased and unbiased thermodynamic quantities can alternatively be derived just as for the case of umbrella sampling [3].

It was shown that the accelerated molecular dynamics using this new smoothing function by Hamelberg et al. can be extended to all-atom biomolecular systems. It samples the conformational space more efficiently than normal molecular dynamics simulations and converges to the correct canonical distribution as was shown in the study of the helix-to-coil transition of hepta-alanine and the $\varphi - \psi$ space sampled by alanine dipeptide. This approach has proven to be robust for an all-atom system and has been used to study long-timescale motions, such as cis–trans isomerization of the Ser-Pro ω bond [43].

The accelerated molecular dynamics method of Hamelberg et al. was used to study cis–trans proline isomerization and the preferred backbone conformation of a serine-proline motif before and after phosphorylation of the serine residue. It was demonstrated that, unlike normal molecular dynamics, the accelerated molecular dynamics allows for the system to escape from the trans to cis isomer, and vice versa. Moreover, for both the unphosphorylated and phosphorylated peptides, the statistical thermodynamic properties were recaptured accurately, and the results were consistent with experimental values. Isomerization of the proline ω bond was shown to be asymmetric and strongly dependent on the ψ backbone angle before and after phosphorylation. The rate of isomerization was estimated to decrease with phosphorylation.

3.3.2. Kinetic rates and roughness

According to transition state theory, the motions on the modified surface evolve with a nonlinear timescale as shown in equation (1). Equation (1) allows for the dynamic information of the system on the unmodified surface to be recaptured. However, as stated earlier, the derivation of equation (1) requires that the bias potential is strictly zero close to the saddle points. In the definition of the simpler bias potential by Steiner et al. this condition was not always enforced, but could be corrected for since they knew exactly what the potential energy landscape looked like. However, corresponding insight into the shape of the potential surfaces of biomolecules does not come very easily. Therefore, studying the dynamics of the cis–trans isomerization of the Ser-Pro motif, Hamelberg et al. [44] devised a novel approach to recapture the kinetic information from accelerated molecular dynamics simulations. This was done by taking advantage of the roughness of the potential energy landscape and how it changes with different boost parameters. They established using accelerated dynamics simulations that the effective diffusion coefficient on a rough potential is related to the intrinsic roughness (the root-mean-square roughness, ε) by equation (7)

$$D = D^{\circ} \exp\left[-\left(\frac{\varepsilon}{k_B T}\right)^2\right] \qquad (7)$$

Here k_B is the Boltzmann constant and T is the temperature. Since the way the roughness is being changed in the accelerated molecular dynamics is known, the kinetics on the unmodified potential landscape could be recovered. Earlier, Zwanzig [45] had analytically solved the one-dimensional Smoluchowski equation to show that the form of equation (7) is characteristic of a random Gaussian-distributed roughness. It was shown in Ref. [44] that the accelerated molecular dynamics method can speed up simulations of biomolecules by more than 10^7 at 300 K. Also, the underlying roughness of the potential energy landscape, ε, was determined using equation (7) from several accelerated molecular dynamics simulations performed at different temperatures.

4. CONCLUSIONS

Computational methods like molecular dynamics simulation are presently the only avenue available to observing time evolution of biological molecules at atomistic detail. However, the timescale of conventional molecular dynamics simulations is currently limited to tens of nanoseconds, and simulations of biomolecules appear to be nonergodic because of high energy barriers separating potential energy basins. A class of accelerated molecular dynamics methods that modify the potential energy landscape akin to the umbrella sampling method has shown much promise. This method has been applied to biological systems and is also being used to explore larger proteins in explicit water simulations. By defining a robust bias potential that is not expensive to construct, accelerated molecular dynamics has been shown to accelerate the molecular dynamics simulation by many orders of magnitude.

ACKNOWLEDGEMENTS

This work was supported in part by grants from NSF, NIH, the Center for Theoretical Biological Physics, the National Biomedical Computation Resource, San Diego Supercomputing Center, and Accelrys, Inc.

REFERENCES

[1] M. Karplus and J. A. McCammon, Molecular dynamics simulations of biomolecules, *Nat. Struct. Biol.*, 2002, **9**, 646–652.
[2] J. A. McCammon, B. R. Gelin and M. Karplus, Dynamics of folded proteins, *Nature*, 1977, **267**, 585–590.
[3] J. A. McCammon and S. C. Harvey, *Dynamics of Proteins and Nucleic Acids*, 1st edition, Cambridge Cambridge, University Press, 1988, p. 246.
[4] K. D. Hammonds and J. P. Ryckaert, On the convergence of the shake algorithm, *Comput. Phys. Commun.*, 1991, **62**, 336–351.
[5] J. P. Ryckaert, G. Ciccotti and H. J. C. Berendsen, Numerical-integration of cartesian equations of motion of a system with constraints – molecular-dynamics of N-alkanes, *J. Comput. Phys.*, 1977, **23**, 327–341.
[6] Y. Weinbach and R. Elber, Revisiting and parallelizing SHAKE, *J. Comput. Phys.*, 2005, **209**, 193–206.
[7] E. Barth, K. Kuczera, B. Leimkuhler and R. D. Skeel, Algorithms for constrained molecular-dynamics, *J. Comput. Chem.*, 1995, **16**, 1192–1209.
[8] B. Hess, H. Bekker, H. J. C. Berendsen and J. Fraaije, LINCS: a linear constraint solver for molecular simulations, *J. Comput. Chem.*, 1997, **18**, 1463–1472.
[9] N. Go, Theoretical-studies of protein folding, *Annu. Rev. Biophys. Bioeng.*, 1983, **12**, 183–210.
[10] N. Go and H. Taketomi, Respective roles of short-range and long-range interactions in protein folding, *Proc. Natl. Acad. Sci. USA*, 1978, **75**, 559–563.

[11] V. Tozzini, Coarse-grained models for proteins, *Curr. Opin. Struct. Biol.*, 2005, **15**, 144–150.

[12] M. Wojciechowski and B. Lesyng, Generalized born model: analysis, refinement, and applications to proteins, *J. Phys. Chem. B*, 2004, **108**, 18368–18376.

[13] W. P. Im, M. S. Lee and C. L. Brooks, Generalized born model with a simple smoothing function, *J. Comput. Chem.*, 2003, **24**, 1691–1702.

[14] A. Onufriev, D. A. Case and D. Bashford, Effective Born radii in the generalized Born approximation: the importance of being perfect, *J. Comput. Chem.*, 2002, **23**, 1297–1304.

[15] D. Bashford and D. A. Case, Generalized born models of macromolecular solvation effects, *Annu. Rev. Phys. Chem.*, 2000, **51**, 129–152.

[16] A. Onufriev, D. Bashford and D. A. Case, Modification of the generalized Born model suitable for macromolecules, *J. Phys. Chem. B*, 2000, **104**, 3712–3720.

[17] W. C. Still, A. Tempczyk, R. C. Hawley and T. Hendrickson, Semianalytical treatment of solvation for molecular mechanics and dynamics, *J. Am. Chem. Soc.*, 1990, **112**, 6127–6129.

[18] J. N. Onuchic, Z. LutheySchulten and P. G. Wolynes, Theory of protein folding: the energy landscape perspective, *Annu. Rev. Phys. Chem.*, 1997, **48**, 545–600.

[19] J. N. Onuchic and P. G. Wolynes, Theory of protein folding, *Curr. Opin. Struct. Biol.*, 2004, **14**, 70–75.

[20] R. E. Bruccoleri and M. Karplus, Conformational sampling using high-temperature molecular dynamics, *Biopolymers*, 1990, **29**, 1847–1862.

[21] K. Kuczera, J. Kuriyan and M. Karplus, Temperature dependence of the structure and dynamics of myoglobin. A simulation approach, *J. Mol. Biol.*, 1990, **213**, 351–373.

[22] A. Mitsutake, Y. Sugita and Y. Okamoto, Replica-exchange multicanonical and multicanonical replica-exchange Monte Carlo simulations of peptides. I. Formulation and benchmark test, *J. Chem. Phys.*, 2003, **118**, 6664–6675.

[23] A. Mitsutake, Y. Sugita and Y. Okamoto, Replica-exchange multicanonical and multicanonical replica-exchange Monte Carlo simulations of peptides. II. Application to a more complex system, *J. Chem. Phys.*, 2003, **118**, 6676–6688.

[24] Y. Sugita and Y. Okamoto, Replica-exchange molecular dynamics method for protein folding, *Chem. Phys. Lett.*, 1999, **314**, 141–151.

[25] M. R. Sorensen and A. F. Voter, Temperature-accelerated dynamics for simulation of infrequent events, *J. Chem. Phys.*, 2000, **112**, 9599–9606.

[26] B. J. Berne and J. E. Straub, Novel methods of sampling phase space in the simulation of biological systems, *Curr. Opin. Struct. Biol.*, 1997, **7**, 181–189.

[27] R. Elber and M. Karplus, Enhanced sampling in molecular-dynamics – use of the time-dependent Hartree approximation for a simulation of carbon-monoxide diffusion through myoglobin, *J. Am. Chem. Soc.*, 1990, **112**, 9161–9175.

[28] H. Grubmuller, Predicting slow structural transitions in macromolecular systems: conformational flooding, *Phys. Rev. E*, 1995, **52**, 2893–2906.

[29] T. Huber, A. E. Torda and W. F. van Gunsteren, Local elevation: a method for improving the searching properties of molecular dynamics simulation, *J. Comput. Aided. Mol. Des.*, 1994, **8**, 695–708.

[30] J. Kleinjung, P. Bayley and F. Fraternali, Leap-dynamics: efficient sampling of conformational space of proteins and peptides in solution, *FEBS Lett.*, 2000, **470**, 257–262.

[31] J. Schlitter, M. Engels, P. Kruger, E. Jacoby and A. Wollmer, Targeted molecular-dynamics simulation of conformational change – application to the T – R transition in insulin, *Mol. Simul.*, 1993, **10**, 291–308.

[32] A. F. Voter, Hyperdynamics: accelerated molecular dynamics of infrequent events, *Phys. Rev. Lett.*, 1997, **78**, 3908–3911.

[33] A. F. Voter, A method for accelerating the molecular dynamics simulation of infrequent events, *J. Chem. Phys.*, 1997, **106**, 4665–4677.

[34] G. M. Torrie and J. P. Valleau, Non-physical sampling distributions in Monte-Carlo free-energy estimation – umbrella sampling, *J. Comput. Phys.*, 1977, **23**, 187–199.

[35] G. M. Torrie and J. P. Valleau, Monte-Carlo study of a phase-separating liquid-mixture by umbrella sampling, *J. Chem. Phys.*, 1977, **66**, 1402–1408.

[36] M. M. Steiner, P. A. Genilloud and J. W. Wilkins, Simple bias potential for boosting molecular dynamics with the hyperdynamics scheme, *Phys. Rev. B*, 1998, **57**, 10236–10239.

[37] J. A. Rahman and J. C. Tully, Puddle-skimming: an efficient sampling of multidimensional configuration space, *J. Chem. Phys.*, 2002, **116**, 8750–8760.

[38] J. C. Wang, S. Pal and K. A. Fichthorn, Accelerated molecular dynamics of rare events using the local boost method, *Phys. Rev. B*, 2001, **6308**, art. no.-085403..

[39] Q. F. Fang and R. Wang, Atomistic simulation of the atomic structure and diffusion within the core region of an edge dislocation in aluminum, *Phys. Rev. B*, 2000, **62**, 9317–9324.

[40] S. Pal and K. A. Fichthorn, Accelerated molecular dynamics of infrequent events, *Chem. Eng. J.*, 1999, **74**, 77–83.

[41] X. G. Gong and J. W. Wilkins, Hyper molecular dynamics with a local bias potential, *Phys. Rev. B*, 1999, **59**, 54–57.

[42] D. Hamelberg, J. Mongan and J. A. McCammon, Accelerated molecular dynamics: a promising and efficient simulation method for biomolecules, *J. Chem. Phys.*, 2004, **120**, 11919–11929.

[43] D. Hamelberg, T. Shen and J. A. McCammon, Phosphorylation effects on cis/trans isomerization and the backbone conformation of serine-proline motifs: accelerated molecular dynamics analysis, *J. Am. Chem. Soc.*, 2005, **127**, 1969–1974.

[44] D. Hamelberg, T. Shen and J. A. McCammon, Relating kinetic rates and local energetic roughness by accelerated molecular-dynamics simulations, *J. Chem. Phys.*, 2005, **122**, 241103.

[45] R. Zwanzig, Diffusion in a rough potential, *Proc. Natl. Acad. Sci. USA*, 1988, **85**, 2029–2030.

CHAPTER 13

Principal Components Analysis: A Review of its Application on Molecular Dynamics Data

Sarah A. Mueller Stein,[1] Anne E. Loccisano,[1] Steven M. Firestine[2] and Jeffrey D. Evanseck[1]

[1]Contribution from the Center for Computational Sciences and the Department of Chemistry and Biochemistry Duquesne University, 600 Forbes Avenue, Pittsburgh, PA 15282, USA
[2]Eugene Applebaum College of Pharmacy and Health Science, 3134 Eugene Applebaum Building, Wayne State University, 259 Mack Avenue, Detroit, MI 48201, USA

Contents

1. INTRODUCTION

Molecular dynamics is a proven and powerful tool in the exploration and study of the structure and dynamics that define biomolecular energy

ANNUAL REPORTS IN COMPUTATIONAL CHEMISTRY, VOLUME 2
ISSN: 1574-1400   DOI 10.1016/S1574-1400(06)02013-5

landscapes [1–7]. Technological advances in simulation methodology [8–14] and computer architecture [15,16] have significantly extended both the time scale and length (size) scale of molecular dynamics trajectories [17–22]. Reports in the literature show that the time scale of contemporary molecular dynamics trajectories, carried out with modest computer resources, have increased by roughly four orders of magnitude since the inception of biomolecular simulation. A microsecond simulation has been reported in 2000 [23]; however, after 5 years, this still remains the exception rather than the rule in computational studies. The length scale of practical molecular dynamics simulations has not witnessed such a dramatic increase, since the urgency for larger systems is not as great as for longer time. System sizes have increased by nearly 25 times, where simulations of 25,000 particles are not uncommon.

To put the growth of molecular dynamics simulations into perspective, a rough analogy to Moore's Law [24] can be created. Since the first reported biomolecular simulation over three decades ago, the time scale of reported protein simulations is found to double roughly every 2 years. In terms of length scale, simulations have nearly doubled in size every 6 years. For example, the first molecular dynamics simulation involving bovine pancreatic trypsin inhibitor (BPTI) was carried out for 9.2 picoseconds involving approximately 1082 atoms using a united-atom force field in vacuum [25]. In contrast, it is now fairly routine to simulate models incorporating explicit solvent, periodic boundary conditions, and extended electrostatics with second generation all-atom molecular force fields for 10–100 nanoseconds. As an illustration, lysozyme, a small protein of comparable size to BPTI, has been simulated using a solvated model of explicit waters for 28 nanoseconds involving over 13,000 atoms [26]. Examples including nucleic acid simulation show even greater growth, where a total of 0.6 microseconds of simulation for unique tetranucleotide sequences of DNA containing ~24,000 atoms has been reported [27,28].

It is obvious that the escalation of computing power, resources, and software development has made it easier to create significantly larger and more complex sets of data stemming from molecular dynamics simulations. However, analysis of molecular dynamics trajectories has never been and is currently not trivial. Extracting meaningful information from even the shortest time simulations is an artform requiring solid chemical intuition, physical insight, and technical expertise [29,30]. The increased complexity and size of molecular dynamics trajectories further amplifies an already difficult situation. As such, computational chemists have been searching for new computational tools to mine molecular dynamics data for meaningful information connecting biological function to structure and dynamics. The goal of this review is to demonstrate the need for multivariate analysis in biophysical studies, present how principal components analysis (PCA) can be implemented in the analysis of molecular dynamics data, and provide insights into the pitfalls and common errors associated with multivariate techniques.

2. MULTIVARIATE METHODS

Systematic variation of a single variable is usually desired in scientific study; however, researchers in the biological, chemical, physical, and social sciences frequently collect measurements on several variables simultaneously. This is especially true for molecular dynamics simulations, where the coordinates and momenta of all atoms are typically sampled every few femtoseconds over millions of time steps. Within the context of molecular dynamics simulations, the challenge is to discover the molecular motion(s) responsible for the phenomena of biochemical interest within the vast range of dynamics "noise" [17,18,29,30]. Some progress has been made, where localized molecular motion has been linked to biochemical function as a gateway in acetylcholinesterase [31–33], a hinged-lid in triose phosphate isomerase [34–38], and combined levers and gates in carbonmonoxy myoglobin [39]. A database of more than 120 molecular motions has been reported [40].

   A molecular dynamics trajectory is by definition multivariate data, where a large number of variables (atomic positions) are typically found to be interrelated, correlated, or dependent on each other. To decipher these large data sets, multivariate statistical analysis is one approach that is gaining popularity. References that present an organized overview of multivariate methods highlighting their statistical utility and connection between each of the techniques are available [41–43]. There are also excellent sources on individual multivariate methods giving an in-depth mathematical review coupled with illustrative examples and scientific problems suited for such applications [44,45]. For our purposes, multivariate analysis has been applied to molecular dynamics trajectories in two general ways:

   (1) *Data reduction or structural simplification.* The goal is to reduce the original large number of dependent variables (atomic coordinates) to a smaller and independent set to explain the phenomena of interest. Data reduction through PCA is unique when applied to molecular dynamics trajectories, since three or less principal components, composed of linear combinations of the original Cartesian coordinates, are typically identified to clarify important biomolecular motions.

(2) *Sorting, classification, and grouping.* The goal is to group or classify objects based upon measured characteristics. In this specific application of multivariate analysis, the dimensionality of the data set remains the same. The data set is simply partitioned into different groups to gain a sense of order or classification. For instance, cluster analysis has been used to identify similar geometric or conformational features from molecular dynamics simulations to further understand complex energy landscapes or design new drugs in pharmaceutical drug design studies.

The method of analysis depends heavily on whether one is interested in interrelationships or in comparisons, and on whether variables are qualitative or quantitative. In many situations, there will not be a single best method of analysis. When applied to molecular dynamics trajectories, the major classifications of multivariate analysis involve PCA [39,46–104], factor analysis [105,106], discriminant function analysis [107], cluster analysis [50,107–122], canonical correlation analysis [123–125], and multidimensional scaling [53,112,113,115,126–130].

A full description for each of these methods is beyond the scope of this review and may be found in other sources [41–45]. There is some overlap between a few of the methods where each technique is generally unique in carrying out either reduction or grouping of multivariate data. However, one of the most commonly applied techniques to molecular dynamics data sets is PCA, which will be the focus of this review.

3. PRINCIPAL COMPONENTS ANALYSIS

3.1. Background

Principal components analysis (PCA) is the simplest of multivariate techniques that is used to reduce or simplify large and complicated sets of data. The PCA procedure was first introduced for only a few variables in 1901 by Karl Pearson [131]. With the advent of computers, PCA was extended as a practical computing method by Hotelling in 1933 for a greater number of variables [132]. Since this time, many variations have been proposed and implemented, such as the essential dynamics method, which has been extensively used and reported in the recent literature. However, the underlying mathematical procedure for essential dynamics remains the same as PCA.

The commonly stated goal of PCA is to reduce the dimensionality of a multivariate data set by taking p interrelated variables, $x_1, x_2, \ldots, x_p$, and finding combinations of these based upon variances to produce a transformed set of variables, $z_1, z_2, \ldots, z_p$, that are uncorrelated. The indices z_i are called the principal components (PCs). Statistically, the point of PCA is straightforward, but this type of explanation is far from a physical interpretation that would be meaningful to scientists employing such a technique.

It is important first to realize that PCA is predicated on the assumption that the phenomena of interest can be explained by the *variances* and *covariances* between the p variables in the original data set. Unless the number of variables p is small, it is not possible to examine all of the variances or the covariances between the variables manually. PCA overcomes this limitation and transforms the data such that the uncorrelated variables or principal components are ranked by the variance of the data set in a single analysis. In terms of molecular dynamics simulations, PCA ultimately gives a view of the atoms that move anisotropically to maximize the variance.

3.2. Principal components

Before understanding the mathematical process on how PCA is carried out, it is instructive to define the principal components. The first principal component, z_1, is simply a linear combination (dot product) of the original variables $x_1, x_2, \ldots, x_p,$ with α. Note that the mathematical dot product operator takes two vectors and gives a scalar, or a new variable (principal component) to describe the data.

$$z_1 = \alpha_1^T x = \alpha_{11}x_1 + \alpha_{12}x_2 + \cdots + \alpha_{1p}x_p = \sum_{j=1}^{p} \alpha_{1j}x_j \qquad (1)$$

The weights $(\alpha_{11}, \alpha_{12}, \ldots, \alpha_{1p})$ are mathematically determined to maximize the variation of the original data in x, subject to the normalization constraint that

$$\alpha_{11}^2 + \alpha_{12}^2 + \cdots + \alpha_{1p}^2 = 1 \qquad (2)$$

The constraint is necessary; otherwise, the maximum can simply be increased by increasing any component of α_j. To be discussed later, the weights for a particular component are used to interpret and account for the variability in the data. Next, the second principal component, $z_2 = \alpha_2^T x$, is determined having a maximum variance that is uncorrelated with z_1 subject to the same normalization constraint on α_{2p}, and so on, so that the kth principal component, $z_k = \alpha_k^T x$, has maximum variance subject to being uncorrelated with $z_1, z_2, \ldots, z_{k-1}$. The computed number of principal components will be same as the number of p original variables. However, in highly correlated data sets, most of the variation from x will be accounted for in a few principal components. In uncorrelated data sets, PCA provides no statistical advantage in treating the data. Obviously, it is desirable to have the value of m much less than the value of p to attain a significant reduction in dimensionality of the data set, where m is the number of principal components necessary to account for the majority of the variation in the data set. The lack of correlation between the principal components is a useful property, since the indices can be interpreted as different "dimensions" describing the variation in the data set.

3.3. Covariance matrix

The process of determining the principal components starts with the construction of the $p \times p$ covariance or correlation matrix from a collection of n snapshot structures from molecular dynamics trajectories. The structure matrix x is composed of the Cartesian coordinates for each time stamp that defines each of the rows. The p columns of x are given by the $3N$ Cartesian coordinates for each atom. It is necessary to transform x to remove rotation and translation contamination that does not contribute to the real dynamics of the system. This is accomplished by aligning the structures to a common structure. The reference structure for the alignment process can be an averaged structure, any structure from the trajectory, or an experimental structure. Many techniques have been reported for comparing and overlaying proteins for applications other than for PCA [133–149]. The underlying procedure is essentially the same, where a subset of atoms for the alignment process is selected, and then alignment is carried out using a standard root-mean-square-deviation (*RMSD*) fit on the selected atoms [150]. In studies involving PCA, it is most common to use the alpha carbons or all of the non-hydrogen atoms in the alignment process.

Once x has been aligned, it is possible to compute the covariance matrix elements. The average position $<x_i>$ of the ith atom is computed along the entire trajectory. The convariance between the ith and jth atoms over the collection of n structures can be calculated as shown in equation (3). Each covariance matrix element is determined, as shown in equation (3).

$$c_{ij} = \frac{1}{n}\sum_{k=1}^{n}(x_{ik} - \langle x_i \rangle)(x_{jk} - \langle x_j \rangle) \quad i = 1, 2, \ldots, p \quad j = 1, 2, \ldots, p \quad (3)$$

The diagonal of the matrix is simply the variance of each coordinate. The covariance is the difference between a variable and its mean multiplied by the difference of another variable and its mean. Thus, if variable x_i varies largely from its mean, and variable x_j varies largely in the same direction, then the covariance matrix element, c_{ij}, will be large and positive. However, the covariance matrix element for x_i and x_j will be small, if either or both values are close to their corresponding means. With respect to a molecular system, the covariance matrix element between two atoms will be large and positive, if each of those atoms deviate largely from their equilibrium positions and the deviations are in the same direction. Mathematically, the covariance matrix summarizes the covariance between all variable combinations. This matrix is symmetric, so each row and column represents coordinates from the same structures in the same order, i.e. the kth row contains the same data points as the kth column.

3.4. Index of selectivity

The index of selectivity is simply the set of atoms identified for analysis. The index of selectivity is a modification of the possible values of i and j in equation (3). It is often assumed in the vast majority of studies utilizing PCA that all atoms should be included in the covariance matrix construction. It is important to realize that selection of all atoms, all non-hydrogen atoms, or all alpha carbons *biases* PCA to extract information involving large-scale global motion. Thus, if localized events are important, and all atoms are selected in the analysis, then the principal components method will likely fail to discover the localized motions, forcing an analysis on motion involving all of the atoms. This problem has been shown for the understanding of the dynamics of carbonmonoxy myoglobin [92]. When all of the non-hydrogen atoms were selected for the PCA, isotropic motion was found, where over 15 dimensions were required to understand the dynamics. However, when smaller and smaller volumes centered about the carbon monoxide ligand were used to select a subset of atoms, the amount of variance was found to be a maximum in two dimensions. Thus, two amino acids, histidine 64 and arginine 45, were found to be responsible for a majority of the anisotropic motion. The dynamics of the two residues were found to explain the spectroscopic A-states of carbonmonoxy myoglobin consistent with available kinetic and mutation data [151–155]. Consequently, the index of selectivity is an important step in the proper use of PCA.

3.5. Eigenanalysis

Analysis using PCA simply involves finding the eigenvectors and eigenvalues of the covariance matrix. The computed eigenvalues from the covariance matrix are the principal component variances. The eigenvalues are ordered from the largest to the smallest, so that $\lambda_1 \geqslant \lambda_2 \geqslant \ldots \geqslant \lambda_p \geqslant 0$. Specifically, the kth eigenvalue, λ_k, indicates the magnitude of the variance of the data in the direction of the corresponding kth eigenvector. The resulting eigenvectors provide the coefficients (weights) for the linear combination of observed structures. These eigenvectors are often referred to as the "loadings" for the principal components, and referred to as α_j in our previous discussion above. Thus, the linear combination of observed structures, $z_i = \alpha_i^T \mathbf{x}$, is known as the ith principal component.

$$z_i = \alpha_{i1}x_1 + \alpha_{i2}x_2 + \cdots + \alpha_{ip}x_p \qquad (4)$$

In protein and nucleic acids, the important data variance can be accounted for by a much smaller number of derived variables (principal components) than the p variables from which the analysis begins. For example in the case of nucleic acids, three principal components may account for 85% of the variance in the data [156]. The first two or three principal components often account for enough of the variance that important motions of the protein or nucleic acid can be extracted.

3.6. Scree test dimensionality determination

A key step in PCA is the determination of the number of dimensions to which the data is reduced. This is most easily accomplished by performing the *scree test*, or by creating a *scree plot* [157,158]. This type of plot involves the eigenvalues that are determined in the diagonalization of the covariance matrix. In a scree plot, the *x*-axis is an index of the number of eigenvalues determined. The eigenvalues are ordered from the strongest to weakest. The *y*-axis gives the magnitude of the eigenvalues from the covariance matrix diagonalization. It is customary to scale the eigenvalues such that they sum to unity in order to determine more easily the percent of the variance of the data accounted for the associated eigenvector. To accomplish this, each eigenvalue is divided by the sum of all of the eigenvalues.

To determine the appropriate dimensionality from the resulting analysis, it is necessary to locate the kink in the scree plot, where the variance rapidly falls to a relatively stable value. If the data is highly correlated initially, then the first few dimensions will have large eigenvalues, which indicates that a great amount of variance is described in those dimensions. The variance should drop rapidly and form a relatively flat plateau. The correct dimensionality is typically the dimension prior to the eigenvalue reaching the plateau. The interpretation is such that adding the extra dimension does not

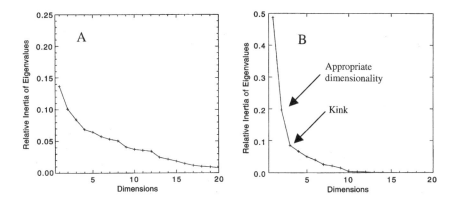

Fig. 1. Scree plots using indices of selectivity that include (a) all heavy atoms and (b) His64, the CO ligand and the heme.

result in any appreciable gain in information (variance) on the system, as compared to the complexity of adding an additional dimension.

Two example scree plots from our earlier work on carbonmonoxy myoglobin are given below [92]. From both plots, it is possible to identify the associated problems with the improper use of the index of selectivity, as commonly assumed (Fig. 1).

When all atoms are used in the PCA, a well-defined kink is never realized. The relative inertia monotonically decreases as the dimension increases. A scree plot with this type of signature indicates that the variance of the molecular system cannot be consolidated under a few dimensions. In using such an index of selectivity, it would be impossible to determine the correct dimensionality for further analysis. However, in Fig. 1b, where a subset of atoms is used to define the index of selectivity, it is clear that a significant portion of the system's variance is captured in the first two dimensions. In fact, approximately 70% of the information is found in the first two principal components. In this specific case, the third dimension delivers additional 10% of information; however, no useful data was found upon examination. The two plots illustrate the problem associated with assuming that all of the atoms should be used in the index of selectivity.

3.7. Visualization

The next step is visualization of the data using the dimensionality determined from the previous step. Projections of the original structures onto the weights (eigenvectors) of the associated principal components are plotted against each other as the scree plot dictates. Consequently, if M structures are collected and used in the covariance matrix construction, then *M* data points will be realized on the plots. The principal components plots give information on the similarity of the *M* structures used to form the covariance matrix. As an example, the two-dimensional plot corresponding to 1045 structures and scree plot in Fig. 1b is given below.

Each point on the plot corresponds to a structure and its relation to all other structures in the dimension(s) plotted. If two points are close to each other on the plot, then those structures are similar. If two points on such a plot are far from each other, then they are dissimilar in some fashion. It is clear that this specific plot yields three general basins of structural similarity. This behavior is consistent with the current ideas of energy landscapes, where multiple minima are clustered into regions that are separated by higher energy barriers [159]. It is at this juncture that the origin of dissimilarity between the three energy basins cannot be derived from the principal components plots alone. All that is known is that the structures are different given the index of selectivity utilized. In this specific instance, the difference was determined to be a result of the structural change of histidine 64, since that was the primary constituent of the index of selectivity. More traditional methods such as constructing the *RMSD* between the two structures from the different energy basins as a function of its sequence can usually pinpoint the molecular reasons of conformational differences. It is through the pair wise comparison of structures from the different basins that a molecular interpretation may be formulated in describing the different conformations sampled by the molecular system. A major result of the Schulze and Evanseck study was that histidine 64 moved in from the solvent to the ligand by ~ 10 Å on a timescale consistent with experiment [151], as shown in Fig. 2b.

When more than three dimensions are indicated by the scree plot, it is possible to examine the variance at the higher dimensions. As an example, when the first and second principal components are determined (using the scree test) to describe large amounts of variance, and when the third and fourth are very close together in magnitude, two separate plots may be created to help characterize molecular motion. The first plot may have the first, second, and third principal components as the axes, and the second plot would use first, second, and fourth as the axes.

4. ESSENTIAL DYNAMICS

4.1. Background

Certain types of internal motions allow proteins to perform their biological functions. These motions may enable the binding of substrates, adaptation

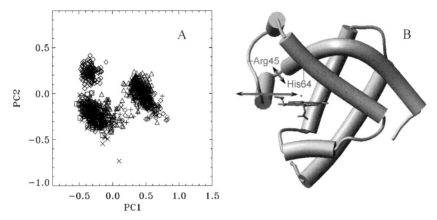

Fig. 2. (a) The two dimensional principal component plot of carbon-monoxy myoglobin using the coordinates of His64, the ligand and heme. The different symbols indicate different starting conditions of the multiple short time trajectories used to form the ensemble of structures. (b) Vectors showing the conformational change extracted from Fig. 2a.

to various environments, or conformational changes that allow binding of a substrate at another site on the protein (allosteric effects). The internal motions may be subtle and can involve complicated correlations between atomic motions, and thus the challenge presented is to identify these motions, determine how they relate to protein function, and to separate the complicated dynamics from the essential degrees of freedom [102,160,161]. Amadei and coworkers first developed the method known as essential dynamics in order to separate the concerted structural rearrangement from irrelevant motions [161]. Their method is based on the hypothesis that by using PCA, atomic positional fluctuations can be used to separate a protein's conformational space into two subspaces: an "essential" subspace which contains only a few degrees of freedom that describe the motions relevant for protein function (e.g., opening and closing and hinge bending motions) and the remaining subspace ("constrained subspace") that describes the irrelevant local fluctuations of the protein. This group used lysozyme as their test case of the essential dynamics method, and they concluded that the essential dynamics of most proteins can be described in a subspace of only a few degrees of freedom, while all other degrees of freedom represent much less important and mostly independent fluctuations of the molecule.

The essential dynamics method involves the use of a covariance matrix constructed from structures sampled throughout a molecular dynamics simulation. By diagonalization of a covariance matrix of the atomic coordinates of the system, the motions of a structure that are responsible for the most variance in atomic position are targeted. The essential sub-space is determined by ranking the eigenvalues elucidated by PCA, of the covariance matrix from the molecular dynamics trajectory. The mathematical equivalence between PCA and essential dynamics has been noted before [88,162–168] and has described within this document.

4.2. Applications to protein systems

Many authors of protein simulation studies have used the essential dynamics method in order to identify important molecular vibrations to understand more about large correlated protein motions and how they are critical to biological function. PCA has been used in a wide array of applications ranging from crystallographic and NMR structure ensembles [63,64,73,80,169–177], protein and peptide folding/unfolding [47,54,66,67,99,167,178–184], structural determinants of transmembrane proteins and channels [49,51,55,69,90,101,185–191], large-scale domain motion [58,77,98,104,192–199], locally accessible conformational sub-states [52,60,92,96,97,103,200], correlated and functional motion [39,56,57,61,71,84,163,166,168,201–215], dynamic effects from mutations and domain swapping [216–219], mutation impact upon binding [220–223], connection between structural similarity and dynamic behavior [87,89,164,224], ligand binding and migration [53,74,82,225–233], conformations of small molecules [72,79,91], protonation effects on dynamics [234], liquid behavior and spectroscopy [48,75,76], testing and development of methodology [46,59,62,65,78,83,85,86,235], protein docking algorithms [68,70,236–238], homology modeling [100], and atomic and molecular properties [50,95].

4.3. Applications to nucleic acids

PCA has been shown to be a powerful tool in evaluation of DNA flexibility in molecular dynamics simulations [162,239–241]. This technique has been employed to examine nucleic acid flexibility [239,240,242], flexibility of hybrid nucleic acids [243], flexibility of DNA in the crystal environment [240], behavior of A-tract DNA [93], electrostatic interactions of nucleic acids [83,156], sequence effects [27,28], DNA containing chemical modifications [81,244–246], broken strand DNA [247], base flipping [248], and nucleic acid mispairs [242]. The potential energy surface of nucleic acid conformational changes have also been investigated using PCA [156]. As new techniques in molecular dynamics simulations emerge, PCA has been used to evaluate the quality of simulations [249–251].

5. RELATED METHODS

5.1. Independent component analysis

Independent component analysis (ICA) is a multivariate technique that is used to separate independent variables in a data set [252,253]. Unlike PCA, ICA is not typically used as a dimensionality reduction technique. In ICA, the data must be fit to a model (not necessarily a linear model) [254] in which the derived variables are as statistically independent as possible. In chemical applications, it is generally favorable if the number of derived variables (principal components, latent variables) is much smaller than the number of original observations collected. Therefore, a data reduction technique such as PCA may be performed before standard ICA is carried out [252,255]. Thus, the focus of ICA is on the subspace accounting for the most variance in the data set when the analysis begins [252]. Westad and Kermit investigated validation methods for ICA and found that cross-validation was a valuable tool for determining the number of principal components to use from the preliminary reduction step and the number of ICs to extract in the actual ICA [256]. Yadava and Chaudhary applied ICA to determine analyte solvation parameters on polymer-coated surface acoustic wave vapor sensors [255]. ICA was employed because PCA did not yield derived variables that were interpretable for this particular type of experiment. ICA has been used in analysis of spectroscopic data [257,258]. Medical image processing is also an area in which ICA has been used [259]. Other uses of ICA include analysis of natural systems such as seismological and atmospheric data [260] and atmospheric aerosol content [261].

5.2. Singular value decomposition

The singular value decomposition (SVD) technique was established by several mathematicians who worked independently to develop the theory leading to the efficient diagonalization of a matrix [262]. Although SVD has many uses, it is commonly used to extract eigenvalues from a symmetric matrix [263]. As such, the technique has been used in PCA [94,264,265]. SVD may be used as a tool to execute PCA on a variety of systems including NMR spectroscopy [194,266] and X-ray photoelectron spectro-microscopy [265]. Andrews and coworkers used the SVD algorithm to perform PCA on myoglobin. In their work, SVD was chosen because it is computationally efficient. SVD was carried out on the internal coordinates of the myoglobin, which gave similar results as the SVD of the Cartesian coordinates [94]. Tomfohr and coworkers used SVD to diagonalize a matrix for dimensionality reduction of gene expression data [264]. SVD may also be used to carry out Gaussian network model analysis [267].

6. LIMITATIONS AND COMMON ERRORS

Multivariate techniques can be very powerful in data analysis. However, there are only a few papers that critically examine the possible weaknesses of multivariate analyses [102,268]. When using these statistical tools on molecular dynamics simulations, one should realize that there exist potential sources of error that could bias the analysis and provide misleading or wrong interpretations of the data.

The first and most important source of error deals with the well-documented sampling issues with molecular dynamics simulations [8,9,11,13,39]. The goal of applying PCA to molecular dynamics trajectories is to extract and understand the dynamics of the system. Consequently, if the trajectory samples only a portion of available structures from the true ensemble, then PCA will extract and provide information on the incomplete representation of phase space. Multivariate analysis will not create data to correct problems with the generation of the original data set.

Secondly, the index of selectivity is crucial to a successful PCA, which is often overlooked in a majority of studies utilizing dimensionality reduction and molecular dynamics. Care needs to be exercised in atom selection, where all atoms, all nonhydrogen atoms, or all alpha carbons of proteins are typically used for analysis. Selection based upon all atoms is correct, as long as low-frequency, large-scale motions are desired. However, it should be clear that molecular motion need not be large scale. As mentioned before, many well-understood examples show that local-motion is connected with function, as gateways [31–33], hinged-lids [34–38], and combined levers and gates [39]. Therefore, important motions could be localized and only a subset of the atoms is needed within the range of molecular motions. In carbonmonoxy myoglobin, it was necessary to modify the index of selectivity, based upon previous knowledge of the binding site, in order to discover the local motion responsible for the spectroscopic A-states [39]. Indices of selectivity can bias multivariate analysis, where it is necessary to have a course idea of the type of dynamics of interest, i.e., local or global motion, in molecular dynamics simulations.

Lastly, when working with PCA, it is essential to bear in mind that the major assumption is that the sources of largest variance are of importance to the problem being addressed. However, caution needs to be exercised in mixed data sets that involve more than the atomic coordinates from molecular dynamics trajectories. For example, differences in the units could be involved, where the original data may be composed of differently measured characteristics. For example, the variation in angstroms in atomic position is obviously different than the variation of pH or temperature. Even when the same units are used, it is plausible that one measured quantity may have a completely different range of behavior compared to another. Consider the variation in covalent bond length versus the variation in intermolecular hydrogen bonding. When variables with large variance are compared with variables of small variance, those with larger associated variance will be weighted more heavily in construction of the principal components. This weighting is simply due to the fact that the goal in constructing the principal components is to maximize variance. In cases with variables with widely ranging variance, using a covariance matrix of standardized variables, or correlation matrix to determine the principal components may help to alleviate this issue [45].

7. CONCLUSION

The continued advances in readily available computer power coupled with the desire to explore dynamics at longer time scales means that the magnitude and complexity of accessible dynamics data will keep growing. By necessity, methods to reduce the size of this data will continue to be valued by computational chemists. In this review, we have sought to highlight the utility of PCA to reduce the complexity of variables describing the dynamics data. PCA and the mathematically identical essential dynamics, have proved useful in the detection of important motions in biomolecules ranging from proteins to nucleic acids. Provided that appropriate care is taken with the use of these methods, computational chemists should find PCA useful in managing large, complex data sets and discovering molecular motions that are biochemically relevant.

ACKNOWLEDGMENTS

This work was funded in part by the National Science Foundation (CHE-0321147, CHE-0354052, AAB/PSC CHE-030008P), Department of Education (P116Z040100 and P116Z050331), SGI and Clarix Corporations, the National Institutes of Health (GM069549-01), and the Center for Computational Sciences at Duquesne University.

REFERENCES

[1] M. Karplus and J. Kuriyan, Molecular dynamics and protein function, *Proc. Natl. Acad. Sci.*, 2005, **102**, 6679–6685.

[2] T. Hansson, C. Oostenbrink and W. F. van Gunsteren, Molecular dynamics simulations, *Curr. Opin. Struc. Biol.*, 2002, **12**, 190–196.

[3] M. Karplus, Molecular dynamics simulations of biomolecules, *Acc. Chem. Res.*, 2002, **35**, 321–323.

[4] M. Karplus and J. A. McCammon, Molecular dynamics simulations of biomolecules, *Nat. Struct. Biol.*, 2002, **9**, 646–652.

[5] W. Wang, O. Donini, C. M. Reyes and P. A. Kollman, Biomolecular simulations: Recent developments in force fields, *simulations of enzyme catalysis, protein-ligand, protein-protein, and protein-nucleic acid noncovalent interactions. Annu. Rev. Biophys. Biomol. Struct.*, 2001, **30**, 211–243.

[6] M. Karplus and G. A. Petsko, Molecular dynamics simulations in biology, *Nature*, 1990, **347**, 631–639.

[7] M. Karplus, Molecular dynamics simulations of proteins, *Phys. Today*, 1987, **40**, 68–70.

[8] X. Cheng, G. Cui, V. Hornak and C. Simmerling, Modified replica exchange simulation methods for local structure refinement, *J. Phys. Chem. B*, 2005, **109**, 8220–8230.

[9] A. E. Loccisano, O. Acevedo, J. DeChancie, B. G. Schulze and J. D. Evanseck, Enhanced sampling by multiple molecular dynamics trajectories: carbonmonoxy myoglobin 10 microsecond $A_0 -> A_{1-3}$ transition from ten 400 picosecond simulations, *J. Mol. Graph. Model*, 2004, **22**, 369–376.

[10] P. Minary, M. E. Tuckerman and G. T. Martyna, Long time molecular dynamics for enhanced conformational sampling in biomolecular systems, *Phys. Rev. Lett.*, 2004, **93**, 1520201/1–1520201/4.

[11] I. Andricioaei, A. R. Dinner and M. Karplus, Self-guided enhanced sampling methods for thermodynamic averages, *J. Chem. Phys.*, 2003, **118**, 1074–1084.

[12] T. Schlick, *Molecular Modeling and Simulation*, Springer, New York, 2002.

[13] Z. Zhu, M. E. Tuckerman, S. O. Samuelson and G. T. Martyna, Using novel variable transformations to enhance conformational sampling in molecular dynamics, *Phys. Rev. Lett.*, 2002, **88**, 100201/1–100201/4.

[14] H. Grubmuller, Predicting slow structural transitions in macromolecular systems: Conformational Flooding, *Phys. Rev. E*, 1995, **52**, 2893–2906.

[15] G. Bhanota, D. Chen, A. Gara and P. Vranas, The BlueGene/L supercomputer, *Nucl. Phys. B (Proc. Suppl.)*, 2003, **119**, 114–121.

[16] F. Bodin, P. Boucaud, N. Cabibbo, G. Cascino, F. Calvayrac, M. Della Morte, A. Del Re, R. De Pietri, P. Deriso and F. Di Carlo, APE computers – past, present and future, *Comput. Phys. Commun.*, 2002, **147**, 402–409.

[17] A. H. Zewail, Femtochemistry, Atomic-scale dynamics of the chemical bond using ultrafast lasers Nobel lecture. In *Les Prix Nobel* (ed. T. Frangsmyr), Almqvist and Wiksell International, Stockholm, 2000, pp. 110–203.

[18] R. M. Hochstrasser, Ultrafast spectroscopy of protein dynamics, *J. Chem. Educ.*, 1998, **75**, 559–564.

[19] V. Reat, H. Patzelt, M. Ferrand, C. Pfister, D. Oesterhelt and G. Zaccai, Dynamics of different functional parts of bacteriorhodopsin: H-2 H labeling and neutron scattering, *Proc. Natl. Acad. Sci.*, 1998, **95**, 4970–4975.

[20] M. Ben-Nun, J. Cao and K. R. Wilson, Ultrafast X-ray and electron diffraction: Theoretical considerations, *J. Phys. Chem. A*, 1997, **101**, 8743–8761.

[21] E. Chen, R. A. Goldbeck and D. S. Kliger, Nanosecond time-resolved spectroscopy of biomolecular processes, *Annu. Rev. Biophys. Biomol. Struct.*, 1997, **26**, 327–355.

[22] T. Schlick, E. Barth and M. Mandziuk, Biomolecular dynamics at long timesteps: Bridging the timescale gap between simulation and experimentation, *Annu. Rev. Biophys. Biomol. Struct.*, 1997, **26**, 181–222.

[23] Y. Duan and P. A. Kollman, Pathways to a protein folding intermediate observed in a 1-microsecond simulation in aqueous solution, *Science*, 1998, **282**, 740–744.

[24] G. E. Moore, Cramming more components onto integrated circuits, *Electronics*, 1965, **38**, 114–117.

[25] J. A. McCammon, B. R. Gelin and M. Karplus, Dynamics of folded proteins, *Nature*, 1977, **267**, 585–590.

[26] M. Marchi, F. Sterpone and M. Ceccarelli, Water rotational relaxation and diffusion in hydrated lysozyme, *J. Am. Chem. Soc.*, 2002, **124**, 6787–6791.

[27] S. B. Dixit, D. L. Beveridge, D. A. Case, T. E. Cheatham III, E. Giudice, F. Lankas, R. Lavery, J. H. Maddocks, R. Osman, H. Sklenar, K. M. Thayer and P. Varnai, Molecular dynamics simulations of the 136 unique tetranucleotide sequences of DNA oligonucleotides. II: Sequence context effects on the dynamical structures of the 10 unique dinucleotide steps, *Biophys. J.*, 2005, **89**, 3721–3740.

[28] D. L. Beveridge, G. Barreiro, K. S. Byun, D. A. Case, T. E. Cheatham III, S. B. Dixit, E. Giudice, F. Lankas, R. Lavery, J. H. Maddocks, R. Osman, E. Seibert, H. Sklenar, G. Stoll, K. M. Thayer, P. Varnai and M. A. Young, Molecular dynamics simulations of the 136 unique tetranucleotide sequences of DNA oligonucleotides, I. Research design and results on d(CpG) steps, *Biophys. J.*, 2004, **87**, 3799–3813.

[29] C. L. Brooks, III, M. Karplus and B. M. Pettitt, *Proteins: A Theoretical Perspective of Dynamics, Structure, and Thermodynamics*, Wiley, New York, 1988.

[30] J. A. McCammon and S. C. Harvey, *Dynamics of Proteins and Nucleic Acids*, Cambridge University Press, Cambridge, 1988.

[31] T. Y. Shen, T. Kaihsu and J. A. McCammon, Statistical analysis of the fractal gating motions of the enzyme acetylcholinesterase, *Phys. Rev. E*, 2001, **63**, 041902/1–041902/6.

[32] N. A. Baker and J. A. McCammon, Non-Boltzmann rate distributions in stochastically gated reactions, *J. Phys. Chem. B*, 1999, **103**, 615–617.

[33] H.-X. Zhou, S. T. Wlodek and J. A. McCammon, Conformation gating as a mechanism for enzyme specificity, *Proc. Natl. Acad. Sci.*, 1998, **95**, 9280–9283.

[34] J. Sun and N. S. Sampson, Understanding protein lids: Kinetic analysis of active hinge mutants in triosephosphate isomerase, *Biochemistry*, 1999, **38**, 11474–11481.

[35] P. Derreumaux and T. Schlick, The loop opening/closing motion of the enzyme triosephosphate isomerase, *Biophys. J.*, 1998, **74**, 72–81.

[36] K. Yuksel, A. Sun, R. Gracy and K. Schnackerz, The hinged lid of yeast triosephosphate isomerase. Determination of the energy barrier between the two conformations, *J. Biol. Chem.*, 1994, **269**, 5005–5008.

[37] N. S. Sampson and J. R. Knowles, Segmental motion in catalysis: Investigation of a hydrogen bond critical for loop closure in the reaction of triosephosphate isomerase, *Biochemistry*, 1992, **31**, 8488–8494.

[38] D. Joseph, G. A. Petsko and M. Karplus, Anatomy of a conformational change: Hinged "lid" motion of the triosephosphate isomerase loop, *Science*, 1990, **249**, 1425–1428.

[39] B. G. Schulze, H. Grubmuller and J. D. Evanseck, Functional significance of hierarchical tiers in carbonmonoxy myoglobin: Conformational substates and transitions studied by conformational flooding simulations, *J. Am. Chem. Soc.*, 2000, **122**, 8700–8711.

[40] M. Gerstein and W. Krebs, A database of macromolecular motions, *Nucleic Acids Res*, 1998, **26**, 4280–4290.

[41] L. G. Grimm and P. R. Yarnold, *Reading and Understanding Multivariate Statistics*, American Psychological Association, Washington, DC, 1998.

[42] B. F. J. Manly, *Multivariate Statistical Methods: A Primer*, Chapman and Hall, London, 1994.

[43] R. A. Johnson and D. W. Wichern, *Applied Multivariate Statistical Analysis*, Prentice Hall, Upper Saddle River, 1992.

[44] I. T. Jolliffe, *In Principal Component Analysis*, 2nd ed, Springer, New York, 2002.

[45] G. H. Dunteman, In: M.S. Lewis-Beck (Ed.), Principal Components Analysis, 1st Ed., vol. 69, Sage, Newbury Park, 1989, p. 96–97.

[46] C. P. Barrett and M. E. M. Noble, Dynamite extended: Two new services to simplify protein dynamic analysis, *Bioinformatics*, 2005, **21**, 3174–3175.

[47] C. Chen, Y. Xiao and L. Zhang, A directed essential dynamics simulation of peptide folding, *Biophys. J.*, 2005, **88**, 3276–3285.

[48] M. D'Abramo, M. D'Alessandro, A. Di Nola, D. Roccatano and A. Amadei, Characterization of liquid behavior by means of local density fluctuations, *J. Mol. Liq.*, 2005, **117**, 17–21.

[49] S. Haider, A. Grottesi, B. A. Hall, F. M. Ashcroft and M. S. P. Sansom, Conformational dynamics of the ligand-binding domain of inward rectifier K channels as revealed by molecular dynamics simulations: Toward an understanding of Kir channel gating, *Biophys. J.*, 2005, **88**, 3310–3320.

[50] O. Horovitz and C. Sarbu, Characterization and classification of lanthanides by multivariate analysis methods, *J. Chem. Ed.*, 2005, **82**, 473–483.

[51] A. Hung, K. Tai and M. S. P. Sansom, Molecular dynamics simulation of the M2 helices within the nicotinic acetylcholine receptor transmembrane domain: Structure and collective motions, *Biophys. J.*, 2005, **88**, 3321–3333.

[52] A. Leo-Macias, P. Lopez-Romero, D. Lupyan, D. Zerbino and A. R. Ortiz, An analysis of core deformations in protein superfamilies, *Biophys. J.*, 2005, **88**, 1291–1299.

[53] Y. Li, Z. Zhou and C. B. Post, Dissociation of an antiviral compound from the internal pocket of human rhinovirus 14 capsid, *Proc. Natl. Acad. Sci.*, 2005, **102**, 7529–7534.

[54] J. T. MacDonald, A. G. Purkiss, M. A. Smith, P. Evans, J. M. Goodfellow and C. Slingsby, Unfolding crystallins: The destabilizing role of a β-hairpin cysteine in βB2-crystallin by simulation and experiment, *Protein Sci*, 2005, **14**, 1282–1292.

[55] S. Oyama, Jr., P. Pristovsek, L. Franzoni, A. Pertinhez Thelma, E. Schinina, C. Lucke, H. Ruterjans, C. Arantes Eliane and A. Spisni, Probing the pH-dependent structural features of α-KTx12.1, a potassium channel blocker from the scorpion Tityus serrulatus, *Protein Sci*, 2005, **14**, 1025–1038.

[56] P. W. Pan, R. J. Dickson, H. L. Gordon, S. M. Rothstein and S. Tanaka, Functionally relevant protein motions: Extracting basin-specific collective coordinates from molecular dynamics trajectories, *J. Chem. Phys.*, 2005, **122**, 034904.

[57] G. R. Smith, M. J. Sternberg and P. A. Bates, The relationship between the flexibility of proteins and their conformational states on forming protein-protein complexes with an application to protein-protein docking, *J. Mol. Biol.*, 2005, **347**, 1077–1101.

[58] Z. Zhou, M. Madrid, J. D. Evanseck and J. D. Madura, Effect of a bound non-nucleoside RT inhibitor on the dynamics of wild-type and mutant HIV-1 reverse transcriptase, *J. Am. Chem. Soc.*, 2005, **127**, 17253–17260.

[59] L. Afzelius, F. Raubacher, A. Karlen, F. S. Jorgensen, T. B. Andersson, C. M. Masimirembwa and I. Zamora, Structural analysis of CYP2C9 and CYP2C5 and an evaluation of commonly used molecular modeling techniques, *Drug Metab. Dispos.*, 2004, **32**, 1218–1229.

[60] B. Alakent, P. Doruker and M. C. Camurdan, Application of time series analysis on molecular dynamics simulations of proteins: A study of different conformational spaces by principal component analysis, *J. Chem. Phys.*, 2004, **121**, 4759–4769.

[61] B. Alakent, P. Doruker and M. C. Camurdan, Time series analysis of collective motions in proteins, *J. Chem. Phys.*, 2004, **120**, 1072–1088.

[62] C. P. Barrett, B. A. Hall and M. E. M. Noble, Dynamite: A simple way to gain insight into protein motions, *Acta Cryst. D.*, 2004, **60**, 2280–2287.

[63] F. Corzana, S. Motawia Mohammed, C. Herve du Penhoat, F. van den Berg, A. Blennow, S. Perez and B. Engelsen Soren, Hydration of the amylopectin branch point. Evidence of restricted conformational diversity of the α-$(1->6)$ linkage, *J. Am. Chem. Soc.*, 2004, **126**, 13144–13155.

[64] E. G. Emberly, R. Mukhopadhyay, C. Tang and N. S. Wingreen, Flexibility of β-sheets: Principal component analysis of database protein structures, *Proteins*, 2004, **55**, 91–98.

[65] D. Flock, I. Daidone and A. Di Nola, A molecular dynamics study of acylphosphatase in aggregation-promoting conditions: The influence of trifluoroethanol/water solvent, *Biopolymers*, 2004, **75**, 491–496.

[66] N. J. Marianayagam and S. E. Jackson, The folding pathway of ubiquitin from all-atom molecular dynamics simulations, *Biophys. Chem.*, 2004, **111**, 159–171.

[67] A. Palazoglu, A. Gursoy, Y. Arkun and B. Erman, Folding dynamics of proteins from denatured to native state: Principal component analysis, *J. Comp. Biol.*, 2004, **11**, 1149–1168.

[68] R. Tatsumi, Y. Fukunishi and H. K. Nakamura, A hybrid method of molecular dynamics and harmonic dynamics for docking of flexible ligand to flexible receptor, *J. Comp. Chem.*, 2004, **25**, 1995–2005.

[69] Y. S. Watanabe, Y. Fukunishi and H. K. Nakamura, Modelling of third cytoplasmic loop of bovine rhodopsin by multicanonical molecular dynamics, *J. Mol. Graph. Model*, 2004, **23**, 59–68.

[70] M. Zacharias, Rapid protein–ligand docking using soft modes from molecular dynamics simulations to account for protein deformability: Binding of FK506 to FKBP, *Proteins*, 2004, **54**, 759–767.

[71] G. Chillemi, P. Fiorani, P. Benedetti and A. Desideri, Protein concerted motions in the DNA-human topoisomerase I complex, *Nucleic Acids Res.*, 2003, **31**, 1525–1535.

[72] X. Fradera, M. Marquez, B. D. Smith, M. Orozco and F. J. Luque, Molecular dynamics study of [2]rotaxanes: Influence of solvation and cation on co-conformation, *J. Org. Chem.*, 2003, **68**, 4663–4673.

[73] J.-C. Hus, W. Peti, C. Griesinger and R. Bruschweiler, Self-consistency analysis of dipolar couplings in multiple alignments of ubiquitin, *J. Am. Chem. Soc.*, 2003, **125**, 5596–5597.

[74] A. Nijnik, R. Mott, D. P. Kwiatkowski and I. R. Udalova, Comparing the fine specificity of DNA binding by NF-κB p50 and p52 using principal coordinates analysis, *Nucleic Acids Res.*, 2003, **31**, 1497–1501.

[75] R. A. Wheeler and H. Dong, Optimal spectrum estimation in statistical mechanics, *ChemPhysChem*, 2003, **4**, 1227–1230.

[76] R. A. Wheeler, H. Dong and S. E. Boesch, Quasiharmonic vibrations of water, water dimer, and liquid water from principal component analysis of quantum and QM/MM trajectories, *ChemPhysChem*, 2003, **4**, 382–384.

[77] N. P. Barton, C. S. Verma and L. S. D. Caves, Inherent flexibility of calmodulin domains: A normal-mode analysis study, *J. Phys. Chem. B.*, 2002, **106**, 11036–11040.

[78] L. S. D. Caves and C. S. Verma, Congruent qualitative behavior of complete and reconstructed phase space trajectories from biomolecular dynamics simulation, *Proteins Struct. Funct. Genet.*, 2002, **47**, 25–30.

[79] M. D'Alessandro, A. Tenenbaum and A. Amadei, Coherent dynamics in a butane molecule, *Phys. Rev. E*, 2002, **66**, 020901/1–020901/4.

[80] R. Dvorsky, V. Hornak, J. Sevcik, G. P. Tyrrell, L. S. D. Caves and C. S. Verma, Dynamics of RNase Sa: A simulation perspective complementary to NMR/X-ray, *J. Phys. Chem. B*, 2002, **106**, 6038–6048.

[81] H. Ishida, Molecular dynamics simulation of 7,8-dihydro-8-oxoguanine DNA, *J. Biomol. Struct. Dyn.*, 2002, **19**, 839–851.

[82] M. J. Millan, L. Maiofiss, D. Cussac, V. Audinot, J. A. Boutin and A. Newman-Tancredi, Differential actions of anti-Parkinson agents at multiple classes of monoaminergic receptor. 1. A multivariate analysis of the binding profiles of 14 drugs at 21 native and cloned human receptor subtypes, *J. Pharm. Exp. Ther.*, 2002, **303**, 791–804.

[83] M. Nina and T. Simonson, Molecular dynamics of the tRNA Ala acceptor stem: Comparison between continuum reaction field and Particle-Mesh Ewald electrostatic treatments, *J. Phys. Chem. B.*, 2002, **106**, 3696–3705.

[84] J. T. A. Saarala, K. Tuppurainen, M. Perakyla, H. Santa and Laatikainen, Correlative motions and memory effects in molecular dynamics simulations of molecules: Principal components and rescaled range analysis suggest that the motions of native BPTI are more correlated than those of its mutants, *Biophys. Chem.*, 2002, **95**, 49–57.

[85] N. Ota and D. A. Agard, Enzyme specificity under dynamic control II. Principal components analysis of a-lytic protease using global and local solvent boundary conditions,, *Protein Sci.*, 2001, **10**, 1403–1414.

[86] R. Dvorsky, J. Sevcik, L. S. D. Caves, R. E. Hubbard and C. S. Verma, Temperature effects on protein motions: A molecular dynamics study of RNase-Sa, *J. Phys. Chem. B*, 2000, **104**, 10387–10397.

[87] A. Giuliani, R. Benigni, P. Sirabella, J. P. Zbilut and A. Colosimo, Nonlinear methods in the analysis of protein sequences: A case study in rubredoxins, *Biophys. J.*, 2000, **78**, 136–148.

[88] B. Hess, Similarities between principal components of protein dynamics and random diffusion, *Phys. Rev. E*, 2000, **62**, 8438–8448.

[89] M. A. Ceruso, A. Amadei and A. Di Nola, Mechanics and dynamics of B1 domain of Protein G: Role of packing and surface hydrophobic residues, *Protein Sci.*, 1999, **8**, 147–160.

[90] J. M. Koshi and W. J. Bruno, Major structural determinants of transmembrane proteins identified by principal components analysis, *Proteins*, 1999, **34**, 333–340.

[91] H. Lanig, M. Gottschalk, S. Schneider and T. W. Clark, Conformational analysis of tetracycline using molecular mechanical and semiempirical MO-calculations, *J. Mol. Mod.*, 1999, **5**, 46–62.

[92] B. G. Schulze and J. D. Evanseck, Cooperative role of Arg45 and His64 in the spectroscopic A3 state of carbonmonoxy myoglobin: Molecular dynamics simulations, multivariate anlaysis and quantum mechanical computations, *J. Am. Chem. Soc.*, 1999, **121**, 6444–6454.

[93] E. C. Sherer, S. A. Harris, R. Soliva, M. Orozco and C. A. Laughton, Molecular dynamics studies of DNA A-tract structure and flexibility, *J. Am. Chem. Soc.*, 1999, **121**, 5981–5991.

[94] B. K. Andrews, T. Romo, J. B. Clarage, B. M. Pettitt and G. N. Phillips, Jr., Characterizing global substates of myoglobin, *Structure*, 1998, **6**, 587–594.

[95] E. Bolzacchini, V. Consonni, R. Lucini, M. Orlandi and B. Rindone, High-performance size-exclusion chromatographic behavior of substituted benzoylpoly L-lysines by principal component analysis and molecular dynamics simulations, *J. Chromatogr. A*, 1998, **813**, 255–265.

[96] L. S. D. Caves, J. D. Evanseck and M. Karplus, Locally accessible conformations of proteins: Multiple molecular dynamics simulations of crambin, *Protein Sci.*, 1998, **7**, 649–666.

[97] R. Laatikainen, J. T. A. Saarala, K. Tuppurainen and T. Hassinen, Internal motions of native lysozyme are more organized than those of mutants: A principal component analysis of molecular dynamics data, *Biophys. Chem.*, 1998, **73**, 1–5.

[98] S. Hayward, A. Kitao and H. J. C. Berendsen, Model-free methods of analyzing domain motions in proteins from simulation: A comparison of normal mode analysis and molecular dynamics simulation of lysozyme, *Proteins*, 1997, **27**, 425–437.

[99] T. Lazaridis, I. Lee and M. Karplus, Dynamics and unfolding pathways of a hyperthermophilic and a mesophilic rubredoxin, *Protein Sci*, 1997, **6**, 2589–2605.

[100] K. Ogata and H. Umeyama, Prediction of protein side-chain conformations by principal component analysis for fixed main-chain atoms, *Protein Eng.*, 1997, **10**, 353–359.

[101] S. T. Wlodek, T. W. Clark, L. R. Scott and J. A. McCammon, Molecular dynamics of acetylcholinase dimer complexed wtih tacrine, *J. Am. Chem. Soc.*, 1997, **119**, 9513–9522.

[102] M. A. Balsera, W. Wriggers, Y. Oono and K. Schulten, Principal component analysis and long time protein dynamics, *J. Phys. Chem.*, 1996, **100**, 2567–2572.

[103] S. Hayward, A. Kitao and N. Go, Harmonic and anharmonic aspects in the dynamics of BPTI: A normal mode analysis and principal component analysis, *Protein Sci.*, 1994, **3**, 936–943.

[104] A. E. Garcia, Large-amplitude nonlinear motions in proteins, *Phys. Rev. Lett.*, 1992, **68**, 2696–2699.

[105] M. Kronen, H. Gorls, H.-H. Nguyen, S. Reissman, M. Bohl, J. Suhnel and U. Grafe, Crystal structure and conformational analysis of ampullosporin A, *J. Pept. Sci.*, 2003, **9**, 729–744.

[106] J. Hanus, I. Barvik, K. Ruszovz-Chmelova, J. Stepanek, P.-Y. Turpin and J. Bok, I. Rosenberg and M. Petrova-Endova, -CH2-lengthening of the internucleotide linkage in the ApA dimer can improve its conformational compatibility with its natural polynucleotide counterpart, *Nucleic Acids Res.*, 2001, **29**, 5182–5194.

[107] Y. K. Reshetnyak, Y. Koshevnik and E. A. Burstein, Decomposition of protein tryptophan fluorescence spectra into log-normal components. III. Correlation between fluorescence and microenvironment parameters of individual tryptophan residues, *Biophys. J.*, 2001, **81**, 1735–1758.

[108] J. Gsponer, U. Haberthur and A. Caflisch, The role of side-chain interactions in the early steps of aggregation: Molecular dynamics simulations of an amyloid-forming peptide from the yeast prion Sup35, *Proc. Natl. Acad. Sci.*, 2003, **100**, 5154–5159.

[109] G. Colombo, D. Roccatano and A. E. Mark, Folding and stability of the three-stranded β-sheet peptide Betanova: Insights from molecular dynamics simulations, *Proteins*, 2002, **46**, 380–392.

[110] R. B. Best, B. Li, A. Steward, V. Daggett and J. Clarke, Can non-mechanical proteins withstand force? Stretching barnase by atomic force microscopy and molecular dynamics simulation, *Biophys. J.*, 2001, **81**, 2344–2356.

[111] Y. Fan, L. M. Shi, K. W. Kohn, Y. Pommier and J. N. Weinstein, Quantitative structure-antitumor activity relationships of camptothecin analogues: Cluster analysis and genetic algorithm-based studies, *J. Med. Chem.*, 2001, **44**, 3254–3263.

[112] F. A. Hamprecht, C. Peter, X. Daura, W. Thiel and W. F. van Gunsteren, A strategy for analysis of (molecular) equilibrium simulations: Configuration space density estimation, clustering, and visualization, *J. Chem. Phys.*, 2001, **114**, 2079–2089.

[113] M. Vankatarajan and W. Braun, New quantitative descriptors of amino acids based on multidimensional scaling of a large number of physical chemical properties, *J. Mol. Mod.*, 2001, **7**, 445–453.

[114] Z. Zhang, Y. Zhu and Y. Shi, Molecular dynamics simulations of urea and thermal-induced denaturation of S-peptide analogue, *Biophys. Chem.*, 2001, **89**, 145–162.

[115] L. Carlacci, Conformational analysis of a farnesyltransferase peptide inhibitor, CVIM, *J. Comput.-Aided Mol. Des.*, 2000, **14**, 369–382.

[116] P. Ferrara, J. Apostolakis and A. Caflisch, Thermodynamics and kinetics of folding of two model peptides investigated by molecular dynamics simulations, *J. Phys. Chem. B*, 2000, **104**, 5000–5010.

[117] D. K. Klimov and D. Thirumalai, Mechanisms and kinetics of β-hairpin formation, *Proc. Natl. Acad. Sci.*, 2000, **97**, 2544–2549.

[118] A. Li and V. Daggett, Identification and characterization of the unfolding transition state of chymotrypsin inhibitor 2 by molecular dynamics simulations, *J. Mol. Biol.*, 1996, **247**, 412–419.

[119] S. Mariappan, A. Garcoa and G. Gupta, Structure and dynamics of the DNA hairpins formed by tandemly repeated CTG triplets associated with myotonic dystrophy, *Nucleic Acids Res.*, 1996, **24**, 775–783.

[120] E. M. Boczko and C. L. Brooks III, First-principle calculation of the folding free energy of a three-helix bundle protein, *Science*, 1995, **269**, 393–396.

[121] A. Li and V. Daggett, Characterization of the transition state of protein unfolding by use of molecular dynamics: Chymotrypsin inhibitor 2, *Proc. Natl. Acad. Sci.*, 1994, **91**, 10430–10434.

[122] M. E. Karpen, D. J. Tobias and C. L. Brooks III, Statistical clustering techniques for the analysis of long molecular dynamics trajectories: Analysis of 2.2 ns trajectories of YPGDV, *Biochemistry*, 1993, **32**, 412–420.

[123] N. Bruant, D. Flatters, R. Lavery and D. Genest, From atomic to mesoscopic descriptions of the internal dynamics of DNA, *Biophys. J.*, 1999, **77**, 2366–2376.

[124] D. Genest, Correlated motions analysis from molecular dynamics trajectories: Statistical accuracy on the determination of canonical correlation coefficients, *J. Comp. Chem.*, 1999, **20**, 1571–1576.

[125] D. Genest, Motion of groups of atoms in DNA studied by molecular dynamics simulation, *Eur. Biophys. J.*, 1998, **27**, 283–289.

[126] Y. Xia and M. Levitt, Funnel-like organization in sequence space determines the distributions of protein stability and folding rate preferred by evolution, *Proteins*, 2004, **55**, 107–114.

[127] O. Ivanciuc, C. H. Schein and W. Braun, SDAP: Database and computational tools for allergenic proteins, *Nucleic Acids Res.*, 2003, **31**, 359–362.

[128] D. Mihailescu, J. Reed and J. C. Smith, Convergence in peptide folding simulation: Multiple trajectories of a potential AIDS pharmacophore, *Biopolymers*, 2003, **70**, 121–133.

[129] G. E. Sims and S.-H. Kim, Global mapping of nucleic acid conformational space: Dinucleoside monophosphate conformations and transition pathways among conformational classes, *Nucleic Acids Res.*, 2003, **31**, 5607–5616.

[130] M. Feher and J. M. Schmidt, Metric and multidimensional scaling: Efficient tools for clustering molecular conformations, *J. Chem. Inf. Comput. Sci.*, 2001, **41**, 346–353.

[131] K. Pearson, On lines and planes of closest fit to a system of points in space, *Phil. Mag.*, 1901, **2**, 559–572.

[132] H. Hotelling, Analysis of a complex of statistical variables into principal components, *J. Educ. Psych.*, 1933, **24**, 417–441.

[133] J. Roach, S. Sharma, M. Kapustina and C. W. Carter, Structure alignment via Delaunay tetrahedralization, *Proteins*, 2005, **60**, 66–81.

[134] V. Alexandrov and M. Gerstein, Using 3D hidden Markov models that explicitly represent spatial coordinates to model and compare protein structures, *BMC Bioinform.*, 2004, 5(2).

[135] T. R. Scheider, Domain identification by iterative analysis of error-scaled difference distance matrices, *Acta Cryst. D*, 2004, **60**, 2269–2275.

[136] Y. Ye and A. Godzik, Database searching by flexible protein structure alignment, *Protein Sci.*, 2004, **13**, 1841–1850.

[137] A. I. Jewett, C. C. Huang and T. E. Ferrin, MINRMS: An efficient algorithm for determining protein structure similarity using root-mean-squared-distance, *Bioinformatics*, 2003, **19**, 625–634.

[138] V. Kotlovyi, W. L. Nichols and L. F. T. Eyck, Protein structural alignment for detection of maximally conserved regions, *Biophys. Chem.*, 2003, **105**, 595–608.

[139] T. R. Scheider, A genetic algorithm for the identification of conformationally invariant regions in protein molecules, *Acta Cryst. D*, 2002, **58**, 195–208.

[140] M. Shatsky, R. Nussinov and H. J. Wolfson, Flexible protein alignment and hinge detection, *Proteins*, 2002, **48**, 242–256.

[141] J. A. Irving, J. C. Whisstock and A. M. Lesk, Protein structural alignments and functional genomics, *Proteins*, 2001, **42**, 378–382.

[142] J. A. Cuff and G. J. Barton, Application of multiple sequence alignment profiles to improve protein secondary structure prediction, *Proteins*, 2000, **40**, 502–511.

[143] W. G. Krebs and M. Gerstein, The morph server: a standardized system for analyzing and visualizing macromolecular motions in a database framework, *Nucleic Acids Res.*, 2000, **28**, 1665–1675.

[144] C. Notredame, D. G. Higgins and J. Heringa, T-coffee: A novel method for fast and accurate multiple sequence alignment, *J. Mol. Biol.*, 2000, **302**, 205–217.

[145] A. F. Neuwald, J. S. Liu, D. J. Lipman and C. E. Lawrence, Extracting protein alignment models from the sequence database, *Nucl. Acids Res.*, 1997, **25**, 1665–1677.

[146] W. L. Nichols, B. H. Zimm and L. F. T. Eyck, Conformation-invariant structures of the a1b1 human hemoglobin dimmer, *J. Mol. Biol.*, 1997, **270**, 598–615.

[147] W. Wriggers and K. Schulten, Protein domain movements: Detection of rigid domains and visualization of hinges in comparisons of atomic coordinates, *Proteins*, 1997, **29**, 1–14.

[148] M. Gerstein and R. B. Altman, Average core structures and variability measures for protein families: Application to the immunoglobins, *J. Mol. Biol.*, 1995, **251**, 161–175.

[149] J. Hein, An algorithm combining DNA and protein alignment, *J. Theor. Biol.*, 1994, **167**, 169–174.

[150] H. Carlson, Personal Communication, 2005.

[151] J. Johnson, D. Lamb, H. Frauenfelder, J. Muller, B. McMahon, G. Nienhaus and R. Young, Ligand binding to heme proteins. VI. Interconversion of taxonomic substates in carbonmonoxymyoglobin, *Biophys. J.*, 1996, **71**, 1563–1573.

[152] W. D. Tian, J. T. Sage, P. M. Champion, E. Chien and S. G. Sligar, Probing heme protein conformational equilibration rates with kinetic selection, *Biochemistry*, 1996, **35**, 3487–3502.

[153] T. Li, M. L. Quillin, G. N. Phillips, Jr. and J. S. Olson, Structural determinants of the stretching frequency of CO bound to myoglobin, *Biochemistry*, 1994, **33**, 1433–1446.

[154] S. Balasubramanian, D. G. Lambright, M. C. Marden and S. G. Boxer, Carbon monoxide recombination to human myoglobin mutants in glycerol-water solutions, *Biochemistry*, 1993, **32**, 2202–2212.

[155] D. Braunstein, K. Chu, K. Egeberg, H. Frauenfelder, J. Mourant, G. Nienhaus, P. Ormos, S. Sligar, B. Springer and R. Young, Ligand binding to heme proteins: III. FTIR studies of His-E7 and Val-E11 mutants of carbonmonoxymyoglobin, *Biophys. J.*, 1993, **65**, 2447–2454.

[156] K. M. Elsawy, M. K. Hodgson and L. S. D. Caves, The physical determinants of the DNA conformational landscape: an analysis of the potential energy surface of single-strand dinucleotides in the conformational space of duplex DNA, *Nucleic Acids Res*, 2005, **33**, 5749–5762.

[157] R. Cattell, The meaning and strategic use of factor analysis. In *Handbook of Multivariate Experimental Psychology* (ed. R. B. Cattell), Rand McNally, Chicago, 1966, pp. 174–243.

[158] R. B. Cattell, The scree test for the number of factors, *Multivar. Behav. Res.*, 1966, **1**, 245–276.

[159] D. J. Wales, *Energy landscapes with applications to clusters, biomolecules and glasses*, Cambridge University Press, Cambridge, 2003.

[160] R. Kazmierkiewicz, C. Czaplewski, B. Lammek and J. Ciarkowski, Essential dynamics/factor analysis for the interpretation of molecular dynamics trajectories, *J. Comput.-Aided Mol. Des.*, 1999, **13**, 21–33.

[161] A. Amadei, A. B. Linssen and H. J. Berendsen, Essential dynamics of proteins, *Proteins*, 1993, **17**, 412–425.

[162] A. Noy, T. Meyer, M. Rueda, C. Ferrer, A. Valencia, A. Perez, X. d. I. Cruz, J. M. Lopez-Bes, R. Pouplana, J. Fernandez-Recio, F. J. Luque and M. Orozco, Data mining of molecular dynamics trajectories of nucleic acids, *J. Biomol. Struct. Dyn.*, 2006, **23**, 447–455.

[163] S. Nunez, C. Wing, D. Antoniou, V. L. Schramm and S. D. Schwartz, Insight into catalytically relevant correlated motions in human purine nucleoside phosphorylase, *J. Phys. Chem. A*, 2006, **110**, 463–472.

[164] N. J. Marianayagam and S. E. Jackson, Native-state dynamics of the ubiquitin family: Implications for function and evolution, *J. Royal Soc. Interface*, 2005, **2**, 47–54.

[165] A. Perez, J. R. Blas, M. Rueda, J. M. Lopez-Bes, X. De la Cruz and M. Orozco, Exploring the essential dynamics of B-DNA, *J. Chem. Theory Comput.*, 2005, **1**, 790–800.

[166] K. Arora and T. Schlick, In silico evidence for DNA polymerase-beta's substrate-induced conformational change, *Biophys. J.*, 2004, **87**, 3088–3099.

[167] J. E. Ollerenshaw, H. Kaya, H. S. Chan and L. E. Kay, Sparsely populated folding intermediates of the Fyn SH3 domain: Matching native-centric essential dynamics and experiment, *Proc. Natl. Acad. Sci.*, 2004, **101**, 14748–14753.

[168] L. V. Mello, B. L. De Groot, S. Li and M. J. Jedrzejas, Structure and flexibility of Streptococcus agalactiae hyaluronate lyase complex with its substrate. Insights into the mechanism of processive degradation of hyaluronan, *J. Biol. Chem.*, 2002, **277**, 36678–36688.

[169] R. Yang, M. C. Lee, H. Yan and Y. Duan, Loop conformation and dynamics of the Escherichia coli HPPK apo-enzyme and its binary complex with MgATP, *Biophys. J.*, 2005, **89**, 95–106.

[170] D. Komander, S. Kular Gursant, W. Schuttelkopf Alexander, M. Deak, K. R. C. Prakash, J. Bain, M. Elliott, M. Garrido-Franco, P. Kozikowski Alan, R. Alessi Dario and M. F. van Aalten Daan, Interactions of LY333531 and other bisindolyl maleimide inhibitors with PDK1, *Structure*, 2004, **12**, 215–226.

[171] P. Barthe, C. Roumestand, H. Demene and L. Chiche, Helix motion in protein C12A-p8MTCP1: Comparison of molecular dynamics simulations and multifield NMR relaxation data, *J. Comp. Chem.*, 2002, **23**, 1577–1586.

[172] R. M. Biondi, D. Komander, C. C. Thomas, J. M. Lizcano, M. Deak, D. R. Alessi and D. M. F. van Aalten, High resolution crystal structure of the human PDK1 catalytic domain defines the regulatory phosphopeptide docking site, *EMBO J.*, 2002, **21**, 4219–4228.

[173] D. M. F. van Aalten, C. R. Chong and L. Joshua-Tor, Crystal structure of carboxypeptidase A complexed with D-cysteine at 1.75-Å–inhibitor-induced conformational changes,, *Biochemistry*, 2000, **39**, 10082–10089.

[174] D. M. F. van Aalten, W. Crielaard, K. J. Hellingwerf and L. Joshua-Tor, Conformational substates in different crystal forms of the photoactive yellow protein – Correlation with theoretical and experimental flexibility, *Protein Sci.*, 2000, **9**, 64–72.

[175] S. Hayward, Structural principles governing domain motions in proteins, *Proteins*, 1999, **36**, 425–435.

[176] R. Abseher, L. Horstink, C. W. Hilbers and M. Nilges, Essential spaces defined by NMR structure ensembles and molecular dynamics simulation show significant overlap, *Proteins*, 1998, **31**, 370–382.

[177] B. L. de Groot, S. Hayward, D. M. van Aalten, A. Amadei and H. J. Berendsen, Domain motions in bacteriophage T4 lysozyme: a comparison between molecular dynamics and crystallographic data, *Proteins*, 1998, **31**, 116–127.

[178] L. Ragona, G. Colombo, M. Catalano and H. Molinari, Determinants of protein stability and folding: Comparative analysis of β-lactoglobulins and liver basic fatty acid binding protein, *Proteins*, 2005, **61**, 366–376.

[179] Y. Sugita and Y. Okamoto, Molecular mechanism for stabilizing a short helical peptide studied by generalized-ensemble simulations with explicit solvent, *Biophys. J.*, 2005, **88**, 3180–3190.

[180] A. Merlino, G. Graziano and L. Mazzarella, Structural and dynamic effects of α-helix deletion in Sso7d: Implications for protein thermal stability, *Proteins*, 2004, **57**, 692–701.

[181] D. Roccatano, I. Daidone, M.-A. Ceruso, C. Bossa and D. Nola Alfredo, Selective excitation of native fluctuations during thermal unfolding simulations: Horse heart cytochrome c as a case study, *Biophys. J.*, 2003, **84**, 1876–1883.

[182] J. Lee and S. Shin, Two-dimensional correlation analysis of peptide unfolding: Molecular dynamics simulations of β hairpins, *J. Phys. Chem. B*, 2002, **106**, 8796–8802.

[183] B. L. de Groot, X. Daura, A. E. Mark and H. Grubmuller, Essential dynamics of reversible peptide folding: Memory-free conformational dynamics governed by internal hydrogen bonds, *J. Mol. Biol.*, 2001, **309**, 299–313.

[184] L. D. Creveld, A. Amadei, R. C. van Schaik, H. A. Pepermans, J. de Vlieg and H. J. Berendsen, Identification of functional and unfolding motions of cutinase as obtained from molecular dynamics computer simulations, *Proteins*, 1998, **33**, 253–264.

[185] R. J. Law, R. H. Henchman and J. A. McCammon, A gating mechanism proposed from a simulation of a human α7 nicotinic acetylcholine receptor, *Proc. Natl. Acad. Sci.*, 2005, **102**, 6813–6818.

[186] A. Grottesi and S. P. Sansom Mark, Molecular dynamics simulations of a K+ channel blocker: Tc1 toxin from Tityus cambridgei, *FEBS lett*, 2003, **535**, 29–33.

[187] D. P. Tieleman, B. Hess and M. S. P. Sansom, Analysis and evaluation of channel models: Simulations of alamethicin, *Biophys. J.*, 2002, **83**, 2393–2407.

[188] R. D. Lins and T. P. Straatsma, Computer simulation of the rough lipopolysaccharide membrane of Pseudomonas aeruginosa, *Biophys. J.*, 2001, **81**, 1037–1046.

[189] G. H. Peters and R. P. Bywater, Influence of a lipid interface on protein dynamics in a fungal lipase, *Biophys. J.*, 2001, **81**, 3052–3065.

[190] I. H. Shrivastava, C. E. Capener, L. R. Forrest and M. S. P. Sansom, Structure and dynamics of K channel pore-lining helices: A comparative simulation study, *Biophys. J.*, 2000, **78**, 79–92.

[191] D. Cregut, G. Drin, J. P. Liautard and L. Chiche, Hinge-bending motions in annexins: Molecular dynamics and essential dynamics of apo-annexin V and of calcium bound annexin V and I, *Protein Eng.*, 1998, **11**, 891–900.

[192] M. C. Lee, J. Deng, J. M. Briggs and Y. Duan, Large-scale conformational dynamics of the HIV-1 integrase core domain and its catalytic loop mutants, *Biophys. J.*, 2005, **88**, 3133–3146.

[193] I. Daidone, D. Roccatano and S. Hayward, Investigating the accessibility of the closed domain conformation of citrate synthase using essential dynamics sampling, *J. Mol. Biol.*, 2004, **339**, 515–525.

[194] I. Stoica, Solvent interactions and protein dynamics in spin-labeled T4 lysozyme, *J. Biomol. Struct. Dyn.*, 2004, **21**, 745–760.

[195] N. E. Labrou, L. V. Mello and Y. D. Clonis, Functional and structural roles of the glutathione-binding residues in maize (Zea mays) glutathione S-transferase I, *Biochem. J.*, 2001, **358**, 101–110.

[196] D. Roccatano, A. E. Mark and S. Hayward, Investigation of the mechanism of domain closure in citrate synthase by molecular dynamics simulation, *J. Mol. Biol.*, 2001, **310**, 1039–1053.

[197] T. A. Soares, J. H. Miller and T. P. Straatsma, Revisiting the structural flexibility of the complex p21ras-GTP: The catalytic conformation of the molecular switch II, *Proteins*, 2001, **45**, 297–312.

[198] C. R. Watts, G. Toth, R. F. Murphy and S. Lovas, Domain movement in the epidermal growth factor family of peptides, *Theochemistry*, 2001, **535**, 171–182.

[199] D. M. F. van Aalten, P. C. Jones, M. De Sousa and J. B. C. Findlay, Engineering protein mechanics: Inhibition of concerted motions of the cellular retinol binding protein by site-directed mutagenesis, *Protein Eng.*, 1997, **10**, 31–37.

[200] C. Arcangeli, A. R. Bizzarri and S. Cannistraro, Molecular dynamics simulation and essential dynamics study of mutated plastocyanin: Structural, dynamical and functional effects of a disulfide bridge insertion at the protein surface, *Biophys. Chem.*, 2001, **92**, 183–199.

[201] L. Stella, E. E. Di Iorio, M. Nicotra and G. Ricci, Molecular dynamics simulations of human glutathione transferase P1-1: Conformational fluctuations of the apo-structure, *Proteins*, 1999, **37**, 10–19.

[202] A. Pandini and L. Bonati, Conservation and specialization in PAS domain dynamics, *Prot. Eng. Des. Sel.*, 2005, **18**, 127–137.

[203] A. Merlino, L. Vitagliano, A. Ceruso Marc and L. Mazzarella, Subtle functional collective motions in pancreatic-like ribonucleases: From ribonuclease A to angiogenin, *Proteins*, 2003, **53**, 101–110.

[204] M. Sulpizi, U. Rothlisberger and P. Carloni, Molecular dynamics studies of caspase-3, *Biophys. J.*, 2003, **84**, 2207–2215.

[205] A. Grottesi, M.-A. Ceruso, A. Colosimo and A. Di Nola, Molecular dynamics study of a hyperthermophilic and a mesophilic rubredoxin, *Proteins*, 2002, **46**, 287–294.

[206] M. J. Jedrzejas, L. V. Mello, B. de Groot and S. Li, Mechanism of hyaluronan degradation by *Streptococcus pneumoniae* hyaluronate lyase, *J. Biol. Chem.*, 2002, **277**, 28287–28297.

[207] M. Otyepka and J. Damborsky, Functionally relevant motions of haloalkane dehalogenases occur in the specificity-modulating cap domain, *Protein Sci.*, 2002, **11**, 1206–1217.

[208] B. S. Sanjeev and S. Vishveshwara, Essential dynamics and sidechain hydrogen bond cluster studies on eosinophil cationic protein, *Eur. Phys. J. D.*, 2002, **20**, 601–608.

[209] C. Arcangeli, A. R. Bizzarri and S. Cannistraro, Concerted motions in copper plastocyanin and azurin: An essential dynamics study, *Biophys. Chem.*, 2001, **90**, 45–56.

[210] R. D. Lins, T. P. Straatsma and J. M. Briggs, Similarities in the HIV-1 and ASV integrase active sites upon metal cofactor binding, *Biopolymers*, 2000, **53**, 308–315.

[211] P. L. Chau, D. M. F. van Aalten, R. P. Bywater and J. B. C. Findlay, Functional concerted motions in the bovine serum retinol-binding protein, *J. Comput.-Aided Mol. Des.*, 1999, **13**, 11–20.

[212] B. L. de Groot, G. Vriend and H. J. Berendsen, Conformational changes in the chaperonin GroEL: New insights into the allosteric mechanism, *J. Mol. Biol.*, 1999, **286**, 1241–1249.

[213] L. Horstink, R. Abseher, M. Nilges and C. W. Hilbers, Functionally important correlated motions in the single-stranded DNA-binding protein encoded by filamentous phage Pf3, *J. Mol. Biol.*, 1999, **287**, 569–577.

[214] R. D. Lins, J. M. Briggs, T. P. Straatsma, H. A. Carlson, J. Greenwald, S. Choe and J. A. McCammon, Molecular dynamics studies on the HIV-1 integrase catalytic domain, *Biophys. J.*, 1999, **76**, 2999–3011.

[215] D. M. F. van Aalten, W. D. Hoff, J. B. C. Findlay, W. Crielaard and K. J. Hellingwerf, Concerted motions in the photoactive yellow protein, *Protein Eng.*, 1998, **11**, 873–879.

[216] A. Merlino, L. Vitagliano, M. A. Ceruso and L. Mazzarella, Dynamic properties of the N-terminal swapped dimer of ribonuclease A, *Biophys. J.*, 2004, **86**, 2383–2391.

[217] M. A. Ceruso, A. Grottesi and A. Di Nola, Dynamic effects of mutations within two loops of cytochrome c551 from Pseudomonas aeruginosa, *Proteins*, 2003, **50**, 222–229.

[218] G. Settanni, A. Cattaneo and P. Carloni, Molecular dynamics simulations of the NGF-TrkA domain 5 complex and comparison with biological data, *Biophys. J.*, 2003, **84**, 2282–2292.

[219] J. Lee, K. Lee and S. Shin, Theoretical studies of the response of a protein structure to cavity-creating mutations, *Biophys. J.*, 2000, **78**, 1665–1671.

[220] A. Brigo, K. W. Lee, G. I. Mustata and J. M. Briggs, Comparison of multiple molecular dynamics trajectories calculated for the drug-resistant HIV-1 integrase T66I/M154I catalytic domain, *Biophys. J.*, 2005, **88**, 3072–3082.

[221] K. S. Chakrabarti, B. S. Sanjeev and S. Vishveshwara, Stability and dynamics of domain-swapped bovine-seminal ribonuclease, *Chem. Biodiv.*, 2004, **1**, 802–818.

[222] R. G. Efremov, Y. A. Kosinsky, D. E. Nolde, R. Tsivkovskii, A. S. Arseniev and S. Lutsenko, Molecular modelling of the nucleotide-binding domain of Wilson's disease protein: Location of the ATP-binding site, domain dynamics, and potential effects of the major disease mutations, *Biochem. J.*, 2004, **382**, 293–305.

[223] F. Fraternali, L. Cavallo and G. Musco, Effects of pathological mutations on the stability of a conserved amino acid triad in retinoschisin, *FEBS Lett.*, 2003, **544**, 21–26.

[224] M. L. Sforca, S. Oyama, Jr., F. Canduri, C. C. B. Lorenzi, T. A. Pertinhez, K. Konno, B. M. Souza, M. S. Palma, N. J. Ruggiero, W. F. Azevedo, Jr. and A. Spisni, How C-terminal carboxyamidation alters the biological activity of peptides from the venom of the eumenine solitary wasp, *Biochemistry*, 2004, **43**, 5608–5617.

[225] A. Crespo, A. Marti Marcelo, G. Kalko Susana, A. Morreale, M. Orozco, L. Gelpi Jose, F. J. Luque and A. Estrin Dario, Theoretical study of the truncated hemoglobin HbN: Exploring the molecular basis of the NO detoxification mechanism, *J. Am. Chem. Soc.*, 2005, **127**, 4433–4444.

[226] M. Fuxreiter, C. Magyar, T. Juhasz, Z. Szeltner, L. Polgar and I. Simon, Flexibility of prolyl oligopeptidase: Molecular dynamics and molecular framework analysis of the potential substrate pathways, *Proteins*, 2005, **60**, 504–512.

[227] C. Bossa, M. Anselmi, D. Roccatano, A. Amadei, B. Vallone, M. Brunori and A. Di Nola, Extended molecular dynamics simulation of the carbon monoxide migration in sperm whale myoglobin, *Biophys. J.*, 2004, **86**, 3855–3862.

[228] M. L. Barreca, K. W. Lee, A. Chimirri and J. M. Briggs, Molecular dynamics studies of the wild-type and double mutant HIV-1 integrase complexed with the 5CITEP inhibitor: Mechanism for inhibition and drug resistance, *Biophys. J.*, 2003, **84**, 1450–1463.

[229] G. I. Mustata, T. A. Soares and J. M. Briggs, Molecular dynamics studies of alanine racemase: A structural model for drug design, *Biopolymers*, 2003, **70**, 186–200.

[230] A. Pang, Y. Arinaminpathy, S. P. Sansom Mark and C. Biggin Philip, Interdomain dynamics and ligand binding: Molecular dynamics simulations of glutamine binding protein, *FEBS lett.*, 2003, **550**, 168–174.

[231] S. K. Ludemann, V. Lounnas and R. C. Wade, How do substrates enter and products exit the buried active site of cytochrome P450cam? 2. Steered molecular dynamics and adiabatic mapping of substrate pathways, *J. Mol. Biol.*, 2000, **303**, 813–830.

[232] G. H. Peters, T. M. Frimurer, J. N. Andersen and O. H. Olsen, Molecular dynamics simulations of protein-tyrosine phosphatase 1B. II. Substrate-enzyme interactions and dynamics, *Biophys. J.*, 2000, **78**, 2191–2200.

[233] G. H. Peters, D. M. van Aalten, A. Svendsen and R. Bywater, Essential dynamics of lipase binding sites: The effect of inhibitors of different chain length, *Protein Eng.*, 1997, **10**, 149–158.

[234] I. Eberini, A. M. Baptista, E. Gianazza, F. Fraternali and T. Beringhelli, Reorganization in apo- and holo-β-lactoglobulin upon protonation of Glu89: Molecular dynamics and pKa calculations, *Proteins*, 2004, **54**, 744–758.

[235] R. Gargallo, P. H. Huenenberger, F. X. Aviles and B. Oliva, Molecular dynamics simulation of highly charged proteins: Comparison of the particle-particle particle-mesh and reaction field methods for the calculation of electrostatic interactions, *Protein Sci.*, 2003, **12**, 2161–2172.

[236] D. Mustard and W. Ritchie David, Docking essential dynamics eigenstructures, *Proteins*, 2005, **60**, 269–274.

[237] S. Sharma, P. Pirila, H. Kaija, K. Porvari, P. Vihko and A. H. Juffer, Theoretical investigations of prostatic acid phosphatase, *Proteins*, 2005, **58**, 295–308.

[238] S. Ferrari, P. M. Costi and R. C. Wade, Inhibitor specificity via protein dynamics insights from the design of antibacterial agents targeted against thymidylate synthase, *Chem. Biol.*, 2003, **10**, 1183–1193.

[239] A. Noy, A. Perez, F. Lankas, F. J. Luque and M. Orozco, Relative flexibility of DNA and RNA: A molecular dynamcis study, *J. Mol. Biol.*, 2004, **343**, 627–638.

[240] A. Perez, A. Noy, F. Lankas, F. J. Luque and M. Orozco, The relative flexibility of B-DNA and A-RNA duplexes: Database analysis, *Nucleic Acids Res.*, 2004, **32**, 6144–6151.

[241] M. Orozco, A. Perez, A. Noy and F. J. Luque, Theoretical methods for the simulation of nucleic acids, *Chem. Soc. Rev.*, 2003, **32**, 350–364.

[242] V. Cojocaru, R. Klement and T. M. Jovin, Loss of G-A base pairs is insufficient for achieving a large opening of U4 snRNA K-turn motif, *Nucleic Acids Res.*, 2005, **33**, 3435–3446.

[243] A. Noy, A. Perez, M. Marquez, F. J. Luque and M. Orozco, Structure, recognition properties, and flexibility of the DNA.RNA hybrid, *J. Am. Chem. Soc.*, 2005, **127**, 4910–4920.

[244] R. Soliva, V. Monaco, I. Gomez-Pinto, N. J. Meeuwenoord, G. A. V. d. Marel, J. H. V. Boom, C. Gonzalez and M. Orozco, Solution structure of a DNA duplex with a chiral alkyl phosphonate moiety, *Nucleic Acids Res.*, 2001, **29**, 2973–2985.

[245] A. Ninaber and J. M. Goodfellow, DNA conformation and dynamics, *Radiat. Environ. Biophys.*, 1999, **38**, 23–29.

[246] H. Yamaguchi, D. M. F. Van Aalten, M. Pinak, A. Furukawa and R. Osman, Essential dynamics of DNA containing a cis.syn cyclobutane thymine dimer lesion, *Nucleic Acids Res.*, 1998, **26**, 1939–1946.

[247] H. Yamaguchi, J. G. Siebers, A. Furukawa, N. Otagiri and R. Osman, Molecular dynamics simulation of a DNA containing a single strand break, *Radiat. Prot. Dosimetry.*, 2002, **99**, 103–108.

[248] D. M. F. van Aalten, D. A. Erlanson, G. L. Verdine and L. Joshua-Tor, A structural snapshot of base-pair opening in DNA, *Proc. Natl. Acad. Sci.*, 1999, **96**, 11809–11814.

[249] S. Jha, P. V. Coveney and C. A. Laughton, Force field validation for nucleic acid simulations: Comparing energies and dynamics of a DNA dodecamer, *J. Comp. Chem.*, 2005, **26**, 1617–1627.

[250] M. Rueda, S. G. Kalko, F. J. Luque and M. Orozco, The structure and dynamics of DNA in the gas phase, *J. Am. Chem. Soc.*, 2003, **125**, 8007–8014.

[251] V. Tsui and D. A. Case, Molecular dynamics simulations of nucleic acids with a generalized born model, *J. Am. Chem. Soc.*, 2000, **122**, 2489–2498.

[252] M. G. Gustafsson, Independent component analysis yields chemically interpretable latent variables in multivariate regression, *J. Chem. Inf. Model.*, 2005, **45**, 1244–1255.

[253] P. Comon, Independent component analysis, a new concept?, *Signal Processing*, 1994, **36**, 287–314.

[254] A. Hyvarinen, Survey on independent component analysis, *Neural Comput. Surveys*, 1999, **2**, 94–128.

[255] R. D. S. Yadava and R. Chaudhary, Solvation Transduction and independent component analysis for pattern recognition in SAW electronic nose, *Sens. Actuators B*, 2006, **113**, 1–21.

[256] F. Westad and M. Kermit, Cross validation and uncertainty estimates in independent component analysis, *Anal. Chim. Acta.*, 2003, **490**, 341–354.

[257] F. S. de Edelenyi, A. W. Simonetti, G. Postma, R. Huo and L. M. C. Buydens, Application of independent component analysis to 1H MR spectroscopic imaging exams of brain tumors, *Anal. Chim. Acta.*, 2005, **544**, 36–46.

[258] A. Pichler and M. G. Sowa, Blind phase projection as an effective means of recovering pure component spectra from phase modulated photoacoustic spectra, *Vib. Spectrosc.*, 2005, **39**, 163–168.

[259] M. Alrubaiee, M. Xu, S. K. Gayen, M. Brito and R. R. Alfano, Three-dimensional optical tomographic imaging of scattering objects in tissue-simulating turbid media using independent component analysis, *Appl. Phys. Lett.*, 2005, **87**, 191112–191113.

[260] E. De Lauro, S. De Martino, M. Falanga, A. Ciaramella and R. Tagliaferri, Complexity of time series associated to dynamical systems inferred from independent component analysis, *Phys. Rev. E*, 2005, **72**, 046712/1–046712/14.

[261] S. De Martino, M. Falanga and L. Mona, Stochastic resonance mechanism in aerosol index dynamics, *Phys. Rev. Lett.*, 2002, **89**, 128501/1–128501/4.

[262] G. W. Stewart, On the early history of the singular value decomposition, *SIAM Rev*, 1993, **35**, 551–566.

[263] M. E. Wall, A. Rechtsteiner and L. M. Rocha, Singular value decomposition and principal component analysis. In *A Practical Approach to Microarray Data Analysis* (eds D. P. Berrar, W. Dubitzky and M. Granzow), Kluwer, Norwell, MA, 2003, pp. 91–109.

[264] J. Tomfohr, J. Lu and T. B. Kepler, Pathway level analysis of gene expression using singular value decomposition, *BMC Bioinform.* 6 (2005).

[265] J. Walton and N. Fairley, Noise reduction in X-ray photoelectron spectromicroscopy by a singular value decomposition sorting procedure, *J. Electr. Spectr. Relat. Phenom.*, 2005, **148**, 29–40.

[266] N. Trbovic, S. Smirnov, F. Zhang and R. Bruschweiler, Covariance NMR spectroscopy by singular value decomposition, *J. Magn. Reson.*, 2004, **171**, 277–283.

[267] S. Maguid, S. Fernandez-Alberti, L. Ferrelli and J. Echave, Exploring the common dynamics of homologous proteins. Application to the globin family, *Biophys. J.*, 2005, **89**, 3–13.

[268] J. A. Hanley, Appropriate uses of multivariate analysis, *Annu. Rev. Public Health*, 1983, **4**, 155–180.

CHAPTER 14

Solvent Effects on Organic Reactions from QM/MM Simulations

Orlando Acevedo and William L. Jorgensen

Department of Chemistry, Yale University, 225 Prospect Street, New Haven, CT 06520-8107, USA

Contents

A review is provided examining the effects of solvation on the reactants, transition structures, and rates for three organic reactions: Menshutkin, nucleophilic aromatic substitution (S_NAr), and Kemp decarboxylation. QM/MM calculations for the reactions in protic and dipolar aprotic solvents readily elucidate the origin of variations in reaction rates using two-dimensional potentials of mean force (PMF) derived from free energy perturbation calculations in Monte Carlo simulations (MC/FEP). Free energies of activation in several solvents are computed consistently to be in close agreement with experiment. The overall quantitative success for the reactions with differing substitution and elimination mechanisms support the present QM/MM/MC approach, highlighting the PDDG/PM3 semiempirical method.

1. INTRODUCTION

Theoretical models have profoundly impacted the understanding of organic reactions in solution, including mechanism elucidation, transition state stabilization, and solute–solvent interactions [1,2]. For many reactions the role of solvent has been assumed to be static, hence its effect is basically thought to be a contribution of solvation energy to the total free energy of the system. However, direct participation of solvent molecules may occur in which a few critical solvent molecules bind to the transition

ANNUAL REPORTS IN COMPUTATIONAL CHEMISTRY, VOLUME 2
ISSN: 1574-1400   DOI 10.1016/S1574-1400(06)02014-7

structure and lower the activation energy or an electric field created by the solvent changes the shape of the potential energy surface. The effect of solvent on such chemical transformations is highly sensitive, typically giving noticeable improvement in rate acceleration and stereoselectivity when transferring from water to dipolar aprotic solvents. In extreme cases the reaction path itself can be perturbed, reinforcing the need for thorough studies on the intermolecular interactions occurring between solvent and reactions.

Much effort has gone into the development of improved methodology to accurately reproduce energies and geometries for condensed phase reactions [3]. Various approaches for modeling solvation are available; a popular technique is the use of a continuum model characterized by the dielectric constant [4,5] such as the conductor-like polarizable continuum model (CPCM) [6]. CPCM in combination with *ab initio* quantum mechanics is computationally efficient and provides good accuracy, e.g., Houk and coworkers recently found a mean absolute deviation from experiment for solvation free energies of 2.6 kcal/mol for 70 different organic molecules in aqueous solution [7]. However, continuum models tend to give poor results when differentiating between rates of reaction in protic versus aprotic solvents owing to the lack of specific information on intermolecular interactions, such as hydrogen bonding.

A QM/MM approach, where reactants are treated quantum mechanically in the presence of a large number of explicit solvent molecules modeled with molecular mechanics, is better suited to explore solute–solvent interactions [2,8]. The use of *ab initio* calculations for the QM method is generally impractical since a QM/MM study of a typical reaction requires ca. 50,000,000 single-point QM calculations. The recent development of an improved semiempirical treatment, the PDDG/PM3 method, [9] has proved valuable in reproducing the rate data for several organic reactions in solution at a fraction of the cost [10–13]. This article will focus on our recent efforts determining the origin of solvent effects for three different organic reactions: Menshutkin, nucleophilic aromatic substitution (S_NAr), and Kemp decarboxylation; comparisons of the QM/MM methodology to other alternatives are included.

2. METHODS

Mixed quantum and molecular mechanical (QM/MM) calculations, as implemented in BOSS 4.6 [14], were carried out with the reacting systems treated with the PDDG/PM3 method [9]. PDDG/PM3 has been extensively tested for gas-phase structures and energetics [9]. The solvent molecules are represented with the united-atom OPLS force field [15] for the non-aqueous solvents and with the TIP4P water model [16]. The systems consisted of the reactants, plus 395 solvent molecules for the non-aqueous solvents, or 740 molecules for water. To locate the minima and maxima on the free energy surface for the reaction, a two-dimensional free energy map was constructed for each reaction. Free-energy perturbation (FEP) calculations were performed in conjunction with Metropolis Monte Carlo (MC) simulations at 25°C and 1 atm. In this QM/MM implementation, the solute intramolecular energy is treated quantum mechanically using PDDG/PM3; computation of the QM energy and atomic charges is performed for every attempted solute move, occurring every 100 configurations. Each MC/FEP simulation consisted of 2.5–10 M configurations of equilibration followed by 5 M configurations of averaging. For electrostatic contributions to the solute–solvent energy, CM3 charges [17] obtained for the solute in the PDDG/PM3 calculations were used with a scale factor of 1.08 for neutral systems and unscaled for ions. Solute–solvent and solvent–solvent intermolecular cutoff distances of 12 Å were employed.

3. MENSHUTKIN REACTION

The Menshutkin reaction is regarded as a fundamental example for studying solvent effects upon the rates of reactions; there have been numerous prior experimental [18] and theoretical [19–28] investigations. The reaction between methyl chloride and ammonia (Scheme 1) is the prototypical example of the biomolecular reaction, in which uncharged reactants proceed to form ions allowing for a fundamental understanding of solvation on emerging charges. Large rate accelerations are observed for such Menshutkin reactions in protic over dipolar aprotic solvents.

Changes in free energy for the $NH_3 + CH_3Cl$ reaction in water and DMSO were calculated using the present QM/MM approach by perturbing the distance between the nitrogen and the carbon (R_{NC}) and the distance between the chlorine and the carbon (R_{CCl}) (Fig. 1a). The free energy map in water (Fig. 1b) was obtained using initial ranges for R_{NC} of 1.45–2.40 Å and R_{CCl} of 1.75–2.35 Å with an increment of 0.05 Å. The transition structure was refined and smoothly connected to the reactants and products with a separation distance of 5.1 Å using increments of 0.01 Å. Ewald sums were used to model long-range electrostatics [29]

$$H_3N + CH_3Cl \longrightarrow H_3NCH_3^+ + Cl^-$$

Scheme 1. Menshutkin reaction between ammonia and methyl chloride.

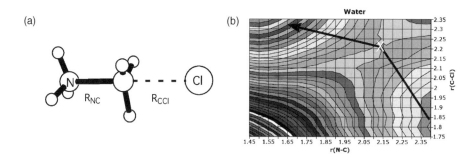

Fig. 1. (a) Distance variables, R_{NC} and R_{CCl}, in the Menshutkin reaction between ammonia and methyl chloride. (b) Two-dimensional potential of mean force in water. X marks the transition structure. The arrow follows the reaction path toward product. Distances in Å.

crucial in reproducing the free energy of reaction for the large charge separation at the products.

The Menshutkin reaction between ammonia and methyl chloride has been studied by a variety of methods implementing numerous solvation models (Table 1). Several dielectric continuum studies have been reported; Dillet *et al.* developed a multipole expansion method used to explore the reaction at the HF level [20]. Truong *et al.* employed the generalized conductor-like screening model (GCOSMO) in conjunction with MP2 and DFT [21]. Fradera *et al.* used the polarizable continuum model (PCM) and MP2 to analyze changes on the potential energy surface in water [22]. Amovilli *et al.* also utilized PCM but with the computationally intensive complete active space self-consistent field (CASSSCF) method; the active space was generated distributing four electrons in four orbitals of a_1 type [30].

QM/MM studies on the Menshutkin reaction began with work by Gao [2,23,24]. In Gao's earlier work, reactants followed a gas-phase minimum energy path using *ab initio* single points at the MP4SDTP/6-31 + G(d) level [23]. Free energies of hydration were then computed by following the path in a box of TIP4P water molecules. A subsequent hybrid QM/MM model followed, using AM1/TIP3P, that allowed polarization of the solutes by the solvent [24]. Recent work by Ruiz-Pernía *et al.* uses dual-level QM/MM calculations, where two QM methods (AM1 and MP2) are used to evaluate the energy during the PMF calculation [28]. Results were improved over AM1 alone, primarily due to the semiempirical method's inaccuracy for the overall energetics.

As an intermediate between continuum and QM/MM approaches, the reference interaction site model self-consistent field (RISM-SCF) method has been used by Kato and coworkers to explore the Menshutkin reaction [25]. RISM–SCF combines the RISM integral equation theory for molecular

Table 1. Computed free energies (kcal/mol) and transition state geometries (Å) for the Menshutkin reaction between $NH_3 + CH_3Cl$ in water

	R_{NC}	R_{CCl}	ΔG_{rxn}	$\Delta G^{\ddagger}$	Ref.
HF/6-31G(d,p)[a]	2.20	2.29	−28.1	28.7	[20]
HF/6-311G(d,p)[a]	2.24	2.28	−34.2	16.8	[30]
BH&HLYP/6-31G(d,p)[a]	2.22	2.18	−16.5	24.8	[21]
MP2/3-21G(d,p)[a]	2.24	2.20	−55.7	20.7	[22]
MP2/6-31G(d,p)[a]	2.16	2.17	−19.8	31.4	[21]
CAS(4,4)/6-311G(d,p)[a]	2.17	2.32	−29.1	20.5	[30]
MP4SDTQ/6-31 + G(d)// HF/6-31 + G(d)/TIP4P[b]	1.90	2.47	−37.0	25.6	[23]
AM1/TIP3P[b]	1.96	2.09	−18.0	26.3	[24]
MP2(fc)/6-31G + (d,p)/ AM1/TIP4P (UIC)[b,c]	–	–	−31.1	23.8	[28]
MP2(fc)/6-31G + (d,p)/ AM1/TIP4P (PIC)[b,d]	–	–	−27.4	19.1	[28]
RISM-HF[e]	2.26	2.26	−27.8	17.7	[25]
RISM-MP2[e]	–	–	−22.1	20.9	[25]
RISM-HF + MD[e,f]	2.17	2.28	−17.8	24.2	[26]
PDDG/PM3/TIP4P[b]	2.14	2.18	−21.9	25.8	This work
Exptl.	–	–	−34 ± 10	23.5[g]	[23,34]

[a] Water modeled with continuum solvation methods.
[b] QM/MM method.
[c] Unperturbed interpolated corrections.
[d] Perturbed interpolated corrections.
[e] Reference interaction site model.
[f] Molecular dynamics with SPC water model.
[g] Reaction between $NH_3 + CH_3I$.

solvents with QM methods for the solute electronic structures, describing local solute–solvent interactions [31]. Recent work by Kato, used RISM–SCF for the reacting system combined with molecular dynamics (MD) for bulk solvent giving good agreement with reported continuum and QM/MM work [26]. Gordon *et al.* also explored a compromise between continuum and QM/MM models through development of the effective fragment potential method (EFP); treating the solutes with *ab initio* methods and introducing discrete water molecules through potentials added as one-electron terms directly into the *ab initio* Hamilton [32]. The HF/DZVP level with EFP was used to study the effect of 2, 4, 6, and 8 explicit water molecules on the reaction between ammonia and methyl bromide with good results [27,33].

Our QM/MM work using the PDDG/PM3 method, yielded the free-energy results in Table 2 for the Menshutkin reaction in water and DMSO. The results obtained in water compare well with many of those obtained through vastly different approaches, i.e., continuum, RISM, dual-level

Table 2. Free energies (kcal/mol) and transition-structure geometries (Å) for the Menshutkin reaction between $NH_3 + CH_3Cl$ in water and DMSO from QM/MM/MC simulations using PDDG/PM3

	R_{NC}	R_{CCl}	ΔG_{rxn}	$\Delta G^{\ddagger}$
Water	2.14	2.18	−21.9	25.8
DMSO	2.02	2.20	21.4	30.1

QM/MM, as well as experiment (Table 1). Dramatic solvent effects were found for both the transition state and the products. In the protic solvent, the reaction results in free ions with a large computed exothermic free energy of reaction, ΔG_{rxn}, of −21.9 kcal/mol representing the strong inter-actions of water with the charged ions. However, for the dipolar aprotic solvent a product ion-pair is more likely formed, as the ΔG_{rxn} is highly unfavorable at 21.4 kcal/mol, pointing to poorer solvation of the separated ions in DMSO. The activation barrier in water is also significantly lower than in DMSO, highlighting the protic solvent's ability to stabilize the emerging charges in the transition structure. Gao reported that increases in the strength and total number of hydrogen bonds are critical for the stabilization of the transition state and products in water [24]. This is evident when comparing the larger R_{NC} distance for the transition struc-ture in water over DMSO, 2.14 Å versus 2.02 Å, respectively (Table 2). The aqueous solution facilitates stabilization of the developing charges, allowing for an earlier transition structure than in DMSO. Consistent with the later R_{NC} in the aprotic solvent, the QM/MM charges for $CH_3NH_3^+$ and Cl^- at the transition state in DMSO are 0.63 and −0.63, respectively, compared to 0.56 and −0.56 in water.

Overall, the good agreement with experimental data for this prototypical Menshutkin reaction supports the reliability of the present QM/MM approach. The computational efficiency of the semiempirical PDDG/PM3 method compared to *ab initio* alternatives offers an attractive approach for computing solvent effects on reactions.

4. NUCLEOPHILIC AROMATIC SUBSTITUTION

Nucleophilic aromatic substitution reactions have been shown to proceed through an addition–elimination mechanism (S_NAr) involving the formation of an intermediate Meisenheimer complex [35–37]. Our recent investiga-tion of an S_NAr reaction in solution explored the reaction between azide ion and 4-fluoronitrobenzene (Scheme 2) in water, methanol, acetonitrile, and DMSO [11]. The rates of S_NAr reactions with anionic nucleophiles

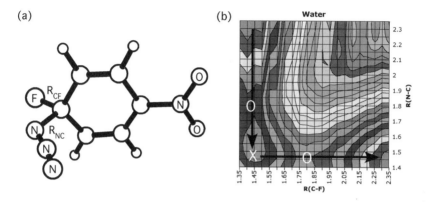

Scheme 2. S_NAr reaction between azide ion and 4-fluoronitrobenzene.

Fig. 2. (a) Distance variables, R_{CF} and R_{NC}, for the S_NAr reaction between azide ion and 4-fluoronitrobenzene. (b) Two-dimensional potential of mean force in water. X marks the intermediate complex, and O symbols mark the transition structures. The arrows follow the reaction path toward product. All distances in Å.

were found to be particularly sensitive to medium effects, with rate accelerations observed for dipolar aprotic over protic solvents [37]. In this case, increased charge delocalization in proceeding to the transition state is unfavorable in hydrogen-bonding media.

To study the detailed origins of the solvent effects, changes in free energy were calculated by perturbing the distance between the closest nitrogen of the azide and the attacked carbon of 4-fluoronitrobenzene (R_{NC}) and the distance between the fluorine and the attacked carbon (R_{CF}) (Fig. 2a). The resultant free energy map for the reaction in water (Fig. 2b) was constructed using initial ranges for R_{NC} and R_{CF} of 1.35–2.35 Å with an increment of 0.05 Å. In all cases, transition structures for the addition (TS1) and elimination (TS2) steps and the intermediate complex (IC) were readily located and refined using increments of 0.01 Å.

Activation barriers and the relative free energy of the intermediate were computed by extending R_{NC} to 5 Å and smoothly connecting the reactants, transition structures, and intermediate using increments of 0.02 Å (Table 3, Fig. 3). Uncertainties in the free energy values are calculated by propagating the standard deviation (σ_i) on each individual ΔG_i and lead to errors below ± 0.6 kcal/mol. The computed $\Delta G^{\ddagger}$ values for either TS are in reasonable agreement with experimental data and

Table 3. Free energies, ΔG (kcal/mol), relative to reactants for the S_NAr reaction from QM/MM/MC simulations

	TS1	IC	TS2	Exptl. [38]
H_2O	30.8	18.1	35.3	28.1
CH_3OH	26.1	10.6	27.5	27.5
CH_3CN	17.5	−2.94	21.1	21.8
DMSO	17.0	−5.02	19.9	21.8

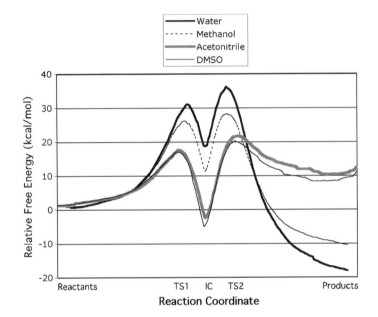

Fig. 3. Potentials of mean force for the S_NAr reaction in the four solvents from the QM/MM/MC calculations.

reproduce well the large rate accelerations in progressing from the protic to the dipolar aprotic solvents.

The QM/MM/MC calculations find that the elimination step (TS2) has the highest barrier in all solvents. This may have relevance in clearing up discourse on whether the rate-limiting step lies at the addition of the nucleophile or elimination of the leaving group [35–37,39]. However, semiempirical QM methods tend to overestimate activation barriers for S_N2 reactions in which fluoride is the nucleophile or the leaving group [10]. To address this concern, density functional theory (DFT) was also applied to the S_NAr reaction. Specifically, the B3LYP/6-31 + G(d) level of theory [40] was used to characterize the transition structures and intermediates in vacuum using Gaussian 03 [41]. Frequency calculations verified

Table 4. Free energies, ΔG (kcal/mol) relative to reactants for the $S_N Ar$ reaction from B3LYP/6-311++G(2d,p) and PCM calculations

	TS1	IC	TS2	Exptl. [38]
H_2O	27.6	25.1	16.4	28.1
CH_3OH	27.9	25.6	17.4	27.5
CH_3CN	27.1	24.9	16.9	21.8
DMSO	27.9	25.5	17.5	21.8

stationary points and provided thermodynamic corrections. The effect of solvent was approximated using single point energy calculations in conjunction with the polarizable continuum model (PCM) [5] and a larger basis set, 6-311++G(2d,p).

The $\Delta G^{\ddagger}$ values computed using DFT/PCM for TS1 in protic solvents show good agreement with experiment (Table 4), and attainment of TS1 is predicted to be the rate-determining step. However, the high dielectric constants lead the DFT/PCM results to, in essence, be the same in all four solvents, not reproducing the substantial solvent effects observed experimentally. The observed variability of the stability of the intermediate in different media is also not reflected in the DFT/PCM results [36,37]. In contrast, the QM/MM/MC calculations find the intermediate to be similar in free energy to the reactants in the dipolar aprotic solvents, whereas it has relative free energies of 11 and 18 kcal/mol in methanol and water (Fig. 3). The explicit representation of solvent molecules and hydrogen bonding in the QM/MM/MC methodology leads to improved results for the solvent effects. However, differences between DFT/PCM and QM/MM/MC results leave open the question on the rate-controlling step. Lower rates are attributed primarily to greater differential stabilization of azide ion than the more charge delocalized transition structures via hydrogen bonding in water and methanol; a detailed thermodynamic analysis of the system can be found in reference [11].

5. KEMP DECARBOXYLATION

The Kemp decarboxylation of 3-carboxybenzisoxazole (**1** in Scheme 3) has been shown to exhibit dramatic rate accelerations by 7–8 orders of magnitude upon transfer from a protic to polar aprotic solvent [42,43]; however, the inclusion of an internal hydrogen bond can effectively inhibit the reaction with near solvent independence [43]. These dramatic kinetic effects emphasize the strong role hydrogen bonding plays on the decarboxylation. QM/MM simulations were recently carried out on the reactions of **1–3** and the effects of inter- and intramolecular hydrogen bonding

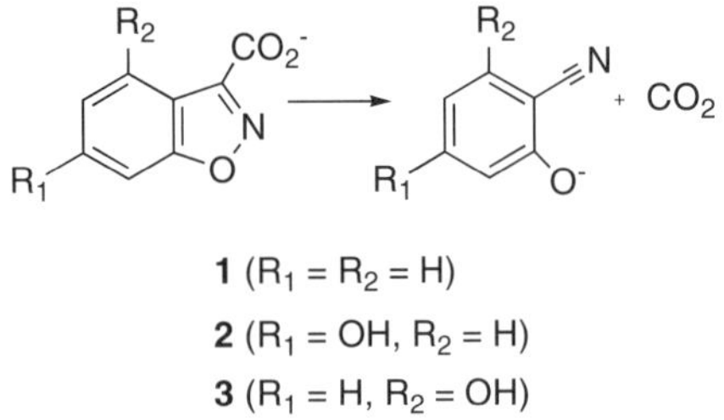

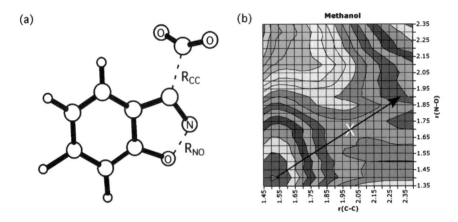

1 ($R_1 = R_2 = H$)

2 ($R_1 = OH, R_2 = H$)

3 ($R_1 = H, R_2 = OH$)

Scheme 3. Kemp decarboxylation for derivatives of benzisoxazole-3-carboxylic acid.

Fig. 4. (a) Distance variables, R_{NO} and R_{CC}, for the Kemp decarboxylation of 3-carboxybenzisoxazole. (b) Two-dimensional potential of mean force in methanol. X marks the transition structure. The arrow follows the reaction path toward product. All distances in Å.

for reactant and transition structures were examined in water, methanol, chloroform, acetonitrile, THF, and DMSO [12].

To investigate the effect of solvation on the Kemp reaction, changes in free energy were calculated by perturbing the distance between the nitrogen and oxygen of the isoxazole (R_{NO}) and the distance between the C3 and carboxylate carbon atoms (R_{CC}), shown in Fig. 4a. The initial ranges for R_{NO} and R_{CC} were 1.35–2.35 Å with an increment of 0.05 Å; the resultant map for 2-D potential of mean force for the reaction of **1** in methanol is shown in Fig. 4b. Critical points for the reactions of **1–3** in several solvents were found with similar maps, and the regions surrounding the free energy minima and maxima were refined with increments of 0.01 Å.

The computed activation barriers for the reaction of 3-carboxybenzisoxazole (**1**) are summarized in Table 5 The statistical uncertainties

Table 5. Free energy of activation, $\Delta G^{\ddagger}$ (kcal/mol), for the Kemp decarboxylation of **1** from QM/MM/MC simulations

	Calc.	Exptl. [42]
Water	24.9	26.4 ($\pm$ 1.5)
Methanol	22.5	24.7
Chloroform	14.8	24.0
Acetonitrile	15.5	19.4
THF	12.1	19.1

in the computed free-energy barriers are below 0.3 kcal/mol. The computed $\Delta G^{\ddagger}$ values reproduce well the large rate enhancements in progressing from protic to dipolar aprotic solvents with good quantitative accord. An interesting point with the Kemp reaction is that it seems anomalously slow in chloroform [42], whereas our PDDG/PM3 based QM/MM calculations with the united-atom OPLS–UA chloroform model (four-site, no H) predict a much faster rate, comparable to an aprotic solvent. The suggestion was made that chloroform may be acting as a hydrogen bond donor [42]. To address this issue a new five-site OPLS–AA model for chloroform was created; facilitating hydrogen bonding through the explicit inclusion of a hydrogen.

The all-atom chloroform model was then used in analogous QM/MM calculations for the reaction of **1**. However, this did not solve the dilemma, as the resultant free energy of activation (14.2 kcal/mol) was nearly identical to the result with the united-atom model (14.8 kcal/mol). Another possibility is that the chloroform was slightly wet in the experiments, although much care appears to have been taken by drying the chloroform through distillation over phosphorus pentoxide [42]. Initial QM/MM calculations for the reaction of **1** with the united-atom chloroform model including the addition of a water molecule were performed; however, the increase in free energy was modest, ca. 1 kcal/mol.

Thus, we turned our attention to possible ion-pairing with the 1,1,3,3-tetramethylguanidinium (TMG) counterion lending preferential stabilization to the reactant. In previous theoretical calculations by Zipse et al., complexation of TMG to the carboxylate group in **1** did yield an increase in the $\Delta\Delta G^{\ddagger}$ values between acetonitrile and THF from -3.8 to -1.5 kcal/mol with and without TMG, respectively, while the experimental difference is -0.3 kcal/mol [44]. In experimental work, Kemp and Paul observed that the strong base, TMG, had little to no influence on the rates of reaction in nearly all dipolar aprotic solvents, but in aprotic solvents of low polarity, such as chloroform, the observed rate constants were not cation independent [42]. Thus, the QM/MM simulations were repeated for the reaction of **1** in chloroform with the addition of a TMG ion initially placed

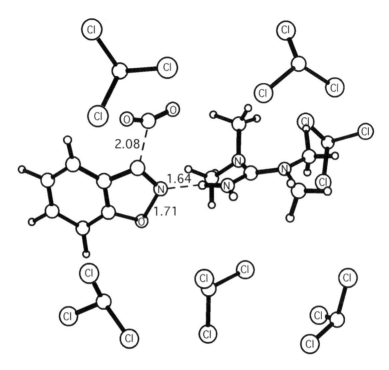

Fig. 5. Snapshot of a transition structure for the reaction of **1** with a TMG counterion in united-atom chloroform (nearby solvent molecules are illustrated) from the QM/MM simulation. Distances in Å.

Table 6. Influence of the addition of a tetramethylguanidinium ion on the computed $\Delta G^{\ddagger}$ (kcal/mol) for the decarboxylation of **1**

	CHCl$_3$-UA	CHCl$_3$-UA + TMG	Exptl. [42]
$\Delta G^{\ddagger}$	14.8	27.7	24.0

near the carboxylate group of the reactant (Fig. 5). Both ions were treated quantum mechanically (PDDG/PM3) as separate, fully flexible solutes in a box of 395 chloroform molecules. Excellent agreement with experiment is now obtained for the activation-free energy (Table 6); inclusion of the counterion does account for the slow rate observed in chloroform.

Hydrogen bonding to the reactant by protic solvents and counterions is the major factor inhibiting reactivity. If the rate acceleration of dipolar aprotic solvents is a result of lessened stabilization, then a reactant with an intramolecular hydrogen bond is expected to be less reactive in all solvents. Indeed, Kemp and coworkers observed that the internally hydrogen-bonded 4-hydroxy-3-carboxybenzisoxazoles such as **3** exhibit essentially

Table 7. Free energies of activation, $\Delta G^{\ddagger}$ (kcal/mol), for the Kemp decarboxylation of **2** and **3** from QM/MM/MC simulations

	2	Exptl. [43]	3	Exptl. [43]
Water	25.8	25.8[a]	25.2	25.6
DMSO	15.9	15.9	23.4	23.6
Acetonitrile	15.6	19.4[b]	22.4	26.3

[a] $R_1 = OCH_3$, $R_2 = H$, ref. [42].
[b] $R_1 = H$, $R_2 = H$.

identical reaction rates in water, acetonitrile, and DMSO [43]. Accordingly, our computational results for **3** agree very well with experiment, where the results are nearly identical in water and DMSO in view of the uncertainties, ± 0.3 kcal/mol (Table 7). An estimate of the strength of intramolecular hydrogen bond in **3** can be obtained from the difference in the free energy of activation relative to the isomer **2**; in DMSO, the computed and experimental values are 7.5 and 7.7 kcal/mol, while they are 6.8 and 6.9 kcal/mol in acetonitrile.

Hydrogen bonding was determined to be the most important factor reducing the rates of reaction through preferential stabilization of the reactant via intermolecular interactions in protic solvents or intramolecular hydrogen bonding in **3**. A detailed thermodynamic analysis of reactions **1–3** can be found in reference [12].

6. CONCLUSION

QM/MM/MC simulations have been applied to a series of organic reactions with good success in reproducing the observed substrate and solvent effects on free energies of activation and reaction. The overall quantitative success supports the utility of the present QM/MM/MC approach using PDDG/PM3 as the QM method. The importance of variations in specific solute–solvent interactions along the reaction paths is evident in the ion pairing in chloroform for the Kemp decarboxylation, in the failure of DFT/PCM calculations to reproduce the rate retardation in the S_NAr reaction, and in the rate enhancement computed for the Menshutkin reaction in water over DMSO.

ACKNOWLEDGEMENT

Gratitude is expressed to the National Science Foundation (CHE-0130996) and the National Institutes of Health (GM032136) for support of this research.

REFERENCES

[1] (a) D. Lim, C. Jensen, M. P. Repasky and W. L. Jorgensen, *Solvent as catalyst: Computational studies of organic reactions in solution in ACS Symposium series (Transition state modeling for catalysis)*, 1999, **721**, 74–85; (b) W. L. Jorgensen, Free energy calculations: A breakthrough for modeling organic chemistry in solution, *Acc. Chem. Res.*, 1989, **22**, 184–189.

[2] J. Gao, Hybrid quantum and molecular mechanical simulations: An alternative avenue to solvent effects in organic chemistry, *Acc. Chem. Res.*, 1996, **29**, 298–305.

[3] M. Orozco and F. J. Luque, Theoretical methods for the description of the solvent effect in biomolecular systems, *Chem. Rev.*, 2000, **100**, 4187–4226.

[4] (a) R. Benoit (ed. Q. M. Becker), *Implicit Solvent Models in Computational Biochemistry* and *Biophysics*, Marcel Dekker, Inc., New York, 2001, pp. 133–151; (b) C. J. Cramer and D. G. Truhlar, Implicit solvation models: Equilibria, structure, spectra, and dynamics, *Chem. Rev.*, 1999, **99**, 2161–2200.

[5] J. Tomasi and M. Persico, Molecular interactions in solution: An overview of methods based on continuous distributions of the solvent, *Chem. Rev.*, 1994, **94**, 2027–2094.

[6] V. Barone, M. Cossi and J. Tomasi, A new definition of cavities for the computation of solvation free energies by the polarizable continuum model, *J. Chem. Phys.*, 1997, **107**, 3210–3221.

[7] Y. Takano and K. N. Houk, Benchmarking the conductor-like polarizable continuum model (CPCM) for aqueous solvation free energies of neutral and ionic organic molecules, *J. Chem. Theory Comput.*, 2005, **1**, 70–77.

[8] J. Gao and X. Xia, A priori evaluation of aqueous polarization effects through Monte Carlo QM–MM simulations, *Science*, 1992, **258**, 631–635.

[9] (a) M. P. Repasky, J. Chandrasekhar and W. L. Jorgensen, PDDG/PM3 and PDDG/MNDO: Improved semiempirical methods, *J. Comp. Chem.*, 2002, **23**, 1601–1622; (b) I. Tubert-Brohman, C. R. W. Guimarães, M. P. Repasky and W. L. Jorgensen, Extension of the PDDG/PM3 and PDDG/MNDO semiempirical molecular orbital methods to the halogens, *J. Comp. Chem.*, 2003, **25**, 138–150; (c) I. Tubert-Brohman, C. R. W. Guimarães and W. L. Jorgensen, Extension of the PDDG/PM3 semiempirical molecular orbital method to sulfur, silicon, and phosphorus, *J. Chem. Theory Comput.*, 2005, **1**, 817–823.

[10] G. Vayner, K. N. Houk, W. L. Jorgensen and J. I. Brauman, Steric retardation of S_N2 reactions in the gas phase and solution, *J. Am. Chem. Soc.*, 2004, **126**, 9054–9058.

[11] O. Acevedo and W. L. Jorgensen, Solvent effects and mechanism for a nucleophilic aromatic substitution from QM/MM simulations, *Org. Lett.*, 2004, **6**, 2881–2884.

[12] O. Acevedo and W. L. Jorgensen, Influence of inter- and intramolecular hydrogen bonding on Kemp decarboxylations from QM/MM simulations, *J. Am. Chem. Soc.*, 2005, **127**, 8829–8834.

[13] O. Acevedo and W. L. Jorgensen, Cope elimination: Elucidation of solvent effects from QM/MM simulations, *J. Am. Chem. Soc.*, 2006, **128**, (in press).

[14] W. L. Jorgensen, *BOSS, Version 4.6*, Yale University, New Haven, CT, 2004.

[15] (a) W. L. Jorgensen, J. M. Briggs and M. L. Contreras, Relative partition coefficients for organic solutes from fluid simulations, *J. Phys. Chem.*, 1990, **94**, 1683–1686; (b) J. M. Briggs, T. Matsui and W. L. Jorgensen, Monte Carlo simulations of liquid alkyl ethers with the OPLS potential functions, *J. Comp. Chem.*, 1990, **11**, 958–971; (c) W. L. Jorgensen and J. M. Briggs, Monte Carlo simulations of liquid acetonitrile with a three-site model, *Mol. Phys.*, 1988, **63**, 547–558.

[16] W. L. Jorgensen, J. Chandrasekhar, J. D. Madura, W. Impey and M. L. Klein, Comparison of simple potential functions for simulating liquid water, *J. Chem. Phys.*, 1983, **79**, 926–935.

[17] J. D. Thompson, C. J. Cramer and D. G. Truhlar, Parameterization of charge model 3 for AM1, PM3, BLYP, and B3LYP, *J. Comp. Chem.*, 2003, **24**, 1291–1304.

[18] (a) J. D. Reinheimer, J. D. Harley and W. W. Meyers, Solvent effects in the Mensc-hutkin reaction, *J. Org. Chem.*, 1963, **2**, 1575–1579; (b) P. Haberfield, A. Nudelman, A. Bloom, R. Romm and H. Ginsberg, Enthalpies of transfer of transition states in the Menshutkin reaction from a polar protic to a dipolar aprotic solvent, *J. Org. Chem.*, 1971, **36**, 1792–1795; (c) M. H. Abraham and R. J. Abraham, Application of reaction field theory to the calculation of solvent effects on the Menshutkin reaction of trip-ropylamine with methyl iodide, *J. Chem. Soc., Perkin Trans. 2*, 1975, **15**, 1677–1681; (d) M. H. Abraham and P. L. Grellier, Substitution at saturated carbon. Part XX. The effect of 39 solvents on the free energy of Et_3N, EtI, and the $Et_3N–EtI$ transition state. Comparison with solvent effects on the equilibria $Et_3N + EtI$ <-> $Et_4N^+I^-$ and $Et_3N + EtI$ <-> $Et_4N^+ + I^-$, *J. Chem. Soc., Perkin Trans. 2*, 1976, **14**, 1735–1741.

[19] U. Maran, T. A. Pakkanen and M. Karelson, Semiempirical study of the solvent effect on the Menshutkin reaction, *J. Chem. Soc., Perkin Trans.*, 1994, **12** (2), 2445–2452.

[20] V. Dillet, D. Rinaldi, J. Bertrán and J. L. Rivail, Analytical energy derivatives for a realistic continuum model of solvation: Application to the analysis of solvent effects on reaction paths, *J. Chem. Phys.*, 1996, **104**, 9437–9444.

[21] T. N. Truong, T. T. Truong and E. V. Stefanovich, A general methodology for quantum modeling of free-energy profile of reactions in solution: An application to the Men-shutkin NH3CH3Cl reaction in water, *J. Chem. Phys.*, 1997, **107**, 1881–1889.

[22] X. Fradera, L. Amat, M. Torrent, J. Mestres, P. Constans, E. Besalú, J. Martí, S. Simon, M. Lobato, J. M. Oliva, J. M. Luis, J. L. Andrés, M. Solá, R. Carbó and M. Duran, Analysis of the changes on the potential energy surface of Menshutkin re-actions induced by external perturbations, *J. Mol. Struc. (Theochem.)*, 1996, **371**, 171–183.

[23] J. Gao, A priori computation of a solvent-enhanced S_N2 reaction profile in water: The Menshutkin reaction, *J. Am. Chem. Soc.*, 1991, **113**, 7796–7797.

[24] J. Gao and X. Xia, A two-dimensional energy surface for a type II S_N2 reaction in aqueous solution, *J. Am. Chem. Soc.*, 1993, **115**, 9667–9675.

[25] K. Naka, H. Sato, A. Morita, F. Hirata and S. Kato, RISM–SCF study of the free-energy profile of Menshutkin-type reaction $NH_3 + CH_3Cl$ -> $NH_3CH_3^+ + Cl^-$ in aque-ous solution, *Theor. Chem. Acc.*, 1999, **102**, 165–169.

[26] K. Ohmiya and S. Kato, Solution reaction path Hamiltonian based on reference interaction site model self-consistent field method: Application to Menshutkin-type reactions, *J. Chem. Phys.*, 2003, **119**, 1601–1610.

[27] M. S. Gordon, M. A. Freltag, P. Bandyopadhyay, J. H. Jensen, V. Kalrys and W. J. Stevens, The effective fragment potential method: A QM-based MM approach to modeling environmental effects in chemistry, *J. Phys. Chem. A*, 2001, **105**, 293–307.

[28] J. Ruiz-Pernía, E. Silla, I. Tuñón, S. Martí and V. Moliner, Hybrid QM/MM potentials of mean force with interpolated corrections, *J. Phys. Chem. B*, 2004, **108**, 8427–8433.

[29] T. A. Darden, D. York and L. Pedersen, Particle-mesh Ewald: An N.log(N) method for Ewald sums in large systems, *J. Chem. Phys.*, 1993, **98**, 10089–10092.

[30] C. Amovilli, B. Mennucci and F. M. Floris, MCSCF study of the SN_2 Menshutkin reaction in aqueous solution within the polarizable continuum model, *J. Phys. Chem. B*, 1998, **102**, 3023–3028.

[31] (a) S. Ten-no, F. Hirata and S. Kato, A hybrid approach for the solvent effect on the electronic structure of a solute based on the RISM and Hartree-Fock equations, *Chem. Phys. Lett.*, 1993, **214**, 391–396; (b) S. Ten-no, F. Hirata and S. Kato, Ref-erence interaction site model self-consistent field study for solvation effect on car-bonyl compounds in aqueous solution, *J. Chem. Phys.*, 1994, **100**, 7443–7453.

[32] P. N. Day, J. Jensen, M. S. Gordon, S. P. Webb, W. J. Stevens, M. Krauss, D. Garmer, H. Basch and D. Cohen, An effective fragment method for modeling solvent effects in quantum mechanical calculations, *J. Chem. Phys.*, 1996, **105**, 1968–1986.

[33] S. P. Webb and M. S. Gordon, Solvation of the Menshutkin reaction: A rigorous test of the effective fragment method, *J. Phys. Chem. A*, 1999, **103**, 1265–1273.

278   O. Acevedo and W.L. Jorgensen

[34] K. Okamoto, S. Fukui and H. Shingu, Kinetic studies of biomolecular nucleophilic substitution 6. Rates of Menschutkin reaction of Methyl Iodide with Methylamines and Ammonia in aqueous solutions, *Bull. Chem. Soc. Jpn.*, 1967, **40**, 1920.
[35] J. F. Bunnett and R. E. Zahler, Aromatic nucleophilic substitution reactions, *Chem. Rev.*, 1951, **49**, 273–412.
[36] J. Miller and A. J. Parker, Dipolar aprotic solvents in bimolecular aromatic nucleophilic substitution reactions, *J. Am. Chem. Soc.*, 1961, **83**, 117–123.
[37] A. J. Parker, Protic-dipolar aprotic solvent effects on rates of biomolecular reactions, *Chem. Rev.*, 1969, **69**, 1–32.
[38] B. G. Cox and A. J. Parker, Solvation of ions. 17. Protic-dipolar aprotic solvent effects on the free energies, enthalpies, and entropies of activation of an SnAr reaction, *J. Am. Chem. Soc.*, 1973, **95**, 408–410.
[39] J. F. Bunnett, E. W. Garbisch, Jr. and K. M. Pruitt, The element effect as a criterion of mechanism in activated aromatic nucleophilic substitution reactions, *J. Am. Chem. Soc.*, 1957, **79**, 385–391.
[40] (a) A. D. Becke, Density-functional thermochemistry. III. The role of exact exchange, *J. Chem. Phys.*, 1993, **98**, 5648–5652; (b) C. Lee, W. Yang and R. G. Parr, Development of the Colle-Salvetti correlation-energy formula into a functional of the electron density, *Phys. Rev.*, 1988, **37**, 785–789.
[41] M. J. Frisch, G. W. Trucks, H. B. Schlegel, G. E. Scuseria, M. A. Robb, J. R. Cheeseman, J. A. Montgomery, Jr., T. Vreven, K. N. Kudin, J. C. Burant, J. M. Millam, S. S. Iyengar, J. Tomasi, V. Barone, B. Mennucci, M. Cossi, G. Scalmani, N. Rega, G. A. Petersson, H. Nakatsuji, M. Hada, M. Ehara, K. Toyota, R. Fukuda, J. Hasegawa, M. Ishida, T. Nakajima, Y. Honda, O. Kitao, H. Nakai, M. Klene, X. Li, J. E. Knox, H. P. Hratchian, J. B. Cross, C. Adamo, J. Jaramillo, R. Gomperts, R. E. Stratmann, O. Yazyev, A. J. Austin, R. Cammi, C. Pomelli, J. W. Ochterski, P. Y. Ayala, K. Morokuma, G. A. Voth, P. Salvador, J. J. Dannenberg, V. G. Zakrzewski, S. Dapprich, A. D. Daniels, M. C. Strain, O. Farkas, D. K. Malick, A. D. Rabuck, K. Raghavachari, J. B. Foresman, J. V. Ortiz, Q. Cui, A. G. Baboul, S. Clifford, J. Cioslowski, B. B. Stefanov, G. Liu, A. Liashenko, P. Piskorz, I. Komaromi, R. L. Martin, D. J. Fox, T. Keith, M. A. Al-Laham, C. Y. Peng, A. Nanayakkara, M. Challacombe, P. M. W. Gill, B. Johnson, W. Chen, M. W. Wong, C. Gonzalez and J. A. Pople, *Gaussian 03, Revision A.01*, Gaussian, Inc., Pittsburgh PA, 2003.
[42] D. S. Kemp and K. G. Paul, The physical organic chemistry of benzisoxazoles. III. The mechanism and the effects of solvents on rates of decarboxylation of benzisoxazole-3-carboxylic acids, *J. Am. Chem. Soc.*, 1975, **97**, 7305–7312.
[43] D. S. Kemp, D. D. Cox and K. G. Paul, The physical organic chemistry of benzisoxazoles. IV. The origins and catalytic nature of the solvent rate acceleration for the decarboxylation of 3 -carboxybenzisoxazoles, *J. Am. Chem. Soc.*, 1975, **97**, 7312–7318.
[44] H. Zipse, G. Apaydin and K. N. Houk, A quantum mechanical and statistical mechanical exploration of the thermal decarboxylation of Kemp's other acid (benzisoxazole-3-carboxylic acid). The influence of solvation on the transition state geometries and kinetic isotope effects of a reaction with an awesome solvent effect, *J. Am. Chem. Soc.*, 1995, **117**, 8608–8617.

CHAPTER 15

Structure-Based Design of New Antibacterial Agents

Haihong Ni and John Wendoloski

Computational Chemistry Group, Infection Discovery, AstraZeneca R&D Boston, Waltham, MA 02451, USA

Contents

1. INTRODUCTION

Four decades ago, the battle against infectious disease was considered won, and as a result, drug companies were not investing substantially in antimicrobial research and development. During the intervening years, very few examples of novel antibiotics were introduced into market: Linezolid [1], an oxazolidinone introduced in 2000, represented the first significant synthetic compound class brought to market in more than 25 years since the successful introduction of fluoroquinolones [2]. However, the unmet medical need posed by drug resistance as well as newly emerging infectious diseases such as SARS, has revived the interest in and funding for the discovery and development of novel antibacterials [3].

This renewed interest in infectious diseases has been aided by signifi-cant improvements in technologies such as genomics and computational

ANNUAL REPORTS IN COMPUTATIONAL CHEMISTRY, VOLUME 2
ISSN: 1574-1400   DOI 10.1016/S1574-1400(06)02015-9

approaches. Advances in microbial genomics [4] resulted in the rapid identification of new antibacterial targets, enabling target-based approaches to be applied at the earliest stages of drug discovery, in contrast to classical whole-cell screening, which identified an active compound first and established its cellular target later. As genomic data increase the supply of potential targets, the combination of focused libraries, high-throughput screening (HTS), computational modeling and structure-based design will be crucial in expediting the discovery of novel lead compounds. Moreover, due to the rapidly increasing amount of three-dimensional (3D) information about receptors, techniques for exploiting structural data will continue to gain in importance over random screening methods [5,6].

This report surveys the application of computational approaches to the design of potent new antibacterial agents for two well-validated infection targets: DNA gyrase and peptide deformylase. In each case, extensive information from both enzyme and enzyme-inhibitor X-ray structures is available to elucidate how inhibitors bind to their target at atomic level as well as to identify specific interactions that are important in molecular recognition. Using the examples from these two infection targets, this survey will describe how structural knowledge combined with various computational tools profoundly influences and accelerates drug discovery by either *de novo* design of leads or the improvement of existing leads.

2. THE DESIGN OF ANTIBACTERIAL AGENTS THAT INHIBIT DNA GYRASE AT B SUBUNIT

2.1. Background

DNA gyrase is a member of the type II family of topoisomerases that controls the topological state of DNA in cells [7]. It uses the free energy from ATP hydrolysis to alter the topology of DNA by introducing transient double-stranded breaks in the DNA, catalyzing strand passage through the break and resealing the DNA. DNA gyrase is an essential, conserved enzyme in bacteria and is unique among topoisomerases in its ability to introduce negative supercoils in DNA. The enzyme consists of two subunits, encoded by *gyrA* and *gyrB*, forming an A_2B_2 tetrameric complex. The A subunit of gyrase (GyrA) is involved in DNA breakage and resealing and contains a conserved tyrosine residue that forms the transient covalent link to DNA during strand-passage. The B subunit (GyrB) catalyzes the hydrolysis of ATP and interacts with the A subunit to translate the free energy from hydrolysis to the process of conformational change in the enzyme that enables strand-passage and DNA resealing.

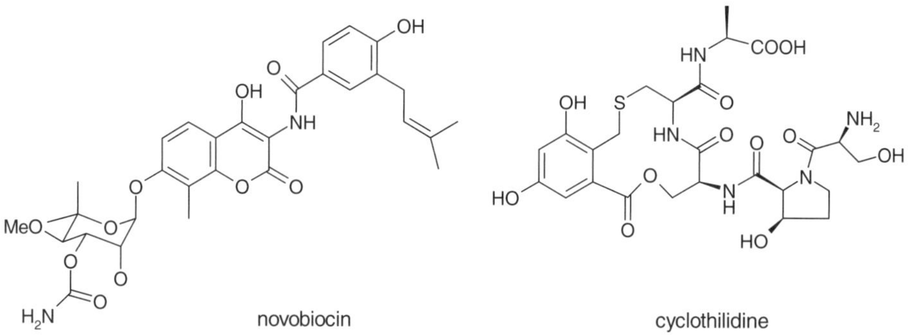

Fig. 1. Chemical structures of natural product gyrase B inhibitors.

DNA gyrase is a validated target of antibacterials – antibiotics such as the coumarins and the fluoroquinolones target the Gyrase B and A subunits, respectively [8]. The coumarins (e.g., novobiocin) (Fig. 1) are examples of natural products isolated from *Streptomyces* spp. in the 1950s that inhibit DNA gyrase by competing with ATP for binding to the GyrB subunit of the enzyme. However, novobiocin has limited usage due to limited spectrum, toxic side effects and development of resistance during the course of treatment [9,10]. Over the past decade, many studies aimed at identifying potent antibacterial agents targeting gyrase B have been disclosed in the patent literature and other publications, and most of them utilized structural information to discover new inhibitors. These inhibitors are largely divided into two classes (Fig. 2): novel chemotypes (compound **1–6**) [11–17], and inhibitors derived from modification of naturally occurring antibacterials (compound **7–8**) [18–20]. A "first in class" Gyrase B inhibitor, which is structurally related to compound **4,** was recently reported to have entered clinical development by Vertex [15].

2.2. Structural features of the GyrB active site

A number of X-ray structures of the ATPase domain of DNA gyrase complexed with ADPNP, novobiocin and cyclothialidine are available (see Fig. 1) [21–23]. These X-ray structures reveal that inhibitors bind to the same general binding pocket as ADPNP; however, they differ considerably in their mode of binding. Consequently, the amino acids which interact with one or the other of the three ligands are quite different and provide a large area which can be explored for the design of novel inhibitors. Despite differences, they do share a common binding motif, the adenine-binding pocket (Fig. 3). Each of the ligands donates a hydrogen bond to an aspartic acid side chain and accepts an H-bond from one ordered water

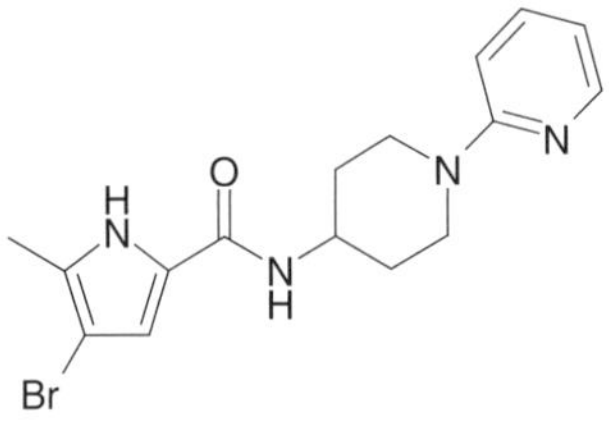

Fig. 2. Chemical structures of published gyrase B inhibitors.

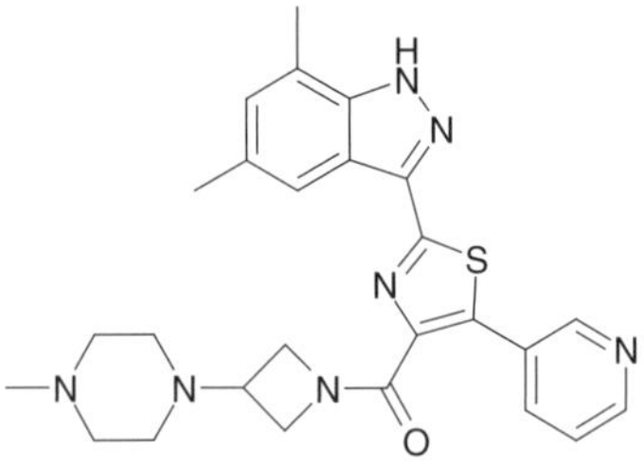

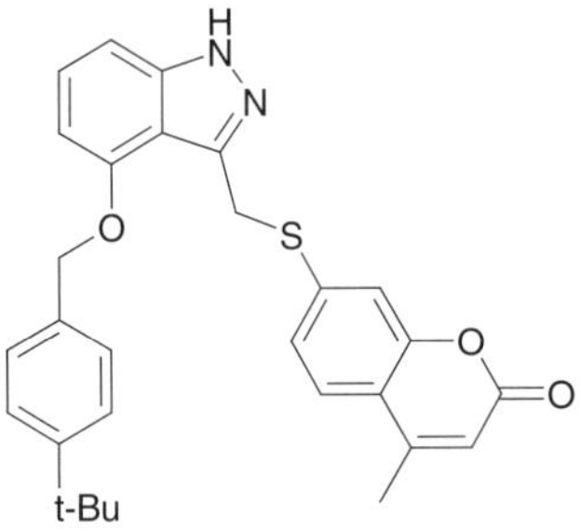

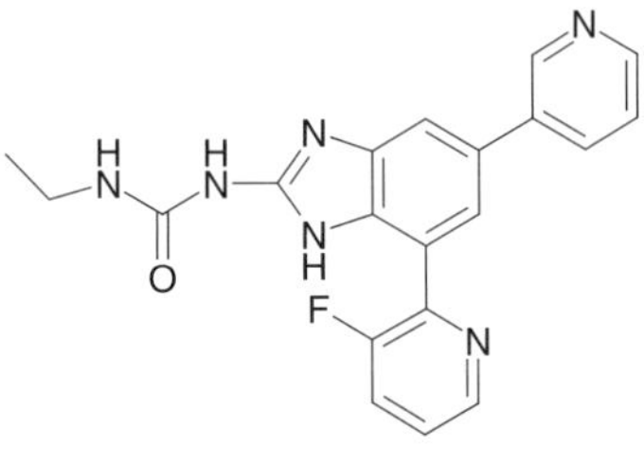

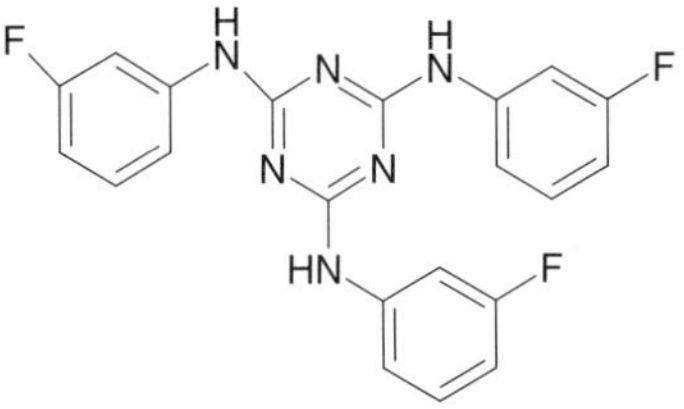

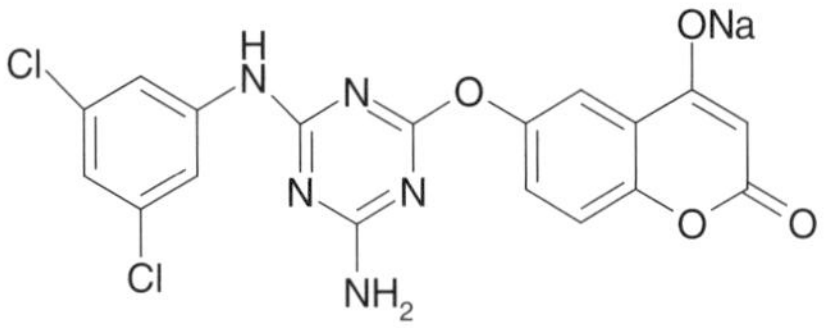

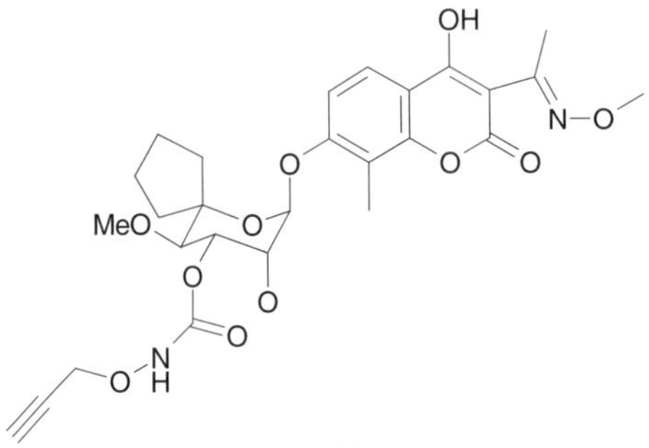

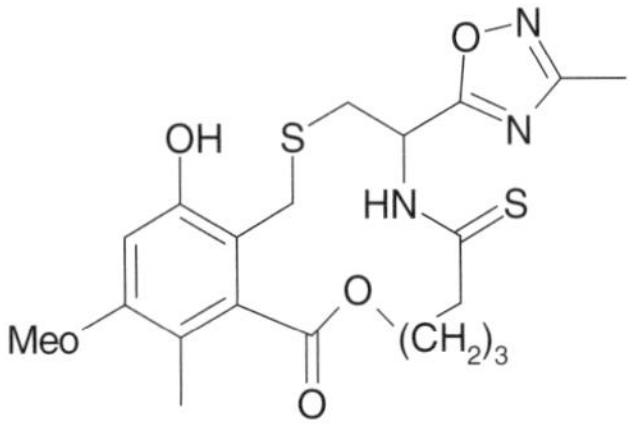

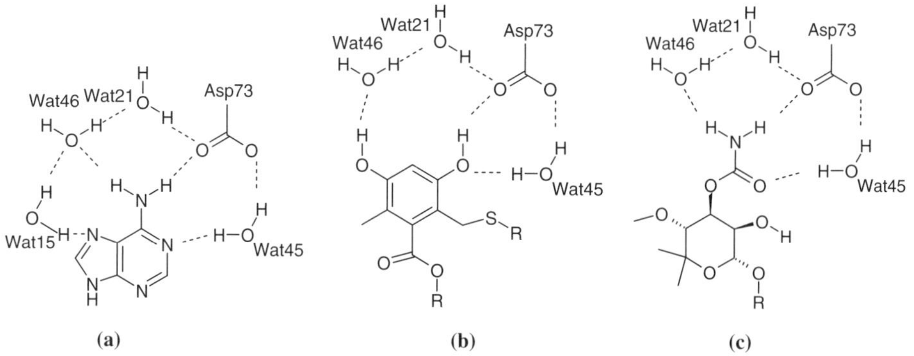

Fig. 3. The common hydrogen bond network between three different ligands and DNA gyrase, including water, determined by X-ray analysis. (a) adenine part of ADPNP, (b) phenolic moiety of cyclothialidine and (c) carbamate moiety of novobiocin.

which is conserved in all the three structures. Because of the high degree of overlap of the binding site, the ligands have some of the same binding site interactions, which lead to competitive binding.

2.3. Hot spot identification

In order to identify novel moieties that might occupy the GyrB active site as starting points for new leads, Schechner *et al.* [24], used the program MCSS to obtain energetically favorable binding positions for a number of functional group probes. MCSS, developed by Karplus and his colleagues [25], yields exhaustive information on possible binding sites and orientations for small chemical or functional groups in the GyrB protein structure. From that, consensus maps for functional group binding in the ATP binding site were constructed using a total of 23 functional groups with different chemical characteristics, such as charged, polar, hydrophobic, aromatic and aliphatic groups. In order to account for the conformational flexibility of the GyrB active site, the calculations were repeated for three different conformations of the 24 KDa subdomain of DNA Gyrase B: two X-ray structure conformers and a third conformer generated by a molecular dynamics simulation. The final consensus maps indicated that those functional group binding sites were insensitive to the various protein conformations. On the other hand, binding energies and orientations for small functional groups were sensitive to protein conformations. In the adenine binding pocket, it was striking to find that the most favorable binding affinity for all groups tested was a phenol forming an H-bond with Asp73, making phenol interesting both as a scaffold and as a substituent on a larger compound. Interestingly, cyclothialidine places a similar aromatic ring close to Asp73. The maps also demonstrated that functional groups other than those found in the known ligands would bind competitively in the binding sites of known ligands. For example, the calculations indicated the possibility of using aromatic ligands to target the phosphate binding site. In addition, they showed the existence of a deep hydrophobic binding pocket near the ATP binding site. The possibility of linking this hydrophobic pocket to the ATP/coumarin-binding site is of interest, especially in the optimization of existing compounds which bind in the vicinity of the pocket.

2.4. Overview of structure-based virtual screening

Structure-based virtual screening methods play an increasing role in lead identification, especially with the availability of numerous software tools for small molecule docking. The docking algorithms used in these programs can be grouped into three major classes. The first class simultaneously optimizes the conformation and orientation of the molecule in the binding site. Docking programs based on such algorithms (e.g., GOLD [26] and Autodock [27]) can predict very accurate binding modes even for large and flexible ligands. The second algorithm pre-calculates low-energy ligand conformers, places the rigid conformers in the binding site, and then optimizes only the remaining six rotational and translational degrees of freedom (e.g., FRED [28]). The third class of docking algorithm, used in programs such as FleXX [29], exploits the fact that most molecules contain at least one small, rigid fragment that is able to form specific, directed interactions with a receptor. Docking is then built from those initial fragment positions in an incremental construction process, followed by an exploration of the conformational space of the newly added fragments. Since there are many ways to combine docking algorithms and scoring functions, it is important to investigate which is the best option for any given protein target, and in this case, which is the best choice for Gyrase B.

To address these issues, a number of evaluations of docking programs and scoring functions have been published in recent years [30,31]. Computational chemists at GSK examined the performance of nine docking programs across seven protein types, including Gyrase B. Their results indicated that there was no one program that was universally applicable for all the targets investigated – different programs docked the same ligand well for some targets and poorly for others. For Gyrase B, it was found that GOLD, GLIDE and FlexX predicted the pose well, while QXP [32] and Fred could not predict the binding mode at all. Similarly, Stahl and Schulz-Gasch at Roche [31] also published their studies evaluating the three docking programs FRED, GLIDE [33] and FlexX against seven protein targets to assess their accuracy in virtual screening. Interestingly, they found that while FlexX predicted the binding mode of GyrB inhibitors well, both FRED and GLIDE failed to generate correct inhibitor binding modes.

2.5. Identification of novel inhibitors by structure-based virtual screening

De novo design of inhibitors of DNA gyrase reported by Boehm et al. at Roche [16] is one example of a successful application of structure-based virtual screening. Virtual screening was employed after searches for novel inhibitors of DNA gyrase by HTS failed. Detailed analysis of the binding interactions of novobiocin co-crystal structures revealed a common binding motif: each of the ligands forms an H-bond with an aspartic side chain (Asp73) and with a conserved water. It was hypothesized that a novel inhibitor would have the same two critical H-bonds. A 3D database search of 350,000 compounds from the Available Chemical Database (ACD) and their own in-house collection was performed using LUDI [34] and CAT-ALYST [35] to identify low molecular weight (MW < 300) compounds that matched this binding motif. After clustering and manual selection, 600 compounds were tested, along with close analogs of the initial hits. Overall, 3000 compounds were screened, and 150 hits were identified, which clustered into 14 classes. The maximal noneffective concentrations (MNEC) of the hits were in the range of 5–64 µg/ml, 2–3 orders of magnitude higher than that of novobiocin, but with much lower MW. Activity of one of the top hits (**9**), an indazole fragment, was validated by protein NMR, and a co-crystal structure of the fragment bound to GyrB was obtained to verify the binding at the ATP site. The preliminary SAR of the validated hits, the SAR for cyclothialidines and coumarins, and the 3D structural knowledge of the active site were then used to guide further optimization (Fig. 4). Structural and docking analysis suggested that introduction of an additional H-bond with Arg136 would produce a more potent second generation of indazole (**10**). However, just minor improvements in activity were observed. A third series of indazoles (**3**) was prepared to exploit the potential van der Waals interactions between ligands and the lipophilic surface formed by Ile78, Pro79 and Ile94. In this case, a pronounced improvement of inhibition was achieved, and the proposed binding mode was confirmed by the X-ray structure of the inhibitor complexed to the 24 kDa fragment of Gyrase B. The final compound achieved a MNEC of 0.03 µg/ml, which was 10 times more active than novobiocin (MNEC = 0.25 µg/ml), and the structure was much simpler.

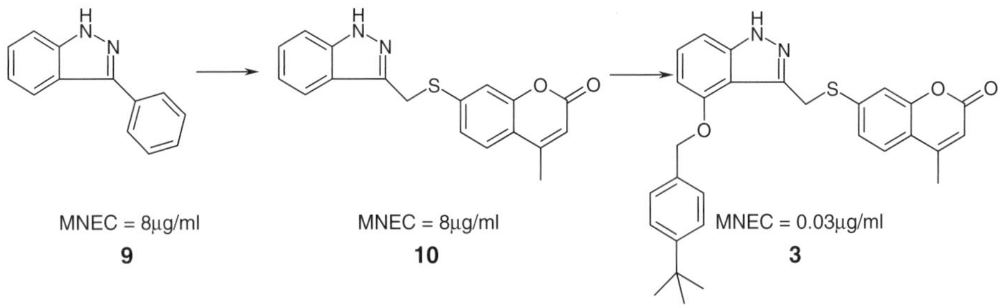

Fig. 4. Schematic drawing of weak gyrase hit identified *in silico* by needle screening and its evolution into a potent inhibitor.

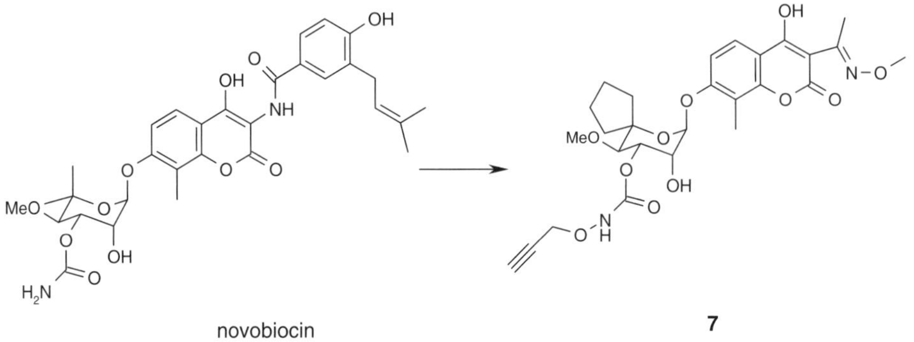

novobiocin   7

Fig. 5. Potent inhibitor optimized based on novobiocin structure.

2.6. Structure-based improvements of existing leads

Scientists at Hochest Marison Roussel [18] utilized X-ray structures to guide their design efforts in search of coumarin antibiotics with improved pharmacological profiles and physicochemical properties (Fig. 5). SAR had demonstrated the critical influence of the 5′, 5′-dimethyl group of noviose in determining the antibacterial spectrum of coumarins. Structural analysis of the 24-kDa N-terminal fragment of DNA Gyrase B and sequence comparison of 12 Gram-positive strains indicated that there was a larger hydrophobic pocket in Gram-positive strains, consisting of Val94 and Phe95, compared to the pocket in the Gram-negative species, *Escherichia coli*. This feature was exploited by studying dialkyl substituents at the 5′, 5′ position of noviose. This led to the identification of the 5′, 5′ spirocyclopentylnoviose (**7**) as the most potent analog, and also exhibited promising safety and pharmocokinetic profiles.

A similar strategy has been applied to identify cyclothialidine derivatives. Cyclothialidine is a potent gyrase inhibitor, but barely exhibits any growth inhibitory activity against intact bacterial cells, presumably due to insufficient permeation of the cytoplasmic membrane. Using both structural data and SAR, scientists at Roche [20] identified a simple hydroxylated benzyl sulfide as the minimal structural requirement for cyclothialidine. Analogs were then made based on that feature. The best activities were displayed by 14-membered lactones. One example, compound (**8**), has improved PK properties and lowered lipophilic properties, including efficacy *in vivo*.

A hybrid approach for creating novel inhibitors is to combine key binding fragments from individual inhibitors. Overlays of the structures of novobiocin and triazine (**5**) [11] led to a hypothesis that a combination of fragments of the two compounds might be active. This hybrid yielded a very active compound (**6**). This is one of the most potent DNA gyrase inhibitors known with activities 3-fold better than novobiocin. Unfortunately, this potency is not reflected in the antibacterial activity. Such a hybridization approach has typically been done manually. Recently, Pierce *et al.* at Vertex reported a simple but powerful automated approach to structure-based hybridization, called BREED, which allows quickly generated hybrid structures from a large diverse set of ligands [36]. This automated approach may be useful for generating novel hybrid Gyrase B inhibitors.

3. THE DESIGN OF PEPTIDE DEFORMYLASE (PDF) INHIBITORS

3.1. Background

In bacteria, protein synthesis starts with *N*-formylmethionine, and as a result, newly synthesized polypeptides carry a formylated N-terminus [37]. PDF is responsible for removing the *N*-formyl group from the N-terminal methionine following translation. This formylation–deformylation cycle is essential for bacterial growth and is conserved among all bacterial species. However, PDF does not have a functionally equivalent gene in mammalian cells, making it a selective antibacterial target [38–39]. PDF is a metallopeptidase [40], which utilizes a ferrous ion (Fe^{2+}) to catalyze amide bond hydrolysis. However, due to the rapid oxidation of Fe^{2+}, the enzyme is unstable and difficult to work with. The substitution of Ni^{2+} and Co^{2+} for Fe^{2+} gives a highly stable enzyme while retaining almost full catalytic activity. Several X-ray crystal structures of PDF and its complex with inhibitors have been determined [41–43]. Based on those structures, PDF represents a novel class of metalloenzyme when compared to the matrix metalloprotease (MMP) superfamily. The availability of PDF crystal structures and knowledge of the basic principles of metalloprotease inhibition [44] has facilitated the discovery of PDF inhibitors. Numerous PDF inhibitors have been reported; essentially all of them are metal chelators. Based on the chelator structure, they can be classified into three different types (Fig. 6): thiols [45,46] (**11**), hydroxamates [47–49] (**12, 14–17**) and *N*-formyl-hydroxylamines [41,50–52] (**13, 18–20**). Recently, LBM415 (NVP PDF-713) [50–52] and BB-83698, [53] *N*-formyl-hydroxylamines derivatives, were reported to be the first members of the PDF inhibitor class to enter clinical development for the treatment of respiratory tract and skin and soft tissue infections caused by susceptible Gram-positive and Gram-negative organisms.

3.2. Structural features at the binding site

X-ray structures of actinonin (**12**) and other inhibitors [44,47] complexed with PDF indicate that the metal ion is penta-coordinated by the side chains of Cys90, His132, His136 and two O atoms from *N*-formyl-hydroxylamine (Fig. 7). The structural similarity of the metal-binding site of PDFs to that of MMPs suggested that the nature of the metal chelating groups is critical for PDF inhibitory activity. H-bonds are made between the chelator and the side chains of Glu133, Gln50 and NH of Leu91. The metal-binding site is adjacent to a deep hydrophobic pocket which forms a favorable hydrophobic interaction with the P1′ hydrophobic side chain. H-bonds are also formed between the NH of Ile44 with the P1′carbonyl group, and between the NH and carbonyl of Gly89 with carbonyl and NH at P2′, respectively. The structures also suggested that the P2′ and P3′ positions are highly solvent exposed and make little contact with the PDF enzyme, providing a good area for enhancing the physicochemical properties and optimizing the microbiological profile.

3.3. Rational design of novel PDF inhibitors based on strategies used with MMP inhibitors

Since PDF is a metalloprotease, one approach to the design of PDF inhibitors is to use a nonspecific chelating pharmacophore that binds to the catalytic metal ion and is coupled with a second moiety that binds to the active site, correctly positioning the chelator and providing the necessary selectivity. Such an approach has been successfully applied to the design of inhibitors of many other therapeutically important metalloproteases [44]. Following this principle, Chen *et al.*, at Vicuron constructed and screened focused chelator-based chemical libraries [48]. VRC3375(**14**) was identified as the inhibitor having the most favorable

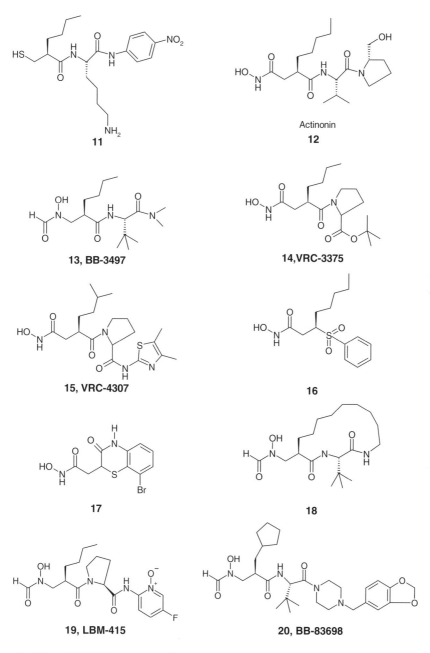

Fig. 6. Chemical structures of published PDF inhibitors.

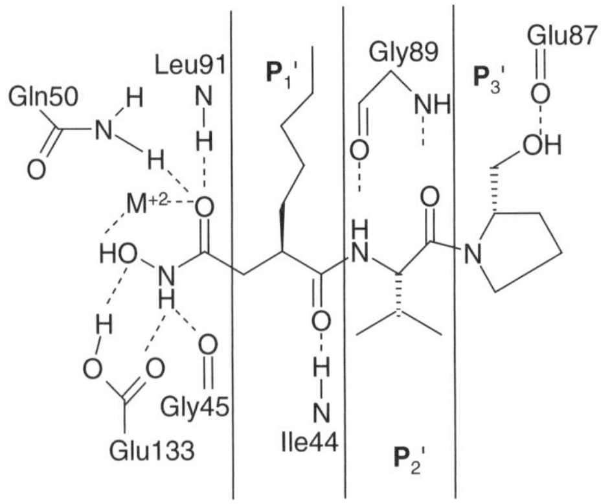

Fig. 7. Schematic drawing of the binding interactions between ligand and PDF, including metal ion, as determined by X-ray.

properties, with a K_i of 0.24 nM against the *E. coli* PDF enzyme. Similarly, Clements *et al.* [41] screened a focused library of metallo-enzyme inhibitors and identified a potent 7 nM selective inhibitor (**13**) of *E. coli* PDF.

In order to elucidate the interactions that contribute to the binding affinity of these inhibitors and to understand the SAR, several computational approaches were taken. QM/MM density functional methods [54] (which have been used to provide useful insights on structures, reactivities and reaction mechanisms in metallo enzymes) were used to calculate the optimum geometry and protonation state in the PDF active site [55]. The calculation reproduced the experimental geometry well for the PDF–inhibitor complex. The calculation also predicted the transfer of an acidic OH proton of hydroxamic acid to the carboxylate O of Glu133 side chain. The requirement for protonation of the active site glutamate anion was found to be an important factor in understanding the potency of the inhibitor.

3.4. Structure-based design of novel macrocyclic inhibitors

Analysis of PDF crystal structures has facilitated the design of novel macrocyclic inhibitors [56,57]. For example, most typical inhibitors are bound in an extended conformation with the P1′ and P3′ side chains similarly oriented and interacting with the enzyme. The P1′ side chain fits into a deep hydrophobic pocket, while the P3′ side chain makes hydrophobic contacts with a shallow pocket nearby as well as one side of the P1′ side chain. Therefore, it seemed that covalent cross-linking of the P1′ and P3′ side chains would be accommodated in the active site. Moreover, the rigidity introduced by cyclization would lock the inhibitor into the bioactive conformation, and thus improve binding affinity. Molecular modeling using QXP [32] confirmed that such cross-linked ligands could indeed fit into the active site. It also suggested that a 9-atom linker group would have sufficient length to link the P1′ alpha carbon and P3′ amino group, while maintaining the extended conformation of the peptide backbone. This led to the synthesis of **18**, with a $K_i = 0.67$ nM, which is 10-fold more potent than the acyclic parent compound. The cyclic inhibitors showed potent inhibitory activity and antibacterial activity against both Gram-positive and Gram-negative bacteria. As compared to their acyclic counterparts, the cyclic inhibitors also displayed improved selectivity for PDF over other metalloproteases, and improved the metabolic stability against proteolytic degradation.

3.5. Structure-based optimization

Screening of the Novartis compound collection [58] for inhibitory activity against *Staphylococcus aureus* Ni-PDF led to the discovery of a very potent inhibitor (**17**) with $IC_{50} < 5$ nM. However, this compound had poor antibacterial activity. Crystal structures in combination with molecular modeling suggested that the synthesis of various analogs with substitution at the nitrogen of the benzothiazinone ring and the modification of the heterocycle would not only maintain high binding affinity, but also potentially improve the antibacterial activity. This hypothesis resulted in the synthesis of small focused library. The compounds synthesized indeed maintained and improved enzyme inhibitory activity, with two compounds exhibiting increased antibacterial activity.

To understand the effects of P2′ and P3′ substituents on PDF activity in both the cell-free enzyme and the whole-cell system, and to identify structural differences between PDF and MMP binding sites, 2D QSAR studies of β-sulfonyl and β-sulfinyl hydroxamic acid derivatives (**16**) have been carried out [59]. The comparison of the QSAR indicated that an increase in hydrophobicity resulted in an increase in whole-cell activity. The study also suggested the possibility of introducing selectivity in these acid derivatives for PDF by substitution on the P3′ position.

Davies *et al.* [52,60,61] also explored the SAR around **13**. X-ray crystallographic data revealed that PDF would tolerate a diverse range of substitutions at the P2′ and P3′ side chains. Therefore, systematic modifications of these regions with a variety of sterically demanding and/or polar substituents were explored. Increasing hydrophobicity at P3′ of the inhibitor led to an improvement of both enzymatic and whole-cell activities. These findings ultimately led to much better PDF inhibitors, including BB-83698 (**20**), which has entered human phase I clinical development.

4. CONCLUSIONS

Computational methods in conjunction with structural information have been used to guide the design of novel antibacterial agents. Analysis of crystal structures and structure-based virtual screening has allowed identification of novel hits and leads in the early stages of drug-discovery projects. Iterative use of structural information and various computational methods has resulted not only in designing more potent enzyme inhibitors, but also in optimizing physicochemical properties and antibacterial activity. Despite the successes outlined above, there are still many challenges ahead in optimizing computational methods, such as improving scoring functions, accounting for protein flexibility, and proper calculation of solvation. One of the additional challenges of designing antibacterial agents is to overcome multidrug resistance, which is conferred by a number of transporters that pump drugs out of cells. In the future, with the use of X-ray crystal structures of the transporters, one could in principle design inhibitors that do not bind to transporters [62,63]. Overcoming these challenges should allow structure-based design an even greater impact on drug discovery.

REFERENCES

[1] D. I. Diekema, Oxazolinonones: a review, *Drugs*, 2000, **59**, 7–16.
[2] P. C. Applebaum and P. A. Hunter, The fluoroquinolone antibacterials: past, present and future perspective, *Int. J. Antimicrob. Agents*, 2000, **16**, 5–15.
[3] G. H. Cassell and J. Mekalanos, Development of antimicrobial agents in the era of new and reemerging infectious diseases and increasing antibiotic resistance, *J. Am. Med. Assoc.*, 2001, **285**, 601–605.
[4] S. Mills, The role of genomics in antimicrobial discovery, *J. Antimicrob. Chemother.*, 2003, **51**, 749–752.
[5] D. Bailey and D. Brown, High-throughput chemistry and structure-based design: survival of the smartest, *Drug Discov. Today.*, 2001, **6**, 57–59.
[6] G. Schneider and H. J. Böhm, Virtual screening and fast automated docking methods, *Drug Discov. Today*, 2002, **7**, 64–70.
[7] J. J. Champoux, DNA topoisomerases: structure, function, and mechanism, *Ann. Rev. Biochem.*, 2001, **70**, 369–413.
[8] A. Maxwell, DNA gyrase as a drug target, *Trends Microbiol.*, 1997, **5**, 102–109.
[9] F. O'Grady, Coumarins. In: *Antibiotic and Chemotherapy* (ed.), F. O'Grady, H. P. Lambert, R. G. Finch and L. S. Greenwood), Churchill Livingstone, Edinburgh, 1997, 7th edition, pp. 333–335.
[10] M. Steiger, P. Angehren, B. Wohlgensinger and H. Gmunder, GyrB mutations in *Staphylococcus aureus* strains resistant to cyclothialidine, coumermycin, and novobiocin, *Antimicrob. Agents Chemother.*, 1996, **40**, 1060–1062.
[11] M. Block and W. Nichols, Design of antibacterial agents, *Mol. Med. Microbiol.*, 2002, **1**, 609–626.
[12] A. L. Breeze, O. M. Green, K. G. Hull, H. Ni, S. I. Hauck, G. B. Mullen, N. J. Hales and D. Timms, Preparation of pyrroles as antibacterial agents, *PCT Int. Appl.*, 2005, WO 2005026149.

[13] K. Yager, S. Chu, K. Appelt and X. Li, Preparation of thiazolylindazoles as inhibitors of bacterial DNA gyrase B inhibitors, *U.S. Pat. Appl. Publ.*, 2005, US2005 054697.
[14] P. Charifson, D. D. Deininger, J. Drumm, A. Grillot and Y. Liao, P. Oliver-Shaffer, D. Stamos, Preparation of 2-ureido-6-heteroaryl-3H-benzimidazole-4-carboxylic acid derivatives and related compounds as gyrase and/or topoisomerase IV inhibitors for the treatment of bacterial infections, *U.S. Pat. Appl. Publ.*, 2004, US2004 0235886.
[15] A. Grillot, D. Stamos, T. Grossman, Y. Bi, M. Carver, D. Deininger, J. Drumm, C. Gross, A. Letiran, Y. Liao, N. Mani, J. Moore, D. Nicolau, E. Olson, J. Parsons, J. Partaledis, E. Perola, S. Ronkin, Q. Tang, S. Tian, P. Tessier, T. Wang, Y. Wei, H. Zhang, and P. Charifson, A new class of dual targeting inhibitors of GyrB and ParE. F-1951, 44th ICAAC, 2004.
[16] H. Boehm, M. Boehringer, D. Bur, H. Gmuender, W. Huber, W. Klaus, D. Kostrewa, H. Kuehne, T. Luebbers, N. Meunier-Keller and F. Mueller, Novel inhibitors of DNA gyrase: 3D structure based biased needle screening, hit validation by biophysical methods, and 3D guided optimization. A promising alternative to random screening, *J. Med. Chem.*, 2000, **43**, 2664–2674.
[17] A. Tanitame, Y. Oyamada, K. Ofuju, Y. Kyoya, K. Suzuki, H. Ito, M. Kawasaki, K. Nagai, M. Wachi and J. Yamagishi, Design, synthesis and structure-activity relationship studies of novel indazole analogues as DNA gyrase inhibitors with Gram-positive antibacterial activity, *Bioorg. Med. Chem. Lett.*, 2004, **14**, 2857–2862.
[18] B. Musicki, A. M. Periers, P. Laurin, D. Ferroud, Y. Benedetti, S. Lachaud, F. Chatreaux, J. L. Haesslein, A. Iltis, C. Pierre, J. Khider, N. Tessot, M. Airault, J. Demassey, C. Dupuis-Hamelin, P. Lassaigne, A. Bonnefoy, P. Vicat and M. Klich, Improved antibacterial activities of coumarin antibiotics bearing 5′, 5′-dialkylnoviose: biological activity of RU79115, *Bioorg. Med. Chem. Lett.*, 2000, **10**, 1695–1699.
[19] S. C. Annedi and L. P. Kotra, RU-79115 Aventis Pharma, *Curr. Opin. Investig. Drugs*, 2001, **2**, 752–754.
[20] P. Angehrn, S. Buchmann, C. Funk, E. Goetschi, H. Gmuender, P. Hebeisen, D. Kostrewa, H. Link, T. Luebbers, R. Masciadri, J. Nielsen, P. Reindl, F. Ricklin, A. Schmitt-Hoffmann and F. P. Theil, New antibacterial agents derived from the DNA gyrase inhibitor cyclothialidine, *J. Med. Chem.*, 2004, **47**, 1487–1513.
[21] R. J. Lewis, O. M. P. Singh, C. V. Smith, T. Skarzynski, A. Maxwell, A. J. Wonacott and D. B. Wigley, The nature of inhibition of DNA gyrase by the coumarins and the cyclothialidines revealed by X-ray crystallography, *EMBO J.*, 1996, **15**, 1412–1420.
[22] F. T. Tsai, O. M. P. Singh, T. Skarzynski, A. J. Wonacott, S. Weston, A. Tucker, R. A. Pauptit, A. L. Breeze, J. P. Poyser, R. O'Brien, J. E. Ladbury and D. B. Wigley, The high-resolution crystal structure of a 24-kDa gyrase B fragment from *E. coli* complexed with one of the most potent coumarin inhibitors, clorobiocin, *Proteins*, 1997, **28**, 41–52.
[23] D. B. Wigley, G. Davis, E. J. Donson, A. Maxwell and G. Dodson, Crystal structure of an N-terminal fragment of the DNA gyrase B protein, *Nature*, 1991, **351**, 624–629.
[24] M. Schechner, F. Sirockin, R. H. Stote and A. P. Dejaegere, Functionality maps of the ATP binding site of DNA Gyrase B: generation of a consensus model of ligand binding, *J. Med. Chem.*, 2004, **47**, 4373–4390.
[25] A. Miranker and M. Karplus, Functionality maps of binding sites: a multiple copy simultaneous search method, *Prot.: Struc., Func. Genet.*, 1991, **11**, 29–34.
[26] G. Jones, P. Willett, R. C. Glen, A. R. Leach and R. Taylor, Development and validation of a genetic algorithm for flexible docking, *J. Mol. Biol.*, 1997, **267**, 727–748.
[27] G. M. Morris, D. S. Goodsell, R. Huey and A. J. Olsen, Distributed automated docking of flexible ligands to proteins: parallel application of AutoDock 2.4, *J. Comput.-Aided Mol. Des.*, 1996, **10**, 293–304.
[28] FRED OpenEye, Santa Fe NM, 2003. http://www.eyesopen.com/
[29] M. Rarey, B. Kramer, T. Lengauer and G. Klebe, A fast flexible docking method using an incremental construction algorithm, *J. Mol. Biol.*, 1996, **261**, 470–489.

[30] G. L. Warren, C. W. Andrews, A. Capelli, B. Clarke, J. LaLonde, M. H. Lambert, M. Lindvall, N. Nevins, S. F. Semus, S. Senger, G. Tedesco, I. D. Wall, J. M. Woolven, C. E. Peishoff and M. S. Head, A critical assessment of docking programs and scoring functions, J. Med. Chem., 2005, ASAP Article. http://pubs3.acs.org/acs/journals/doilookup?in_doi = 10.1021/jm050362n.

[31] T. Schulz-Gasch and M. Stahl, Binding site characteristics in structure-based virtual screening: evaluation of current docking tools, J. Mol. Model., 2003, 9, 47–57.

[32] C. McMartin and R. J. Bohacek, QXP: powerful, rapid computer algorithms for structure-based drug design, J. Comput.-Aided Mol. Des., 1997, 11, 333–344.

[33] R. A. Friesner, J. L. Banks, R. B. Murphy, T. A. Halgren, J. J. Klicic, D. T. Mainz, M. P. Repasky, E. H. Knoll, M. Shelley, J. K. Perry, D. E. Shaw, P. Francis and P. S. Shenkin, Glide: a new approach for rapid, accurate docking and scoring. 1. Method and assessment of docking accuracy, J. Med. Chem., 2004, 47, 1739–1749.

[34] H. -J Böhm, The computer program LUDI: a new method for the de novo design of enzyme inhibitors, J. Comput.-Aided Mol. Des., 1992, 6, 61–78.

[35] P. Sprague, Automated chemical hypothesis generation and database searching with CATALYST, Perspect, Drug Discov. Des., 1995, 3, 1–20.

[36] A. C. Pierce, G. Rao and G. W. Bemis, BREED: generating novel inhibitors through hybridization of known ligands, J. Med. Chem., 2004, 47, 2768–2775.

[37] T. Meinnel, Y. Mechulam and S. Blanquet, Methionine as translational start signal: a review of the enzymes the pathway in, E. coli, Biochimie., 1993, 75, 1061–1075.

[38] Z. Yuan, J. Trias and R. J. White, Deformylase as a novel antibacterial target, Drug Discov. Today, 2001, 6, 954–961.

[39] A. S. Waller and J. M. Clements, Novel approaches to antimicrobial therapy: peptide deformylase, Curr. Opin. Drug Discov. Dev., 2002, 5, 785–792.

[40] P. T. R. Rajagopalan, X. C. Yu and D. Pei, Peptide deformylase: a new type of mononuclear iron protein, J. Am. Chem. Soc., 1997, 119, 12418–12419.

[41] J. M. Clements, R. P. Beckett, A. Brown, G. Catlin, M. Lobell, S. Palan, W. Thomas, M. Whittaker, S. Wood, S. Salama, P. J. Baker, H. F. Rodgers, V. Barynin, D. W. Rice and M. G. Hunter, Antibiotic activity and characteristic of BB-3497, a novel peptide deformylase inhibitor, Antimicrob. Agents Chemother., 2001, 45, 563–570.

[42] B. Hao, W. Gong, P. T. R. Rajagopalan, Y. Zhou, D. Pei and M. K. Chan, Structural basis for the design of antibiotics targeting peptide deformylase, Biochemistry, 1999, 38, 4712–4719.

[43] J. –P. Guilloteau, M. Mathieu, C. Giglione, V. Blanc, A. Dupuy, M. Chevrier, P. Gil, A. Famechon, T. Meinnel and V. Mikol, The crystal structures of four peptide deformylases bound to the antibiotic actinonin reveal two distinct types: a platform for the structural-based design of antibacterial agents, J. Mol. Biol., 2002, 320, 951–962.

[44] R. P. Beckett, A. H. Davidson, A. H. Drummond, P. Huxley and M. Whittake, Recent advances in matrix metalloproteinase inhibitor research, Drug Discov. Today, 1996, 1, 16–26.

[45] T. Meinnel, L. Patiny, S. Ragusa and S. Blanquet, Design and synthesis of substrate analogue inhibitors of peptide deformylase, Biochemistry, 1999, 38, 4287–4295.

[46] Y. Wei, T. Yi, K. M. Huntington, C. Chaudhury and D. Pei, Identification of a potent peptide deformylase inhibitor from a rationally designed combinatorial library, J. Comb. Chem., 2000, 2, 650–657.

[47] D. Z. Chen, D. V. Patel, C. J. Hackbarth, W. Wang, G. Dreyer, D. Young, P. S. Margolis, C. Wu, Z. J. Ni, J. Trias, R. White and Z. Yuan, Actinonin, a naturally occurring antibacterial agent, is a potent deformylase inhibitor, Biochemistry, 2000, 39, 1256–1262.

[48] D. Z. Chen, C. Hackbarth, Z. J. Ni, C. Wu, W. Wang, R. Jain, Y. He, K. Bracken, B. Weidmann, D. V. Patel, J. Trias, R. J. White and Z. Yuan, Peptide deformylase inhibitors as antibacterial agents: identification of VRC-3375, a proline-3-alkylsuccinyl hydroxomate derivative, by using an integrated combinatorial and medicinal chemistry approach, Antimicrob. Agents Chemother., 2004, 48, 250–261.

[49] C. M. Apel, D. W. Banner, D. Bur, M. Dietz, T. Hirata, C. Hubschwerlen, H. Locher, M. G. P. Page, W. Pirson, G. Rosse and J. L. Specklin, Hydroxamic acid derivatives as potent peptide deformylase inhibitors and antibacterial agents, *J. Med. Chem.*, 2000, **43**, 2324–2331.

[50] J. A. McIntyre, J. Castaner and L. Martin, LBM-415 antibacterial peptide deformylase inhibitor, *Drug Future*, 2005, **30**, 23–28.

[51] T. R. Fritsche, H. S. Sader, R. Cleeland and R. N. Jones, Comparative antimicrobial characterization of LBM-415 (NVP PDF-713), a new peptide deformylase inhibitor of clinical importance, *Antimicrob. Agents Chemother.*, 2005, **49**, 1468–1476.

[52] S. J. Davies, A. P. Ayscough, R. P. Beckett, J. M. Clements, S. Doel, L. M. Pratt, A. M. Spavold, S. W. Thomas and M. Whittaker, Structure-activity relationships of the peptide deformylase inhibitor BB-3497: modification of the methylene spacer and the P1′ side chain, *Bioorg. Med. Chem. Lett.*, 2003, **13**, 2715–2718.

[53] R. Jain, D. Chen, R. J. White, D. V. Patel and Z. Yuan, Bacterial peptide deformylase inhibitors: a new class of antibacterial agents, *Curr. Med. Chem.*, 2005, **12**, 1607–1621.

[54] R. B. Murphy, D. M. Philipp and R. A. Friesner, Mixed quantum mechanics/molecular mechanics (QM/MM) method for large-scale modeling of chemistry in protein environment, *J. Comp. Chem.*, 2001, **21**, 1442–1457.

[55] V. Madison, J. Duca, F. Bennett, S. Bohanon, A. Cooper, M. Chu, J. Desai, V. Girijavallabhan, R. Hare, A. Hruza, S. Hendrata, Y. Huang, C. Kravec, B. Malcolm, J. McCormick, L. Miesel, L. Ramanathan, P. Reichert, A. Saksena, J. Wang, P. C. Weber, H. Zhu and T. Fischmann, Binding affinities and geometries of various metal ligands in peptide deformylase inhibitors, *Biophys. Chem.*, 2002, **101–102**, 239–247.

[56] X. Hu, K. T. Nguyen, V. C. Jiang, D. Lofland, H. Moser and D. Pei, Macrocyclic inhibitors for peptide deformylase: a structure-activity relationship study of the ring size, *J. Med. Chem.*, 2004, **47**, 4941–4949.

[57] X. Hu, K. T. Nguyen, C. L. M. J. Verlinde, W. G. Hol and D. Pei, Structure-based design of a macrocyclic inhibitor for peptide deformylase, *J. Med. Chem.*, 2003, **46**, 3771–3774.

[58] V. Molteni, X. He, J. Nabakka, K. Yang, A. Kreusch, P. Gordon, B. Bursulaya, I. Warner, T. Shin, T. Biorac, N. S. Ryde, R. Goldberg, J. Doughty and Y. He, Identification of novel potent bicyclic peptide deformylase inhibitors, *Bioorg. Med. Chem. Lett.*, 2004, **14**, 1477–1481.

[59] M. K. Gupta, P. Mishra, P. Prathipati and A. K. Saxena, 2D-QSAR in hydroxamic acid derivatives as peptide deformylase inhibitors and antibacterial agents, *Bioorg. Med. Chem. Lett.*, 2002, **10**, 3713–3716.

[60] H. K. Smith, R. P. Beckett, J. M. Clements, S. Doel, S. P. East, S. B. Launchbury, L. M. Pratt, Z. M. Spavold, W. Thomas, R. S. Todd and M. Whittaker, Structure-activity relationships of the peptide deformylase inhibitor BB-3497: modification of the metal binding group, *Bioorg. Med. Chem. Lett.*, 2002, **12**, 3595–3599.

[61] S. J. Davies, A. P. Ayscough, R. P. Beckett, R. A. Bragg, J. M. Clements, S. Doel, C. Grew, S. B. Launchbury, G. M. Perkins, L. M. Pratt, H. K. Smith, Z. M. Spavold, S. W. Thomas, R. S. Todd and M. Whittaker, Structure-activity relationships of the peptide deformylase inhibitor BB-3497: modification of the methylene spacer and the P1′ side chain, *Bioorg. Med. Chem. Lett.*, 2003, **13**, 2709–2713.

[62] G. Chang and C. B. Roth, Structure of MsbA from *E. coli*: a homolog of the multidrug resistance ATP binding cassette, *Science*, 2001, **293**, 1793–1800.

[63] H. Akama, T. Matsuura, S. Kashiwagi, H. Yoneyama, S. Narita, T. Tsukihara, A. Nakagawa and T. Nakae, Crystal structure of membrane fusion protein, MexA, of the multidrug transporter in *Pseudomonas aeruginosa*, *J. Biol. Chem.*, 2004, **279**, 25939–25942.

CHAPTER 16

Recent Evaluations of High Throughput Docking Methods for Pharmaceutical Lead Finding – Consensus and Caveats

Wendy D. Cornell

Merck Research Laboratories, P.O. Box 2000, Rahway, NJ 07065, USA

Contents

ANNUAL REPORTS IN COMPUTATIONAL CHEMISTRY, VOLUME 2
ISSN: 1574-1400   DOI 10.1016/S1574-1400(06)02016-0

1. INTRODUCTION

Selecting among available software for high throughput docking (HTD) is a challenging problem. A number of papers evaluating HTD software have appeared in the recent literature from molecular modeling research groups in academia [1,2] and the pharmaceutical industry [3–10]. These evaluations are useful because they provide a side-by-side comparison of the performance of these programs using data sets composed of pharmaceutically interesting protein targets and drug-like candidate ligands. Here we summarize the results of HTD evaluations published from 2003 to early 2006, along with wisdom from related papers, and present consensus findings and caveats.

2. BACKGROUND

Automated methods for protein–ligand docking were first developed by Kuntz *et al.* in the early 1980s [11]. Early validation studies focused on reproducing the crystallographically observed binding mode of a given ligand in its cognate protein structure. As the field matured, more relevant objectives were pursued, namely the reproduction of binding modes using a protein structure not derived from a co-complex with the target ligand, ranking of active compounds, and screening of databases with the aim of producing a list of database molecules enriched in actives. These are three very different goals. Indeed, the first corresponds to a type of virtual structural biology, the second to lead optimization, and the third to high throughput screening (HTS). The third, HTD, is sometimes also referred to as structure-based "virtual screening" and it is that topic we review here. Examples of novel drug leads discovered using HTD have been reviewed elsewhere by Alvarez [12].

3. METHODS

3.1. Docking programs

In general, docking programs generate poses for each candidate ligand, a pose being defined by the ligand conformation plus orientation within the binding site. Poses can be ranked using a scoring function internal to the program that generates the poses or one from another source. Once the "best" pose has been identified for each ligand, different ligands can be ranked relative to each other using the same scoring function used to select the best pose for each ligand, another scoring function internal to the program, or a scoring function from an outside source.

The docking programs assessed in the aforementioned HTD evaluations are summarized in Table 1. They include AutoDock [13], DOCK [11,14], DockIt [15], DockVision [16,17], FlexX [18], Flo + [19], FRED [20], Glide [21,22], GOLD [23], ICM [24], LigandFit [25], MOEDock [26], SLIDE [27], and Surflex [28]. HTD studies usually assume a rigid protein, since allowing for a flexible protein would be too computationally expensive. Ligand conformational space is explored through the use of pre-generated conformers or by flexing "on-the-fly." This is in contrast with early docking studies where a single low-energy conformation was typically used for each ligand.

3.2. Scoring functions

Scoring functions are generally classified into three types – force field, empirical, and knowledge based. Force field-based scoring functions are derived from standard molecular mechanics force fields. Examples include DOCK Energy [29], GoldScore [23], and the objective function used to rank poses for each ligand in Glide (Emodel) [21]. Empirical scoring functions such as ChemScore [30], GlideScore [22], LigScore [25], FlexX [31], and X-Score [32] include terms that are weighted to reproduce sets of experimental binding energies. Finally, knowledge-based scoring functions are derived from the statistics of atomic interactions in proteins and protein–ligand complexes in the PDB [33]. These include PMF [34] and DrugScore [35]. Scoring functions can be further characterized as "hard" (e.g. ChemScore, FlexX, and force field-based scoring functions) or "soft" (e.g. PMF, PLP, DrugScore, and Gaussian shape), based on their sensitivity to small changes in the ligand position. Hardness arises from repulsive terms and angular components of attractive terms [3]. Some docking programs will include their own scoring function as well as ones from outside sources. In the latter case, the scoring function may be implemented somewhat differently from its original form and may not produce the same results.

3.3. Resource requirements

HTD calculations are CPU intensive simply due to the need to evaluate thousands or millions of ligands, but memory requirements are small relative to protein molecular dynamics or small molecule quantum chemical calculations. Consequently, HTD calculations are frequently carried out on Linux clusters rather than SMP (shared memory processing) machines. Some groups (e.g. BMS, GSK, and Novartis) have made use of a GRID of

Table 1. Docking programs assessed in recent published HTD evaluations

	AutoDock	DOCK	DockIt	Dock Vision	FlexX	Flo +	FRED	Glide	GOLD	ICM	LigandFit	MOEDock	SLIDE	Surflex
Schulz-Gasch et al., Hoffman LaRoche					X	X	X	X						
Klon et al., Novartis					X			X						
Bursulaya et al., Scripps	X	X			X				X	X				
Kellenberger et al., CNRS		X			X	X	X	X	X				X	X
Perola et al., Vertex								X	X	X				
Muegge et al., B-I/Bayer		X						X			X			
Cummings et al., J&J		X		X				X	X					
Kontoyianni et al., J&J		X			X			X			X			
Warren et al., GSK		X	X		X	X	X	X	X		X	X		
Chen et al., AstraZeneca					X			X		X				

desktop PCs within the company. While such GRIDs can make good use of the otherwise idle CPU cycles of a large number of existing machines, they may present software licensing and access control issues relative to using a small number of more powerful machines specialized for modeling work, e.g. dedicated clusters [36]. These issues should be taken into account when considering the price-performance value of a desktop PC GRID relative to other hardware configurations. HTD calculations can require significant disk space since one pose is typically saved for each ligand which docks successfully, i.e. is able to fit into the binding site.

3.4. Protein structures

HTD is a structure-based technique and consequently the choice of protein structure and active site definition significantly impacts the results. For example, in a HTD screen of the Estrogen receptor, a protein structure derived from an antagonist-bound complex will have an open active site and thus be able to accommodate both agonists and antagonists, whereas a protein structure from an agonist-bound complex would not be able to accommodate canonical antagonists such as tamoxifen. In an HTD screen of a kinase, a protein structure of the unactivated kinase may be preferable to that of the generic activated form since there is greater active site variation across unactivated kinases and therefore greater potential to identify a selective inhibitor. The user's choice of protonation state for amino acid chains in the protein is also important and has significant impact on results.

Shoichet *et al.* have compared the performance of the DOCK program when using protein structures derived from holo- and apo-crystal structures and homology models of nine targets – DHFR, PNP (with and without PO_4^-), PARP, Thrombin, GART, SAHH, AR, AchE, and TS [37]. Using the MDDR as a source of actives and inactives for each target and "% of database screened to find 25% of known ligands" as the objective measurement, they found that the holo structures performed best in seven out of ten cases, the apo structure in two, and the modeled structure in one case. Further, in the cases of Thrombin and TS, the modeled structure did not perform appreciably worse than the best experimental structure. These results were somewhat surprising, since one might have expected the experimental structures to always perform better than the modeled structure and for the holo structure to outperform the apo due to tighter packing in and pre-organization of the binding site in the former.

Kairys *et al.* investigated the performance of different homology models and templates for Carboxypeptidase, Factor Xa, PPARα, CDK2, and

AchE [38]. They also found that the modeled structures performed quite well. Using 13–22 known ligands for each target derived from the PDB or the literature, the NCI diversity set of compounds [39] as decoys, and average rank $<r>$ of actives as the performance measurement, the authors found that one of the modeled structures outperformed the experimental structure in three of the five cases. Moreover, the model that performed best was not necessarily the one most similar to the target in sequence.

Table 2 shows the variation of enrichment factors with choice of protein structure. Muegge and Enyedy [6] compared the enrichments obtained using two different crystal structures for CDK2 and SRC kinases and found they varied typically from 0% to 50% (at 10% subsetting), depending on the docking program used (DOCK, Glide, or LigandFit) and the decoy set. Halgren et al. [22] demonstrated the improvement of Glide 2.5 relative to earlier versions by calculating enrichment factors for nine targets, in 5 cases using two or three crystal structures per target. Using the enrichment factor obtained for the top scoring 10% of compounds as the performance measurement, they also observed variations from 0% to 50%. For the 14 examples shown in Table 2, the average ratio of minimum to maximum enrichment observed is approximately 0.75, so this number is employed here as a rough error estimate when comparing reported enrichments.

3.5. Ligand data sets

When evaluating the results of HTD studies or indeed any computational chemistry prediction against experiment, the accuracy of the experimental data must be considered. Primary HTS data, for instance, is notoriously noisy and is not a very good source of "active compounds" for comparing docking methods. Preferably one should use only those compounds for which one can demonstrate concentration-dependent binding in a confirmatory binding assay. The actives employed in the evaluations reviewed here were culled from a variety of sources (Table 3).

Given an active compound identified through any means, it is straightforward to identify related compounds through a topological similarity search of the compound database. What makes docking methods useful is their ability to retrieve actives from different structural classes, and performance is often measured by that criterion. Presumably, it is of more value to identify three total actives from different structural classes than tenactives from a single class.

It is standard practice as part of a HTD evaluation to assemble inactive or "decoy" compounds from sources such as the MDDR or ACD by

Table 2. Variation of enrichment factors with choice of protein structure

	Program	Decoys	PDB 1	Enrichment 1 (E1)	PDB 2	Enrichment 2 (E2)	Min(E1,E2)/ Max (E1,E2)
CDK2	Glide		1dm2	6.0	1aq1	6.0	1.00
Estrogen receptor	Glide		3ert	8.0	1err	9.0	0.89
P38 MAP kinase	Glide		1a9u	2.4	1bl7	4.1	0.59
Thrombin	Glide		1dwc	9.4	1ett	9.0	0.96
HIV RT	Glide		1rt1	6.4	1vrt	5.8	0.91
CDK2	Glide	MDDR	1e9h	5.1	1qmz	3.6	0.71
CDK2	Glide	ACD	1e9h	7.7	1qmz	7.7	1.00
CDK2	Glide	Kinase-like	1e9h	5.6	1qmz	3.6	0.64
CDK2	DOCK	MDDR	1e9h	2.8	1qmz	3.6	0.78
CDK2	DOCK	ACD	1e9h	4.9	1qmz	6.4	0.77
CDK2	DOCK	Kinase-like	1e9h	4.5	1qmz	4.7	0.96
CDK2	LigandFit	MDDR	1e9h	0.6	1qmz	3.3	0.18
CDK2	LigandFit	ACD	1e9h	1.8	1qmz	3.1	0.58
CDK2	LigandFit	Kinase-like	1e9h	1.5	1qmz	2.9	0.52
SRC	Glide	MDDR	1byg	3.3	1src	4.4	0.75
SRC	Glide	ACD	1byg	6.6	1src	5.9	0.89
SRC	Glide	Kinase-like	1byg	4.3	1src	3.8	0.88
SRC	DOCK	MDDR	1byg	7.7	1src	6.9	0.90
SRC	DOCK	ACD	1byg	8.9	1src	9.9	0.90
SRC	DOCK	Kinase-like	1byg	8.7	1src	7.8	0.90
SRC	LigandFit	MDDR	1byg	1.2	1src	0.9	0.75
SRC	LigandFit	ACD	1byg	2.5	1src	1.2	0.48
SRC	LigandFit	Kinase-like	1byg	1.5	1src	0.9	0.60
Average							0.76

Table 3. Description of active and inactive compounds employed in HTD evaluations

	Number targets	Number publicly available structures	Number actives (N_a) per target	Sources of actives	Potency range	Number inactives	Ratio of inactives to actives	Source of inactives
Bursulaya et al. [a]	11	37	2–8	PDB In-house	nM – Low μM	10,037		ACD
Schulz-Gasch et al. [b]	7	3	36–128	PDB Review articles		7528	209	WDI
Perola et al. [c]	3	0	142–247	In-house	Low nM – High μM	10,000-N_a	40–70	Commercial DB
Muegge et al. [d]	2	4	52–492	Literature In-house	Low nM – μM	1) 10,000 2) 10,000 3) 10,000	20–192	1) MDDR 2) Kinase inhibs 3) ACD
Klon et al. [e]	2	2	266–13-27	Literature Patents In-house	NA	179,805	135–676	ACD
Kellenberger et al. [f]	1	1	10	L. Scapozza, ETH	Sub-μm-200 μM	990	99	ACD
Cummings et al. [g]	5	5	5–14	In-house	NA	1049	75–210	MDDR Actives for other targets
Kontoyianni et al. [h]	6	6	8–10	Literature	0.1 nM – 1 μM	996	124–100	ACD and MDDR
Warren et al. [i]	8	0	138–218	In-house Literature	Low nM – μM	1303-N_a	6–9	In-house Commercially available
Chen et al. [j]	12	4	17–622	In-house	nM – Low μM	22,743-N_a	37–1338	Actives for other targets

applying filters for drug-likeness and then selecting a diverse subet. Further consideration is sometimes given to the physical properties of the decoys. Verdonk *et al.* [40] demonstrated the importance of choosing "focused" decoy libraries having 1D property profiles similar to those of the actives. Failure to do this will result in ligand scores based on not only active site complementarity but also non-specific 1D properties. The clearest example is molecular weight, which has been shown to correlate with almost any docking score [34,41].

4. PERFORMANCE MEASUREMENTS

Lead finding is an exercise in the classification of compounds into actives and inactives. In HTD, as with HTS, it is not necessary to obtain an accurate measure of the binding energy or relative rank of each compound. An accurate classification will suffice.

In an ideal HTD search for leads, all N active compounds would be ranked from 1 through N with all inactives receiving clearly worse scores. In reality, the performance is much less than ideal and a number of approaches have been applied to measuring how close the actives are to the top of the list. Some of the measures provide a complete and complex picture of active retrieval, while others are more limited but provide a straightforward answer to practical questions such as "Which method provides more actives if I am willing to screen 10% of my database?" and "What percentage of my database do I need to screen in order to find 80% of the actives?"

4.1. Fraction actives found in top scoring *N*%

If active compounds are randomly distributed within a larger set, then *N*% of the actives should be found in a random sample of *N*% of the total compounds. Most of the HTD evaluations summarized here reported the fraction actives identified or enrichment (see below) in the top scoring 10% of compounds. Here the ideal value is 100% recovery, although this is only possible when the number of compounds tested is greater than or equal to the number of actives present. Values greater than 10% correspond to better than random identification of actives.

4.2. Percentage of database screened to find *M*% of actives

This metric provides an answer to the question, "What fraction of the database would I need to screen in order to find, for example, 80% of the actives?"

4.3. Enrichment factor

An alternative formulation of the fraction actives found is the enrichment factor observed for the top scoring N%. If $2*N$% of the actives are found in the top scoring N% of the database, then an enrichment of 2 is seen at N%. Many of the HTD evaluations cited also show "enrichment" or "cumulative recall curves" which plot % actives found vs. % compounds tested.

4.4. Maximum enrichment factor

This metric indicates the highest ratio of actives to inactives found in the ranked list.

4.5. Percentage of database where maximum enrichment factor occurred

This metric indicates at what point in the ranked list the highest ratio of actives to inactives is found.

4.6. Cumulative recall or accumulation curves

In this graphical representation, the number of actives found is plotted against the number of compounds tested. When the number of actives is much smaller than the total number of compounds and the retrieval is much less than ideal (which is true for most cases), this graph approximates the ROC curve.

4.7. ROC curves

In an HTD study on Metabotropic Glutamate Receptor Subtype 4, Triballeau et al. [42] described the application of the receiver operator characteristic (ROC) curve method to compare different docking protocols. In this method, the selectivity (S_e) of given method is plotted against $1-$sensitivity (S_p). Sensitivity is calculated as the ratio of true positives (TP) to the sum of true positives plus false negatives (FN).

$$S_e = N_{\text{selected actives}}/N_{\text{total actives}} = \text{TP}/(\text{TP} + \text{FN})$$

Specificity is calculated as the ratio of true negatives to the sum of true negatives plus false positives.

$$S_p = N_{\text{discarded inactives}}/N_{\text{total inactives}} = \text{TN}/(\text{TN} + \text{FP})$$

Area under the curve (AUC) can be calculated, with an AUC of 1.0 corresponding to ideal recovery of actives, 0.5 to random, and 0.9 to randomly chosen actives outscoring random inactives 90% of the time. The authors claim that the ROC curve is superior to the more commonly used accumulation curve in that it is independent of the number of actives included and provides more information overall. Further, the accumulation curve provides information on selectivity but not specificity.

4.8. Average rank

Kairys *et al.* [38] defined the quantity of average rank to capture the performance at identifying all actives.

$$\langle r \rangle = \frac{100\%}{N_{\text{bind}} N_{\text{tot}}} \sum_{i=1}^{N_{\text{bind}}} r_i$$

4.9. RIE

Sheridan *et al.* have proposed Robust Initial Enhancement (RIE) as an alternative measurement, which defines the density of actives among the highest scoring compounds [43].

$$\text{RIE} = \frac{S}{\langle S \rangle}$$

$$S = \sum_i^{\text{actives}} e^{(-\text{rank}(i)/a)}$$

a is a user-specified constant $\ll N$, e.g. 0.01*N

The RIE has the advantage over using a sharp cutoff (say enrichment at a particular percent compounds tested) in that the front of the list is upweighted and also the measure is less sensitive to 1 or 2 actives moving across the borderline).

4.10. Evaluation metric employed in this review

Most of the HTD evaluations included in this review reported performance statistics for (sometimes among other things) the top-scoring 10% of the compounds. This may or may not be a relevant measure for a particular "real world" application of the software. For example, if HTD is used to select approximately 1000 compounds out of 1,000,000 compounds for benchtop screening, then performance in the top-scoring 0.1% fraction of the database is more realistic. If HTD is used to select approximately 10,000 compounds for more detailed computational investigation, then the top-scoring 1% fraction would be of interest. Thus the convention of using 10% may make methods look much better than they really are for practical applications.

5. EVALUATIONS

HTD evaluations reported in ten recent publications are summarized below. The active and inactive/decoy compounds from each study are summarized in Table 3. Protein targets and HTD programs are summarized in Table 4 along with enrichments obtained in the top scoring 10% of compounds. Finally, the number of targets for which each program was a top performer in a given study are shown in Table 5.

5.1. Bursulaya et al. (Scripps)

One of the earliest HTD comparisons was published by Bursulaya et al. at Scripps [1]. In this study, DOCK 4.0, FlexX 1.8, and ICM 2.8 were compared in virtual database screening studies using the proteins Trypsin, Cytochrome P450, Neuraminidase, Carboxypeptidase A, L-arabinose binding protein, Thrombin, Thermolysin, Penicillopepsin, intestinal FABP, Ribonuclease T1, and Carbonic anhydrase II. For each protein, from two to eight PDB structures were tested. The positional ranking of the cognate ligand was reported relative to a list of decoys consisting of 10,000 molecules from the ACD and 36 ligands from the remaining PDB complexes. DOCK and FlexX were able to identify, respectively, seven and eight cognate ligands and ICM found 17 within the top scoring 1% of solutions. Because this study was limited to the identification of the single cognate ligand for each protein structure, the data are not included in Table 4.

In the later HTD evaluations reported below, the number of actives included for a given protein ranged from 5 to 1327. These later studies thus went beyond the ability of a program to recognize a single active in its pre-formed cognate protein structure.

Table 4. Enrichment values obtained for top scoring 10% of compounds from recent HTD evaluations

		DOCK	DockIt	Dock Vision	FlexX	Flo+	FRED	Glide	GOLD	ICM	LigandFit	MOEDock
Kinases	CDK2	4.0 1E9H B$_{2.8}$ 4.0 1QMZ B$_{3.6}$						2.5 1E9H B$_{5.1}$ 2.5 1QMZ B$_{3.6}$			4.6 1E9H B$_{0.6}$ 4.6 1QMZ B$_{3.3}$	
	Chk1 Kinase	4.0 ^{i}G$_{1.4}$	1.0 ^{i}G$_{4.2}$		1.10,1 G$_{7.0}$	8020 G$_{5.6}$	1.2,1 G$_{2.9}$	2.0 ^{i}G$_{6.3}$	1.2 ^{i}G$_{0.1}$		4.7 ^{i}G$_{3.3}$	02.03 ^{i}G$_{3.9}$
	GSK3b				1.10 ^{i}A$_{1.9}$			3.5 ^{i}A$_{1.7}$	2.2 ^{i}A$_{1.2}$	3.2.01 ^{i}A$_{4.7}$		
	JNK3				1.10 ^{i}A$_{1.8}$			3.5 ^{i}A$_{1.5}$	2.2 ^{i}A$_{1.4}$	3.2.01 ^{i}A$_{5.0}$		
	P38 Kinase				1.10 ^{i}A$_{2.1}$			3.5 ^{i}A$_{0.8}$	2.2 ^{i}A$_{2.1}$	3.2.01 ^{i}A$_{7.3}$		
	Protein Kinase B	4.0 1O6K N$_{0.2}$			1.9,2 H$_{5.7}$ 1.10 1O6K N$_{1.0}$		1.1 ^{i}H$_{7.9}$	1.8 ^{i}H$_{7.5}$ 2.5 1O6K N$_{4.8}$				
	Src Kinase	4.0 1BYG B$_{7.7}$ 4.0 2SRC B$_{6.9}$						2.5 1BYG B$_{3.3}$ 2.5 1BYG B$_{4.4}$			4.6 1BYG B$_{1.2}$ 4.6 1BYG B$_{0.9}$	
	Thymidine Kinase	4.0 1KIM C$_{3.0}$			1.11 1KIM C$_{8.0}$	1.11 1KIM C$_{2.0}$	1.1 1KIM C$_{2.0}$	2.0 1KIM C$_{6.0}$	2.0 1KIM C$_{10.0}$		4.7 1KIM K$_{6.7}$	
Metallo-enzymes	Carbonic Anhydrase				1.9 7KIM K$_{3.3}$ 1.9 1BMN K$_{5.0}$			3.5 ^{i}A$_{5.7}$			4.7 1KMN K$_{3.0}$	
	Carboxy-peptidase				1.10 ^{i}A$_{3.9}$				2.2 ^{i}A$_{4.5}$	3.2.01 ^{i}A$_{6.5}$		
	Gelatinase A				1.9,2 1CK7 H$_{6.7}$		1.1 1CK7 H$_{4.4}$	1.8 1CK7 H$_{6.2}$				
	PDF (E. coli)	4.0 ^{i}G$_{0.9}$	1.0 ^{i}G$_{0.2}$		1.10,1 G$_{0.8}$	0802 G$_{1.5}$	1.2,1 G$_{3.2}$	2.0 ^{i}G$_{0.6}$	1.2 ^{i}G$_{1.0}$		4.7 ^{i}G$_{2.9}$	
	PDF (strep)	4.0 ^{i}G$_{0.8}$	1.0 ^{i}G$_{0.0}$		1.10,1 G$_{0.8}$	0802 G$_{0.8}$	1.2,1 G$_{1.2}$	2.0 ^{i}G$_{0.4}$	1.2 ^{i}G$_{0.1}$		4.7 ^{i}G$_{1.7}$	
	Stromelysin				1.9 1SLN K$_{4.0}$						4.7 1SLN K$_{5.0}$	02.03 ^{i}G$_{2.1}$
	Thermolysin				1.9 2TMN K$_{6.3}$						4.7 2TMN K$_{6.3}$	02.03 ^{i}G$_{0.6}$

Table 4. (*Continued*)

Family	Target	DOCK	DockIt	Dock Vision	FlexX	Flo+	FRED	Glide	GOLD	ICM	LigandFit	MOEDock
Serine Proteases	Factor Xa	$_{4.0}^{i}G_{4.1}$	$_{1.0}^{i}G_{2.0}$		$_{1.10}^{i}A_{3.7}$			$_{3.5}^{i}A_{8.7}$	$_{2.2}^{i}A_{3.6}$	$_{3.2.01}^{i}A_{9.3}$		$_{02.03}^{i}G_{0.6}$
	Thrombin	$1QBV\,_{4.0}^{i}J_{7.0}$; $1HVR\,_{4.0}^{i}J_{0.0}$			$_{1.10,1}^{i}G_{2.2}$; $1DWD\,_{1.10,2}^{i}A_{7.5}$; $1DWD\,_{1.9,2}^{i}H_{8.3}$	$8020\,^{i}G_{2.7}$	$_{1.2,1}^{i}G_{4.1}$; $1DWD\,^{i}H_{7.8}$	$_{2.0}^{i}G_{5.4}$; $1DWD\,_{3.5}^{i}A_{9.8}$; $1DWD\,_{1.8}^{i}H_{8.7}$	$_{1.2}^{i}G_{4.1}$; $1DWD\,_{2.2}^{i}A_{1.4}$	$1DWD\,_{3.2.01}^{i}A_{8.8}$	$_{4.7}^{i}G_{1.9}$	$_{02.03}^{i}G_{0.0}$
	uPA			$1QBV\,_{2}^{i}J_{3.0}$				$1QBV\,_{2.5}^{i}J_{8.0}$	$1QBV\,_{1.2}^{i}J_{2.0}$			
Aspartyl Protease	HIV Protease	$1HVR\,_{4.0}^{i}J_{0.0}$		$_{2}^{i}J_{2.0}$; $1HVR\,_{2}^{i}J_{0.0}$				$_{2.5}^{i}J_{4.0}$; $1HVR\,_{2.5}^{i}J_{6.0}$	$_{1.2}^{i}J_{9.0}$; $1HVR\,_{1.2}^{i}J_{0.0}$		$2BPX\,_{4.7}^{i}J_{8.0}$	
Nuclear Receptors	Estrogen Receptor				$1ERR\,_{1.10}^{i}A_{0.8}$; $1ERR\,_{1.9,2}^{i}H_{5.7}$		$1ERR\,_{1.1}^{i}H_{7.9}$	$1ERR\,_{3.5}^{i}A_{3.9}$; $1ERR\,_{1.8}^{i}H_{7.5}$	$1ERR\,_{2.2}^{i}A_{0.8}$	$1ERR\,_{3.2.01}^{i}A_{6.2}$		
	PPARδ	$_{4.0}^{i}G_{1.7}$	$_{1.0}^{i}G_{3.2}$		$_{1.10,1}^{i}G_{5.2}$	$0802\,^{i}G_{3.6}$	$_{1.2,1}^{i}G_{1.1}$	$_{2.0}^{i}G_{4.8}$	$_{1.2}^{i}G_{2.5}$		$_{4.7}^{i}G_{1.2}$	
Oxido-reductases	COX2				$1CX2\,_{1.10}^{i}A_{0.5}$		$_{1.1}^{i}H_{6.4}$	$1CX2\,_{3.5}^{i}A_{3.1}$; $_{1.8}^{i}H_{6.2}$	$1CX2\,_{2.2}^{i}A_{3.6}$	$1CX2\,_{3.2.01}^{i}A_{7.1}$		
	nNOS				$_{1.9,2}^{i}H_{4.4}$; $_{1.10}^{i}A_{0.1}$; $_{1.10}^{i}A_{1.4}$			$_{3.5}^{i}A_{6.7}$; $_{3.5}^{i}A_{1.6}$	$_{2.2}^{i}A_{0.1}$; $_{2.2}^{i}A_{0.9}$	$_{3.2.01}^{i}A_{4.7}$; $_{3.2.01}^{i}A_{2.3}$		
Hydrolases	PTP1B	$1C84\,_{4.0}^{i}J_{0.0}$; $1C88\,_{4.0}^{i}N_{4.5}$		$1C84\,_{2}^{i}J_{8.0}$	$1C88\,_{1.1}^{i}J_{7.2}$			$1C84\,_{2.5}^{i}J_{6.0}$; $1C88\,_{2.5}^{i}N_{8.4}$	$1C84\,_{1.2}^{i}J_{9.0}$			
	sPLA2				$1DB4\,_{1.10}^{i}A_{1.9}$			$1DB4\,_{3.5}^{i}A_{10.0}$	$1DB4\,_{2.2}^{i}A_{0.0}$	$1DB4\,_{3.2.01}^{i}A_{7.6}$		
Glycosyl Hydrolase	Neuraminidase				$_{1.9,2}^{i}H_{6.6}$		$_{1.1}^{i}H_{8.5}$	$_{1.8}^{i}H_{9.7}$				

Class	Target									
Isomerase	Gyrase B	$_{4.0}^{i}G_{1.7}$	$_{1.0}^{i}G_{2.0}$	$_{1.10,1}^{i}G_{5.8}$ $_{1.9,2}^{i}H_{7.1}$	$_{0802}^{i}G_{2.3}$	$_{1.2,1}^{i}G_{1.9}$	$_{2.0}^{i}G_{1.0}$	$_{1.2}^{i}G_{4.0}$	$_{4.7}^{i}G_{2.8}$	$_{02.03}^{i}G_{0.0}$
Transferase	HCV Polymerase	$_{4.0}^{i}G_{1.8}$	$_{1.0}^{i}G_{1.0}$	$_{1.10,1}^{i}G_{0.9}$ $_{1.1}^{i}H_{4.1}$	$_{0802}^{i}G_{3.4}$	$_{1.2,1}^{i}G_{2.0}$	$_{1.8}^{i}H_{5.6}$ $_{2.0}^{i}G_{1.0}$	$_{1.2}^{i}G_{0.0}$	$_{4.7}^{i}G_{1.8}$	$_{02.03}^{i}G_{0.0}$
Ligase	HDM2	$_{4.0}^{i}J_{6.4}$		$^{i}J_{6.4}$				$_{1.2}^{i}J_{3.6}$		
Racemase	HPMur1			$_{1.10}^{i}A_{0.5}$			$_{3.5}^{i}A_{2.6}$	$_{2.2}^{i}A_{1.1}$	$_{3.2,01}^{i}A_{4.9}$	
Reductase	DHFR			$_{1.9}^{3DFR}K_{7.8}$ $_{1.10,1}^{i}G_{3.9}$					$_{4.7}^{3DFR}K_{7.8}$	
Aminoacyl tRNA Synthetase	Met tRNA Synthetase	$_{4.0}^{i}G_{4.2}$	$_{1.0}^{i}G_{1.0}$	$_{1.10,1}^{i}G_{3.9}$	$_{0802}^{i}G_{1.7}$	$_{1.2,1}^{i}G_{0.6}$	$_{2.0}^{i}G_{5.3}$	$_{1.2}^{i}G_{0.0}$	$_{4.7}^{i}G_{2.9}$	$_{02.03}^{i}G_{1.0}$

Note: A (Astra-Zeneca)[10], B (Boehringer-Ingelheim/Bayer)[6], C (CNRS)[2], G (GSK)[9], H (Hoffman LaRoche)[3], J (J&J, Exton)[7], K (J&J, Spring House)[8], and N (Novartis)[4]. Left superscript – PDB code or "i" in case of internal, proprietary structure. Left subscript – software version number. Right subscript – enrichment for top scoring. Grey shading – Best enrichment with vendor sw for target within a given (horizontal) study plus any enrichment within 25% confidence limit. B – MDDR decoy results; H, K – Enrichment reported for best performing scoring function for given docker on particular target.

Table 5. Number of targets for which program was a top performer (best score or within 75%)

	DOCK	DockIt	Dock vision	FlexX	Flo+	FRED	Glide	GOLD	ICM	Ligand Fit	MOE Dock
Schulz-Gasch et al.[a]				3/7		5/7	7/7				
Klon et al.				1/2			2/2				
Kellenberger et al.				1/1				1/1			
Cummings et al.	3/5		2/5	3/6			2/5	2/5			
Kontoyianni et al.[a]										5/6	
Warren et al.	2/8	0/8		3/8	2/8	2/8	4/8	2/8		2/8	
Chen et al.				1/11			5/11	0/11	11/11		0/8

[a]Based on enrichments calculated using best performing scoring function within a given program for each target.

5.2. Schulz-Gasch *et al.* (Hoffman LaRoche)

Schulz-Gasch *et al.* of Hoffman LaRoche [3] compared the performance of the FlexX 1.9.2, FRED 1.1, and Glide 1.8 programs against seven protein targets – COX-2, Estrogen receptor, p38 MAP kinase, Gyrase B, Thrombin, Gelatinase A, and Neuraminidase. Between 36 and 128 actives were used for each target, culled from in-house drug discovery programs, review articles, and the PDB. A total of 7528 inactives were taken from the WDI.

Each docking program was tested in combination with three different scoring functions. FlexX was assessed with FlexXScore [31], PLP [44], and ScreenScore; FRED with ChemScore, PLP, and ScreenScore; and Glide with GlideScore, GlideComp, and ScreenScore. The objective function used during the docking phase for each program was FlexXScore for FlexX, Gaussian shape for FRED, and GlideScore and OPLS-AA for Glide. The FRED implementation of ScreenScore omits the angular term for metal contacts and includes an additional penalty for protein–ligand clashes. ScreenScore is not implemented in Glide, so it was applied within FlexX to the top scoring pose from Glide.

Enrichment factors reported in Table 4 were obtained through visual inspection of the bar graphs shown in the published study. Values reported are for the best performing scoring function for each program, namely, ScreenScore for FlexX, ChemScore for FRED, and GlideScore for Glide. Across all targets, Glide performed best with an average enrichment of 6.7, compared to 6.0 for FlexX and 5.9 for FRED. The authors note, however, that the reported enrichment factors "should be interpreted with caution" since "most of the known inhibitors were extracted from crystal structures or built by modeling ligands into binding sites, and therefore are already close to the native ligand". Glide was a top performer on all 7 targets, COX2 (6.2), Estrogen receptor (7.5), Gelatinase A (6.2), Gyrase B (5.6), Neuraminidase (9.7), p38 (7.5), and Thrombin (8.7). FRED was a top performer on 5, COX2 (6.4), Estrogen receptor (7.9) Neuraminidase (8.5), p38 (7.9), and Thrombin (7.8), and FlexX on 3, Gelatinase A (6.7), Gyrase B (7.1), and Thrombin (8.3).

5.3. Perola *et al.* (Vertex)

Perola *et al.* at Vertex [5] assessed the performance of Glide, GOLD, and ICM on three targets: HIV-1 Protease, IMPDH, and p38 MAP Kinase. Between 142 and 247 actives were selected for each target from internal research programs. 10,000–N decoy compounds were selected from commercial databases, where N equals the number of actives for a given target. The top scoring pose generated by each of the three docking programs was re-scored using the ChemScore, GlideScore, and OPLS-AA scoring functions both prior to and after OPLS-AA minimization. Results from this study are not included in Table 4 since enrichment data was not reported for the top scoring 10%.

Results were presented for the top scoring 3% of compounds. For HIV-1 protease, enrichments ranging from 8.3 to 10.5 were obtained using each docker in combination with ChemScore. Limited improvement was seen with ChemScore following OPLS minimization, but more significant improvement was seen for GlideScore using GOLD and ICM poses and OPLS-AA using Glide, GOLD, and ICM poses. For IMPDH, enrichments of 16.4 and 14.1 were obtained with GlideScore using Glide and ICM poses, with minimal improvement obtained through minimization. Minimization did improve the results obtained with ChemScore using Glide and ICM poses and OPLS using Glide, GOLD, and ICM poses. Finally, in the case of p38 kinase, best results ranged from 8.5 to 9.0 and were obtained with GlideScore using Glide, GOLD, and ICM and for OPLS using ICM poses. Some improvement was seen upon minimization for ChemScore on ICM poses and GlideScore on GOLD poses.

5.4. Kellenberger *et al.* (CNRS)

Kellenberger *et al.* from CNRS [2] investigated the performance of eight docking programs, Dock, FlexX, FRED, Glide, GOLD, SLIDE, Surflex, and QXP, against a single target, Thymidine kinase (TK). The ligand test set consisted of 10 actives and 990 inactives from the ACD. For the top scoring 10% of the compounds, GOLD and Surflex performed best, finding all hits (enrichment factor of 10.0). Lesser enrichment factors were seen for FlexX (8.0), Glide (6.0), DOCK (3.0), FRED (2.0), QXP (2.0), and SLIDE (0.0).

The SLIDE calculations were repeated by Zavodsky and Kuhn, in whose lab SLIDE was developed, and they obtained significantly improved results running SLIDE in standard mode and using ligand conformations generated with OMEGA [45]. The results obtained by Kellenberger for TK using SLIDE and Surflex are omitted from Table 4 since these programs were not applied to any other protein targets in this evaluation and they were not included in the other evaluations considered here.

5.5. Klon *et al.* (Novartis)

Klon *et al.* at Novartis [4] compared the programs DOCK, FlexX, and GLIDE against two targets – PTP1B and Protein Kinase B (PKB). Publicly available crystal structures were used for each target. The ligand test set included 266 actives for PKB, 1327 for PTP-1B and 179,805 inactives from the ACD. The authors found that Glide performed best against both PTP-1B and PKB, with enrichment factors of 8.4 and 4.8, while FlexX yielded enrichment factors of 7.2 and 1.0, and Dock 4.5 and 0.2. In this study the authors introduced the concept of applying machine-learning methods by training a naïve Bayes classifier using 2D fingerprints found in high-scoring compounds and then rescoring all compounds using this model. This approach improves enrichment values seen for the top scoring 10% of compounds for PTP-1B, especially with the Dock program. ROC curve AUC values are also reported and reflect the same improvement.

5.6. Muegge and Enyedy (Boehringer-Ingelheim/Bayer)

Muegge and Enyedy at Boehringer-Ingelheim and Bayer [6] evaluated the performance of the DOCK, Glide, and LigandFit programs against CDK2 and Src Kinases. They further explored the effects of choice of PDB structure and source of decoy compounds for each protein. Fifty-two actives were culled from the literature for CDK2 and 492 were collected for Scr from an in-house program. Three sets of 10,000 inactives each were employed, assembled from the MDDR, ACD, and compounds known to be or similar to kinase inhibitors.

  Using the MMDR inactives with the CDK2 1e9h and 1qmz crystal structures, enrichment factors of 2.8 and 3.6 were obtained using DOCK, 5.1 and 3.6 with Glide, and 0.6 and 3.3 using LigandFit with the LigandFit score. Use of the ACD inactives led to enrichments of 4.9 and 6.4, 7.7 and 7.7, 1.8, and 3.1, respectively, with the three programs and two crystal structures. Similar results were seen for SRC kinase. *These numbers demonstrate the accuracy of the enrichment values reported in* Table 4, *since with Glide or Dock the enrichment obtained can vary by 50% according to choice of crystal structure and by greater than 100% according to choice of inactives.*

5.7. Cummings *et al.* (J&J)

Cummings *et al.* at J&J [7] compared the performance of DOCK, Dock-Vision, GLIDE and GOLD against five targets. Publicly available crystal structures were employed for three of the five proteins, HIV Protease, PTP1B, and Thrombin, while proprietary in-house structures were used for HDM2 and uPA. From 5 to 14 actives were employed for each ligand, mostly from in-house programs, with 1049 inactives assembled from the MDDR together with the actives from the four remaining targets.

The average enrichments for the top scoring 10% of compounds across the five targets were similar – GLIDE (5.1-fold), DOCK (4.9), DOCKVISION (4.9), and GOLD (4.7). Enrichments varied for individual targets. For example, GLIDE found three of the five actives for HIV-Protease whereas none were found by the other three programs. In contrast, for HDM2, GLIDE found only one of 14 actives whereas DOCK and DOCKVISION each found nine and GOLD found five. For PTP1B, GOLD, and DOCK identified nine of ten actives while DockVision found eight. For Thrombin, Glide and DOCK found eight and seven of ten actives. Finally, for uPA, GOLD found nine of ten actives.

Overall, DOCK was a top performer for three targets, HDM2 (6.4), PTP1B (9.0), and Thrombin (7.0). DockVision was a top performer for two, HDM2 (6.4) and PTP1B (8.0), as were Glide, HIV Protease (6.0), Thrombin (8.0); and GOLD, PTP1B (9.0) and uPA (9.0).

5.8. Kontoyianni *et al.* (J&J)

Kontoyianni *et al.* at J&J [8] evaluated the four docking programs DOCK, FlexX, Glide, and LigandFit in combination with ten different scoring functions against six target proteins from the PDB. The scoring functions included Ligscore1, Ligscore2, PLP1, PLP2, ChemScore, FlexX, PMF (Cerius2), PMF (Tripos), DOCK (Tripos), and GOLD (Tripos). Eight to ten actives were assembled for each protein from the literature spanning a range of potencies from "10^{-1} to 10^3 nM." A decoy set of 996 compounds was selected from the ACD and MDDR using drug-like filters.

For Thermolysin, best results were obtained using (1) LigandFit in combination with either GOLD score as implemented by Tripos, PMF as implemented by Accelrys, or LigScore1; or (2) FlexX in combination with PMF as implemented by Tripos or GOLD score as implemented by Tripos. For Stromelysin, best results were obtained using LigandFit/LigScore1, LigandFit/GOLD(Tripos), Glide/DOCK(Tripos), or FLexX/ChemScore. For DHFR, best results were obtained from the following docker/scorer combinations: FlexX/FlexXScore, FlexX/PMF(Tripos), LigandFit/LigScore1, LigandFit/PMF(Tripos), Glide/LigandScore1, Glide/PMF(Accelrys), and Dock/PMF(Tripos).

For HIV Protease, best results were obtained with LigandFit/GOLD(Tripos), LigandFit/PMF(Accelrys), LigandFit/DOCK(Tripos), LigandFit/PMF(Tripos), LigandFit/LigScore2, and Glide/GOLD(Tripos). In the case of Carbonic anhydrase, best results were obtained using LigandFit/GOLD(Tripos). Finally, in the case of Thymidine kinase, best results were obtained with LigandFit/LigScore1 and LigandFit/LigScore2.

5.9. Warren *et al.* (GSK)

Warren *et al.* at GSK [9] assessed the performance of ten docking programs, DOCK 4.0, DockIt 1.0, DockVision 2, FlexX 1.10.1, Flo + 0802, FRED 1.2.1, Glide 2.0, GOLD 1.2, LigandFit 4.7, MOEDock 02.03, and their internal program MVP, against eight proteins. All reported studies were carried out using proprietary in-house protein crystal structures. Between 138 and 218 compounds were selected from in-house programs for each protein, in each case spanning 2–5 congeneric series. For a given target, fewer than 20% of the compounds were inactive and fewer than 20% were highly active. Decoys consisted of the compounds from the 1303 selected not associated with a particular target.

Averaging enrichment factors across all targets for the top scoring 10% of compounds, the MVP program performed best with 5.7. Among the programs available outside of GSK, FlexX performed best with an enrichment of 3.3, followed closely by Glide (2.9) and Flo + (2.7). Rounding at the list were LigandFit (2.3), DOCK and FRED (2.1), GOLD (2.0), DockIt (1.7), and MOEDock (1.0, i.e. no improvement over random).

Glide with GScore performed best or among the best on four targets: Chk1 (6.3), Factor Xa (3.4), MRS (5.3), and PPARδ (4.8). FlexX performed best on 3 targets, Chk1 (7.0, TotalScore), Gyrase B (5.8, GoldScore), and PPARδ (5.2, ChemScore). Five programs performed best on 2 targets: DOCK with Energy, Factor Xa (4.1) and MRS (4.2); Flo +, Chk1 (5.6), and HCVP (3.4); FRED with ScreenScore, Factor Xa (4.1), and E. coli PDF (3.2); GOLD with Fitness, Factor Xa (4.1) and PPARδ (5.5); and LigandFit with Dreiding/DScore, *E. coli* PDF (2.9) and Strep PDF (1.7). DockIt performed best only on Chk1 (4.2), while MOEDock did not perform best on any targets.

The authors further assessed the performance of the programs at recovering higher potency compounds and compounds from different ligand classes. They found that changing the definition of an active from $\leqslant 1\,\mu M$ to $\leqslant 10\,\mu M$ or $\leqslant 100\,nM$ did not significantly affect the enrichments, with the exception of Chk1 where one of the two ligand classes did not include any actives which satisfied the 100 nM threshold. Lead identification performance was represented by percent of the list screened to recover at least one active for all compound classes. Median values for each program across the eight targets were Flo + (3.6), DockIt (6.4), MOEDock (7.0), Glide (7.2), FlexX (9.0), Dock (9.5), GOLD (21.5), LigandFit (32.3), and FRED (35.2).

5.10. Chen *et al.* (Astra-Zeneca)

The most recent HTD evaluation in the literature is from Chen *et al.* at Astra-Zeneca [10]. These researchers assessed the performance of

FlexX 1.10, GOLD 2.2, GLIDE 3.5, and ICM 3.2.01 against 12 protein targets using 17–622 actives per target and a decoy set consisting of ~22,000 compounds from commercially available sources plus actives from the other targets. Publicly available crystal structures were used for COX-2, ER, and Thrombin, whereas proprietary in-house structures were used for Carboxypeptidase, Factor Xa, GSK3B, HPMur1, JNK3, nNOS, p38 Kinase, PTP1B, and sPLA1.

Using the native scoring function for each program, they found that when assessing the top scoring 10% of compounds, on average ICM performed best (6.1-fold enrichment) followed by GLIDE_Emodel (4.6), GLIDE_Score (4.3), FlexX (2.2), and GOLD (1.7). Looking at individual targets and allowing for ties, ICM performed best against 10 targets: Carboxypeptidase (6.5-fold enrichment), COX2 (7.1), ER (6.2), Factor Xa (9.3), GSK3B (4.7), HPMur1 (3.9), JNK3 (5.0), p38 Kinase (7.3), PTP1B (2.3), and Thrombin (8.8). Glide performed best for five targets: Carboxypeptidase (5.7), Factor Xa (8.7), nNOS (6.7) sPLA1 (10.0), and Thrombin (9.8). Finally, FlexX was a top performer for a single target, Thrombin (7.5), while GOLD was for none. Significant enrichments were clearly achieved for sPLA1, Thrombin, Factor Xa, p38 Kinase, and COX-2, while PTP1B was the least tractable target. Calculation of average enrichment factors for the top scoring 1% of compounds led to similar trends, i.e. ICM (34), GLIDE/Gscore (23), and GLIDE/Emodel (21).

The authors assessed the value of structure-based lead finding by comparing the above enrichment results with those obtained using the ROCS and ISIS ligand-based methods. Averaged across all targets, ROCS and ISIS showed enrichment values for the top scoring 10% of compounds of 4.6 and 3.5, respectively. The enrichment of 4.6 for ROCS is less than that of the best performing docking program, ICM (6.1), equal to the second best, GLIDE_Emodel (4.6), and better than GLIDE_Gscore (4.3), FlexX (2.2), and GOLD (1.7). ROCS performed better than or as well as the best docking methods for three targets: HPMur1 (5.7), COX2 (8.1), and JNK3 (2.9).

5.11. Consensus and caveats

The collective wisdom from these studies can be summarized as follows:

• The comparative performance of different HTD programs for use in lead finding is of interest to multiple pharmaceutical companies as evidenced by their recently published evaluations, e.g. AstraZeneca, Boehringer-Ingelheim, Bayer, GSK, Hoffman LaRoche, J&J, Merck (manuscript in preparation), Novartis, and Vertex.

- Glide, FlexX, DOCK, and GOLD (in that order) were the most commonly evaluated programs.
- In the seven published evaluations summarized in Table 5, the following programs were top performers on the greatest number of targets:
  ○ Glide in three out of the seven evaluations: Schulz-Gasch *et al.* (5/7), Warren *et al.* (5/8), and Klon *et al.* (2/2),
  ○ ICM in the Chen *et al.* evaluation (10/11),
  ○ LigandFit in the Kontoyianni *et al.* evaluation (5/6),
  ○ DOCK in the Cummings *et al.* evaluation (3/5),
  ○ FlexX in the Kellenberger *et al.* evaluation (1/1).
- Top performing programs can be identified for major target classes:
  ○ Kinases – Glide, DOCK, ICM, LigandFit, FlexX, GOLD,
  ○ Metalloenzymes – FlexX, LigandFit, Glide, FRED, ICM,
  ○ Serine Proteases – Glide, DOCK, FlexX, FRED, GOLD, ICM,
  ○ Nuclear Receptors – Glide, FlexX, FRED, GOLD, ICM.
- Homology models can sometimes yield enrichment factors as good as or better than X-ray crystal structures, however, the best results are not necessarily obtained with the highest homology templates.
- Enrichment factors are sensitive to the choice of PDB structure.
- Enrichment factors are sensitive to the choice of decoy set.
- The HTD evaluations discussed here were derived using decoy sets consisting of diverse sets of molecules from the ACD, other commercial sources, WDI, MDDR, or in-house collections and/or actives from other targets in the evaluation. Different results are possible (indeed likely) when searching in-house collections.
- Even though the active set compounds ranged in potency from nM to μM, most authors (Warren *et al.* excepted) did not report retrieval success as a function of potency. This information is important for assessing lead finding performance since most potential lead compounds fall into the μM rather than the nM range.

6. POST-PROCESSING

Some of the HTD evaluations discussed above included rescoring with non-native scoring functions. While that data is not reviewed here due to the combinatorics involved, this approach can be useful when one program is good at generating poses, but another program or scoring function performs better at relative scoring of different molecules. Other post-processing approaches have been explored as well. Jansen and Martin [46] have reviewed the application of target-biased approaches and expert systems in docking. They identify four key areas of application. Filtering tools can automate the common but laborious process of visually inspecting poses. Expert systems can classify poses based on protein–ligand interaction patterns. The docking process itself can be further optimized to select target-biased poses. Finally, scoring functions can be re-optimized based on statistical analysis of known ligands [47] or known protein–ligand interactions [48].

The machine learning approach employed by Springer *et al.* [48] included vdW and electrostatic terms from the DOCK scoring function, SASA terms, and hydrogen bonding, metal binding, lipophilic, and rotatable bond terms from the ChemScore scoring function. Using the random forest method, they were able to correctly classify 39 of 44 active binding complexes and 42 of 44 decoy complexes in a test set of diverse protein targets. They further noted that for most descriptor combinations explored in this study, a higher success rate was seen for identification of decoys than actives. This observation suggests that for successful application of HTD for lead finding, one need not necessarily get the "right result" (classification of actives/inactives) for the "right reason" (correct pose of actives).

7. FUTURE DIRECTIONS

Cole *et al.* recently reviewed the literature on docking evaluations in an article entitled "Comparing Protein–Ligand Docking Programs is Difficult" and presented recommendations for improving these evaluations [49]. They noted, "Some of these recommendations are strong; that is, we believe that current, common practice is flawed and clearly open to improvement." Specifically, they suggest that the statistical significance of HTD results must be established if the data are to be interpreted with any certainty. In addition, they identify the importance of decoy set selection as well as technical details such as ligand conformation generation and active site definition.

It is clear that a significant amount of time has gone into this recent round of HTD evaluations, on the part of both the industrial practitioners and also the academic and commercial developers who understandably wanted to ensure their programs were deployed in optimal fashion. Further, docking and scoring continue to be active areas of research, with improvements continually being made and integrated into the available software. While these improvements are welcome, they render data from HTD evaluations stale relatively quickly. It can also be unclear whether a particular target was employed in fine-tuning the algorithm or the scoring function.

In the interest of reducing time spent on future evaluations, it would be useful to establish a standardized set of benchmarks such as the ones employed by computer hardware vendors. This would not be a trivial task, indeed, new benchmarks might need to be released annually, however, it would potentially offer significant benefits to both developers and users of these methods. To that end, some representatives from molecular modeling groups in the pharmaceutical industry have undertaken discussions with the NIH about the possibility of carrying out the evaluations in the public sector using proprietary data sets released by industry [50]. While preliminary, these discussions underscore the importance of these methods to industry and suggest the possibility of shorter cycle times for methodology improvement in the future.

ACKNOWLEDGEMENTS

WDC thanks R Sheridan, J-F Truchon, McGaughey, and R Torres for helpful comments on the manuscript.

REFERENCES

[1] B. D. Bursulaya, M. Totrov, R. Abagyan and C. L. Brooks, III., Comparative study of several algorithms for flexible ligand docking, *J. Comput. Aided. Mol. Des.*, 2003, **17**, 755–763.

[2] E. Kellenberger, J. Rodrigo, P. Muller and D. Rognan, Comparative evaluation of eight docking tools for docking and virtual screening accuracy, *Proteins*, 2004, **57**, 225–242.

[3] T. Schulz-Gasch and M. Stahl, Binding site characteristics in structure-based virtual screening: Evaluation of current docking tools, *J. Mol. Model (Online).*, 2003, **9**, 47–57.

[4] A. E. Klon, M. Glick, M. Thoma, P. Acklin and J. W. Davies, Finding more needles in the haystack: A simple and efficient method for improving high-throughput docking results, *J. Med. Chem.*, 2004, **47**, 2743–2749.

[5] E. Perola, W. P. Walters and P. S. Charifson, A detailed comparison of current docking and scoring methods on systems of pharmaceutical relevance, *Proteins*, 2004, **56**, 235–249.

[6] I. Muegge and I. J. Enyedy, Virtual screening for kinase targets, *Curr. Med. Chem.*, 2004, **11**, 693–707.

[7] M. D. Cummings, R. L. DesJarlais, A. C. Gibbs, V. Mohan and E. P. Jaeger, Comparison of automated docking programs as virtual screening tools, *J. Med. Chem.*, 2005, **48**, 962–976.

[8] M. Kontoyianni, G. S. Sokol and L. M. McClellan, Evaluation of library ranking efficacy in virtual screening, *J. Comput. Chem.*, 2005, **26**, 11–22.

[9] G. L. Warren, C. W. Andrews, A.-M. Capelli, B. Clarke, J. LaLonde, M. H. Lambert, M. Lindvall, N. Nevins, S. F. Semus, S. Senger, G. Tedesco, I. D. Wall, J. M. Woolven, C. E. Peishoff, M. S. Head, *J. Med. Chem.*, A critical assessment of docking programs and scoring functions, 2005, ASAP Article, DOI: 10.1021/jm050362n.

[10] H. Chen, P. D. Lyne, F. Giordanetto, T. Lovell and J. Li, On evaluating molecular-docking methods for pose prediction and enrichment factors, *J. Chem. Inf. Model.*, 2006, **46**, 401–415.

[11] I. D. Kuntz, J. M. Blaney, S. J. Oatley, R. Langridge and T. E. Ferrin, A geometric approach to macromolecule–ligand interactions, *J. Mol. Biol.*, 1982, **161**, 269–288.

[12] J. C. Alvarez, High-throughput docking as a source of novel drug leads, *Curr. Opin. Chem. Biol.*, 2004, **8**, 365–370.

[13] G. M. Morris, D. S. Goodsell, R. S. Halliday, R. Huey, W. E. Hart, R. K. Belew and A. J. Olson, Automated docking using a Lamarckian genetic algorithm and an empirical binding free energy function, *J. Comput. Chem.*, 1998, **19**, 1639–1662.

[14] T. J. M. Ewing, S. Skillman and A. G. Kuntz, I.D. DOCK 4.0: Search strategies for automated molecular docking of flexible molecule databases,, *J. Comput. Aided. Mol. Des.*, 2001, **15**, 411–428.

[15] J. M. Blaney, and J. S. Dixon, 1.0 eds, Metaphorics, LLC, Mission Viejo, CA.

[16] T. N. Hart and R. J. Read, A multiple-start Monte Carlo docking method, *Proteins*, 1992, **13**, 206–222.

[17] T. N. Hart, S. R. Ness and R. J. Read, Critical evaluation of the research docking program for the CASP2 challenge, *Proteins*, 1997, **Suppl 1**, 205–209.

[18] M. Rarey, B. Kramer, T. Lengauer and G. Klebe, A fast flexible docking method using an incremental construction algorithm, *J. Mol. Biol.*, 1996, **261**, 470–489.

[19] C. McMartin and R. S. Bohacek, QXP: Powerful, rapid computer algorithms for structure-based drug design, *J. Comput. Aided. Mol. Des.*, 1997, **11**, 333–344.

[20] M. R. McGann, H. R. Almond, A. Nicholls, J. A. Grant and F. K. Brown, Gaussian docking functions, *Biopolymers*, 2003, **68**, 76–90.

[21] R. A. Friesner, J. L. Banks, R. B. Murphy, T. A. Halgren, J. J. Klicic, D. T. Mainz, M. P. Repasky, E. H. Knoll, M. Shelley, J. K. Perry, D. E. Shaw, P. Francis and P. S. Shenkin, Glide: A new approach for rapid, accurate docking and scoring. 1. Method and assessment of docking accuracy, *J. Med. Chem.*, 2004, **47**, 1739–1749.

[22] T. A. Halgren, R. B. Murphy, R. A. Friesner, H. S. Beard, L. L. Frye, W. T. Pollard and J. L. Banks, Glide: A new approach for rapid, accurate docking and scoring. 2. Enrichment factors in database screening, *J. Med. Chem.*, 2004, **47**, 1750–1759.

[23] G. Jones, P. Willett, R. C. Glen, A. R. Leach and R. Taylor, Development and validation of a genetic algorithm for flexible docking, *J. Mol. Biol.*, 1997, **267**, 727–748.

[24] R. T. Abagyan and M. R. Kuznetsov, ICM – A new method for protein modeling and design: Applications to docking and structure prediction from the distorted native conformation, *J. Comput. Chem.*, 1994, **15**, 488–506.

[25] C. M. Venkatachalam, X. Jiang, T. Oldfield and M. Waldman, LigandFit: A novel method for the shape-directed rapid docking of ligands to protein active sites, *J. Mol. Graph. Model.*, 2003, **21**, 289–307.

[26] Chemical Computing Group, Montreal, QC, Canada.

[27] M. I. Zavodszky, P. C. Sanschagrin, R. S. Korde and L. A. Kuhn, Distilling the essential features of a protein surface for improving protein–ligand docking, *scoring, and virtual screening, J. Comput. Aided. Mol. Des.*, 2002, **16**, 883–902.

[28] A. N. Jain, Surflex: Fully automatic flexible molecular docking using a molecular similarity-based search engine, *J. Med. Chem.*, 2003, **46**, 499–511.

[29] E. C. Meng, D. A. Gschwend, J. M. Blaney and I. D. Kuntz, Orientational sampling and rigid-body minimization in molecular docking, *Proteins*, 1993, **17**, 266–278.

[30] M. D. Eldridge, C. W. Murray, T. R. Auton, G. V. Paolini and R. P. Mee, Empirical scoring functions: I. The development of a fast empirical scoring function to estimate the binding affinity of ligands in receptor complexes, *J. Comput. Aided. Mol. Des.*, 1997, **11**, 425–445.

[31] M. Rarey, S. Wefing and T. Lengauer, Placement of medium-sized molecular fragments into active sites of proteins, *J. Comput. Aided. Mol. Des.*, 1996, **10**, 41–54.

[32] R. Wang, L. Lai and S. Wang, Further development and validation of empirical scoring functions for structure-based binding affinity prediction, *J. Comput. Aided. Mol. Des.*, 2002, **16**, 11–26.

[33] H. M. Berman, J. Westbrook, Z. Feng, G. Gilliland, T. N. Bhat, H. Weissig, I. N. Shindyalov and P. E. Bourne, The protein data bank, *Nucleic Acids Res.*, 2000, **28**, 235–242.

[34] I. Muegge, Y. C. Martin, P. J. Hajduk and S. W. Fesik, Evaluation of PMF scoring in docking weak ligands to the FK506 binding protein, *J. Med. Chem.*, 1999, **42**, 2498–2503.

[35] R. Wang, Y. Lu, X. Fang and S. Wang, An extensive test of 14 scoring functions using the PDBbind refined set of 800 protein–ligand complexes, *J. Chem. Inf. Comput. Sci.*, 2004, **44**, 2114–2125.

[36] R. K. Scott, Assessing the impact of high-performance computing on the drug discovery and development process, *DDT, Biosilico*, 2004, **2**, 175–179.

[37] S. L. McGovern and B. K. Shoichet, Information decay in molecular docking screens against holo, apo, and modeled conformations of enzymes, *J. Med. Chem.*, 2003, **46**, 2895–2907.

[38] V. Kairys, M. X. Fernandes and M. K. Gilson, Screening drug-like compounds by docking to homology models: A systematic study, *J. Chem. Inf. Model.*, 2006, **46**, 365–379.

[39] G. W. Milne, M. C. Nicklaus, J. S. Driscoll, S. Wang and D. Zaharevitz, National Cancer Institute Drug Information System 3D database, *J. Chem. Inf. Comput. Sci.*, 1994, **34**, 1219–1224.

[40] M. L. Verdonk, V. Berdini, M. J. Hartshorn, W. T. Mooij, C. W. Murray, R. D. Taylor and P. Watson, Virtual screening using protein–ligand docking: Avoiding artificial enrichment, *J. Chem. Inf. Comput. Sci.*, 2004, **44**, 793–806.

[41] Y. Pan, N. Huang, S. Cho and A. D. MacKerell, Jr., Consideration of molecular weight during compound selection in virtual target-based database screening, *J. Chem. Inf. Comput. Sci.*, 2003, **43**, 267–272.

[42] N. Triballeau, F. Acher, I. Brabet, J. P. Pin and H. O. Bertrand, Virtual screening workflow development guided by the "receiver operating characteristic" curve approach. Application to high-throughput docking on metabotropic glutamate receptor subtype 4, *J. Med. Chem.*, 2005, **48**, 2534–2547.

[43] R. P. Sheridan, S. B. Singh, E. M. Fluder and S. K. Kearsley, Protocols for bridging the peptide to nonpeptide gap in topological similarity searches, *J. Chem. Inf. Comput. Sci.*, 2001, **41**, 1395–1406.

[44] D. K. Gehlhaar, G. M. Verkhivker, P. A. Rejto, C. J. Sherman, D. B. Fogel, L. J. Fogel and S. T. Freer, Molecular recognition of the inhibitor AG-1343 by HIV-1 protease: Conformationally flexible docking by evolutionary programming, *Chem. Biol.*, 1995, **2**, 317–324.

[45] M. Zavodszky, L. He, S. Arora and L. A. Kuhn, manuscript in preparation.

[46] J. M. Jansen and E. J. Martin, Target-biased scoring approaches and expert systems in structure-based virtual screening, *Curr. Opin. Chem. Biol.*, 2004, **8**, 359–364.

[47] M. Jacobsson, P. Liden, E. Stjernschantz, H. Bostrom and U. Norinder, Improving structure-based virtual screening by multivariate analysis of scoring data, *J. Med. Chem.*, 2003, **46**, 5781–5789.

[48] C. Springer, H. Adalsteinsson, M. M. Young, P. W. Kegelmeyer and D. C. Roe, PostDOCK: A structural, empirical approach to scoring protein ligand complexes, *J. Med. Chem.*, 2005, **48**, 6821–6831.

[49] J. C. Cole, C. W. Murray, J. W. Nissink, R. D. Taylor and R. Taylor, Comparing protein–ligand docking programs is difficult, *Proteins*, 2005, **60**, 325–332.

[50] J. Wehrle, Report of the NIGMS Workshop on Challenges in Docking and Virtual Screening, August 26, 2005. http://www.nigms.nih.gov/News/Reports/DockingWorkshop082505.htm; http://www.nigms.nih.gov/News/Reports/DockingMeeting022406.htm.

SUBJECT INDEX